People's Law and State Law
The Bellagio Papers

Antony Allott and Gordon R. Woodman (eds.)

PEOPLE'S LAW AND STATE LAW

The Bellagio Papers

1985
FORIS PUBLICATIONS
Dordrecht - Holland/Cinnaminson - U.S.A.

Published by:
Foris Publications Holland
P.O. Box 509
3300 AM Dordrecht, The Netherlands

Sole Distributor for the U.S.A. and Canada:
Foris Publications U.S.A.
P.O. Box C-50
Cinnaminson N.J. 08077
U.S.A.

Published for the Commission on Folk Law and Legal Pluralism of the International Union of Anthropological and Ethnological Sciences.

ISBN 90 6765 100 1

© 1985 By the authors

Printed in the Netherlands by ICG Printing, Dordrecht.

Dedication to Geert van den Steenhoven, Professor of Folk Law and initiator of the Commission on Folk Law and Legal Pluralism

From left to right:
front: A. Allott, K. Kludze, S. Conn, M. Galanter, G. van den Steenhoven,
R. Alum, R. Verdier, M. Chiba, H. van de Put.
second row: K. von Benda-Beckman, H. Slaats, K. Portier, M. Koesnoe,
R. Schott, J. Bayly, J. Starr, F. Snyder.
standing: H. Finkler, G. Woodman, R. Bolton, N. Singer, A. Mensah-
Brown, E. van Rouveroy van Nieuwaal, F. von Benda-Beckmann, P.
Fitzpatrick, F. Strijbosch, R. Abel, E. le Roy, U. Baxi, J. Griffiths.

Contents

Introduction

Antony Allott and Gordon R. Woodman

The papers in this volume were presented at the first conference of the Commission on Folk Law and Legal Pluralism at Bellagio, Como, Italy, from 21st to 25th September 1981.

Folk Law and Legal Pluralism as a Field of Study

The first steps in the establishment of a new field of enquiry comprise the delimitation of the field and the attribution of a name to it. The two operations are part of a single act. It is not by chance that Genesis records that one of the first activities of the first man was to name every beast. The first step in connection with the field covered by the present volume was taken when the Commission on Folk Law and Legal Pluralism was set up through a Dutch initiative. As the list of our present authors discloses, the range of the Commission is now worldwide; but just as strikingly the subjects which they have chosen to discuss are spread as widely in kind and orientation. Is this a case where the field is so wide (one thinks of "Comparative Law", which has become almost a synonym for "Law, preferably foreign") as to cease to have relevance; or can one truthfully say that the world of legal and social science must now take in and work from a new map, linking institutions and processes formerly conceived of as distinct?

It was naturally the hope of the organizers of the Bellagio conference, as it is of the editors of the present volume, that the latter alternative was the more correct. That is, E.M. Forster's plea, "Only connect!", must now serve to link studies and researchers in areas previously far apart. Two worlds meet in the papers which follow: on the one hand, the world of "primitive" or customary laws - of the laws of peoples who use neither writing nor codified or recorded laws, and who, in parallel, probably lack modern technologies and systems of government; and on the other hand, the world of the paralegal or quasi-legal forms of reglementation to be found embedded within state or official legal systems, being the "laws" of groups or communities operating outside the regular systems of courts and state law. Customary and other similar laws were official laws, in the sense that they were (and indeed often still are) the generally recognised legal systems within the societies which they governed. Unofficial "laws" and codes within state systems are precisely what the adjective suggests, viz. bodies of rules and modes of settlement at best tolerated and at worst prohibited by the official state power. In this sense, as many of the papers disclose, unofficial laws can be found within the most sophisticated polity as well as the less developed.

The term "folk law" has a number of approximate synonyms - people's law, customary law, unofficial law and indigenous law are the most prominent in this volume - but no agreed definition (see also Griffiths, Introduction to Part I). According to a common view folk law is the normative self-regulation of a semi-autonomous social field (e.g. Allott, Galanter; cf. Moore 1973). But this may have insufficient scope, since it arguably excludes "imposed law" (whether imposed by an external force or by a dominant section of the social field itself). Perhaps there is general agreement on two propositions: that the law of modern states is not, or does not consist wholly of, folk law; and that folk law includes any law which is not state law, without necessarily excluding all types of state law.

Implicit in the notion is the contention that a study of law in society may usefully adopt a broad conception of law, and should focus particularly on non-state law, a subject which has been relatively neglected. It denies the axiom of western legal theory which confines the concept of "law" to state law (and which then finds considerable difficulty in providing an analytical basis for this ideological preference). Students of folk law find that some of the other problems of western legal theory prove in practice to be of little consequence. None of the papers in this volume, for example, encounters difficulty over the much-discussed distinction between law and positive morality, nor over the alleged need for an ultimate unifying source of norms in a legal system. The experience of folk law studies suggests that these issues may be the concerns only of an ethnocentric legal positivism.

Every member of the human race is claimed as a subject by at least one state legal system. It is extremely unlikely that anyone is not also claimed as a subject by at least one folk law. Therefore the relations between folk law and state law are of concern to students of both types of law. Consequently some prefer to define the field of study as "legal pluralism". This term is of course not to be interpreted to mean only state law with multiple sources or bodies of norms (Griffiths 1981).

The label of legal pluralism has the merit of asserting the universal fact of the non-monopoly of state law over the legal arena. It may be criticised for offering admission to state law, whereas "folk law" excludes it. Perhaps a weightier criticism is that the emphasis on pluralism suggests that in the study of any law, the principal external factors for examination (for example, as cause or effect of the law) must be other laws. Papers in this volume show that the study of a law may be most illuminating if it is considered in its entire context, not merely in that aspect of its context identified as legal pluralism.

Not only do different kinds of law meet here; but two (or indeed more) kinds of students of them. Habitually the laws of technologically simple societies have been the province of the anthropologist, and less frequently of the lawyer, who now often join forces in the study of what is termed "legal anthropology", or "ethno-jurisprudence", while what goes on in technologically complex societies in unofficial arenas has been traditionally the province of the sociologist, or more recently the "law and society" lawyer. Awareness of common features and the use of similar methods of investigation and conceptualisation tend to bring these groups of investigators, whatever their parent discipline, closer together.

In addition to developments in anthropology, sociology and legal science, several further factors have served to strengthen the development of the field. The colonial experience, which produced the global extension of states and state law, also led colonial powers and colonised peoples for practical reasons to investigate scientifically the indigenous laws which so often continued to flourish independently of the granting or withholding of state recognition. Legal history, while far from abandoning the analysis of formal doctrine, has branched into social history and come upon folk customs and laws which it can no longer disregard. Finally, marxist theory has made advances in the investigation of contemporary international capital and of non-capitalist modes of production, and has found legal phenomena to be significant.

These streams are now gradually mingling in a growing mutual awareness. Progress was delayed only briefly by the fashion for law and development studies, which often made an ill-considered, dismissive evaluation of folk law. Today institutions are emerging to foster the field of study: we may instance both the Commission on Folk Law and Legal Pluralism and the *Journal of Legal Pluralism and Unofficial Law* with which the Commission is now institutionally associated. Today the prospects are of worthwhile advances in each of the areas mentioned as it makes use of the perspectives of the others (cf. Roberts 1977, evidencing less interaction between anthropologists and lawyers in a seminar in 1974 than existed in the Bellagio conference of 1981).

The field of folk law and legal pluralism today contains a great variety of topics of study, many of which are illustrated in this book. Some of the divisions of the field are standard in law and society studies. Thus there is no novelty in distinguishing such topics as the content of contemporary laws, the emergence of laws, the effects (as social control or otherwise) of laws, and the change over time of laws and their relations to other social facts. Moreover, it may be assumed that every serious study involves explicitly or by implication instances of comparison, whether over a wide or narrow scale, and whether synchronic, diachronic or both. (On some of the considerable problems in making scientific comparisons, see F. von Benda-Beckmann.) A number of further distinctions are possible within the field of folk law and legal pluralism. It is possible to make many permutations.

1. A distinction may be between (a) the study which focuses on a single folk law (e.g. Alum, Bolton), and (b) that which examines the interaction between different laws (illustrated by virtually all the papers other than the two mentioned). Type (a) need not and cannot omit comparative studies. Neither need it fail to take account of factors external to the laws or the society on which it focuses. It is distinguished by its primary focus on issues other than the interaction between laws. Studies of type (b) have usually considered the interaction between a folk law and a state law, although they could consider that between two or more folk laws. They may consider issues of "choice of law", conflict between laws, "incorporation" or "recognition" of one law by another, or "influence" of one upon another.

2. A distinction may be made between (a) studies of normative systems, and (b) studies of dispute processes. This is sometimes posed as a distinction between alternative and exclusive conceptualisations or definitions of law. It indeed appears that there exist conflicting claims to two such conceptualisations, but it seems possible to adopt a comprehensive view accommodating both. Type (a) may view the normative system as a body of beliefs (e.g. Koesnoe in part), as practices (e.g. Baxi, Bayly), or as both (see Alum, who contrasts them). Type (b) may view the processes from the viewpoint of a disputing party (e.g. K. von Benda-Beckmann, Starr, Strijbosch), or from that of a third party, either mediator, judge, social administrator or other (e.g. Abel, Griffiths, Singer).

3. Distinctions may be drawn between the varieties of folk laws. It seems not useful to attempt an exhaustive classification, but it seems that most current study is concerned with three broad types: (a) so-called "traditional laws", or folk laws which developed before state laws claimed jurisdiction over the societies, which may have been transformed during subsequent social changes, and which in the typical case is the folk law of the entirety of the inhabitants of a territorial area (e.g. Kludze, Schott; cf. Le Roy, arguing that a traditional law has become an ingredient in the new category of "local law"); (b) unofficial, relatively new laws of groups whose members are predominantly within technologically complex state societies (e.g. Allott, Galanter); and (c) "indigenous laws", or folk laws similar in origin to type (a) but of groups which find themselves today within technologically complex state societies, and which are typically the folk laws of minority ethnic groups (e.g. Bayly, Conn, Finkler, Kirby).

4. A distinction may be made between (a) studies which aim primarily to develop speculative theory (e.g. Abel, Chiba, Podgorecki, Snyder), and (b) studies which aim primarily to develop fairly immediately practical policies to assist or stimulate activity (e.g. Bayly, Conn, Finkler, Kirby, who happen to be all those in this volume who are concerned with indigenous laws). Much

of the impetus for folk law studies has historically come from demands for type (b) studies. We have expressed the distinction here in terms of "primary" aims. It would seem that in principle one study could simultaneously seek to achieve both, although in practice this is likely to prove difficult.

These types of studies can be accomplished through various methods, many studies requiring combinations of method. The observational and descriptive study of an aspect of one social group is particularly associated with anthropology. Whether directed to dispute processes or to a normative system, it may use a case method as pioneered by anthropologists (one thinks of Gluckman) and some lawyers (one thinks of Llewellyn); but it need not do so exclusively (see e.g. Kirby, Schott). The method of doctrinal and conceptual analysis is associated on the other hand with lawyers (e.g. Kludze, Woodman). The usefulness of this second method cannot be adequately debated here. It may only be suggested that it is not purely ideological; that it is based upon empirical investigation in the first place, in that analysis takes as its material the facts of believed-in or practised norms; and that it is necessary for a true description of any law which exhibits a degree of autonomy or rationality. The method of archival research is likely to be used by the historian studying change over time. It is frequently used by those who have thoroughly exploited other methods (e.g. Baxi, Starr). The study of the writings of others is a further method, which may produce valuable syntheses, or enable the development of new theoretical or practical insights (e.g. F. von Benda-Beckmann, Fitzpatrick, both papers based upon this method by writers who have made notable contributions elsewhere through other methods). Finally, as one paper argues, the method of film can deepen understanding and communicate it more fully (van Rouveroy van Nieuwaal).

Two questions remain for the future. The less important is the name which the Commission has given to its chosen field. The more important question is, "where do we go from here"? As to the name, while the inclusion of both folk law and legal pluralism avoids the question of a choice between them, the former phrase is not beyond criticism. The speakers of the Germanic languages have the advantage over the speakers of English. "Folk law" when translated into German or Dutch does not have the same rather antiquarian air as it has in English. Folk law is primarily people's law - law generated or accepted by the people, whether the whole people as in customary-law societies, or a fraction of the people, as in legally pluralist societies. The political and functional advantages of people's law are an important area of future discussion and research, centred around the twin concepts of acceptance and effectiveness. If (and one must not prejudge the issue) folk laws have value even in highly developed state systems, then it must be practically as well as theoretically rewarding to discover how they operate, how they change over time, what the secret of their success - if such it is - may be, and how and in what areas of life in community parallel systems of folk-generated law can be usefully developed or allowed to flourish.

We do not deny the notable progress now occurring if we venture to suggest some weaknesses in the current stage. First, there is too little research into folk law and legal pluralism in history, a weakness which may be as much a loss to legal historians as to us. Obviously some methods of investigation are - in the absence of working time-machines - excluded from this area. Nevertheless it would be of interest in particular to study the role of folk law in a society where it is the sole law of that society. Every society now known has, whether through colonial impact, the transfer of institutions and ideas, or participation in the wider world, eaten the apple of state law, so that a pure folk system is hard to find. And yet all the known legal systems of the world had as their ancestors exactly such pristine folk systems. It is as rewarding to the legal analyst to trace the origins and development of legal systems from such a past as it is for the student of human language to uncover the processes of language development.

Secondly, less than sufficient use is made of political science, perhaps in part because it is associated with the study of the state. However, if, as suggested, folk law is to be defined partly by contrast with state law, and if furthermore the interaction between folk law and state law is to be studied, it must be necessary to conceptualise precisely the notion of "state", its attributes, and types of states such as the "modern" state. Political science might assist us to refine these terms. Moreover, studies aimed at producing political activity require an understanding of the constraints upon and potential consequences of political action. Thirdly, there is perhaps a tendency to view folk law groups as monolithic social groups in which folk law is formed by a general consensus, becomes thoroughly internalised, and generally claims exclusive authority over all activity. Each of these alleged characteristics needs to be questioned (cf. Abel, Galanter). Fourthly, and closely related to the previous weakness, there is a tendency to assume universal value-judgements of the kind characterised at the conference by Antony Allott, by analogy with a slogan in Orwell's *Animal Farm*, as: "Folk law good; state law bad". These result perhaps from a healthy desire to repudiate "statist" assumptions, but suffer from the same lack of discrimination. Fifthly, despite the recent progress there is still insufficient awareness among students of each other's work, and so insufficient critical interaction. There is some tendency for work to continue in isolation from other highly relevant findings. When discoveries, approaches and insights are disseminated, the communication sometimes seems to stop at the boundaries of particular national or linguistic groups of students. To advance this criticism is to ask only for more communication, not to doubt the value of diversity nor to deny that it is a strength of work in this field at present.

In the foreseeable future the study of folk law and legal pluralism is likely to bring advances both in law and society studies and in legal theory. Law and society research appears to have become concentrated lately in intensive work on relatively small areas: in industrialised societies these are areas such as crime and deviance, dispute processes, and economic relations; while in the third world the decline of the law and modernisation movement has left little of any programme for law and society study - except in the area of folk law. The study of folk law and legal pluralism offers new perspectives on each of the areas hitherto studied within their present social contexts, also the means of extending each area to a wider range of societies, and furthermore the opening of a number of relatively untouched, fundamental topics. Legal theory in the west appears to be engaged either in ever more intricate and sterile conceptual analysis of formal state law, or in increasingly obsessive analysis and evaluation of judicial processes in state courts. Legal theory in the third world seems engaged largely in investigating how far western theory applies outside the west. The jurists concerned with the definition of law and of its normative prescriptions will, with the advancing study of folk law and legal pluralism, be obliged to expand and refine their theory to accommodate the incidents of folk systems, as well as those of the state systems which legal thinkers, guided by Bentham on the one hand or Napoleon on the other, have tended to regard as the sole valid forms of law. The new areas, reasonably well-defined yet extensive and socially important, offer possibilities for theory to integrate empirical investigation and doctrinal analysis, and furthermore to contribute to pressing political issues by way of theory, tactical appraisal, and advocacy. Folk law and legal pluralism should soon become an essential field of study for both legal philosophers and legal activists.

This Volume

Some information on the Commission on Folk Law and Legal Pluralism is given on the last page of this book. The conference to which these papers were presented was on "State Institutions and Their Use of Folk Law". The papers are published here grouped in Parts corresponding to the conference sessions. The introduction to each Part has been written by the chairperson of the session, and reports or comments on both the papers and the discussion at the session.

The editors have tried to retain as far as reasonably possible the variety of style, content and philosophical basis of the original papers. Accordingly most have been revised only to the extent of accepting minor authorial amendments, setting them into a broadly similar format, and asking the authors of the lengthiest to abbreviate them. Similarly the varying approaches of the chairpersons have not been standardised.

The categorisation of the papers, and the provision of titles for the conference sessions were necessary, if inevitably somewhat arbitrary. We did not find ourselves able to produce a better division of the material. It will not surprise the reader to be told that there was considerable leakage between the sessions; many of the papers could as readily have been discussed under the one head as the other. But, in justification of the breakdown adopted, it can be said that every permutation of aspects of the field was reviewed in turn: informal law outside state courts; folk law in state courts; the relations between state and unofficial law; questions of legal policy in the face of juristic pluralism; and a session, somewhat out of fit with this pattern, which reviewed the methodological perceptions of marxian thought when applied to this field. E.A.B. van Rouveroy van Nieuwaal showed his film at a separate session, and provided preliminary notes on it. They have been included as a separate section of Part III.

The Commission on Folk Law and Legal Pluralism was instituted through the efforts of Geert van den Steenhoven, Professor of Folk Law and Director of the Institute of Folk Law at the Catholic University of Nijmegen, The Netherlands, until his retirement in 1981. The conference was organised primarily by him and the Secretary of the Commission, Fons Strijbosch. The Chairperson of the Commission during and since the conference has been Marc Galanter. The Commission was provided with accommodation and facilities for the conference by the Rockefeller Foundation at its Study and Conference Centre, Villa Serbelloni, Bellagio.

The Commission appointed a Publication Committee charged with securing the publication of the papers, consisting of Antony Allott (chairperson and editor), Rolando A. Alum Jr., Stephen Conn, A.K.P. Kludze, and Keebet von Benda-Beckmann (secretary). Gordon Woodman was later co-opted as a member and appointed a co-editor.

Finally, some words of thanks are due from the editors. The first must go to the original organisers of the Bellagio conference, who boldly seized this new idea and developed it. Those who contributed papers, and those who edited and improved them for publication, naturally receive the thanks of the editors, since without them there would be no publication. But in this instance the thanks are more than conventional. One of the editors (ANA) would like to thank the other (GRW) for the ever-growing contribution which he has made to the eventual preparation of the text, which has been a long and laborious task. Lastly, the secretary of the Publication Committee has earned our gratitude for acting as negotiator and channel of communication with the publishers, in which burdensome task she has been assisted by the understanding and forbearance shown by the publishers towards the delays and other difficulties caused by the editors.

REFERENCES

(Undated references are to papers in this volume.)

Griffiths, J.
  1981   'What is legal pluralism?', paper delivered at the annual meeting of the Law and
              Society Association, Amherst, Massachusetts, 12-14 June.
Moore, S.F.
  1973   'Law and social change: the semi-autonomous social field as an appropriate
              subject of study', *Law & Society Review*, 7, 718-46; reprinted in: S.F. Moore, *Law
              as Process*, London: Routledge & Kegan Paul (1978).
Roberts, S.A. (ed.)
  1977   *Law and the Family in Africa*, The Hague: Mouton.

Part I
Informal social control

Introduction

J. Griffiths

This introduction takes the form of a report of the symposium discussion on the papers reproduced or summarised in this Part. The discussion is freely reproduced and in many places condensed and edited.

Chairman's Introduction

Why are we beginning a conference on "folk law in state courts" with a session on "informal social control"? The purpose must be to focus upon this problem: What is the nature of that thing - "folk law" - which we suppose to exist outside of "state courts", but in some circumstances to be capable of entering into or affecting the operations of a "state court"? In short, we must confront a preliminary question for this conference: the nature of "folk law" *outside* of "state courts".

The papers for discussion in this session offer food for discussion with respect to at least two sub-questions of the general problem just defined:

(1) How can the phenomenon of "folk law" be conceptualized?

(2) How can the interaction of "folk" and "state law" be conceptualized? We can arrange the various papers according to their explicit or implicit answers to these two questions.

(1) Conceptualization of the phenomenon of "folk law". Here we see in the papers a contrast between two ways of approaching the phenomenon. Folk law can be regarded as an aspect of social organization, the self-reglementation of social fields (Galanter), or as a matter of ideas and attitudes (Podgorecki) and of practices associated with ideas and attitudes (Alum; Allott) without it being necessary that those ideas and attitudes be actually imbedded in social organization. Another contrast in the approaches to folk law represented here is between the typological approach of Allott, for example, which regards folk law as a distinct type of law, and Galanter's approach, which places all legal phenomena on a continuous dimension of relative organization and differentiation. Finally, there is a question of the scientific perspective which one adopts, consciously or not, in observing and analyzing folk law and its institutions. Allott, especially, adopts a "state's-eye-view" of folk law, as reflected in the central place he gives to categorizations of folk law such as its consistency or inconsistency with state law. Galanter, on the

other hand, seems to want to treat all legal phenomena - "state" or "folk" - as equivalent for purposes of scientific study, and to reject the idea that the substantive requirements of one normative order can be used in describing and analyzing the others.

(2) Conceptualization of the interaction between state and folk law. Here again the question of the appropriateness of the "state's-eye-view" is important - do we take as *scientific* problems the *political* problems of interaction as defined by the concerns of state institutions, as Allott, for instance, seems to do?

An important aspect of the interaction between different legal orders, for which Allott's paper affords a very nice instance, can best be conceptualized, I believe, in terms of a distinction of Eugen Ehrlich's between "rules for decision" and "rules of conduct" - a piece of analytic equipment which I miss in the papers even of those who explicitly invoke Ehrlich. One can look at processes of interaction, among other things, as processes in which rules of conduct affect and become incorporated into rules for decision. This does not necessarily entail a "state's-eye-perspective" (although it certainly did in Ehrlich's case), since state courts are not the only institutions which employ rules for decision; a case is even imaginable, and Galanter could surely give us an example, in which rules of conduct on the level of the state affect rules for decision in some other social field.

Finally, in thinking about interaction the question of reciprocal influences on effectiveness is always central: one can look at the influence of state law on the effectiveness of folk law (Galanter) or of folk law on the effectiveness of state law (Bolton; Allott).

Discussion

Allott: I sought to focus upon the processes which are responsible for observed phenomena of change in the status of norms from unofficial at one end of the scale to official at the other. These processes by which changes work their way up are not limited to changes in judge-made law but carry through into legislation as well. My concern was not with social practice as such, but social norms. I do not regard myself as having adopted the point of view of the state; but it is essential to take account of the law of the state.

Chairman: The "state's-eye-view" does not entail being in favour of the state or its law. The question is (whether one approves of the state and its law or not): is the state central to the conceptual apparatus used for describing and analyzing the phenomena concerned?

(In my response to a question concerning the introduction:) I do not claim to be able to understand the distinction between "subjective" and "objective" concepts of law. I simply note that several writers - especially Podgorecki in his discussion of "intuitive law" - explicitly state that their concept of law is a "subjective" one. Apparently that differs from a concept of law which is not "subjective". Some writers, including also Podgorecki, refer to that thing outside state courts in which they are interested - "folk law" - as being a matter of attitudes, beliefs, and suchlike, whereas Galanter explicitly takes the opposite point of view and concerns himself with "concrete patterns of social ordering to be found in a variety of institutions". This difference between law as attitudes, perceptions, etc. and law as observable patterns of social ordering is very important for the further progress of our discussion.

Galanter. I deliberately used "ordering" instead of "behaviour" because it involves judgments by those concerned that what is going on conforms to certain normative expectations; it thus allows for some incorporation in the concept of law of normative and subjective elements.

Chairman. Saying "normative and subjective" as if they were the same thing begs the question. The question is, what is the meaning of "normative". Things which are judgmental do not have to take place inside the heads of people: making judgments is an observable kind of behaviour. The question is, when we talk about the "normative", are we talking about something which is observable or about something which we can ultimately only get at (if at all) by psycho-analytic techniques?

Snyder. The question is not whether an objective social science is possible, but whether one should do interpretative sociology with the methods appropriate to it, or more behaviouristic, positivistic sociology.

Chairman (in response to question from Alum). I would place Alum partly in the "objective" and partly in the "subjective" category because, like Allott, he refers both to practice and to beliefs and attitudes. But the latter reference is not clear: perhaps he means not matters subjective to the individual, but supra-individual, social phenomena. His description of his questionnaire is not detailed enough to let one know exactly how the relevant questions were formulated. On the other hand, one can doubt whether a questionnaire is a suitable way of investigating social facts as such.

Conn. Persistent criticism of "legal centralism" seems to be the new vogue. The other new theme is that "folk law" has been over-romanticized and state law is better. The original idea of "folk law" recognized, by contrast, that the contest between the two sorts of law is ultimately a political contest - a contest over power.

Galanter. Scepticism concerning the virtues of folk law is every bit as necessary as scepticism concerning the claims of state law to moral pre-eminence. Much of folk law is morally reprehensible and oppressive, as in the case of Indian village life where folk law is nasty and oppressive. The idea that folk law is "people's law" ignores the central question: which people? Except in very egalitarian settings, the "people's choice" is the choice of some people about how to run the lives of others. Often state law is a very liberating force for some part of the population, for lower castes, for women, and so on. Without wanting to be an uncritical partisan of state law, I suggest that in trying to find usable concepts for comparative purposes we would do ourselves a disservice by adopting a romantic notion of folk law as an indwelling, egalitarian social capacity which, if we only remove the intervention of the state, could flourish.

Starr. The factor of power is central both to the local-level, village, folk-law system, and to the state system. There are hierarchies of power in both. Homogeneous, egalitarian societies do not exist - there is always a struggle for power. Different individuals have different abilities to manipulate the various available systems. The choices of individuals and groups for one system or another is an important focus for study.

"Indigenous" as Galanter uses it is a poor word for his purposes since it suggests that the practice in question has a history. Many "self-regulating" systems are not really "indigenous".

Abel. The reason for constructing the opposition between "folk" and "state" lies in the pretension that the activity in which we are engaged is a non-normative, positive social science. Those words are used to cover normative valuations that some law is good and some is bad. For a long time it was believed that state law was good and local folk law bad, and that was why state law was invoked; then there came a reaction and it came widely to be believed that local law was good and state law bad. We would do better to be explicit about our own normative views, and our reasons for favouring one system or the other. That would force us to make explicit the inevitably political nature of the processes which we are discussing. This explicitness was missing in the papers - partly because of a reluctance to engage in normative discussion. Allott's paper, for example, leaves out of the picture the political struggle led by feminist activists - a struggle that has often been very painful, on both sides.

Baxi. I agree that we are ultimately talking about power and the uses of power. Romanticization of folk law is itself a matter for investigation: which people are romanticizing folk law and for what purposes. It does not just happen; it is not just a matter of scientific passion. It is an active political communication strategy.

Woodman. I am not convinced that we are in a position to engage in a fruitful discussion of normative preferences for state or folk law; we should rather try to obtain a clearer understanding of situations which in fact exist in the different societies we are concerned with. The problem of the "state's eye" perspective is not so much that normative preferences creep into our observations, but that we will not obtain an adequate overall view. If we look at state law and folk law only from the state's perspective, then we shall miss certain things - we shall fail to achieve certain insights which we would otherwise have had. This is a danger particularly for someone with a lawyer's training, who has been brought up to look at things from the "state's eye" perspective.

It is also important to avoid the danger of such exclusive devotion to micro-studies that we fail to put our topic in a broader context and to emphasize its social implications. As soon as we put any sort of law into context, it is inevitable - because of the interwining of state and folk law in every society - that we encounter folk law. What we should not forget is the need to see an overall pattern of different types of law as it affects individuals, and not concentrate just on one type of law. Allott's passing reference to the importance of history deserves emphasis. English legal historians seem to be abandoning their past obsession with the state and state courts, and are moving in the direction of looking more fully at folk law. We can learn something from the way in which current historical studies are developing.

Kludze. None of the writers or speakers has been objective. Admittedly they are sympathetic toward folk law, but still they have not been able to shed the prejudice that what you think of as folk law, people's law, or customary law is to be looked at from the point of view of state law. If you reverse the position and go to my village [in the Volta Region of Ghana] and ask the leaders or the chiefs what type of law they are administering, none of them is going to tell you that he is administering folk law and that the courts are administering state law. What is here being called "state law" they would call - in a pejorative sense - "English law", even though it may well have been enacted by the Parliament of Ghana. They regard it as an imposition, as foreign law. To look at the system in such a village in a so-called objective sense and yet to think of it as "folk law" - that is to place one sort of law (state law) on a pedestal and to treat the other as an inferior type of law.

Snyder. Why is it worth trying to define the notion of folk law at all? Is it anything more than an umbrella concept, a symbol, which brought a number of people with different interests together? By placing the necessity of definition at the centre of discussion at the beginning we do bring out a number of issues, clarify a number of people's positions and raise some difficulties, but in another sense it is a red herring, because in the end it is impossible to reach an ahistorical, cross-culturally valid definition of "folk-law". No definition is likely to be very useful. This is partly because definitions which start off from western preoccupations are not useful somewhere else, but also because people's uses of the term and therefore their meanings vary with place and historical period. Without wanting to go so far as to deny the possibility of an ahistorical social science, it may not be for many of us a particularly interesting enterprise.

A dualistic distinction between folk and state law is misleading for a number of reasons. First, and most important, both are fundamentally part of the *same* system in any specific social context; a dichotomy which posits parallel, interacting systems tends to miss this. Second, folk law (as state law) is not necessarily a "system" or "systematic"; Galanter's paper makes clear that folk law in the United States is not generally a "legal system" in the way that in the case of Ghana, for example, one might regard English law - the imposed law - and the law of a particular community both as systems. I myself would go further and argue that in neither case is the law concerned usefully viewed as a system, any more than is state law in the west. Third, both sorts of law are usually intertwined in the same social micro-processes. Finally, they mutually interact - they do not necessarily reinforce or conflict with each other, but they exist together. The concept of a "semi-autonomous social field", for example, is an important notion, whose usefulness lies in its emphasis on the fact that the small communities which are able to generate norms and which have certain processes of dispute settlement are partially autonomous, just as the state system is partially autonomous. But its disadvantage lies in the neglect of the fact that the apparent autonomy of a small social field is itself always shaped and determined by a wider system. This brings us back to the first point: that folk law and state law are parts of the same general system.

Allott. If we were to pursue the discussion of the last speaker much further, we would have to have an extended discussion on what we mean by a "system" and whether a "system" has to be "systematic" (the latter being really a value judgment that can be passed upon systems). Is my living next to my next-door neighbour a system? I think it is. We have a relationship - it is very restricted but it could be developed - so that there is a system. If you consider the structure, not only of society but also of organisms, you find various levels of organization - like skin - which can themselves be analyzed as systems or regarded as parts of a larger system. It is useful to segregate these levels of operation, these different autonomous or non-autonomous systems, recognizing always that they are operating in a given social setting and in that sense must have systematic relations with each other.

No social field - not even the absolutist state - is fully autonomous. What we are discussing is a factor in all regulative systems. Autogenousness, as I would prefer to call it, concerns the extent to which regulative systems are autogenous, that is, generated from within the subject of a particular system rather than arising from outside and imposed upon it. By studying this factor in any system you link what happens at the bottom end of the scale in western society with what happens at the top end of the scale, or with what happens in an Ewe village. We do not have to segregate so-called folk law systems from others; we do have to recognize that some systems are at different places in the hierarchy, some exhibit a greater degree of self-regulation. This, and the question of the relationships which subsist between the different levels, are the important questions.

Woodman. We must not think of folk law as local law, as intra-state law. Traditionally, the folk law of an ethnic group which straddles international boundaries is a well-known phenomenon. But also there is the folk law of games or sports, for example. It may be useful to distinguish between systems of folk law which are territorially delimited, more or less, and those which are not.

Baxi. We do need some conceptualization of the difference between state law and people's law. Those who enforce state law are people, and have beliefs and practices independent of state law. They generate their own law within the framework of the state law. The officials of the state legal systems are capable, we must as scientists recognize, of generating semi-autonomous social fields. Although they are wearing the authority of the state, as people they are creating enclosures of folk law within the state system. To recognize this sort of law as "people's law" side-by-side with the law of non-state groups, would be a mistake. I would not want to recognize the third-degree methods of the police as "people's law", even though the police are people and, scientifically speaking, you have all the required trappings of folk law. I consider their law a part of state law, or in any case (it is, after all, formally prohibited) not the sort of "people's law" I am interested in studying. I want to draw a line between the state and people.

F. von Benda-Beckmann. "Folk law" can never be a good analytic concept. What is important is the making of distinctions of the sort which Baxi has just made, not the names we give to them. Another simple and obvious distinction we need to make, which has hardly been made in the discussion, is between social phenomena in the form of social behaviour and social phenomena in the form of objectified meaning (norms). Whether or not we ultimately combine both into a single definition of folk law, we cannot avoid the necessity of making the distinction and analyzing the two sorts of social phenomena separately, and also their interrelations. Some of the papers - for instance, Allott's - do so.

Starr. The discussion is making it clear that folk law is an analytic, not a taxonomic category. It consists of many different kinds of law, generated by self-regulating groups at many levels of society. We have to be aware of the processes of change in self-regulating groups.

Podgorecki. It is probably impossible to define folk law in terms of a number of essential features, theoretically speaking. But practically speaking we can use the term by contrast with the law of the state, especially in connection with processes of social change and social engineering. When we speak about "folk law", we are always concerned with some process of social change.

Snyder. I agree that use of the term "folk law" is unobjectionable, provided we do not talk about it: which seems a ridiculous position on its face. Abel's suggestion (in the *Newsletter* of the Commission on Folk Law and Legal Pluralism) is the most useful, so far as the choice of a single term is concerned: "legal pluralism" is the most general term that we can live with. So far as practical uses of "folk law" are concerned, we have to recognize that there is a variety of not-necessarily-consistent political purposes which those who use it may have. Just to say that the term can be used for practical purposes, while obviously important, does not deal with this problem of quite distinct practical purposes. "Legal pluralism" has rather more theoretical content - at least, there seems to be more written in English on "legal pluralism" than on "folk law".

Chairman. To sum up, there seems to have been some crystallization on at least one aspect of the subject, and this result can perhaps be stated in the following proposition: It is not useful to think of "folk law" as a distinct category of legal phenomena. While various speakers have given a variety of different reasons why this is so, everyone seems to agree on the ultimate conclusion. We seem also to be agreed that it is more useful to identify a number of different sorts of variation in legal phenomena. Some of these variations have been identified during the discussion: many can be summed up in Galanter's terms as having to do with the differentiation and organization of the generation and application of norms; also important is the degree to which, in Allott's terms, the generation of norms is autogenous; etc. Most of this variation - with the exception, perhaps, of Woodman's variable, geographic boundaries - can best be thought of as continuous. If I am right, then, we are at least all agreed that it is preferable to think about our subject in this way rather than to take our object - "folk law" - as a phenomenon fundamentally distinct from other sorts of law, especially "state law". I do not mean to suggest that there is nothing we can observe and identify as "folk law" if we wish. But there is no such *type* of law, no such analytically distinct sort of legal phenomenon, which we can usefully separate for scientific purposes from the rest of legal phenomena. None of the dichotomous distinctions which have been suggested - state versus folk law, state versus people's law, formal versus informal law, official versus intuitive law - will be fruitful for our purposes. Instead, we can recognize a number of kinds of dimensions of variation, none of which coincides very well with the notion of folk law: folk law is not necessarily more "local" than state law; some non-state law is just as highly organized and differentiated as state law (e.g. church law); and so forth. There is no characteristic which consistently follows the supposed distinction between state and folk law.

F. von Benda-Beckmann. I agree that on the theoretical level typological distinctions cannot be made. But in empirical reality we can readily distinguish different forms of law. Obviously we can distinguish between a law which is generated by a state's legislature and a law which is generated on the village level. On the theoretical level we require concepts which refer to continuous sorts of variation in law; but in empirical reality we observe actual, historically-specific forms of law, which we can readily distinguish from each other while recognizing that they coexist within a larger system.

Popular law-making in western society

Antony Allott

I. THE SCOPE OF THE TOPIC

We are all familiar with law-creation in societies ruled by customary law, though there have been few analytical accounts of the processes involved in such law-creation. There are many good studies, naturally mostly by anthropologists, of the *mechanisms* in such societies for the making of law; but one may suggest that the analyst must go further than merely recording these mechanisms and their operation, and that part of his task is almost philosophical, viz. to lay bare the *processes* which underlie these mechanisms, and which can account for the way in which sentiments, practices and rulings can "become" legal norms and institutions. If one were seeking a parallel from the physical sciences, biologists (or rather, "naturalists") had provided good descriptions of the birth and evolution of life forms, as seen from the outside, long before advances in genetics at the cell level and in biochemistry allowed scientists to explain the underlying biological and chemical processes which enabled these developments to occur. One feels, in other words, that study and understanding of law-creation processes are still largely at the observational, "naturalist" level only.

Studies, therefore, of how norms and institutions of customary laws emerge and take on the character which they possess are urgently needed. There is agreement that habitual practices, popular sentiment, and the dictates of authority, together with the inputs derived from the physical and psychological background, somehow combine to generate new legal institutions in such societies. Custom (what people do), mores (how people judge, by approval or disapproval, what people do), moral and religious notions and practices thus have a major part in law-formation in customary societies.

When we turn to so-called non-customary societies, those of the western world particularly, where legislation and clear law-making authority appear to be paramount, it would seem that there is no room for a parallel enquiry, since it is not conceded that habitual practices and popular sentiment play a part in law-formation - or at most it is accepted that they do so indirectly. The transmuting of one to the other, of what is into what ought to be, does not seem a suitable field for investigation. If this were so, then observation of the mechanisms would be at the same time a sufficient account of the processes.

However, there has been a growing realisation, fed by many studies from those of Ehrlich onwards, that processes similar to those which prevail in customary-law societies are at work in the developed systems too. Hence, indeed, the conference at which these papers were presented, and the creation of the Commission which sponsored it.

There is an urgent need, in other words, to investigate more deeply the processes of law-generation and law-modification in western societies, in which the popular role is much more pervasive and important than standard teaching and practice usually recognise. I would assert that this is as true of the civil-law as of the common-law systems, of the socialist and authoritarian as of the liberal democratic types of regime.

It would seem an easy task to isolate and describe the processes of emergence and development of law in the so-called common-law legal systems, because in such systems the function of the superior judge as proclaimer of law is open and evident. Whatever the previous rationalisations of the judge's role in earlier times, when it was asserted or assumed that he merely found and declared the law and did not "make" it, it is now well accepted and even trite that the judge makes law constantly in the course of the processes of litigation and adjudication. But - to revert to our earlier question - how? And, as a subsidiary question, what are the materials upon which he draws, and how precisely are popular values and practices fed into the law-making machine? The pressure of public opinion, direct or indirect, upon the processes of legislation by a parliament or other legislative authority is also a familiar story, though of a different kind and with different mechanisms. That similar processes are at work in systems which accord no such status to judge-made law and which assert the unchallengeable pre-eminence of the official law-maker, be he authoritarian or representative, requires slightly more justification and explanation.

The field and its name

Terminology, I would submit, is not the last, but the first, act of analytical activity in creating a field of study. This is because the choice of terms defines (=limits, directs) both what one wishes to look at, and how one looks at it. One must therefore avoid preselecting a term which presupposes a particular viewpoint- in other words, the term selected should be "open" and capable of extension or qualification, rather than "closed". Of course, what happens in reality is that there is a dialogue between the topic or field studied and the terms used to talk about it. This means that one must first provisionally settle in one's mind the general field, and then find terms which do not exclude, but, as closely as can be arranged, embrace this field. If this is the correct order of proceeding, it is important to agree first of all what is our field. Our field, it seems to me, is twofold: (1) on the one hand, it comprises the processes by which popular material is inserted into the official law or legal system, in the ways which have just been mentioned; (2) on the other hand, it looks at the extent to which the legal system allows, or is incapable of preventing, subidiary norm-making by those subject to the law, whether such norm-making is in conformity with the official law or not. A comprehensive account would cover both (1) and (2). Because of lack of space, and because less attention has perhaps been paid to the description and analysis of subsidiary norm-making, this paper will be restricted to the second aspect.

That is, the field is the processes by which bodies of whatever size evolve their own rules for their own regulation, such rules operating both at the primary level (allocation of claims and responsibilities) and at the secondary level (settlement of disputes about such allocations). Some of these bodies are dignified by being labelled "states", identifiable by their claim to monopoly within a wide area of regulation (though probably no state, however totalitarian, has ever claimed to regulate *everything* - e.g. domestic arrangements within a household - in detail). The constituted regulative system of a "state" may be conveniently referred to as a law or legal system.

This is not to beg the question whether regulative systems in autonomous societies which we are not prepared to call states are also laws. I think that they should be so called. At this stage one does not beg either the question of the limits of the term "law", and whether the regulative systems of bodies within a state can or should also be called laws.

What interests me is the process of self-regulation. In tyrannies and autocracies, whatever the rhetoric, the claim of the state to speak for the people, thus claiming that the system is self-regulatory, is fraudulent. In societies with genuine and total participation by the people in the processes of government (consensus societies), there may be self-regulation at this level, and also - so far as it obtains - at the topmost level. This provides the link, which to me is vital and interesting, between some customary-law societies and "folk-law" activities in other types of society.

Such self-regulation at lower levels may be either licit or illicit. In the next section of this paper I examine licit and illicit self-regulation under the heading of "catanomic" and "paranomic" norm-making. This divide does not correspond exactly to the division between "official" and "unofficial" law, since much that is done informally at the lowest level of the system is not official in any sense, but may be either law-conforming or law-contradicting. What is more, as we shall see, such lower-level norm-creation and behaviour can move from the illicit to the licit category - and we are interested in what makes them move and how the move is recognised by the system.

Many terms, none satisfactory, are proposed for this field. The injection of material derived from those subject to the law into the law at the highest official level contributes, as already remarked, to self-regulation; whilst at the lowest level norm-creation and norm-conformity *are* self-regulation.

"Folk-law" not only has a medieval ring about it but does not discriminate in the way I should like between these various phenomena. "Popular law" might have served; but here again there is a risk of confusion, because an unpopular law can still be law.

The domain of study is that of "regulation". The sub-domain is that regulation which is created and administered by those subject to it. In other words, the regulation is self-generated or "autogenous". Our field, I would suggest, is therefore that of *autogenous regulation*. If a single word is sought, one possibility is *autonomics*, which may be taken to mean a spontaneous and self-regulating system. By choosing either or both of these terms, one can avoid begging all sorts of questions - whether something is "law" or no law, who are the folk, and so on. If there is any danger of confusion with systems of self- regulation studied solely at the mechanical level in the scientific field, then one might qualify the term as *social autonomics*. (It is worth mentioning that the *Shorter Oxford English Dictionary* gives a quotation from 1854 which conveys the meaning one wants: "Reason is thus ever autonomic; carrying its own law within itself".)

II. THE ESSENCE OF THE PROBLEM

Confining, then, our attention henceforward to law-making in western society (though reserving the right to look back at practice in customary societies if this can illuminate the processes), we are seeking to isolate and describe those normative elements within the legal system in a western country which are popular in the sense that they are made by the people directly, i.e. without the intervention of the legislator. When one mentions "people", the reference is to the mass of those subject to the law and who do not possess special authority to make law. In *The Limits of Law* I coined two new terms (though made out of old elements), so as to enable one to distinguish between norm-making at the popular level which is in conformity with the execution of the official legal system, and norm-making which is non-conforming. I proposed the terms "catanomic" - in accordance with, not in defiance of, the law, and "paranomic" - apparently in contradiction or defiance of the existing legal system. Catanomic norm-creation includes a whole range of permitted activities and possibilities, such as the making of contracts generally under the law of contract, the dispositive parts of the law of property, and the setting up of a variety of associations whose framework only is laid down by law, the details and indeed the purposes being filled in by those who associate together. Paranomic norm-creation occurs whenever an individual or body within the society purports to make norms, and the legal system either does not permit such making of norms or does not permit the sorts of norms purportedly made. It may be asked why one does not use terms like "legal/illegal", "licit/illicit", for such a distinction. The reason is simple. We are interested in norm-creation, not an act or action as such; many instances of "illegal" activity comprise, not the setting up of a normative system in rivalry to the law, but the commission of a single illegal act. In other words, the illegal operator does not purport to legislate for others. As for "illicit", the function of this term is so vague as to be useless. It can cover acts which are manifestly illegal, as well as those which are merely morally wrong. If we take a cardinal example of a paranomic relationship, such as that of association of a man and a woman outside marriage in a continuing quasi-matrimonial relationship ("cohabitation"), this is certainly (or rather *was*) morally illicit. It was "illegal" in English law to the extent that the law would recognise no rights flowing from the association, and would invalidate a contract arising out of the relationship on the principle, *ex turpi causa non oritur actio*. But it is not, and has not been for many years, illegal in the sense that it may attract criminal sanctions. In other words, "illegal" is a word of too many, too vague, and insufficiently apposite meanings to be helpful here. Hence the need for a neologism.

Rule-making, norm-making, then, can be carried out by ordinary people. Much of what they do never encounters the legal system: one thinks of the vast body of social regulations and conventional practices which are not intended to have a legal purpose or effect, like the rules of card-games, the running of a society, domestic arrangements of one sort or another. These are certainly catanomic, in that they fall foul of no law; at the same time, they appear to be outside the ambit of the law, and hence outside the ambit of our study. But - and this is one of the fascinating features of this whole enquiry - such regulation of mores or social intercourse or association can easily move into the legal domain. The regulation can firstly be involved in the legal domain when what is regulated is quoted, cited, relied on or queried in a court of law or legal process by way of *indirect reference*. Thus if a club-member alleges that another member has cheated at cards, and a libel action is set on foot, then the rules of the game of cards, though themselves not intended to be legally binding, will have to be scrutinised by the court. Similarly if a football-player brings a criminal charge of assault against an opposing player for a tackle which offended the rules of football - the rules of football are not as such legal rules; but by a form of indirect reference they are brought into the legal domain and subjected to the characteristic forms of legal analysis.

Regulation of private associations, societies and activities can be brought within the legal domain by *direct reference* also, whenever one of those participating seeks direct legal enforcement of the rules in question. Private societies, we have said, are often informal associations whose members never contemplated that their relationship should be governed and determined by law; and yet the affairs of such societies and clubs may in England be brought before the courts directly if a member alleges a breach of the rules, and if he can establish a property consequence of such a breach. The English law of trusts operates to constrain those who hold office in such clubs and societies to manage the affairs of the association in the interests of its members, and especially so as to protect their property interests as beneficiaries.

Three stages can thus be discerned: (1) private autonomic regulation, which may be paranomic or not; "it is our affair, and the law should not interfere"; (2) indirect involvement of the law: "it is still our business how we do things, but please protect us"; (3) direct involvement of the law: "these norms, purportedly non-legal, create interests which we ask the law to protect". A fourth stage may then occur: (4) the norms, and indeed the association, become a part of the legal system.

If we turn to paranomic self-regulation, it is clear that the first stage, just cited, is not only possible but necessary: parties cannot be heard in a court of law asking the court to take note of that which the law disallows. The second stage, that of indirect involvement, is the interesting one. The law is sucked into an area out of which it has kept until now, or from which it has been positively excluded. What should be the posture of the official agencies of the law when confronted with such a situation? The likely response, if the court is willing to contemplate any recognition of the situation at all, is that, although the paranomic regulation is something which the law cannot countenance directly, yet it might lead to still greater injustice, especially to innocent third parties, if the paranomic situation were not reckoned as part of the background against which the rights and duties of the parties were to be ascertained and tested. By the time we move to the third stage, the Rubicon has been crossed. The parties are now asking the court to declare that their relationship has catanomic, and paranomic, status. If the request is acceded to, the result is an addition to the legal system of a new institution or set of rights and duties.

Quasi-matrimonial relationships

This, I would submit, is exactly what has happened, and is happening, with regard to informal relationships between a man and a woman of a quasi-matrimonial type. This development is worldwide, and not restricted to Britain, Europe, or North America; it includes the developing world, where the breakdown of traditional marriage patterns is also going on. I have selected this example not only because of its great intrinsic interest and because we can see the process of change occurring before our very eyes, but because of its fundamental importance, both for the legal system which must adjust to it, and for the society which is causing this process to occur. Marriage, one need hardly remark, is a central social institution in every society we know. From the least advanced to the most advanced, it could truthfully be said up to now that the legal system (and society through its social customs and mores) accorded a special status and a special protective apparatus of rights and responsibilities to a permanent or durable association between a man and a woman, provided that association had been created in accordance with the norms assigned in that society for its formation, and provided no contrary event had occurred which had caused the relationship to come to an end. Marriage everywhere creates a framework, the contents of which are partly filled in by the law, which prescribes the rights and duties of the parties (not just the spouses themselves, of courses, in many societies) - this we would call "status"; and partly by the parties themselves within the marriage, exercising their contractual or ordaining power to settle many of the details in the relationship. It is most important to note that the protected and recognised legal status of marriage is so protected and recognised not only *inter partes* but *in rem*: others are affected by the relationship and must observe it, be they adulterers, creditors or landlords. Marriage is thus a catanomic status+contract relationship or association.

Begun consensually as it is (though the consents are in some instances those of families or guardians instead of or in addition to those of the actual spouses), marriage has an affinity to other sorts of consensual relationship between a man and a woman, who may agree to live together in every way like husband and wife except for the fact that the formalities which the law requires have not been complied with. How may one distinguish between these two states? Obviously the fact that formalities have been observed or not observed is decisive. However, although it does not affect the position in the developed countries of which we now write, in some customary laws it is possible, or even usual, for a relationship to mature or be perfected over time, to move, in other words, from informal unapproved association to formal marriage. So a man and woman who live together without the approval of the respective parents or the appropriate payments ("marriage considerations"; dowry; "bride-price") having been made can cure these defects at any time if the consents are obtained and the payments made. In some cases, payments may even be deferred till the next generation. The effect of such a perfecting of their relationship is often related back to the first period of it, thus legitimising children who would otherwise be illegitimate, and so on. The social and legal consequences of this possibility of perfecting an informal relationship are to diminish the paranomic character of the original relationship. That such a possibility is not confined to some African customary laws and that it can occur now in developed society too is evidenced by case-law from England. Thus in *Foley* v *Foley*[1] it was held that a judge was entitled, in considering what lump sum to award to a wife payable by the husband on the dissolution of their marriage, to take into account a period of cohabitation between them prior to their getting formally married in determining what was, in the statutory phrase, "the duration of the marriage". But it was also held that, although perhaps "a very weighty factor", the premarital cohabitation was to be distinguished from the marriage proper: "Ten years of cohabitation would not necessarily have the same effect as ten years of marriage", according to Eveleigh, LJ.

In *The Limits of Law* I devoted Chapter 8 to exploring the growth, in the law of England, of the relationship of the "the 'house-mate' or common-law wife" - so there is no point in my repeating the detail of what I wrote there. The very title of the chapter, however, exposes some of the problems which a legal system must face in coping with this kind of development. In the last decade or so the American expression "common-law wife" has come into common popular use to refer to a woman living with a man as his wife without being formally married to him. The term has become popular because the institution has spread, or become more generally recognised and admitted. It is legally a misnomer, since the common law does not, and did not, recognize two persons associating together in a quasi-matrimonial relationship as being husband and wife to each other in any sense. Either (as in the old law) they had, though not celebrating their marriage before a priest, taken each other as husband and wife, and then became legally husband and wife, or they had not; in the latter case, their relationship was concubinage and not marriage. Since 1753 the former possibility has been unrecognised by the law. As to the term "house-mate", I adopted this to refer to the relationship because there comes a moment in time in the evolution of a new institution or relationship or phenomenon when it must be given a specific name by which it may be mentioned, ordered and discussed. For the reasons I develop in my book (and some of which are raised below), this moment has now come in English law and this name seemed the least inappropriate.

The development of what I call the "house-mate" relationship proceeds apace in most developed legal systems. Academic and practical concern with this development is evidenced by the flood of articles, studies and new books devoted to the topic. Two recent ones which one may cite as typical are *Marriage and Cohabitation in Contemporary Societies* (with the sub-title "Areas of legal, social and ethical change") edited by John M. Eekelaar and Sanford N. Katz; and *The Cohabitation Guide*, by Pat Clayton.[2] In adding to the weight of this publication one risks being accused of jumping on an academic bandwaggon; but with respect one may reply in justification that other such writings are concerned with aspects different from the present study. Thus the Eekelaar and Katz book, the fruits of an international symposium, explores in detail the impact on the institution of marriage of these new developments, and the difficulties experienced in the legal regulation, if any, of the new institution; the Clayton book is a compendium of practical advice to those who may find themselves in such a relationship.

Now, while the former sort of study does attempt to relate legal change to social change, and also asks how the law has adapted or should adapt to changing social institutions, it is not concerned with one of our principal questions in this study, viz., what is the process by which the paranomic becomes the catanomic? We look in other words primarily at the growth of new institutions rather than the decay of old ones. Our concern must be with the input of popular wishes into the legal system, and how these inputs are translated into new legal regulation. Naturally the aspects canvassed in Eekelaar and Katz are also of interest to us; while the discussion in detail of what, for instance, the partners in a quasi-matrimonial relationship should do about their joint or several property (as so usefully covered by Clayton) highlights the boundary problem as between law and voluntary individual action.

If one turns one's attentions now solely to English law (though bearing in mind that in Australia, Brazil, Hungary, France, the Netherlands, Canada, Sweden, Switzerland, the United States, West Germany, and Yugoslavia - to quote some of the countries mentioned in the Eekelaar and Katz volume, to which we could add many of the countries of Africa to some extent, and the Caribbean countries to a very pronounced extent - these problems also arise), the recentness and magnitude of the change in attitude of the legal system to such relationships are astonishing. It is little more than a decade or a decade and a half that has seen a more fundamental change sweep over the English legal system in this area than has previously occurred in many centuries. If nothing else, this demonstrates the potency of popular attitudes and practice today in changing law. Undoubtedly this is associated with the individualistic and voluntarist character of social and legal sentiment, which has already been demonstrated by the withdrawal of the law from many areas of private morality and behaviour, such as homosexual relationships and obscene materials. The primacy of the individual will, and the impenetrable privacy accorded to what is done by it so far as it does not affect others, are the principles that are being exemplified and advanced. (The contradiction of this emphasis with the movement towards cutting back on freedom of contract in the interests of consumer protection and state policy is striking.) If broadly individuals are, in the modern polity, to be allowed to do what they like without the interference or control of the law, should what they do be left there, or is there some role for the state legal system in either marking the boundaries of permitted action or in according recognition and protection to the results?

Anyhow, let us briefly review the movement in English legal opinion in this field. A late indication of the classical approach can be found in Lord Devlin's *The Enforcement of Morals*. Published in 1965, it restates the old principle of English law, *ex turpi causa non oritur actio*. In his chapter entitled "Morals and the law of marriage" Lord Devlin says:

"The law does not prohibit sexual unions outside marriage. Marriage, when stripped of its spiritual significance, is simply a special sort of union between a man and a woman to which society gives a special status...

"Is then the State according to our ideas of society entirely free to grant or withold the status of marriage as it is, for example, free to confer or not the status of the peerage? No. A man and a woman who live together outside marriage are not prosecuted under the law but they are not protected by it. They are outside the law. Their union is not recognized, no legal obligation is implicit in it, and an express obligation will not be enforced by the law. Prima facie the individual is entitled to call upon the law to enforce the contracts which he makes ... English law has from the earliest times refused to enforce certain classes of contracts as being against public policy. Irregular sexual unions constitute one of those classes ... The decision [about whether to impose such a restraint on freedom of contract] ... is a political and not a moral one. That means that in a democracy it must, broadly speaking, accord with the will of the majority. Society has a right therefore to define the status of marriage in accordance with the ideas of the majority and to refuse to confer it upon those who do not conform" (Devlin 1965: 77-78).

And at another place, when discussing "Morals and the law of contract", Lord Devlin has this to say:

"Obviously, the law cannot specifically enforce contracts requiring the performance of acts which the law itself forbids to be done. English law extends this embargo to acts which although not contrary to law are contrary to morality, such as fornication. The courts will not enforce a covenant to provide for a mistress. A landlord who discovers his lodgers are living in sin must turn them out or else rely on their sense of honour for the rent. But English law goes further than this. It treats such contracts not merely as unenforceable but as suffering from an infectious disease. It will not even help a man who has acted on the faith of them to get what in justice is his due" (Devlin 1965:52).

It is fair to add that Lord Devlin goes on to deprecate some of these rigours of English law as they affect innocent parties. In particular, he expresses sympathy with a "discarded mistress who seeks to recover money she was promised". But the sympathy was not the law.

How different is the law now, less than 20 years on! Lord Denning, most distinguished of living English judges, whom no one could accuse of being anything less than a pillar and upholder of conventional morality, has this to say when a milkman tried to turn out of his own house the woman with whom he had been living and who had borne him two babies:

"I cannot believe that this is the law. This man had a moral duty to provide for the babies of whom he was the father. I would go further. I think he had a legal duty towards them. Not only towards the babies. But also towards their mother. She was looking after them and bringing them up. In order to fulfil his duty towards the babies, he was under a duty to provide for the mother too."[3]

A man's property rights, in other words, would be overriden in the interests of his mistress; a man could owe, not just a "moral obligation" (an odd phrase when contrasted with what Lord Devlin had to say about immorality!), but a legal obligation to his ex-mistress to provide for her. A total revolution, in other words, in English law, documented in my book. How have we got to this new position?

It was certainly not as a consequence of any formal democratic process. There has been no vote in Parliament, no enacted law which says that a fundamental change in English law should now be made (with the exception of the Domestic Violence and Matrimonial Proceedings Act 1978, which extended the protection accorded to wives to those living as husband and wife). The will of the majority in the matter has never been formally ascertained by referendum or otherwise, and it would be mere speculation to suggest what that will might be. It is social facts, the sum of individual decisions and actions, which have pressed on the courts and persuaded them to change their attitude. Practically none of the principles of law stated so confidently by Lord Devlin in his discussion of law and morality in connexion with contracts, and quoted above, would now obtain. Courts *are* prepared to order the specific performance of an agreement between a man and his mistress; even more, a court has ordered a man to perform a promise to transfer property to his mistress which lacks enforceability as a contract.[4]

III. RESEARCH TASKS

What I have done here is to point to some possible areas of enquiry, especially as they arise in English law (though the same sorts of enquiry could, I am sure, be made in many other western countries too). Quasi-matrimonial relationships are just one possible field for enquiry among many, though the most interesting, radical and challenging. What is one seeking to investigate, and how should one carry on such an investigation?

Hints as to the former question have been scattered through this paper. The processes by which material derived from popular sentiment and practice is gradually incorporated in the fabric of the official law are one such field. To some extent in looking at this field one is repeating or adding to well established topics - after all, Dicey was concerned in the 19th century with the way in which law and public opinion were related to each other; and he was by no means the first, and is certainly not the last, to show an interest in this relationship. I have myself tried to add to the listable means by which popular elements are incorporated in the legal system in *The Limits of Law* in which I mention - for English law: the judicial technique for re-definition of instrumental legal terms to adopt new popular views of what is right and reasonable; the contextual interpretation of statutes, where the context can include contemporary social morality and practices; the jury and lay justices of the peace as intermediaries in the popularisation of law and its administration; and social pressures on the police which influence them in the execution of their duty to apply the criminal law. All this as well as the more obvious and frank attempts at popular modification of law by pressure groups and indeed by the processes of representative democracy. Especially interesting are the unwitting and unspoken modifications of the law by popular practice, where there is no overt attempt to subvert or remould the law, but where the effect of the practice is just as radical. This is what has happened in the house-mate field. There comes a tilting point when what up till then had been a paranomic practice, ignored or reprobated by the official law and its agencies, suddenly wins recognition and acceptance, however limited, from the legal system as operated. I use the adjective "tilting", because this seems to describe the rapidly accelerating process by which the new association or practice is taken on after its slow and at first unaccepted beginning. The law on house-mates in England is now changing so rapidly that one cannot keep abreast of it without reading the latest cases, which are emerging in a steady stream. What is the force, what is the psychological change, which explains the sudden and decisive tilt in the official recognition of a paranomic situation?

For future research into this field I see the main tasks as spotting suitable areas for investigation. Again, I have mentioned a number of possibles in my book, such as squatting and parking on the highway. I suspect that one could always find more by backtracking through legal history, and that one is not concerned with a unique phenomenon of the 20th century. A historical investigation is therefore demanded as well as a current sociological one. The historical approach has the special advantage that we can see what the end result of the process will be, and can trace back from there to its earliest beginnings; whereas with such developments as that of the house-mate system it is not yet clear that it is a system, or what the eventual result, within the law, will be.

As to the *manner* of the investigation, since what is influential is mostly practice rather than statement, only those trained in observing and analysing behaviour will be able to make much progress with their researches. Since that which is influenced is the mind of those who run the official legal system, psychological studies come into play. One has the impression that many studies of the judicial mind are formal and predictive only; what "causes" a judge, and still more a group of judges, to start taking a new line in a radically changed area of the law is still an inscrutable mystery. Speculations about class orientation and professional training are unlikely to yield the sort of results we want. Judges are unlikely to submit themselves for deep analysis; and even if they were, their retrospective rationalisations of why they have now begun to behave as they have do not have any necessary validity.

I mention these considerations without much ability to provide useful answers. This is one important reason for conferring in the way that we did at Bellagio, and attempting to open out a whole new field in the process. That the task is important is a point I briefly develop in the section below.

IV. IMPLICATIONS FOR LEGAL THEORY AND ADMINISTRATION

I am convinced that the task is important. If it were not, the debate on methodology and aims would be profitless. We - that is, those who have been conditioned by being brought up in, perhaps trained in, the legal systems of the western world - perceive "law" in a particular and peculiar way. We have been convinced that law is what the official organs of the state make and administer. We assume that the raw materials for their law are derived by those organs by some rational process and from official and overt sources. What we are now required to accept is that these preconceptions are misleading, and, to speak bluntly, fallacious. Law is not the sole preserve of the official organs of the state; it is a complex of what is said, and what is done, by law-subjects as well as law-givers and law-administrators. What is done by law-subjects often deviates grossly from what is said by law-givers. Previously the assumption was that such deviation was lawless, and that was all. Now it is appreciated that such deviation is law-creating.

It is here that the parallels with the customary-law societies become especially helpful. Again our theoretical image of how such laws work may be erroneous or shortsighted. We may think that in a customary legal system the rules of the law are manufactured out of the practices of the people, that, in other words, practice is in this instance a legitimate source of law, and that practice authenticates and sustains such law. This is not untrue, but neither is it the whole truth. We avoid completely here the immense philosophical problem of describing how what is done becomes that which ought to be done, and look only at the processes by which the customary law becomes re-defined, stretched or altered as practice and social sentiment change. What may not always be appreciated is that, even in a customary-law society, popular practice may be law-disregarding and that paranomic relationships can be created there too. The customary law is subjected to a ceaseless process of adaptation and change, strengthened by popular participation in many societies in law-administration as much as by popular practice outside court. The people in western societies participate in law-administration too, both overtly - as with juries and lay justices - and covertly - as when their ideas and practices influence what the judge decides.

The likely consequence of the prosecution of these lines of enquiry is that our perception of law will be radically altered and our understanding of the way in which laws are actually made and administered will be profoundly enlarged.

NOTES

1.   [1981] Fam. 160, C.A.
2.   And see also Bottomley et al. 1981: this is a most useful guide to every current legal aspect of cohabitation law in England, compiled by a collective of women legal workers.
3.   *Tanner* v. *Tanner* [1975] 3 All E.R. 776, C.A., at p. 779.
4.   *Pascoe* v. *Turner* [1979] 2 All E.R. 945, C.A.

REFERENCES

Allott, A.
    1980   *The Limits of Law*, London: Butterworths.
Bottomley, A., et al.
    1981   *The Cohabitation Handbook: A Woman's Guide to the law*, London: Pluto.
Clayton, P.
    1981   *The Cohabitation Guide*, London: Wildwood House.
Devlin, P.
    1965   *The Enforcement of Morals*, London: Oxford University Press.
Eekelaar, J.M., and S.N. Katz (eds.)
    1980   *Marriage and Cohabitation in Contemporary Societies; Areas of Legal, Social and Ethical Change*, Toronto: Butterworths.

Cultural ideology and empirical reality: case studies in contemporary law management[1]

Rolando A. Alum Jr.

> "The law perverted!... The law become the weapon of every kind of greed! Instead of checking crime, the law itself guilty of the evils it is supposed to punish!" (Bastiat 1979)

I. THEORETICAL CONSIDERATIONS[2]

I have often heard anthropologists say that if they had the opportunity to start their research all over again, they would begin by contrasting the cultural ideology (the ideal culture) with the observable ethnographic behaviour of the population under study (e.g. González 1974:39). The logic behind this approach is not new. Malinowski, the patriarch of legal anthropology, proposed such a strategy in his classic *Crime and Custom in Savage Society* (1926).[3] He postulated that no culture, particularly in its legal aspects, could be properly understood without an exploration of the discrepancies between (a) the ideal of what constituted proper legal behaviour, "the orthodox version", and (b) "its realization", the practice of "actual life" (Malinowski 1926:107). Criticising the then incipient body of legal anthropological literature, Malinowski continued:

> "When the native is asked what he would do in such and such a case, he answers what he should do;... the pattern of possible conduct... His sentiments,... propensities,... bias,... self-indulgences,... he reserves for his behaviour in real life..., [which is] revealed only to the field-worker, who observes native life directly... 'Hearsay Anthropology' is constantly exposed to the danger of ignoring the seamy side of [native] law... The... Hearsay Anthropolog[ist] constructs [the native]... legal doctrine... from... informants' statements, but he remains ignorant of the blurs made by human nature... Truth is a combination of both versions..." (Malinowski 1926:120-21).

Ever since Malinowski's seminal work the bulk of legal anthropological and sociological research has concentrated on the opposite side. Philosophically inspired by European Legal Positivism and the related American Legal Realism, the emphasis has been placed not on the ideal configuration, but on the more or less statistically verifiable "real" legal cases. Underlying this approach has been a twofold inquiry: (i) a perennial pursuit of a cross-culturally valid definition of law[4], and (ii) a search for conflict resolution legal mechanisms. The usual unit of analysis has been the legal case, whether the "trouble" (synchronic) or the "extended" (diachronic) version, or a combination of both.[5]

Critics of the case method have called attention to its limitations;[6] it was not its use, but its abuse, in the exclusion of other perspectives, that concerned many social scientists studying the realm of law in culture and society.[7] Many of the best known anthropologists of law had a wide training in sociology, philosophy, history, and/or jurisprudence (e.g. Póspísil 1971), and have recognised the need to return to Malinowski's earlier view. However, few have succeeded in correcting the one-sided perspective despite their claims. It could be said that there has been a disparity between the ideology advocated and the reality of the work delivered. A few even eventually reverted to Hearsay Anthropology,[8] while others opposed the two-sided perspective.[9]

Nevertheless, we find some adherents of the dual-perspective approach in contemporary legal anthropology. Thus Moore takes into account the ideal-real dimension in her proposed model of "law as process" (Moore 1978:51). Contemporary theoretical support is also found in Lévi-Strauss's French Structuralism. As Moore notes, Lévi-Strauss has put the question: "To what extent does the manner in which a society conceives its orders and their ordering correspond to the real situation?" (Moore 1978:36; Lévi-Strauss 1958:312).[10] According to Nutini, one of Lévi-Strauss's best interpreters, the French Structuralist approach consists precisely of "excavating" into the cultural "deep structural" responses, the results of which should be contrasted with the statistical observational data, in order to build the "mechanical model" that should in turn be submitted to constant scientific testing (Nutini 1970; Alum and Pye 1976).[11]

However, I am not yet satisfied with these theoretical and methodological advances. It seems that the history of legal anthropology parallels that of socio-cultural anthropology (ethnology) in general, at least in one processual sense. Every new school of thought has arisen as a reaction to a previously predominant school, which it has sought to overcome by rejecting the old postulates *in toto* (De Waal Malefijt 1974). Colloquially put, each "threw the baby out with the bath-water". Thus Hearsay Anthropology missed the reality behind the ideological constructs. Then came the casuistic-realist-positivists (for lack of a better label) who missed ideology (or, at best, confused it). Both missed the ideal-real incongruences. We now encounter a new breed that tries to reconcile the previous two approaches by taking into account the ideal-real dichotomy, but does so in an incomplete and rather negative way. The ideal-real contrast is conducted with the *a priori* purpose of "proving" the inconsistencies of the social life of the culture in question.[12]

I intend instead to take a more objective stand that will seek to discover which tenets of the cultural ideology - or of the ideal folk law - are actually effective.[13] Law is but one of the cultural mechanisms for social control (D. Black and Mileski 1973: 4-7).[14] The comparison presented below between the ideal legal culture in a plantation community in the Dominican Republic, and a sample of formal legal cases, reveals that, while in reality some of the ideal tenets (such as non-violence) are little practised, others are still functioning. In other words, if law has many admirable manifestations, as we claim (Bohannan 1957; Hoebel 1954), then we should be pleased to admit that the genuine multidisciplinary, integrative approach used here leads to the discovery of, among other things, the predicted rules (ideal) of local socio-cultural institutions that do in reality perform law-like social control functions - both being part of the sub-culture's folk law.[15] Following Malinowski again, we must also take into consideration the law-abiding patterns in society (Malinowski 1926:56-59).[16] This will represent another improvement on the case method which presents only the law that is violated *and* reported. A fuller study of law should include both what happens and what does not happen in the realm of social control. The presentation that follows is a preliminary testing of such a combined model.[17]

II. THE ETHNOGRAPHIC SETTING

1. The Dominican Republic

The ethnographic field data under analysis here was collected in the Dominican Republic (DR) during a period of 30 months.[18] The DR occupies almost three-quarters of the Caribbean island which Columbus named Hispaniola, and which lies between Cuba to the west, and Puerto Rico and the Atlantic Ocean to the east. The remaining western quarter of the island is the territory of the Republic of Haiti. The DR covers some 19,000 square miles, or slightly more than Denmark or Switzerland. Sugar cane has been historically the major national crop. Most of the cane plantations are located in the dry southern coastal lowlands where I conducted my research. The rate of national economic development in the last decade and a half has been most impressive. Poverty is nonetheless still pervasive, most obviously in the region of the frontier with Haiti and the plantation areas.[19] The population, of which the majority is phenotypically mulatto, is estimated at five and a half million. Neighbouring Haiti, in contrast, with much poorer resources and smaller territory, has a slightly larger population. This fact may explain why thousands of illegal migrant Haitian workers find their way to the DR's plantations every year. The Haitian presence affects the cultural definition of race, which is most intriguing. Negritude is considered undesirable and is primarily identified with Haitians.[20]

Political instability has been the rule during more than a century of republican life. Notwithstanding this, remarkable stability *and* democratisation have been achieved since the mid-1960s. The current constitution establishes a tripartite representative government, consisting of an elected Executive, a bicameral Congress, and an appointed Judiciary. The Code Napoleon, introduced with the French and Haitian invasions in the nineteenth century, is in force (DR/JCE 1966; Wiarda 1968; Alum various).

2. The Community of Batey

Batey (pseudonym)[21] is a typical community of cane workers in the coastal plain, about 40 miles east of Santo Domingo, the capital city. The hamlet is located on one of the state-owned plantations in the cane-growing southeastern region.[22] The factory (*ingenio* or mill) and the Caribbean Sea are some eight kilometers to the south. Most of the residents work in occupations related to the plantation, especially during the *zafra* (harvest). The population is about 800 at the peak season, of whom some 300 are children. There are more men than women, especially among the non-Dominican components, because of the cane-fields' male labour demands. There are some 160 households and one single-room school. Although the plantation owns all lands and some of the residential structures, many families own their houses. The nuclear family plus other kinfolk is the pattern of household composition. Most conjugal relations are of a mutual consent type. Several homes are matrifocal, and illegitimacy is widespread. Ritual kinship in the form of *compadrazgo* (discussed below) is characteristic.

The internal social status differentiation follows ethnic lines. Three distinguishable groups are found here, as in any cane community in the DR. (a) At the highest level are the Dominicans - phenotypically white, mulatto and negroid in order of social ranking. (b) Intermediate are the *cocolos*, the Anglophone blacks who have migrated from elsewhere in the West Indies and have been permanent residents for nearly half a century. (c) The bottom stratum are the Haitians, both those who reside permanently and those who are in the plantation just for the harvest (usually about 100 young, unaccompanied males).

Local authority is diversified between various individuals, some responding to the municipal, provincial or national governments, and others to the internal plantation structure; but all are appointed. Most *Bateyanos* (residents of Batey) are nominally Roman Catholic; a small proportion is Protestant. At the same time, local versions of African-Catholic syncretism, Dominican vodum, and witchcraft practices are prevalent, constituting some of the sources of conflict.

Bateyanos purchase their foodstuffs and other goods from local retail stores.[23] The stores are now owned by local entrepreneurs but informants remember when they were company stores (under Trujillo).[24] Complaints about high prices and low quality on the part of the merchants, and non-payment of debts on the part of the customers, are some of the sources of inter-personal disputes. A few of the residents own small animals, such as pigs, chickens and goats, which roam freely, causing occasional damage to scarce individual possessions such as clothes hung out to dry.

III. RESEARCH DESIGN

1. Background to the Project

I went to the DR to gather data for my doctoral dissertation; I had originally intended to focus on the choice of inter-personal conflict resolution options *a la* Collier (1973; Alum and Miller 1975). My intended strategy consisted of a combination of traditional participant-observation and collection of trouble and extended cases, observed and/or gathered through court archival research, and informal intervieuws. However, I soon realised the practicality of applying sociologically styled surveys. I eventually administered in person five different kinds of questionnaires covering over four-fifths of Batey's households; only one kind, however, is used for this paper.[25]

2. The Field Surveys

The ethnographic portion of this report is based on analyses of the responses given to questions considered to be of a legal-anthropological nature. Formal interviews were conducted in Spanish in early 1978. The sample consisted of 63 informants, 33 women and 30 men, all of them household heads or co-heads. I tried to secure representation of all geographical corners of Batey, types of housing, ethnic and age groups, social status, etc., but this representativeness was implemented in an "artistic" manner, rather than in a statistical fashion. I was able to corroborate my initial assumption that, nationality aside, there is great cultural, social and economic homogeneity. Consequently, this sample, constituting 13% of Batey's adult population and 40% of its households, may be considered more than sufficient to be statistically significant for Batey. Furthermore, Batey is unquestionably representative of Dominican plantation communities in more than one sense, especially of *bateyes* (sugar plantation hamlets) in the typical *canaveral* (cane field) areas of the southeastern strip.[26]

3. The Conflict Cases

I encountered more difficulty in collecting the formal cases than in applying the questionnaires. Batey is located exactly on the borderline between two municipalities. Some cases are taken to the court in the small city of San José, located some 15 kms to the north and the capital of the municipality of its name. Technically its court has jurisdiction over Batey and almost all of the surrounding cane-fields and villages. However, because of proximity, some cases are taken to the factory town's court. Both are *Juzgados de Paz*, Justice of the Peace (JP) Courts, provided for in the 1966 Constitution now in force.[27] Their jurisdiction is to hear minor civil and criminal cases.[28] I initially intended to gather old and current cases arising within Batey or involving people from Batey. However, I encountered problems; I met a strong initial resistance by court officials to cooperating and allowing me to conduct the investigation in the court archives.[29] Countering this took me untold effort and time, to the point that I pondered whether I should not try to research something else. I finally received "clearance", but not before I had involved on my behalf the Ministries of Education and Justice, and the Attorney General in person. I then discovered that the "archives" consisted of an unfurnished room in each JP Court, where records were piled on the floor at random and got wet owing to leaks in the structure, and where rats and roaches roam freely. Moreover, some years' collections had been lost, ruined or destroyed. I then understood some of the reasons for the initial apprehension toward my study. Nevertheless, I continued my documentary search, but discovered that the records contained few cases involving Batey and/or *Bateyanos*. As an alternative, I began collecting cases from or involving residents of nearby, Batey-like communities, in so far as these were accessible in the two courts. I ended up collecting hundreds of those, ranging in date from current cases that I had personally observed in court to as far back as the 1930s.[30]

For practical reasons, however, the sample of cases included here conforms to the following criteria of selection: (a) they are exclusively interpersonal conflict cases (i.e., involving at least one plaintiff and a defendant regardless whether of a civil or criminal nature); (b) they are cases aired at the San José Court; (c) they involve at least one contender from a Batey-like community in Batey's environs, that, moreover, belongs to the same state-owned plantation compound, *Guarina* (pseudonym); and (d) they comprise the first 100 cases collected that met criteria (a), (b) and (c), regardless of other attributes and variables. Notwithstanding, as will be seen shortly, all have the further characteristic (e) of being rather recent (i.e., from 1960s on).[31]

IV. THE IDEAL-REAL CONTRAST

It has already been established that there are often differences between the two faces, the ideal and the real components of culture. The legal culture of a given society is constituted by those socio-cultural aspects which are related to the social control mechanisms, broadly defined, and it represents one of the vital elements of any legal system (Friedman 1977:7). It also contains the dual components of ideology and performance, which may or may not overlap. Thus legal culture involves both (a) the body of beliefs that justifies social control actions, expressed when people say how they should or would like to behave when confronted with particular situations, or in how they believe they do act, as well as (b) the body of empirical information observed or reported about cases that constitutes the manifest social practice.

Some writers appear to identify the legal culture exclusively with the ideal aspect (D. Black and Mileski 1973:10; Bohannan 1957; Collier 1975; Friedman 1977). What we have at stake here is the vital concept of culture itself. *Culture*, whether legal culture or otherwise, is not just a belief system, nor just an ideology (cf. M. Black 1973; M. Black and Metzger 1965); culture involves also performance. J.M. Roberts (1964) and others in the New Anthropology group have advanced a definition of culture that treats the concept as an information system. This version is more suitable for legal culture, since the second aspect, the practice of observable legal behaviour, is culturally bound too, a phenomenon from which even social deviance does not escape. Every individual enculturated in a society has a notion of how far he or she can deviate from the socially acceptable norm before tolerance is breached; or at least, he or she has an idea of what to expect in case of miscalculation. In other words, both dimensions, the ideal and the real, together constitute a fitting, functioning and dynamic system.

Bearing all this in mind, we are now ready to examine the construction of the local cultural ideology through the analysis of questionnaire responses. There are a total of ten questions analysed, most of which presented hypothetical cases. The answers to these (= A) are then compared with the statistical analyses of formal cases (= B) collected in court. The answers have been grouped into five general categories. For answers, N = 63; for cases, N = 100.

1. Robbery. "What do you do when someone steals something that belongs to you?"

A. a. basically do nothing   27
  b. fight/stage uproar/indulge in violence   2
  c. report to authorities (police, etc.)   20
  d. other informal peaceful options (e.g. protest)   6
  e. no answer, no adequate answer, or not applicable (e.g. "I have nothing worth stealing")   8

T=63=N

B. Eight cases involved some kind of accusation of robbery.

2. Debt. "If you lent money or some object to a neighbour and he/she would not return it, what would you do?"

A. a.	basically nothing	38
b.	fight/uproar/violence	0
c.	report to authorities	4
d.	other informal peaceful	11
e.	no answer, etc.	10

B. Only one case (1960) involved a debt, which was for three cents. (See 9A and B.d, below.)

3. Merchants' wrongdoing. "What do you do when you purchase something (from a local retail store) and then realise that you have been cheated on the price, quantity and/or quality?"

A. a.	basically nothing	20
b.	fight/uproar/violence	0
c.	report to authorities	1
d.	other informal peaceful (e.g. present claim)	33
e.	no answer, etc.	9

B. No case had its origins in a merchant's wrongdoing.

4. Animals' actions. "What do you do when your neighbour's animals break into your home?"

A. a.	basically nothing	12
b.	fight/uproar/violence	1
c.	report to authorities	1
d.	other informal peaceful (e.g., call the animal's owner)	42
e.	no answer, etc.	7

B. No case arose from animal's damaging actions.

5. Child abuse. "What do you do when someone hits your child?"

A. a.	basically nothing	13
b.	fight/uproar/violence	5
c.	report to authorities	11
d.	other informal peaceful	15
e.	no answer, etc.	19

B. Three cases involved hitting children. In one the defendant was the school teacher in a hamlet other than Batey.

6. Casting of witches' spells. "What do you do when someone casts a witchcraft spell on you?"

A. a.	basically nothing	19
b.	fight/uproar/violence	2
c.	report to authorities	7

d. other informal peaceful (e.g., reverse spell)   17
e. no answer, etc.   18
B. See subsection B, next Question.

7. *Accusations of withcraft.* "What do you do if someone accuses you of withcraft?"
A. a. basically nothing   29
   b. fight/uproar/violence   0
   c. report to authorities   8
   d. other informal peaceful   17
   e. no answer, etc.   9
B. Only one case (1976) involved an accusation of withcraft.

8. *Mediation in quarrels.* "What is your reaction when you see a quarrel going on in the Batey community?"
A. a. basically nothing   26
   b. join in the fight/uproar/violence   0
   c. report to authorities   8
   d. other informal peaceful (e.g. mediate)   18
   e. "there are never fights here" (see 9A and B.a, and 10A.d, below) 4
   f. no answer, etc.   7
B. Two cases indicated that an attempt was made by a third party to mediate between parties involved in a quarrel. (See also next Question.)

9. *Inter-personal quarrels.* "What types of arguments have you had with your neighbours, local merchants or fellow-workers here?" The answers and the corresponding empirically gathered cases need a comparative tabulation in this case.

		A	B. Cases
A. a.	"none, I never have any arguments (see 8A.e, above and 10A.d, below)	51	–
b.	over children's actions	3	3
c.	over false testimony, "*respeto*", gossip	2	2
d.	over debts	1	1 (see 2B above)
e.	jealousy and other marital	0	20 (incl. 17 involving violence)
f.	other inter-personal (e.g. with co-workers)	1	74
g.	no answer, etc. (e.g. "cannot remember")	5	–
		T=63=N	T=100=N

10. Dominican-Haitian rivalry. "Who do you think fight more, Dominicans or Haitians?" The answers and the corresponding empirically gathered cases need a comparative tabulation in this case.

A.			B. Cases (all);	Cases (violent)
a.	Dominicans among themselves	5	84 (1960-78)	54
b.	Haitans among themselves	17	1 (1975)	1
c.	Dominicans with Haitians & vice versa	6	10 (1962-78)	9
d.	"no-one ever fights here" (*"aquí nunca se pelea"*) (see 8A.e, 9A.a, above)	7		
e.	all fight the same	11		
f.	no answer, etc.	17		
g.	nationality unclear		5	4
		T=63=N	100=N	T=68

V. A PRELIMINARY INTERPRETATION: CULTURAL IDEOLOGY, EMPIRICAL RE-ALITY, AND SOCIAL CONTROL

The contrast presented requires detailed and deep analysis which is not possible within the present constraints of time and space. Nevertheless, a few observations of a preliminary nature may be noted.

1. Of the ten questions, eight elicited "basically will do nothing" as the most frequent response. On this evidence it appears that the standardised local ideology calls for a passive response to the kinds of problems posed, at least at the hypothetical level.

2. Although fighting back, staging a loud uproar, or engaging in violence do not appear to be the cultural expectation, 67% of the cases involved some kind of violence and public uproar (*"escándalo público"*).

3. Reporting to authorities seems to be the behaviour preferred by the standardised ideology only in certain circumstances, such as in cases of robbery. It is not expected in other types of conflicts, such as disputes over merchants' wrongdoings, or over animals' property damage. Moreover, although I do not have statistics, it is clear that very few of the cases registered in the courts were instituted by civilians; almost all were commenced by some representatives of the law enforcement authorities, especially the rural guard.

4. Every question elicited, from at least some of the informants who answered it, responses which were not in any of the three categories just mentioned.[32]

5. In respect of every question some respondents resorted to evasive answers, such as "I have nothing worth stealing/damaging", "that has never

happened to me", "there are never fights here", and the like, all revelatory of the "we-all-get-along-here" ideology.

6. Particularly striking is the difference between the zero percentage answers in category 9A.e (involvement in quarrels arising from jealousy and other marital disputes), reflecting the ideal, and the incidence of 20% jealousy/marital dispute cases, 17 of which involved violence, representing the single largest discernible category.

7. Dominican-Haitian rivalry is revealed in the answers to question 10. Respondents believe that Haitians fight more among themselves than Dominicans fight with Haitians and with other Dominicans.[33] However, the case analysis reveals that 84 cases (= 84%) involved Dominicans among themselves, of which 54 involved some violence (representing 81% of the total 67 violent cases gathered).

8. Notwithstanding the noted incongruities, the comparison further reflects the effectiveness for social control of some aspects of the cultural ideology. For example, many respondents chose other informal redress mechanisms as their preferred answer, as already noted above, a frequency that is in agreement with the empirical case evidence. In two questions, "3. Merchants' wrongdoing" and "4. Animals' actions", the respondents' most preferred answers, "a. nothing" and "d. other informal ways", parallel the case data, since no court cases were found in those two categories in the sample. Having conducted participant-observation research in the region, I find it difficult to believe that no reasons for quarrelling in these two categories ever arose. One is led to conclude then that the injured party actually did nothing about it, or chose other informal redress mechanisms. Similar conclusions could be drawn in regard to questions "2. Debt" (1% of cases) and 6 and 7, the "witchcraft" questions (1% of cases). This leads us to an observation on co-godparenthood's effectiveness, of the social control dimension of the *compadrazgo* ideology.

The social control dimension of the Compadrazgo Ideology In its most limited sense, *compadrazgo* refers to the bonds established between the parents and god-parents of a neophyte. There are, however, many variations throughout the Mediterranean-Latin oriented, predominantly Catholic cultures.[34] Various anthropologists have reported some of the different aspects and dimensions of *compadrazgo*, such as its demographic functions (Nutini and Bell 1980), but the institution has not been studied extensively. While previous studies of mine present the most recent ethnographic analyses of *compadrazgo* in an Antillean society (e.g., Alum 1977, 1981), its functions as a social-control mechanism have been ignored.[35]

The Dominican *compadrazgo* ideology requires, according to informants, that participants have a previous history of amicability. Once established, the relationship is considered sacred, sometimes carrying more force than consanguineal and affinal forms of kinship. This spiritual relationship is supposed to be guided by cordiality and mutual respect ("*respeto*"). Of *compadres* (pl., m. or f.) who quarrel it is said, "God will punish them", and at best the relationship will cease.[36] Most strikingly, I have yet to find evidence of any *compadres* or *comadres* (pl., f.) being involved on opposite sides in a dispute. Although I expect to encounter exceptional cases as further research is conducted, one is led to conclude not that co-godparents never have reasons to clash, but that their differences are never brought into the open. The implications of these findings for the theory of social control and conflict management are obviously immense.[37]

VI. CONCLUSION: TOWARD THE ELUCIDATION OF NEW MODELS IN THE ETHNOLOGY OF LEGAL SYSTEMS

I began by calling attention to Malinowski's criticism of Hearsay Anthropology, but I noted that the empiricist trend represented by the case-method erred in the opposite direction by ignoring the ideological dimension. The few attempts to contrast the two sides have been too narrowly focused, aimed at proving a lack of fit between the ideal and the real, and missing a whole array of other phenomena, such as the law-abiding patterns and the social control effectiveness of institutions such as *compadrazgo*. I have proposed instead an eclectic approach which, while not totally new, combines a number of strategies that correct the previous omissions.[38] This approach both takes account of the ideal-real dichotomy, and also benefits from it by extrapolating a series of testable theoretical and practical generalisations. It has been submitted to initial test here on ethnographic material from the Dominican Republic. Eight generalisations are drawn above; the reader may add others from the data exhibited.

This approach raises the question of the proper study of *law*. Here we can only briefly comment. Writers of anti-scientific inclination have favoured, sometimes inadvertently, an ideographic or particularistic (i.e., artistic) position. Elsewhere I have argued, following Lévi-Strauss 1958, Nutini 1970, and contemporary philosophy of science, that, if we are ever to succeed in bringing the socio-behavioural sciences to the level of true science, we must attempt more generalising, nomothetic analyses. These analyses, rooted in the philosophy of J.S. Mill, allow us to construct cross-culturally and diachronically valid generalisations that could prove to be universally applicable ethnological/social-scientific laws (Alum 1975; Alum and Pye 1976). The integrative ideal-real approach could be replicated in almost every culture. An unusual degree of discrepancy between the ideal and real may be taken as signs of rapid socio-cultural change and can lead to anomie (Berger and Berger 1972; Nisbet 1965).[39]

A replication of my survey in the same plantation some years later could indicate, for instance, changes in the shared values, or, on the other hand, a persistence of traditionalism.[40] Such comparative longitudinal/diachronic studies, however, must be conducted with great care and objectivity.[41] Because of the limited availability of court cases, I did not treat time as a variable, but we could and should do so in future studies in order to discover the pace of socio-cultural dynamics.[42]

In sum, the *integrated, ideal-real* approach could be one vehicle in our search for the social uniformities governing mankind's behaviour, the end toward which we should strive in this multinational and multidisciplinary Commission on Folk Law and Legal Pluralism.[43]

NOTES

1.   Field research for this paper was conducted in the Dominican Republic between 1976 and 1978 under the joint auspices of the fellowship programs of the Social Science Research Council, U.S. Fulbright-Hays, Organization of American States, and the Dominican Fondo Para el Avance de las Ciencias Sociales and the Fundación Carcía-Arévalo (DR). I enjoyed institutional affiliations with the Museo del Hombre Dominicano, the OAS Inter-American Institute of Agricultural Sciences, and the Universidad Nacional P. Henríques-Ureña, as well as the Inter-American Institute of Puerto Rico. Partial funding for data analysis was provided by the University of Pittsburgh and by the Doctorate Association of New York Educators Morgan Award. My visit to Europe was made possible by a grant from the Stichting ter Bevordering van Buitenl., Universitaire Betrekkingen (Foundation for the Advancement of University Foreign Affairs), Catholic University, Nijmegen, The Netherlands. Responsibility for the paper is, however, solely mine.
    This paper is dedicated to all, too numerous to name, who in various ways made my project successful, and in particular to my brother Louis Alum, Esq., and Frank M. Hernández of the Dominican Institute of Applied Research (IDEA), and also to Professor G. van den Steenhoven, founder and retiring Chairman of our Commission, for his exemplary dedication.
2.   This report represents only a summary of the initial findings of a more ambitious project in progress. The present version was revised and updated in Autumn, 1982, a year after its first presentation.
3.   As is known, Malinowski used the terms "savage" and "primitive" interchangeably. Because of their implicit ethnocentrism, we have abandoned them. I am freely substituting the more neutral and acceptable "native" or "folk" law whenever appropriate. (See Malinowski's posthumous *Diary*: Malinowski 1967.)
4.   To the extent that non-anthropologists resort to anthropologists' definition of law (e.g. Friedman 1977:55).
5.   See note 17.
6.   The popularity of the case method was perhaps due in part to Anglo-American anthropologists' own common-law tradition. Cf. D. Black and Mileski's criticisms of the limitations of recent legal sociology: "its theoretical aspirations can go no further than America [i.e., the U.S.A.]"; and the further remark by Black that "*anthropological* literature... has contributed more than sociology to a general theory of law" (D. Black and Mileski 1973: 4-5, 52). Some of the best examples using the case method that are widely cited both by anthropologists and non-anthropologists are: Bohannan 1957; Collier 1973 (cf. Alum and Miller 1975); Jayawardena 1963; Llewellyn and Hoebel 1941; Lowy 1978; Pospisil 1958; Smith and Roberts 1954; and Starr 1978, in this volume.

7.   E.g. some of the synoptic reviews of the literature on the anthropology-sociology of law: Collier 1975; Moore 1978; Nader and Yngvesson 1973; Pospisil 1971; S. Roberts 1979; also Galanter's (1974) prognoses and Allott's (1970) review of African judicial systems.

8.   Lewis *et al.* 1977-78 is a prime example of "Hearsay Anthropology" still among us; see the criticisms in Thomas 1978; Alum 1979.

9.   Aubert sees sociology as "concerned with the study of values... of... preferences" (Aubert 1969), i.e., of ideologies, thus leaving open the possible implication that anthropology should be concerned with the observable ethnographic reality, but predicting no intertwining of the two paths. Indeed, anthropology has traditionally been relegated to the status of a social/behavioural science that studies only how humans really *are* and behave. Philosophy, not sociology, has been assigned the task of concerning itself with how humans ought to be. Cf. Bastiat 1979; Berger and Berger 1972; Hart 1961; Hoebel 1954; Nisbet 1965; Alum 1975; Alum and Pye 1976. See further note 43.

10.   Moore in turn cites Murphy's observation that "social life is... a series of contradictions" (Moore 1978; Murphy 1971:143). Murphy further urges the social scientist to explore more deeply the ethnographic material, to question all the ideologically bound responses from informants, and actually to seek "the extreme opposite" of what we "see and hear" - therein his dialectical exercise. Moore's and Murphy's position appears to be amenable to the logic of Levi-Strauss's French Structuralism.

11.   Nutini and Bell notably succeed in practising the ideal-real contrast approach, e.g., in their recent study of co-godparenthood in Mexico (Nutini and Bell 1980). See also my reference to *compadrazgo* below (see notes 34-36).

12.   As D. Black and Mileski note in assessing the recent work on law as a normative system, the contrast of "legal practices to legal ideals,... has been, at its core, evaluative", failing thus to treat law as an "empirical phenomenon" (D. Black and Mileski 1973:4).

13.   The preceding overview is not intended as a thorough review of the literature on the ideal-real ethnographic (descriptive) contrast analysis, nor even as a synoptic comparison, but rather as a selective review of some representative works, positions and trends, as an introduction to the presentation of my own data.

14.   As Friedman writes, the various functions of law can perhaps all be reduced to the single function of *social control*, a conclusion in agreement with Weber and Pound (Friedman 1977:14; Weber 1922; Pound 1965).

15.   Law is assumed to be a sub-division of culture. As Thompson writes, "Law is the indispensable condition for the existence of a human society" (Thompson 1975:18). Pilon, another philosopher, understands this in calling attention to the relativity of the judicial review process, even in Western-styled societies: "We all wish to live under the rule of law... But there are points in every political order at which... [it] depends critically upon the rule of men" (Pilon 1981:14).

16.   As Póspísil vividly notes, Malinowski came close to Eugen Ehrlich's conception of the "living law" (Pospisil 1971:29).

17.   Póspísil classifies law into: (a) authoritarian (imposed by a ruler or a legislature), and (b) customary (Póspísil 1971, 1978). The transition from one pole to the other, however, is fluid, especially in a typically open society (Popper 1966). Presumably most customary laws were originally authoritarian, though not all authoritarian laws become customary. The distinction is quantitative; it rests on the degree of people's psychological internalisation, which creates what some call ethos, others the body, of folk law. By *folk law* is meant the unwritten customary rules present even in complex Western societies with elaborate written codes: see other papers in this volume, particularly those of Allott and Podgorecki; also cf. Allott 1970; Podgorecki 1974. Moreover, as Weber foresaw, the dynamic center of legal power need not rest in the state in a modern society; legal pluralism is a universal fact (Weber 1922). Indeed, the essence of Pospisil's comparative theory of law lies in the proposition that an individual in any given society is subject to multiple legal systems of different levels, even to the point of conflict and contradiction.

18.   I have drawn freely for this section from some of my other writings (Alum 1977, 1981, 1982, 1983a; Belcher and Alum n.d.). Indeed, this report might be considered one of a series of inter-related papers.

19.   All the properties of dictator Rafael Trujillo (1930-61) were confiscated after his assassination, among them 12 of the 16 sugar factory-and-cane plantation compounds in the DR, including that where "my" community is located. (Of the remaining four that are privately owned, one belongs to Gulf and Western, a multinational corporation, and the other three to the Casa Vicini, owned by a Dominican family of Italian descent.)

20.   The question of Haitian migrants is extremely complicated, since it involves the additional dimensions of skin colour/race and national sovereignty/territoriality. The DR and Haiti have a long history of border tension and disputes, including limited incursions, all-out invasions, and massacres (Hernández 1973).

21.   A term of pre-Columbian indigenous Arawak-Taino origins, *batey* refers to a hamlet in contemporary sugar-cane plantations in the Latin Greater Antilles countries.

22.   See note 19.

23.   This is one of the crucial characteristics that distinguishes rural or agricultural workers from peasants, farmers and urban workers. Mintz has established the paradox that this kind of landless, wage-earning, land-toiling worker cannot engage in subsistence agriculture, which is explicitly discouraged by the plantation authorities, which in this case are the public authorities (since the plantation is owned and administered by the government) (Mintz 1974). Although city politicians and foreign scholars seem to ignore it, *Bateyanos* (residents) resent state ownership. They have various reasons, particularly that (a) they feel themselves in double jeopardy because of the dual role of public-law-enforcer and employer-management of the plantation authorities, and (b) in order to survive they have to succumb to a corrupt system rooted in political patronage and nepotism, the functioning of which is not determined by people's needs or abilities but by its political subservience to a centralised government, no matter how democratic it may otherwise be.

24.   See note 19. Through informants' oral history, available archival documents, including Land Tribunal case records, and published material (Hoetink 1972; Moya-Pons 1977), I was able to reconstruct much of the history of the plantation from its founding, *circa* 1916. (A Cuban-born daughter of one of the two Spanish brothers who founded the compound is still living in the *central* or factory town and was most cooperative during repeated interview sessions.)

25.   I list below in English each of the relevant questions posed. The full original questionnaires are available from me.

26.   I personally visited all the 16 plantations in the DR and all the *bateyes* in Natey's environs. The physical, cultural and human components of the latter are closely comparable to those of Batey (see notes 19 and 31).

27.   DR/JCE 1966. There is a minimum of one JP Court in each municipality. The legislature has created additional courts according to the burden of caes and distance, such as the JP Court in the factory's central *batey*; each is headed by a *juez* (judge).

28.   Grave civil, commercial and penal (criminal) cases are heard by the next higher bench, the Courts of First Instance (one in each province). In addition there are seven Courts of Appeal, a Supreme Court, and several Special Courts, such as the Land, Juvenile, Labour, and Traffic Tribunals (DR/JCE 1966).

29.   This was despite the fact that I was affiliated with the Dominican Museum of Man, a government agency whose Director at the time was a very influential person (Alum 1978a).

30.   In some instances, mostly of very recent cases, I was able to gather supplementary oral information from people who remembered the incident (i.e., the "memory technique") and/or knew the participants, or from the conflict actors themselves or their relatives who were still in the area.

31.   I have good reason to believe that these 100 cases are representative enough and that further inclusion of other cases in future analyses will not alter the outcome. Furthermore, as explained above (text and note 26), there is great uniformity - cultural, demographic, structural/ physical and otherwise - in all the nearby Batey-like communities located in the *Guarina* plantation that contribute cases to our sample. (Officials and scholars familiar with the area, and whom I have been consulting since 1975, all concur with me.) Indeed, a decade earlier Dr. Belcher, a Senior Sociologist from the University of Georgia, had selected Batey for a large statistical survey of levels of living throughout the country, precisely because of its typical nature. The results of our joint longitudinal/diachronic efforts are synthesised in Belcher and Alum n.d. (see note 42).

32.   The original questionnaire was of an open-answer style. I wrote down the informants' verbatim answers, and classified them later.

33.   Dominican court docket documents normally list the actors' nationality. Names are also indicative of nationality and ethnicity, but not always.

34.   Although in north European and north American Catholic communities the actors involved do not normally form a discrete group once the baptism ceremony is consummated, in the Latin World people are drawn into an enduring and regularly exercised kin-like relationship.

35.   See note 11.

36.   The local mythology is revealing. According to informants a pond not far from Batey was formed years ago with the blood of two *compadres* who killed each other in a fight!

37.   Cf. Nisbet's exemplary analysis of kinship, political power and the law (Nisbet 1973); also Alum's review of Meso-American kinship (Alum 1978b), and his study of Equatorial Guinea's polity (Alum 1983b).

38.   I am aware that the reconstruction of hypothetical conflict cases has been included in past case-method neo-classic studies, e.g. Llewellyn and Hoebel 1941, Póspísil 1958, and Smith and Roberts 1954; and that formal questionnaires, which serve in the construction of hypothetical cases, have been used in at least one major work, Karst *et al.* 1973. But, as Nader and Yngvesson write, "if anthropologists who study law have used more tightly structured interviews, they have rarely published them" (Nader and Yngvesson 1973:897).

39.   Records from police and court archives have been widely used as sources not only by bona fide anthropologists (Scaglion 1976) but even by non-scientifically oriented, self-avowed, strict humanists (see Alum 1980).

40.   The dynamic and interdependent characteristics of law were summarised in the last century by Durkheim: "... puisque droit varie toujours comme les relations sociales qu'il règle" (Durkheim 1893:141).

41.   From another perspective, the collection of cases has an ethno-historical dimension if we consider them to constitute documents for the reconstruction of (ethno-)history.

42.   Although the dynamics of the local legal culture have not yet been formally analysed, I study the pace of socio-cultural and material changes in Batey during the ten-year period 1967-77 in another paper (Belcher and Alum n.d.). See also Bolton's revealing paper in this volume, based on ethnographic data from a comparable Latin American sub-culture; and note 31.

43.   Most comments advanced to the first draft of my paper (see note 2) I have attempted to meet in this revised version. The criticism, however, that my writing was allegedly faulty for not "citing" certain authors, is neither novel nor deserving of rebuttal. Those who wish to worship their respective earthly deities, omitted from my project because of their irrelevance, may do so on their own. I was enculturated to be a free-thinking, objective, factual social-scientist (Alum 1975; Popper 1966), not an intimidated, arm-chair ideologue nor a writer of fiction (see note 9).

REFERENCES

Allott, A. (ed.)
1970   *Judicial and Legal Systems in Africa*, London: Butterworths.
Alum, R.A.
1975   'Social sciences and physical sciences; a consideration of equality', *Eureka!*
            (University of Pittsburgh), Apr., 5-8.
1977   'El parentesco ritual en un batey dominicano', *Revista M-M; Estudios Dominica-
            nos*, V(26), 11-36.
1978a   'José A. Caro (Obituary)', *Anthropology Newsletter*, 19(5), 3.
1978b   'The growth of Meso-American and Caribbean Kinship studies', *Boletín de
            Estudios Latinoamericanos y del Caribe; A Journal of Latin American and Caribbe-
            an Studies*, 25, 73-77; revised Spanish version in *Revista de Ciencias Sociales*
            (University of Puerto Rico), 22(1-2), 149-64 (1980).
1979   'A critique of O. Lewis' *Four Women*', *Cuban Studies/Estudios Cubanos*, 9(1),
            64-67.
1980   'Un estudio etno-histórico sobre los anarquistas andaluces', *Ethnica, Revista de
            Antropología*, 16, 122-24; abridged English version in *American Anthropologist*,
            81(3), 677.
1981   'Ritual kinship in the Dominican Republic', *ERIC* (Educational Research Infor-
            mation Center, Teachers College, Columbia University, U.S.A.).
1982   'Dominican Republic', in: *Current History Encyclopedia of Developing Nations*
            New York: McGraw Hill and *Current History*, pp. 293-97.
1983a   'The political system of the Dominican Republic', in: G. Delury (ed.), *World
            Encyclopedia of Political Systems and Parties*, New York: Facts on File.
1983b   'The political system of Equatorial Guinea (W. Africa)', in: G. Delury (ed.),
            World Encyclopedia of Political Systems and Parties, New York: Facts on File.
Alum, R., and R. Miller
1975   'About J. Collier's Law and Social Change in Zinacantán', *Inter-American
            Review of Bibliography* 25(3), 302-3.
Alum, R., and C. Pye
1976   'The ideological bases of Nutini's interpretation of French Structuralism', unpu-
            blished typescript, Anthropology Department, University of Pittsburgh.
Aubert, V.
1969   'Introduction' [to Part III: Case Studies of Law in Western Societies], in: L.
            Nader (ed.), *Law in Culture and Society*, Chicago: Aldine, pp. 273-81.
Bastiat, F.
1979   *The Law* (trans. D. Russell, originally 1853), Irvington- on-Hudson, New York:
            Foundation for Economic Education.
Belcher, J., and R. Alum
n.d.   'Dynamics of life style in rural Dominican Republic', unpublished paper, Soci-
            ology Department, University of Georgia (delivered, Annual Meeting of the
            Society for Applied Anthropology, Philadelphia, March 15-17, 1979, and sub-
            mitted for publication).
Berger, P., and B. Berger
1972   *Sociology; a Biographical Approach*, New York: Basic Books.
Black, D., and M. Mileski (eds.)
1973   *The Social Organization of Law*, New York: Seminar Press.
Black, M.
1973   'Belief systems', in: J. Honigmann (ed.), *Handbook of Social and Cultural Anthro-
            pology*, Chicago: Rand McNally.

Black, M., and D. Metzger
1965   'Ethnographic description and the study of law', in: L. Nader (ed.), *Law in Culture and Society*, Chicago: Aldine, pp. 3-32.
Bohannan, P.
1957   *Justice and Judgment Among the Tiv*, London: Oxford University Press.
Collier, J.
1973   *Law and Social Change in Zinacantán*, Stanford: Stanford University Press.
1975   'Legal processes', in: B. Siegel *et al.* (eds.), *Annual Reviews of Anthropology*, IV, 121-33.
DR/JCE, Dominican Republic, Junta Central Electoral
1966   *Constitución de la República Dominicana*, Santo Domingo: Gobierno Dominicano.
Durkheim, E.
1893   *De la Division du Travail Social*, Paris: F. Alcan.
Friedman, L.
1977   *Law and Society; An Introduction*, Englewood Cliffs, N.J.: Prentice-Hall.
Galanter, M.
1974   'The future of law and social sciences research', *North Carolina Law Review*, 52, 1060-69.
González, N.
1974   'The city of gentlemen: Santiago de los Caballeros', in: G. Foster and G. Kemper (eds.), *Anthropologists in Cities*, Boston: Little Brown, pp. 19-40.
Hart, H.L.A.
1961   *The Concept of Law*, London: Oxford University Press.
Hernández, F.M.
1973   *La Inmigración Haitiana*, Santo Domingo: Ediciones Sargazo.
Hoebel, E.A.
1954   *The Law of Primitive Man; a Study in Comparative Legal Dynamics*, Cambridge, Mass.: Harvard University Press.
Hoetink, H.
1972   *El Pueblo Dominicano: 1850-1900; Apuntes Para su Sociología Histórica*, Santiago de los Caballeros, DR: Universidad Católica Madre y Maestra.
Jayawardena, C.
1963   *Conflict and Solidarity in a Guianese Plantation*, London: Athlone Press.
Karst, M., M. Schwartz and H. Schwartz
1973   *The Evolution of Law in the Barrios of Caracas*, Los Angeles: Latin American Center, UCLA.
Lévi-Strauss, C.
1958   *Anthropologie Structurale*, Paris: Plon.
Lewis, O., R. Lewis and S. Rigdon
1977-78   *Living the Revolution*, Vols. I-III, Urbana: University of Illinois Press.
Llewellyn, K., and E.A. Hoebel
1941   *The Cheyenne Way*, Norman: University of Oklahoma Press.
Lowy, M.
1978   'A good name is worth more than money; strategies of court use in urban Ghana', in: L. Nader and H. Todd (eds.), *The Disputing Process; Law in Ten Societies*, New York: Columbia University Press, pp. 181-208.
Malefijt, A. de Waal
1974   *Images of Man; A History of Anthropological Thought*, New York: A. Knopf.
Malinowski, B.
1926   *Crime and Custom in Savage Society* (repr. 1966), Totowa, NJ: Littlefield, Adams & Co.

1967   *A Diary in the Strict Sense of the Term* (trans. N. Guterman), New York: Harcourt.

Mintz, S.
1974   *Caribbean Transformations*, Chicago: Aldine.

Moore S.F.
1978   *Law as Process; An Anthropological Approach*, London: Routledge & Kegan Paul.

Moya-Pons, F.
1977   *Manual de Historia Dominicana*, Santiago: Universidad Católica Madre y Maestra.

Murphy, R.
1971   *The Dialectics of Social Life*, New York: Basic Books.

Nader, L., and B. Yngvesson
1973   'On studying the ethnography of law and its consequences', in: J. Honigmann (ed.), *Handbook of Social and Cultural Anhropology* , Chicago: Rand McNally, pp. 883-922.

Nisbet, R.
1965   *Émile Durkheim* Englewood Cliffs, N.J.: Prentice-Hall.
1973   'Kinship and political power in first century Rome', in: D. Black and Mileski 1973, pp. 262-77.

Nutini, H.
1970   'Lévi-Strauss's conception of science', in: J. Pouillon et P. Maranda (eds.), *Echanges et Communications; Mélanges Offertes à Claude Lévi-Strauss*, The Hague: Mouton, pp. 543-70.

Nutini, H., and B. Bell
1980   *Ritual Kinship; the Structure and Historical Development of the Compadrazgo System in Rural Tlaxcala*, Vol. I, Princeton: Princeton University Press.

Pilon, R.
1981   'On the foundations of justice', *The Intercollegiate Review*, 17(1), 3-12.

Podgorecki , A.
1974   *Law and Society*, London: Routledge & Kegan Paul.

Popper, K.
1966   *The Open Society and its Enemies*, London: Routledge & Kegan Paul.

Póspísil, L.
1958   *Kapauku Papuans and Their Law*, Publications in Anthropology No. 54, New Haven: Yale University Press.
1971   *Anthropology of Law; a Comparative Theory*, New York: Harper & Row.
1978   *The Ethnology of Law*, Menlo Park, California: B. Cummings.

Pound, R.
1965   *An Introduction to the Philosophy of Law*, New Haven: Yale University Press.

Roberts, J.M.
1964   'The self-management of cultures', in: W. Goodenough (ed.), *Explorations in Cultural Anthropology*, New York: McGraw Hill, pp. 433-54.

Roberts, S.
1979   *Order and Dispute; An Introduction to Legal Anthropology*, Harmondsworth: Penguin.

Scaglion, R.
1976   'Seasonal Patterns in Western Abelam Conflict Management Practices', Ph.D. thesis, University of Pittsburgh, U.S.A.

Smith, W., and J.M. Roberts
1954   *Zuñi Law; A Field of Values*, Peabody Museum Papers 43(1), Rimrock Project Report # 4, Cambridge, Mass.: Harvard University Press.

Starr, J.
1978   *Dispute and Settlement in Rural Turkey; An Ethnography of Law* , Leiden: E.J.
            Brill.
Thomas, H. (Lord)
1978   'Children of Castro; Review of O. Lewis et al., Four Men', *Cuban Studies/Estudi-
            os Cubanos*, 8(1), 53-57.
Thompson, S.
1975   'Law and social continuity', *The Intercollegiate Review*, 10(1), 17-23.
Weber, M.
1922   *Grundrisse der Sozialökonomie, Teil III: Wirtschaft und Gesellschaft*, Tübingen:
            J. Mohr.
Wiarda, H.
1968   'Contemporary constitutions and constitutionalism in the Dominican Republic;
            the basic law within the political process', *Law & Society Review*, II, 385-405.

How the Qolla handle homicide: the demifeud in action

Ralph Bolton

In a curiously entitled book, *Cambios en Puno*, Bourricaud (1967) presented his analyses of observations collected more than two decades ago in the Qollao region of the Peruvian highlands. Most of his perceptions are astute and valid today, including his recognition that among the natives of the Qollao "personal relations are marked by outbursts of violence and by a high degree of instability" (Bourricaud 1967:70-71, my translation). If one aspect of Qolla social life has not changed in these intervening years, it is these "outbursts of violence".

It is my purpose in this paper to discuss some limited dimensions of Qolla violence. Specifically I shall present a brief introduction to the topic of homicide among villagers by speaking about the rates and ramifications of homicide in one Qolla community. Although my main objective is to convey a sense of the pervasiveness of the touch of violent death in the lives of Qolla peasants, I shall also comment on the meaning of this phenomenon as a form of social exchange and communication and I shall point out some possible structural concomitants (causes, if you like) of the homicide rates.

I. HOMICIDE RATES[1]

My study of homicide is focused in the village of Incawatana, located on the shore of Lake Titicaca approximately seventy kilometers north and east of the city of Puno, in the Quechua-speaking zone of the Altiplano. Although the settlement consists of scattered houses, population density is high - more than two hundred persons per square kilometer. Residents of Incawatana engage in intensive agriculture, producing potatoes, barley, beans, and oca as the major crops. Animal husbandry is of slight importance since the villagers have minimal access to pasture lands and *totora* and fishing is carried on by only a few adult males. The incomes derived from subsistence farming are frequently supplemented by wages earned in menial labor during periodic migrations to the regional and coastal cities. The basic social and economic unit in Incawatana is the household, which generally is made up of a single nuclear family, but which, on occasion, has a variant composition.

The calculation of homicide rates depends, of course, on the possibility of obtaining adequate population estimates. Immediately one is faced with the problem of deciding who is and who is not going to enter into the statistics. The geographical mobility of Andean peasants is notorious, in spite of their so-called "attachment to the land". I have attempted to overcome the problem by using three categories of community members and by calculating a number of homicide rates in relation to the population estimates for these different categories.

The population categories which I have found useful are the following: first, resident members of the community actually in residence at the time of the population count; second, resident members of the community who are temporarily absent (e.g. for purposes of working, visiting, studying, soldiering, etc.); third, non-residents who are still considered to be members of the community by virtue of close ties of kinship and property ownership (they may be residing elsewhere because of permanent jobs or marriage to an outsider). The census conducted by the author in the village of Incawatana in 1969 yielded the population figures shown in Table 1. In that table I have also shown my estimates for the average population during the twenty-five year period, 1945-1969, which is the period covered by the homicide data to be discussed. The estimates may be slightly inflated, which will result in conservative estimates of the homicide rates.

Table 1 Population Estimates for Incawatana

Population Category	1969	1945-1969
a) Resident members in residence	1000	800
b) Absentee resident members	250	200
c) Non-resident members	250	200

Official police records are minimally helpful in determining homicide rates in this region and I base my estimates on data obtained in interviews with key informants. The method is not totally reliable, but I have cross-checked all cases and eliminated a number of them for lack of sufficient evidence. The cases retained for analysis have been classified into three categories with respect to my degree of certainty that the event in question did indeed occur. The categories are absolute, probable, and questionable. In Table 2 the homicide rates for both victims and offenders are presented along with the number of cases involved.

The rate which is probably most comparable to those normally calculated for other societies is A.1. in the table, in other words 55 homicide victims per year per 100,000 population. This figure corresponds only to cases of absolute certainty or at least a high probability. If one compares this rate with rates for African societies and most Western European countries, one discovers that the Qolla have an extremely high homicide rate. The highest

Table 2 Homicide Rates and Numbers for 25 Years, 1945-1969, Involving Residents and Members of the Village of Incawatana (adjusted to a hypothetical population of 100,000)

A. Incawatana Victims of Homicide	Number	Rate
1. Resident members, killed inside confines of the village (a)	11	55.0
2. Absentee resident members, killed outside the village (b)	4	16.0
3. Non-resident members, killed outside the village (c)	5	16.5
4. Combination of 1-3, i.e., all persons considered members of Incawatana (c)	20	66.0
B. Incawatana Offenders, Homicide Cases		
1. Resident members prosecuted for involvement in homicide (a)	13	65.0
2. Resident members formally accused of involvement in homicide (a)	19	95.0
3. Resident members suspected of involvement in homicide but not accused nor prosecuted (a)	13	65.0
4. Resident members who in fact probably participated in homicide (a)	21	105.0

The letters in parentheses refer to population estimates upon which the rates are based; see Table 1.

rate reported by Bohannan (1960) for African societies was under 12 per 100,000 (i.e. for the Sebei).

It could be argued, of course, that the methods of obtaining rates which I have used are different from those employed by the contributors to Bohannan's volume. That is the case, since the rates which he reported are based for the most part on court records. For the Qolla of Incawatana the prosecuted rate is 20 homicides per 100,000 population, a figure still almost double the highest African rate. The number of homicides in Incawatana during the past 25 years is given in Table 3 where I have noted whether or not a case was prosecuted. In only 5 of the 21 absolute and probable homicides were formal accusations entered and the offenders prosecuted. One additional case was investigated by the district police (*guardia civil*), but no charges were ever filed.

Table 3 Number of Homicides Involving Members of Incawatana, 1945-1969, Classified by Place of Residence of Victims and Offenders, Degree of Certainty of Events, and Prosecution or Non-prosecution of the Case by the Judicial Authorities

Place of Residence of Victim and Offender	Prosecuted	Not Prosecuted		
	A	A	P	Q
a. Victim and offender are both residents of Incawatana	4	4	3	1
b. Victim is Incawatana resident, offender is an outsider	0	3	1	0
c. Victim is an outsider, offender is Incawatana resident	0	0	0	1
d. Victim is Incawatana absentee resident, offender is an outsider	0	1	0	0
e. Victim is an outsider, offender is Incawatana absentee resident	0	0	0	1
f. Victim is non-resident member of Incawatana, offender is an outsider	1	1	3	0

Note: A = Absolute, P = Probable, Q = Questionable.

It is my impression that police efficiency is considerably higher for most places for which homicide rates are available. Since burial permits are readily obtained in districts of the Qollao, foul play is difficult to detect and costly to prove. Consequently, I would assert that the Qolla homicide rate which is useful for comparative purposes is above 50 victims per 100,000 population.

The offender rate for resident members of Incawatana is approximately 65 per 100,000 population when based upon the numbers of villagers actually prosecuted. I calculate that the true rate of involvement in homicide as offenders is on the order of 105 resident members per year per 100,000 population.

The rates which I have cited for Incawatana are certainly out of line with statistics reported for the whole of Peru. According to the United Nations Yearbook, the Peruvian homicide rate (victims) is under three per 100,000 per year. However, the Incawatana figure is not much exaggerated in comparison to the rest of the Qollao. Cuentas (n.d.) has provided evidence which shows that the homicide rate for the province of Huancane during five years in the fifties was approximately 15 per 100,000, a figure reasonably close to the rate for Incawatana since Cuentas counted only prosecuted cases of homicide.

II. SOCIAL RAMIFICATIONS OF HOMICIDE

What does this high rate of violence mean in terms of the local community? During the 25-year period under consideration the community consisted of about 200 households, the household being, as already mentioned, the basic solidary unit in Qolla society. More than 20% of all households contain an adult member who has been deprived through homicide of at least one close relative, i.e. parent, child, spouse or sibling. An additional 10% of all households have a living adult who has been formally accused of murder or who has probably been involved in an act of homicide; consequently, over 30% of all Incawatana households contain an adult member whose parent, child, spouse or sibling has been involved as an offender in a homicide case. To illustrate further the impact of homicide on the local community I shall describe the case involving the murder of Simon Mamani.

It was the early fifties and Simon Mamani was a not too popular member of the community. He had some known proclivity toward theft. But he was becoming an entrepreneur in legal economic activities, having decided to undertake a small mining operation in the region. He was present at a wedding one day in October and there is said to have had a fight with the owner of the land on which he was planning to operate his mine. That night - the story varies in detail - Simon Mamani was bludgeoned to death by several villagers.

An immediate Qolla response to homicide is for the close relatives of the victim to assault the homes of the presumed perpetrators of the deed and forcibly confiscate their animals (destroying other property in the process). In the case of Simon, his wife, son, and sons-in-law attempted to carry out this revenge. But some of the offenders had already sent their animals out of the village and one offender was hiding his two bulls inside his huts under lock and key. In the morning the police were called from the district capital. They discovered the offender with the hidden cattle. He and other accused persons were arrested - not all of them, however, for some had already fled from the village.

This case was prosecuted. The son of the victim acting for his mother pursued the accused through the courts. Accusations were lodged against more than 25 persons, men and women, most but not all residents in Incawatana. Ten of the accused spent time in jail in Puno, although only three were eventually convicted of the crime. (The son of Simon Mamani maintains today that the principal offenders were not convicted.) In addition to the accused and the kinsmen of the victim the case involved approximately thirty witnesses, many of them residents or members of Incawatana, but a few false witnesses as well, hired from neighbouring communities.

In the study of homicide and violence it might be useful to draw upon the concept of the action-set when trying to demonstrate or measure the ramifications of an event in the life of a community. The action-set of any given ego consists of those persons who can be counted upon to help out that ego when he is in need of assistance. In Qolla society the basic action-sets are attached to households rather than individual egos and normally include the following categories of individuals (with respect to each adult member of the household):

a. parents
b. siblings
c. siblings' spouses
d. children
e. children's spouses
f. parents of children's spouses
g. ritual kinsmen (*compadres*, godchildren, and godparents).

At any given point in time, because of quarrels some members of an action-set may not be willing to participate in self-help activities of the central household involved - even though it would be recognized as their duty to do so in any case. Failure to fulfill obligations is quite common, especially for ritual kinsmen and to some extent for siblings. But, when the centre of the action-set is in serious need - such as when involved in a homicide case - then most members will rally to participate.

In the case of Simon Mamani three important village families were prosecuted for the murder, which means that with the action-set of the victim four major action-sets in all were mobilized to deal with this case. There was some overlap in action-sets, of course, especially among the three defendant sets. These three were closely allied by marital ties. Additionally, ritual kinship ties further obligated them to each other. Parenthetically, however, I might point out that under the duress of the judicial proceedings these ties were severely strained, with each of the defendants denying his complicity in the events and throwing the blame upon others.

Although the major overlapping membership in action-sets occurred among the defendants themselves, there was overlap with the action- set of the accused. Indeed, the brother of the victim was brother-in- law to the central person in two defendant action-sets and the victim's son's marriage godfather (in other words the victim's *compadre*) was one of those prosecuted. But in spite of these and other overlapping memberships in action-sets the case was not dampened but reverberated throughout the community. Involvement was widespread. The four major action-sets concerned drew in approximately 40% of all Incawatana households; if one included witnesses and the action-sets of others accused of the murder, the mobilization of the population of Incawatana would be well over 60%. Mobilization in this instance means that members of an action-set are called upon for moral support, in some cases financial backing and physical presence from time to time.

I noted earlier that a majority of homicides do not lead to this extreme simply because they are not prosecuted. I shall cite only one such case which occurred during our fieldwork. Two youths got into a fight during a school recess; one of the boys, about fifteen years old, used a stone to hit the other boy. The next day the youth who had been hit on the head died. The family of the deceased was distraught, not knowing what to do. Immediately the mother consulted the village school director, who claimed ignorance of the case and noted that the fight had taken place off the property of the school. He advised the woman to consult her brother, a district official. She did so. But in the meanwhile the child's father had arranged a settlement with the parents of the offending youth. Rather than enter a complaint against the offender, the victim's family agreed to cover up the events in question in exchange for the expenses of the funeral which the offender's family would bear.

Two days later this case was finished; the public explanation of the death was innocuous. It was claimed that the youth (completely healthy before) had died from colic which was due to the eating of fresh bread the day before death. A few villagers were aware that the death resulted from injuries sustained in the fight; most were not.

This case did not explode for several reasons: first, the two families (and consequently action-sets) were closely related, victim and offender being first cousins; second, the persons involved were not high status individuals in the community (not even adults); and third - and most important - the family of the victim felt that the pursuit of revenge would be more expensive than it was worth.

III. SOCIAL SIGNIFICANCE OF THE HOMICIDE RATE

The discussion of homicide cases and rates can be intrinsically interesting, but I should like to discuss the meaning of these rates and the erratic methods of handling homicide in Qolla society.

First we can recall the position of Durkheim, Marx, and Mead, all of whom felt that some crime is "good for society" because it calls forth a reaction of moral outrage on the part of other members of the society and thus helps to keep the society united. But in a situation where a case of homicide can mobilize over half the population I doubt that this point of view makes much sense. Moral outrage is minimal and almost every villager's view of the events depends upon his ties to participants in that event or events. Moral condemnation is minimal and the society as a whole does not deal with the matter at the local level in any real sense. If homicide does not unite the village against the offenders, what then is its impact on society?

Lévi-Strauss views society as a series of overlapping communication structures and in his words, "A society consists of individuals and groups which communicate with one another" (Lévi-Strauss 1963:296). Communication takes place on a number of different levels as exchanges, primarily of women, goods and services, and messages. Although he singles out these three types of exchange, he points out that "society includes many things besides marriage, economic, and linguistic exchanges" (Lévi-Strauss 1963:83-84).

I think that it is worth emphasizing that in essence there are only two interesting forms of social communication, those communications or messages which are socially integrative, on the one hand, and those which are socially disruptive, on the other. The former convey a sense of solidarity and the latter convey intentions of enmity and hostility. While Lévi-Strauss and others have contributed enormously to the understanding of certain integrative forms of exchange, notably, in the case of Lévi-Strauss, marriage exchanges, socially disruptive exchanges have received little attention.

It was Sahlins who provided a "scheme of reciprocities" which incorporated the notion of unsociable exchanges as well as socially integrative ones (Sahlins 1965). According to him exchanges can be placed on a spectrum of reciprocities "defined by its extremes and mid-point" as follows:

1. generalized reciprocity, the solidary extreme;
2. balanced reciprocity, the midpoint;
3. negative reciprocity, the unsociable extreme.

To the extent that a high proportion of exchanges in a society fall near the solidary end of the spectrum, that society can be said to be well-integrated. But a society characterized by a high degree of exchanges involving negative reciprocity (i.e., theft, barter, cunning, stealth, violence, etc.) is a minimal society. When applied to local communities rather than the society as a whole, these assertions are even more obviously true.

Examples of negative reciprocity are recorded by most ethnographers, but, as LeVine has noted, theoretical attention to such phenomena is "relatively new in anthropology" (LeVine 1961:3). Exchanges involving negative reciprocity are usually instances of social conflict, at times socially approved and customarily engaged in and at other times disapproved and forbidden.

If attention in anthropology to social conflict processes is of recent vintage, much of that theorizing has been constrictively tied to assertions about the eufunctional character of conflict for the survival of societies. Specifically, LeVine draws our attention to the "silver-lining" approach so prominent in the writings of Gluckman and other Manchester anthropologists (LeVine, 1961:3). Their concern has been with the socially integrative aspects of conflict and not with the socially disruptive.

Only recently, too, have we begun to get studies of negative reciprocity in the Andes. I should point out a fascinating article on field theft in the Andes

written by Gade (1972) in which he comments upon the widespread occurrence of that type of negative reciprocity.

Homicide is a rather extreme example of negative reciprocity, one in which
the person from whom something has been taken (probably his most pre-
cious possession) is in no position ever to reciprocate. Indeed, homicide is
also a basic form of communication, one which relays hostility and fear to
many persons in the society. Hostility is communicated quite dramatically.
Fear is the reaction of others, especially in a situation where the offenders are
rarely caught and punished. And, to me at least, it calls to mind a passage by
Hobbes, quoted on the title page of *The Moral Basis of a Backward Society*:

> "In such condition, there is no place for industry, because the fruit thereof is
> uncertain; and consequently no culture of the earth; no navigation, nor use of the
> commodities that may be imported by sea; no commodious building; no instru-
> ments of moving, and removing, such things as require much force; no know-
> ledge of the face of the earth; no account of time; no arts; no letters; no society;
> and which is worst of all, continual fear, and danger of violent death; and the life
> of man, solitary, poor, nasty, brutish, and short" (Hobbes, quoted Banfield
> 1958).

The condition to which Hobbes was referring, of course, was the absence of a
sovereign authority which could guarantee security and order. Although it is
platitudinous to point out that a Hobbesian state of nature exists nowhere in
reality, to deny the existence of societies which approach that state would be
absurd.

IV. THE WAY HOMICIDE IS HANDLED

Hobbes was wrong, to be sure; society is possible in the absence of a
"sovereign authority". Anthropological studies of acephalous societies at-
test to the actuality of such systems. Yet, on the other hand, Hobbes may
have been right with respect to the conditions of life which prevail in such
societies. The classic example of a "tribe without a ruler" is the Nuer, about
whom Evans-Pritchard has written:

> "As Nuer are very prone to fighting, people are frequently killed ... From their
> earliest years children are encouraged to settle all disputes by fighting, and they
> grow up to regard skill in fighting the most necessary accomplishment and
> courage the highest virtue" (Evans-Pritchard 1940:151).

Although a high level of violence among the Nuer is readily acknowledged
(unfortunately, we do not know anything about rates of violence or homicide
for that society), we are told that *additional* violence is suppressed by the fear
of reprisal and the dread of feud. And Gluckman in a famous lecture even

speaks of the "peace in the feud" (Gluckman 1955). While the feud may serve as a legal mechanism and as the only "sanction for offences such as homicide" in some societies (Middleton and Tait 1958:21), there can be no doubt that the presence of feuding groups is disruptive for a society.

It has been shown that societies with a low level of political integration are likely to engage in feuding if fraternal interest groups are present (Otterbein and Otterbein 1965). A simple level of political integration is not sufficient for the prediction of the occurrence of feuding patterns in a society. Instead a certain degree of subgroup solidarity (i.e., the fraternal interest group) must be present before feuding emerges. Now one must either abandon Hobbes altogether or assume that there are societies without feuding which are characterized by even more socially disruptive violence and by lesser degrees of solidarity among subgroups.

Gluckman has argued, correctly I think, that it is unlikely that the feud was ever practised with any frequency in local communities of any society:

> I may have given the impression that I am arguing that vengeance is never taken and the feud never waged. I don't want to do this. Feud is waged and vengeance taken when the parties live sufficiently far apart, or are too weakly related by diverse ties. Even when they are close together, hotheadedness and desire for prestige may lead to vengeance and constant fighting. But where they are close together, many institutions and ties operate to exert pressure on the quarrellers to reach a settlement (Gluckman 1955:19).

Efficient pursuit of the blood-feud would lead to the decimation of small communities and, most likely, their elimination. In modern parlance one might say that the feud has considerable deterrence value.

The Aymara-Qolla figured in the cross-societal study by the Otterbeins, but they proved to be a deviant case, not fitting the hypotheses. According to the Otterbeins' predictions the Aymara-Qolla should engage in feuding. The authors correctly note that the Aymara-Qolla do not practice the feud (i.e. blood revenge following a homicide). They suggest that the Aymara (in my terminology the Aymara-Qolla) should not have entered into their sample since they are a dependent people and not an independent tribe.

I would argue that the Qolla are only minimally integrated into a larger political unit and that the political forces at the local level do not function in cases of homicide. Additionally because of the nature of the larger political unit (i.e., the Peruvian State) the Qolla seek revenge for injuries by way of an institution analogous to the feud and which I call the demifeud.

Briefly, the demifeud involves the pursuit of revenge by injured parties after a homicide (or for that matter any other injury), but unlike the feud, in which revenge is sought in blood, the revenge wrought through the demifeud involves the confiscation of enemy property by force and the imprisonment of one or more of the offending parties. I suggest that the demifeud is likely to flourish in societies with minimal social solidarity within the local community, and a State system characterized by incomplete penetration and lack of impartiality in the detection and punishment of major criminal behavior.

In the specific instance of Incawatana, except in the case of crimes such as counterfeiting and smuggling, the police do not interfere unless the behaviour is denounced by an interested party. And then the damaged party must be willing to foot the bill in obtaining redress. I have been assured by lawyers that this is indeed a part of the regional legal philosophy even in the case of homicide. Unless an injured party feels sufficiently damaged to finance the "pursuit of justice", it is felt that society has not been seriously offended against. One might suspect that such cases are not sufficiently lucrative to be worth pursuing in a city such as those of the *altiplano*, where the ties are as multiplex as in any village. The demifeud is, in my opinion, more disruptive than the feud, as an institution, perhaps because its effects are so insidious. The parties commit their financial resources until they obtain what they consider a just settlement - or until they exhaust themselves in the struggle - over a period of years. Not willing to engage in the demifeud at the court level, most injured parties permit the offenders to go unpunished.

It is my hypothesis, then, that high rates of violence, such as among the Qolla, are likely to be associated with societies practising the demifeud.

NOTE

1. An extended discussion of the problems associated with determining the homicide rates for societies such as the Qolla appears in the debate between Lewellen and Bolton (Lewellen 1981; Bolton 1984).

REFERENCES

Banfield, E.C.
1958   *The Moral Basis of a Backward Society*, Glencoe, Illinois: The Free Press.
Bohannan, P. (ed.)
1960   *African Homicide and Suicide*, Princeton: Princeton University Press.
Bolton, R.
1984   'The hypoglycemia-aggression hypothesis: debate versus research', *Current Anthropology*, 25, 1-53.
Bourricaud, F.
1967   *Cambios en Puno*, Mexico, D.F.: Instituto Indigenista Interamericano.
Cuentas Gamarra,
n.d.   *Apuntes anthropologicos sociales sobre las zonas aymaras del departamento du Puno*, Puno: Corpuno, Departamento de Integracion Cultural.
Evans-Pritchard, E.E.
1940   *The Nuer*, Oxford: Oxford University Press.

Gade, D.W.
1972   'Cultural-geographical implications of social disorganization: crop theft in high-
            land Peru', *The Geographical Survey*, 1(3), 1-15.
Gluckman, M.
1955   *Custom and Conflict in Africa*, Oxford: Blackwell.
LeVine, R.
1961   'Anthropology and the study of conflict: an introduction', *Journal of Conflict
            Resolution*, 5(1), 3-15.
Lévi-Strauss, C.
1963   *Structural Anthropology*, New York: Basic Books.
Lewellen, T.C.
1981   'Aggression and hypoglycemia in the Andes: another look at the evidence',
            Current Anthropology, 22, 347-61.
Middleton, J.D., and D. Tait (eds.)
1958   *Tribes Without Rulers*, London: Routledge.
Otterbein, K.F., and C.S. Otterbein
1965   'An eye for an eye, a tooth for a tooth: a cross-cultural study of feuding',
            American Anthropologist, 67(6), 1, 1470-1482.
Sahlins, M.
1965   'On the sociology of primitive exchange', in M. Banton (ed.), *The Relevance of
            Models for Social Anthropology*, New York: Frederick A. Praeger.

Indigenous law and official law in the contemporary United States

Marc Galanter

[Editorial Note. The principal substance of the paper presented under this title at the Bellagio symposium has been published: Galanter 1981: especially 8-10, 17-27. The following summary has been prepared by Gordon Woodman.]

Despite the rise of national legal systems, indigenous orderings and law continue to exist. To appreciate their importance and to study them clearly we must discard our habitual "legal centralism". This is the perspective in which state agencies occupy the centre of legal life, and stand in a relationship of hierarchic control to other normative orderings, and in which indigenous law is consequently overlooked.

Indigenous law may be regarded as a regulation of activity by the participants in that activity. Neither state law nor indigenous law is often found in a "pure" form: most regulation involves a combination, having characteristics typical of each type of law. Furthermore, indigenous law is not easily distinguished from social life generally. While social life entails a great variety of regulatory orders, indigenous law may be usefully regarded as characterised by relatively greater organisation and differentiation of norms and sanctions. On the scale of organisation and differentiation it may be convenient to take as a distinguishing point for indigenous law the introduction of a second "layer" of control, or of norms about the application of norms. Nevertheless it must be recalled that rules are not necessarily determinative or explanatory of practice in indigenous orderings any more than in official orderings.

A considerable literature demonstrates the survival and proliferation of indigenous law in the contemporary United States. Palen and Galanter have endeavoured to contribute to these studies by assembling an archive of materials from the popular press on the subject of indigenous self-regulatory activity in various American institutions and social settings. These materials are suggestive of the richness and assessability of data about indigenous law in contemporary industrial societies. They suffer from obvious problems of representativeness as well as from the episodic and fragmentary character of the reporting (not unlike law reports). Notwithstanding these deficiencies, it is believed that these materials can contribute in several ways to our exploration of indigenous law. However, no systematic analysis of these materials has yet been possible.[1]

Exploration of the working of indigenous law has been inhibited by the pretensions of legal centralism, that the official legal system is all-encompassing, uniform, exclusive and controlling. Taking an evolutionary view of legal development, it considers indigenous law to be a feature of society which is displaced or transformed with the growth of the centralised bureaucratic system, and which thereafter emerges again only in deviant, peripheral and transient manifestations. It induces us to organise our perceptions in such ways that we may scarcely even observe the existence of indigenous law. Even those who are not proponents of legal centralism may fail to see indigenous law, since they may look for an inclusive, self-contained (although informal) *Gemeinschaft*, whereas indigenous laws in societies such as the United States operate in a multitude of loosely joined and partly overlapping, partial or fragmentary communities. The indigenous ordering and official law may be not mutually exclusive, but interacting.

Four very preliminary hypotheses may be advanced concerning the interaction of official and indigenous law. First, official law may give effect to indigenous norms, even when not recognising them. The official system confers authorisations and immunities, either expressly or impliedly as a result of its passivity or overcommitment, on many informal regulatory settings. Official institutions may even sometimes be exploited to secure results determined by indigenous norms. Second, official law and its process may be used as a resource for the enforcement of indigenous regulation, for example by a party threatening to have recourse to the former if the latter is not complied with. Third, official intervention may strengthen rather than weaken indigenous regulation - even where the official standards are foreign to the indigenous ones. Fourth, the role of indigenous law may increase with the density of social relations, that is, it may be that the more inclusive in life-space and temporal span a relationship between parties is, the more likely it may be that the relationship will be regulated by some indigenous system. Inclusive and enduring relationships create the possibility of effective sanctions, and the participants are likely to share a value consensus. In contrast, areas of activity in which there are no enduring relationships giving rise to self-regulation are those most accessible to government control. But in these areas official controls can be rendered empty by avoidance precisely because there are no valued rewards or feared sanctions built into those relationships.

NOTE

1.   Galanter showed at the Bellagio symposium a sample of his and Frank Palen's archive, together with a scheme of classification for the material they had assembled. (Ed.)

REFERENCE

Galanter, M.
    1981   Justice in Many Rooms: Courts, Private Ordering, and Indigenous Law', *Journal of Legal Pluralism*, 19, 1-47.

Intuitive law versus folk law

Adam Podgorecki

[*Editorial Note*. The paper presented under this title at the Bellagio symposium has been subsequently published in the *Zeitschrift für Rechtssociologie*. The following summary has been prepared by Gordon Woodman.]

Eugen Ehrlich is usually credited with the first development of the essential distinction between the law in the books, or "positive law", and the law in life, or the "living law". Subsequent studies in the USA and Poland have confirmed his suggestion that relationships within the family, and between the family as an entity and the outside world, would not correspond fully to the norms of positive law, although these studies also reveal differences between the societies in popular opinions, practices and attitudes regarding family relationships. However, Ehrlich did not provide an adequate definition or explanation of living law, although he rightly perceived that it constituted the foundation of the legal order of human society, and hence that knowledge of it would be of extraordinary value. He saw also that it could be studied by the ethnomethodological approach, the historical method, juristic experiment, and psychometry.

There is, however, evidence that the crucial step in moving beyond an understanding of law as a purely normative phenomenon, belonging to the world of "ought", was taken earlier by Leon Petrazycki. He distinguishes between: (1) positive and official law (law used by the courts and upheld by the state), (2) positive and unofficial law (for example, a mediator or unofficial agency resolving a conflict with reference to positive law or normative facts), (3) intuitive and official law (for example, the decision by an English court in a case on the foundation of equity), and (4) intuitive and unofficial law (people's spontaneous behaviour guided by their legal intuitions regarding mutually connected rights and duties).

Positive law virtually coincides with official law, and intuitive law with unofficial law. The two primary aspects of a society's law, official and intuitive, may be mutually supportive, or in conflict. In general, the more homogeneous a social system, the more it tends to provide few precise, formal prescriptions, and to rely upon monolithic social values and informal enforcement, that is, upon intuitive, unofficial law. The more heterogeneous a society, the more it provides precise, codified, formal prescriptions, that is, the more it relies upon positive, official law.

The relationship between intuitive, unofficial law and official, positive law is comparable to that of an eloquent, noisy dwarf sitting upon the shoulders of a dumb giant. The dwarf is respected so long as he is assumed to enjoy the support of the giant, and the power of the giant may be overlooked and attributed to the blustering dwarf. Thus traditional jurisprudence sees only the positive, official law, and assumes that spurious, deviant features of legal life are primary.

Intuitive law may be easily seen operating within such areas of social life as the family, the street corner group, the mafia, or the scientific community. Max Weber argued that the sociologist should analyse laws other than official state law, but he failed to distinguish clearly intuitive from official laws. Intuitive law is not restricted to primitive law, in the sense of legal phenomena of non-state societies, nor to customary law, in the sense of law emerging from persistent practice and not imposed from above. Some students of the law of "primitive man", such as Malinowski, Hartland and to some extent Bohannan, have conceived it in terms similar to those of Petrazycki's intuitive law, although some, such as Hoebel and Pospisil, have stressed the elements of sanction and authority more typical of official law.

What is "folk law"? Bohannan conceives of Tiv law as a "folk system", by which he means a system created by the participants in social events out of their social relationships. In this he takes the position of an insider, adopting the subjective viewpoint characteristic of and specific to intuitive law, which stresses the inner dimension of perceived legal claims and duties. From this theoretical viewpoint folk law is nothing else than intuitive law. From a practical viewpoint it is possible to draw a distinction by holding that folk law is related to legal phenomena in "primitive" societies only. However, as such the notion is rapidly losing its practical value, and moreover is questionable in its designation of some societies as "primitive". Alternatively one might claim that the study of "folk law" should be extended to modern society and to those aspects of it which are not normally the subjects of sociological research. The concept might then include such areas of social life as corrupt practices of legislators, or business practices of directors of private or state enterprises.

Part II
Folk Law in State Courts

Introduction

Rüdiger Schott

CHAIRMAN'S REPORT

This introduction aims to supplement the papers in this Part by summarizing the different views expressed in the discussion on them.

There seem to be optimists and pessimists among the experts on folk law – their outlook depending to a certain degree on local conditions and historical developments which refuted all attempts at generalization.

The discussion touched on many points concerning the relations between folk law and state law in general, i.e. not only in courts.

Responding to the question of a "legal revival", comparable to religious revivals (Galanter), it was stressed that a revival of customary law, pure and simple, is impossible because "you cannot regain your lost innocence" (Allott): customary law has changed under the influence of imposed legal systems during colonial rule, and these changes cannot be undone.

The question was raised: who controls the ones professing to know what *the* customary law is, once the traditional social controls over the "legal experts" has gone: "Who regulates the regulators in these systems?" (Allott). The optimistic experience from Zambia, that chiefs administering law in Local Courts are controlled by literate clerks (Singer), was challenged in a heated discussion which revolved round the problem of dissatisfaction with Local Courts and their rulings.

Customary law was held to be extremely flexible under modern conditions, and it was pointed out that perhaps only one out of a hundred cases regulated according to established folk law was sent to the courts (Conn, F. v. Benda-Beckmann). In opposition to this, the question was raised as to whether a person has in fact an option as to the forum to which he may take his case; in many cases the State itself initiates the procedure (Bayly). Folk law therefore exists only in a very restricted sense.

In contrast to this, the point was made that an individualistic view of folk law as a means of settling disputes by attributing "rights" to single persons in quite inappropriate to the concepts of non-European peoples: "The main purpose of folk law is to make you do your duty as a member of your community *before* disputes arise. From their duties follow their rights; in Western societies it is the other way round." (Koesnoe).

The collective character of folk law was further underlined: "Judgments in traditional courts are not simply the pronouncements of the Chief or of one person: they are the collective wisdom of the entire village; the decisions must reflect the general consensus of the community" (Kludze). This "system of participatory justice" (Kludze) assures the control of the traditional courts *and* the acceptance of their rulings by the people concerned.

It was asked whether the "satisfaction of the users of a system of justice" was a valid "criterion of a good or bad legal system", and if so: "How do we measure satisfaction or dissatisfaction with any particular legal system?" (Allott). It was pointed out that present-day legal systems in Africa "are provisional only: they have changed in the past and they will probably rapidly change in the future according to the satisfaction or dissatisfaction they give." There are many signs of dissatisfaction, such as e.g. the creation of parallel unofficial jurisdictions, the "strike of customers" with regard to official courts, and the allegations of corruption, inefficiency, incompetence, sabotage, inaccessibility, high costs etc. (Allott).

For francophone (West) Africa the situation was said to be essentially the same as in anglophone countries. The "basic or fundamental principles of customary law" were said to be still alive on the village level: "It is a law of judges who adapt the general principles to the situation." (Verdier). The judge in the official State Courts is in a much more difficult situation: he is a lawyer trained in modern law and as such he is not easily accepted by the community. The modern judge stands between the government and the people; he knows little of the customary law of the ethnic group in which he is stationed, and, as a rule, he knows also little of the modern law (Verdier).

It was pointed out that the dissatisfaction with justice is not peculiar to Africa, but is characteristic of Western legal systems as well (Griffiths). An essential difference, however, was seen in the fact that in overseas countries the colonial powers had imposed by force *foreign* laws on the traditional customary laws. There was not only a technical difference between the two laws, but a profound one: for an understanding of folk law and its fundamental principles a knowledge of the world view of the particular people is essential (Schott).

A "gap in understanding" was blamed for the situation of Canadian Indians who will "never go to court unless they are brought there. The incorporation of certain of their customs into our European system of law is not going to solve the problem of their dissatisfaction with the State Courts." (Bayly).

In conclusion, the importance of the population which is concerned with the application of folk law or of state law in courts, and the view *they* take of the matter, was emphasized. Empirical and comparative investigations should be made into the differences of acceptance and of satisfaction or dissatisfaction with customary and/or state laws and court procedures.

The use of folk law in West Sumatran State Courts

Keebet von Benda-Beckmann

State courts in Indonesia work according to procedures based on Dutch procedural law.[1] Substantive law is in criminal cases also statutory, based on French and Dutch law. Civil disputes may also be determined according to statutory law, in part closely similar to Dutch civil law, in part derived from Anglo-American law, and in part newly created Indonesian law without a clear basis in any particular foreign legal system. Such law is mainly used in urban and semi-urban centres, especially where international trade is involved. However, in civil disputes state courts also apply folk law, *adat law*,[2] which varies throughout Indonesia. This is generally the case in rural areas, one of which is West Sumatra, the region to be discussed in this paper. West Sumatra is inhabited by the piously Muslim Minangkabau, a matrilineal ethnic group of approximately 6 million people, half of whom live within the province of West Sumatra, while the remainder live scattered throughout the archipelago.[3] Statistics of court registers show that state courts in the central, rural part of West Sumatra apply *adat* or *adat* law in 86% of all civil disputes (K. von Benda-Beckmann 1982: 39).

In this paper I shall attempt to clarify what it means to "apply *adat* law". Generally speaking this term refers to one particular use of rules, namely that of attaching certain consequences to a given set of facts. If A has happened then norm B determines that C shall be the consequence. The term "law application" is thus closely related to the concept of sanctioning and it refers to the final decision in a dispute. However, during a process of dispute-management disputants and judges make frequent use of norms in a sense quite different from the one mentioned here. Recent publications on the application of folk law show a growing uneasiness with the conventional way in which the term has been used. Perhaps the shift away from the study of rules and decisions towards an orientation to processes and procedures has brought the shortcomings of the conventional model to the surface. As a result, many authors have called attention to various other ways in which substantive rules are used in processes of dispute management. Comaroff and Roberts (1977:85) have argued that parties in a dispute present a "paradigm of argument" by which an attempt is made "to convey a coherent picture of relevant events and actions *in terms of one or more (implicit or explicit) normative referents*" (original italics). Norms are thus used not only as a programme for the attachment of consequences to a set of events, but also to set the parameters of the dispute. Depending on whether the paradigm presented by a party is accepted by the opponent, the ensuing argumentation tends to be put either more in terms of facts or more in terms of norms.[4] Earlier, Abel (1970:62) had questioned the validity of "the central assumption of conventional legal scholarship - concern with the analysis of legal rules" and commented that, if it was true that most disputes concerned disagreement about facts, then evidence was a central part of a dispute which deserved our full attention. In that case "surely legal scholarship should be concerned primarily to discover the critical rules governing the determination of facts and not allow itself to be limited by conventional preoccupations with the study of substantive principles ....." However, Abel does not seem to move far from the conventional model. He merely uses it for the determination of facts rather than for the attachment of consequences. Moore (1978:209) criticized the model from yet another perspective. She suggested in her work on the Chagga that judgments only to a certain extent contained the true reasons for the decisions and should be regarded also as a justification of the consequences attached to the proven events or as a demonstration that the court was a guardian of law and order. She called for a critical examination of the other uses of norms and warned against rash inferences from decisions.

In each of these approaches the need is expressed to do more than simply look at substantive legal rules and their precise content. Each author pays attention to one particular way in which rules and principles are used. In fact, each one looks at a different part of the dispute. Comaroff and Roberts concentrate on the beginning of the dispute at which the parameters are set by a presentation and acceptance or rejection of the paradigm. Abel emphasizes the establishment of facts, which usually occurs at a later stage. Moore writes about the next stage, the decision. It seems to me that it would be more fruitful to look at the various ways in which rules and principles are used throughout the process than to pick out one particular aspect only. This may not be so obvious for processes lasting no longer than a few hours. In such cases it is tempting to select one salient aspect, as Comaroff and Roberts did. However, if one studies processes which last several months or even years, it becomes obvious that each passes through a number of stages which can be distinguished analytically.

It seemed fruitful to me to distinguish four different stages, in each of which substantive and procedural norms are used in different ways.[5]

(i) *Presentation of the claim, definition and specification of the issues*
In this stage the parties explain, modify and specify their version of the events about which they have a conflict. They also give their interpretation of the events and may propose what the judge should do about the dispute. This

stage ends with a preliminary discussion determining what are the issues, which events and interpretations are disputed, and on what matters evidence is needed.

(ii) *Provision and evaluation of evidence*
At this stage each of the parties provides as much support for his assertions as he can. This includes evidence of facts as well as interpretations of facts and rules. Further specification of disputed issues takes place here. The stage ends with a decision that all evidence required and available has been obtained and - more importantly - with an evaluation of this evidence. Two questions must be answered at this stage: Is the evidence reliable? Is it relevant to the issue in dispute?

(iii) *Final decision*
This consists of two parts, one being the court's own version of what happened, its identification of the issues and its evaluation of the evidence. To a large extent these decisions have been made at earlier stages and only take their definite form here. As Gulliver noted: "Decision-making is not limited only to the final outcome of a dispute. Throughout both kinds of process [i.e., arbitration and adjudication] there is a necessity for decisions in both procedural and substantive matters" (1978:37). I would add that most of these can be reversed until the final decision has been made. The other part is formed by the consequences to be attached to the events (cf. van Velsen 1969:144).

(iv) *Realization of the decision*
If we talk about application of norms, we are interested not so much in the final decision as such, as in the final result of the decision-making process. That is to say, we should include in our analysis questions such as to what extent, when and how the consequences pronounced in the decision are carried out. This stage, however, not only concerns the effectiveness of decisions in the narrow sense in which the term is usually employed. At the same time we need to see how the first part of the decision is treated. Do parties attach the same meaning to the court's version of events, to its evaluation of evidence, and to the ascription of rights and duties to the parties, as the court does?

Shifting our attention from the final decision to all stages of a process has another advantage. It forces us to realize that in West Sumatra not only *adat* substantive norms are used, but at the same time non-*adat* procedural norms. This brings me to the second purpose of my paper. In which ways does the Dutch type of state court procedure affect the outcome of disputes? I use the term 'procedure" here in a very broad sense, including the actual course of a dispute as well as the state court organisation, recruitment and education of judges, and their notions of proper procedure.

Both questions will be elaborated by a comparison with village institutions of dispute management, which by and large work according to *adat* procedures. In West Sumatra there are thus two kinds of institutions using *adat* substantive law, one according to the Indonesian law of procedure, the other according to Minangkabau *adat* procedural law (cf. Koesnoe in this volume).

Since the relative influence of procedure and *adat* substantive law is different in each stage, I shall make my comparisons stage by stage. The stages cannot always be neatly separated. At any one time different issues may be in different stages and an issue may go back and forth several times between them. I do think, however, that for analytical purposes the division into stages is useful and allows us to obtain a clearer understanding of what "rule application" means than if we concentrate on decisions only. More particularly it makes it possible to discern the important reasons for the differences in outcome between state courts and village institutions. One such reason is the difference in procedures. The other is that procedural aspects, or action aspects, considered essential elements of *adat* norms in the villages, are disregarded or even willingly cut off from the *adat* norms in state courts.

Village institutions dealing with conflicts in West Sumatra are designed to solve conflicts, whatever the issue at stake. They do so by means of deliberations and negotiations among all people concerned until, ideally, a unanimous decision (Min. *sakato*, Ind. *mupakat*)[6] is reached. Consensus is the main guarantee for a just and correct decision, because the Minangkabau consider it hardly thinkable that all persons involved would agree with something unjust or incorrect. This system can only work when parties and decision-makers know each other well, when the social setting of disputes is familiar to all, when access to information is easy, and when the power of every person involved is properly held in balance by the power of others. Some villages in West Sumatra are still small and coherent enough to make this kind of dispute management possible. In Bukit Hijau,[7] from which I derived most of the information used in this study, it does not work well and many conflicts remain unsolved or come to the state court.

State court procedures are based on very different presumptions. They are meant to guarantee a neutral, impartial, distanced treatment of a dispute, in which legal questions should be addressed by fulltime, salaried officials with a law training. Neutrality and impartiality of judges are guaranteed by restrictions on admissibility of information. Only information presented during formal sessions may be accepted and parties should have equal access to such information. Judges may have no prior knowledge of either the conflict or the parties. In fact, they often have no more than a vague notion of village life. They live in towns, are personally oriented towards semi-urban or urban social life, and many of them greatly dislike the narrow-mindedness of village life. They not only lack the background information which village functionaries have, but they are also restricted in their search for information and evaluation of information.

The rules of evidence used in state courts are designed for a society in which literacy is widespread and where documents are commonly used in transactions. Both admissibility and evaluation of evidence are more restricted than in village institutions. Furthermore, courts are designed to pass a decision, rather than bring parties to an agreement. And the idea is that with the decision a solution is reached for the conflict, which can be simply carried out, if necessary with police support. Even though the Indonesian judges are required to try to bring parties to an agreement at every session, the procedure is not designed for negotiations, nor are judges trained for such activities. They have learned to interpret rules and analyse legal questions, not to negotiate with people. They are trained more to say what the law is than to bring people to a settlement of their problem. This does not mean that judges are never interested in the real conflict, nor that they do not try to promote settlements, but neither their training, nor their ideas of their task as judges, nor the court organization and procedures promote this kind of activity. Judges are in general oriented towards a Dutch type of dispute management, in which legal questions are to be answered and norms should be applied in a clearcut way (cf. K. von Benda-Beckmann 1984).

1. DEFINITION AND SPECIFICATION OF THE ISSUES

Most conflicts already have a long history of unsuccessful settlement attempts by various village institutions such as the lineage head, the clan segment council, the *adat* council, the mayor, the village council or sub-district and district institutions, (police, military officer, district officer)[8], before they are submitted to the state court. In a way state courts are used as a kind of appellate institution. People consider that conflicts should be handled first by village institutions - especially the village council - which may only act as mediators and formally are not allowed to pass judgments.[9] However, in practice the court dispute tends to take on a rather different character from that which the conflict had before it reached the state court (cf. Moore 1977:182 ff.). State courts do not accept all kinds of conflicts; they deal with "civil disputes" only, and a conflict must be formulated to fit this requirement. In general one could say that disputes about village politics and about proper behaviour are never the central issue and are avoided as far as possible. A conflict about the right to be a lineage head, for example, is not considered to be a civil dispute, whereas a conflict about lineage land is. Likewise, a conflict about an omission to pay due respect will not be accepted as a civil dispute, whereas one about land titles will be. If both issues are involved, the latter must be the basis for a claim and the first can at best play a role in the evidence submitted in support of the latter issue. On the other hand, in village institutions disputes tend to be formulated in terms of proper behaviour and procedures (K. von Benda-Beckmann 1981).

A suit usually contains only a factual account of the main events on which the claim is based and a request to the courts to take certain action. It rarely makes explicit reference to any norms. However, implicitly they always structure the formulation of a dispute, especially when a plaintiff takes an opportunity of asking a court clerk or a judge to help him formulate the suit. Judges and clerks have very definite opinions on what kind of issues may be treated. They advise a plaintiff either to withdraw the claim or to define it in such a way that it fits their requirements (Tanner 1971:189 ff.).

Usually the first four sessions are spent reading claims and counterclaims. Thus, this initial exchange of claims and counterclaims is used to specify, modify and adjust each party's claim. Judges usually ask short questions about the meaning of passages and make some suggestions for a better formulation. Too bold claims may be withdrawn and extra arguments added. More importantly, however, in this stage the first selection of relevant facts and issues takes place. Since judges concentrate on legal issues and neglect other complaints, a dispute is moulded according to the judges' ideas of relevance, which may differ markedly from the plaintiff's original ideas. Parties must follow the judges' kind of reasoning and provide them with arguments plausible to them in order to be successful. For many disputants this is a very difficult and frustrating activity, because they have the feeling that judges treat not their conflict but something else.

With the formulation or definition of the dispute thus a first global selection of relevant norms, issues and events is made. This forms the basic structure for the rest of the dispute. In the course of the dispute this is further narrowed down, but the parameters are set at this early stage.[10] When the court gives a summary of the events and issues on which the claim is based and decides what is undisputed and what needs further evidence, this is structured by the normative framework set out in this stage, even though there is still no explicit reference to the norms.

2. PROVISION AND EVALUATION OF EVIDENCE

Once the main issues are defined and it has become clear what are the disputed and undisputed events, the court invites parties to provide evidence in support of their respective standpoints.[11]

There is a strong preference on the part of judges for written evidence, especially contracts and notary deeds. However, sufficient evidence of this type is rarely available. Other kinds of written evidence, such as genealogies, decisions by various village institutions of dispute-management, and letters from village functionaries explaining the situation, are frequently presented, but treated with great distrust by the court. As long as papers do not fulfil the statutory requirements of proper signatures by both parties, they are worth very little.

Most disputes hinge on witnesses' testimonies. The problem with witnesses, however, is that they are usually related in one way or another to at least one of the parties. Whereas in village procedures this is considered normal and even desirable, judges in state courts tend to be suspicious and sometimes reject such witnesses' evidence on the ground that it is against the law of civil procedure to allow close relatives of a party to testify. An important category of witnesses are the *adat* functionaries and other village functionaries, such as the mayor and the village secretary. They are heard not only as regular witnesses, but also as expert witnesses on village life and on the village variant of Minangkabau *adat*. It is especially this role which causes great misunderstanding between judges and *adat* experts. Both consider themselves the only true experts, but they tend to interpret both rules and events rather differently. Moreover, information formally received by an *adat* functionary from his predecessor, and therefore according to *adat* particularly trustworthy and an important basis for their expertise, is often treated as ordinary evidence. Judges in general have a low opinion of *adat* functionaries and tend to over-emphasize the decline during the last 100 years of their prestige and knowledge of local affairs.

It is not always possible to present enough direct evidence to convince the court of one's claim. Hardly any dispute in which the history of a lineage and kin relations are disputed can be decided on direct evidence. Inheritance is the main issue in 29% of all cases according to the court registers, and lineage history and kin relationships are an important element in far more disputes. They can only directly be proven by means of a genealogy recognized by both parties. But these are usually contested, frequently on good grounds. Many genealogies I have seen had been tampered with, often in the crudest way. What remains then is circumstantial evidence, because blood relationships are unobservable, and according to state courts therefore cannot be proven by witnesses. A statement by a lineage head to the effect that both parties belong - or do not belong - to the same lineage within his clan-segment is often regarded as unacceptable evidence in state courts. In village procedures such a statement would be an acceptable basis for a decision.

During the initial stage each party usually has given several reasons to make its standpoint plausible. At this stage the arguments are refined and put more precisely. Usually they run along the same lines of thought, namely that social relationships always have a number of other social and legal implications. However, parties may disagree about the specific implications of a certain relationship, the relevance of certain events for the relationship, or the occurrence of the events. The first two involve an interpretation of norms, whereas the latter is "merely" a question of fact.

In a case described at length elsewhere the dispute evolved around the lineage membership of the two parties (K. von Benda-Beckmann 1984). Each provided a genealogy which differed from the other on the crucial point. The issue of lineage membership was then dissected into several issues from which lineage membership could be deduced or not. Both parties and the court agreed that it implied having common lineage property (*harato pusako*), a common graveyard, a lineage house, etc. The disagreement concerned smaller details. For example, the plaintiff had sent a mattress to the house where the head of the lineage, of which he claimed to be a member, had died. He had intended to fetch the body of the deceased, bring it to his house, and have a ceremony performed appointing him as the new lineage head, after which he would bring the deceased to the graveyard and bury him. However, the mattress was refused and one point of disagreement was about the interpretation of the refusal. Could the mattress be refused on religious grounds only, in which case the refusal would not necessarily amount to a denial that the sender was a lineage member? Or did refusal always mean a denial of lineage membership? The court chose the latter possibility.

Less macabre indications of lineage membership may be provided by the answers to questions such as whether female relatives live closely together; who cared for a deceased during his or her illness or old age; who paid doctor's bills; and questions such as who took part in what function during ceremonies like lineage head installations, weddings and burials. Much of this is common knowledge in village institutions. Parties may even agree about the interpretations in a village setting. But it is not uncommon for them to take standpoints in state court processes which they could not and would not take in village processes. Many of the elements of circumstantial evidence are regarded in village procedure as *tando*, visible signs of something invisible and so as compelling evidence, to be valued more highly than most other evidence, and rebuttable only by the knowledge of an *adat* functionary.

But judges have insufficient access to background information, even though some go into great detail, and clever disputants gamble on a dismissal of evidence. Although some judges pursue the history of the issues under dispute far back and build a whole pyramid of questions, leading to the central issue to be proven, they do not go down to the basic issues, especially when village and lineage politics are involved. Going all the way down could mean that the very points which should prove the issue could only be proved by means of that issue. Thus in the case mentioned above the court did not go as far as to ask whether the plaintiff had legitimately sent over the mattress. The answer to that question would have depended on whether he belonged to the same lineage as the deceased and that was precisely the question under dispute! Judges simply stop short of getting involved in such a vicious circle.

Judges often need an expert on village customs to interpret the events and norms, because norms generally valid throughout Minangkabau may vary in their more specific forms from village to village. Sometimes judges follow the interpretation of *adat* experts, but sometimes they prefer to use a more generally accepted interpretation, much to the chagrin of those experts. In general, they tend to treat every issue separately. If, for example, a series of events is put to them as evidence of lineage membership, they ask as to every event whether it by itself necessarily indicates common lineage membership. If it is an indication for clan segment membership but not necessarily for lineage membership, it is considered irrelevant to the latter issue.[12] Village functionaries on the other hand have a more integrative approach. They do not look at the various aspects as if they were independent issues to each of which a norm could be applied. Even though an event by itself is only a possible indication, the more of such events there are, the more likely there is to be a common lineage membership. The result is that events are considered irrelevant by state courts which are highly relevant in village procedures.

3. FINAL DECISION

The final decision can take either of two forms. One is a settlement between the parties, in which case the parties make the decision and the court only acts as a mediator with more or less influence. However, only 15% of all civil disputes end thus. By far the greater proportion end with an authoritative decision.[13] For a complete description it would be necessary to include settlements in the analysis. In this paper I shall confine myself to formal judgments of the court.

Indonesian judgments have a similar form to Dutch judgments. They start with the list of parties, the claims, defences and counterclaims as they were formulated in the written statements, exchanged at the initial sessions. In contrast to Dutch judgments, they contain a full list of the means of evidence provided by the parties.[14] Then comes the first main part of the judgment, in which the court gives its own version of the disputed and undisputed facts and issues and sums up the disputed facts for which it required evidence. It then gives a summary of each piece of evidence and a discussion of its reliability and relevance. After that comes a final reconstruction of the events, according to the view of the court, followed by decisions on the issues considered to constitute the dispute, in which the rights and obligations of the parties, the validity of transactions, legal positions etc. are decided. The final part is a short list stating the consequences of these decisions. It is thus the direct answer to the original request by the plaintiff to the court to take particular action, and what precedes it is the justification - imaginary or real - for that decision.

The judgment is authoritative in the sense that the court decides independently of whether parties agree to the decision. Generally, at least one party does not agree and often both are dissatisfied. In the section about realization of decisions I shall examine the further consequences of parties' disagreement.

Village functionaries cannot make authoritative judgments. A decision is only valid, or "round", as it is called, when the disputants have agreed to it. If one of the parties is not satisfied with a proposed solution, he refrains from consenting and waits for the other to take further steps or goes to another institution himself. If no other institution is available, the dispute either remains unsolved or is raised above the village level and presented to a state institution. Most decisions by village institutions remain unwritten. They should by custom be affirmed with a ceremonial meal, but often such a meal does not take place and the only way to know whether consensus has been reached is by looking at what the disputants do. However, the village council, installed by the state administration, usually writes a decision in much the same form as state court judgments, the only difference being that the disputants have to sign it, because formally it is a settlement, not a judgment. About half of the decisions drawn up by the village council lack the signature of at least one of the parties. The *adat* council, the highest traditional institution of dispute-settlement, and some of the lower councils as well, sometimes write decisions, the form of which varies greatly. Some are very similar to state court judgments and village council decisions. Others contain a very short statement of what the parties promised to do or refrain from doing.

As I have demonstrated in the preceding sections, *adat* norms play various roles in the final decision. Tentative decisions made in the preceding stages take on their final form here. The final judgment thus contains the last and most definite of a long series of decisions. In the next section I shall discuss the question of how conclusive the decision is.

We have also seen that procedural rules of a non-*adat* character play an important role during the process, in particular at the stage where evidence is evaluated, resulting in a different picture of the disputed events and a different meaning from those they would have in village processes. Since the overwhelming majority of disputes decided by state courts hinge upon the legal relevance and credibility of events and social relationships, the differences between Dutch procedural law and village procedures often result in a different outcome to a dispute. However, the differences in outcome are also caused by differences in the ways in which judges and village functionaries conceive of rules. Although they agree about most rule-statements, they interpret them differently when relating them to concrete events and claims during the process. I discuss this difference at this place, although it has an impact on the two preceding stages as well. Basically the difference lies in two closely related characteristics attributed to rules in *adat*: (1) *adat* rules have a high degree of flexibility in that they are treated as guidelines for decisions rather than as clear prescriptions, as in western legal theory; (2) *adat* theory demands the consideration of all concrete circumstances of the situation to which the rule must be applied. This holds true for all kinds of decisions and not only for decisions in disputes. In village processes of decisionmaking the substantive content of a norm therefore is not sharply distinguished from the decisionmaking process in which the norm is used, even though this "procedural" aspect is not explicit in the norm statement. Under these circumstances proper procedure - and especially the requirement of unanimity - is the main guarantee of a good solution. Functionaries have a rather large discretion in how they use *adat* norms.[15]

With the introduction of the Dutch court system and doctrine of decisionmaking, flexible *adat* rules have been transformed into rather strict, inflexible rules, fitting into the rule model of western continental law. The guarantee for a good decision lies now in the substantive content of the rule and not so much in procedural requirements. Rules of procedure in western legal systems are rules for trouble cases, not for trouble-free decision-making processes. However, since the rules of procedure are statutory, judges feel free to neglect or even cut off the procedural elements of *adat* law, considered essential in that law, from the *adat* substantive rules.[16]

I have described elsewhere this fixation, or transformation of *adat* norms with respect to the division of estates, land titles, the social meaning of the knowledge of *adat* functionaries, and the construction of contracts.[17] In a much more general way the differences between *adat* and state interpretation of norms are reflected in the way compensation is awarded. The state courts have laid down the rule that the risk of inflation should be equally divided between plaintiff and defendant, independently of their individual circumstances such as fault or relative economic prosperity. In order to assess the value of the damage ensuing from inflation, a simple comparison between prices in terms of the rupiah is considered enough. But it may be necessary to compare gold prices, since the value of land and pawning prices are often expressed in gold rupiahs.

The most common claim for compensation is the loss of harvests from the moment of illegal occupation until the final decision. Generally speaking one half of the value of harvests over that period is allowed, with a tendency to fix a maximum limit of 5 years.[18] In this respect the amount of the compensation is fixed in a way similar to the division of an inheritance, i.e. in equal parts. For a consideration of particular circumstances there is substituted the fiction that both parties are equally at fault (or in the case of inheritance have equal needs) and therefore should share the damage.

Of course, village institutions also allow damages to be recovered. But they do not calculate in such a clear-cut way as the courts. They do not simply count the years of illegal occupation and have the harvests paid back. This could perhaps happen if the period of illegal occupation had lasted only a very short time. Otherwise it will depend on the economic situation of both parties and, more specifically, on whether the person entitled to the land has really suffered from the lack of harvest; on how much the illegal occupier can pay; on the personal and social relationships between the parties and their lineages; on an evaluation of how much each party is to be blamed for the existence and continuation of the illegal situation; and of course on the relative negotiating strengths. The total amount of the compensation never becomes as high as in the longer court disputes, not because villagers are particularly nice to each other, but because they are realistic. Too high a debt cannot and will not be paid any way and would only enhance rancour instead of making an end to the conflict. A very realistic calculation and evaluation of what is feasible, and what the consequences will be, is the basis for such decisions.

These considerations hardly play a role in court disputes. Parties usually have gone through considerable frustration because no solution on the village level could be reached. Once they have made the step to go to the court, they fight bitterly to get as much out of it as they can. They do not even expect judges to be considerate. It is not by sheer chance that only a very low percentage of court disputes end with a settlement, especially in land and inheritance cases.

State courts thus often use fictions where village institutions look at the real situation. And since state courts cannot and may not follow the same procedures as village institutions, they do not consider them to be essential elements of *adat* rules. State court *adat* rules, in short, are different from *adat* rules used in village decision-making processes. This is one reason why villagers do not recognize state court law as their own law. However, many disputants appreciate the advantages of state court law and make clever use of its possibilities. They know that judges, even if they tried, could not possibly take all circumstances into consideration, and they take great care to ensure that some circumstances never come to the judges' attention. Furthermore they recognize the value of manipulating witnesses, and know that by simply denying facts, even though these are well known, they can turn a decision in their favour. Not all disputants are will-less victims of ill-meaning judges. And some are victims of the manipulations of their opponents rather than of judges.

4. REALIZATION OF THE DECISION

State court doctrine makes a sharp distinction between a court procedure resulting in a judgment and the execution of the decision. The first is in the hands of judges, whereas the latter is in principle a matter for the parties themselves. Only when necessary can the "strong arm" of the law, the bailiff (Ind. *jurusita*), or the police, be called for assistance. For the court a dispute ends with the judgment, but not for the disputants. They have several options in deciding how to proceed from there. A much used possibility is to appeal to the Court of Appeal in the capital of West Sumatra. Minangkabau disputants are very tenacious once they have made the step to go to the state court. 54% of civil disputes are appealed, and as many as 18% of the decisions by the Court of Appeal are taken to the Supreme Court of Indonesia in Jakarta for cassation. It seems to be worth the trouble. Over 40% of the appealed decisions are reversed (cf. F. von Benda-Beckmann 1979:308)!

Of the 46% contained at the state court level, the judges claim that almost all decisions are adhered to or executed. Unfortunately I have no systematic data on the actual rate of execution. In Bukit Hijau, from where I have information about several disputes from the period after court decisions, there were several ways in which these were "executed" and all decisions had at least some effect. If the court ordered the transfer of a piece of land, the demolition of a lineage house, or anything other than the payment of money, it was usually done. But there were other ways to "execute" the decision. In one case the defendant, who had been ordered to give a plot of rice land back to the plaintiff, continued to work on it, with the implicit understanding that from now onwards she held it on loan and not as her property or in pawn, as she had claimed in court.

I expect that similar kinds of arrangements are quite commonly made, especially in cases in which the court awards compensation for unlawful possession and use of agricultural land. As compensation may be awarded for periods of 30 years or more, sums often reach staggering heights. It seems completely impossible that sums equivaent to US $1000 or more can ever be fully recovered. I assume that disputants usually come to some arrangement and that only a small part of the compensation is actually paid. For the rest the outstanding debt can be conveniently used as a threat in case the main claim is not fulfilled.

Another possibility is that for the time being nothing happens at all. If, for example, the disputed land was pawned or taken in share-cropping by a third person, no immediate action is necessary to execute a decision requiring the land to be transferred to the plaintiff. Its effect is simply that another person is entitled to redemption. The same holds true for all kinds of validation, nullification or determination of the legal status of land or other property, unless the court itself attaches further consequences to it. State court procedures do not require a ceremony in which all participants confirm their consent to the decision, as do village procedures. Thus it is impossible to say whether the decision is executed until someone tries, e.g., to redeem the land or takes action allowed only to an official heir, etc. But that may happen long after the decision. This is not just a technical problem in the sense that an outside observer cannot know for sure whether or not people live according to the decision; for the losing party may also consciously refrain from further action for the time being, until the political situation in the village, and the personal strength of his lineage, have changed in a way which promises good chances for a reversed decision if the case is taken to the court again. This frequently happens in Minangkabau villages. The main disputes are long-standing conflicts between lineages or lineage segments over property, which in slightly different constellations flare up over and over again. In the village dispute processing following a court decision, the previous court decision has enormous prestige. Even if it is generally known that the witnesses have lied and the decision was wrong, a court decision tends to be treated not as a decision between the parties originally concerned, and binding on them alone, but as a more or less absolute establishment of rights and legal positions. It takes the return from abroad of an influential lineage member, or the coming of age of a strong personality in the lineage, for successful action against such a court decision to be taken before a village institution. The effect of state court decisions lies not so much in their direct realization - because so many judgments are reversed on appeal, and of the remainder only a part is fully realized - but rather in this effect they have on village dispute processes. In renewed court proceedings, on the other hand, previous decisions have much less effect. It is rather easy for the disputants to formulate basically the same dispute in such a way that it is accepted as a new dispute by the courts. Very often the judges do not even realize that the disputes concern the same conflict. As the subject-matter is changed by the parties, who are themselves often not the same persons as in the previous case, the courts have no way of avoiding such a repetition, and the rule that a dispute may not be decided twice by the court (*ne bis in idem*) is of little value.

5. CONCLUSIONS

The traditional model according to which legal rules determine the outcome of a dispute in a rather mechanical way does not provide a satisfactory understanding of the role legal rules play in processes of dispute management. Such processes can be better understood if we take a broader look at the various ways in which substantive and procedural rules and principles are used by the participants in such processes.

I have analyzed these different kinds of use by conceiving of a disputing process as consisting of four stages which resemble van Velsen's stages with the exception of his pre-trial and my post-trial stage. I have considered the operation at each stage of both substantive and procedural rules. In the first stage the substantive rules are primarily used to structure the dispute. This is the kind of norm-use Comaroff and Roberts wrote about in their article of 1977. In the second stage substantive norms are used as a standard for relevance and credibility of events. As such they are an important element in the construction of the factual basis for the court's decision. Abel (1970) drew our attention to this kind of norm use in his observations on Kenya's state courts. In the third stage all decisions, tentatively or definitely made at earlier stages, take on their final form. Norms are used here in part in the same way as in earlier stages. But they are also used to justify the consequences attached to the events as constructed by the court. To what extent they are a justification, as Moore suggested (1978), and how far the consequences are determined, though not exclusively, by the norms, can only be evaluated if we look at the final decision as a result of decisions made at previous stages and not as an isolated decision. The second question is how far procedural norms, in the Minangkabau state courts based on Dutch law, influence the outcome of a dispute. This is a complex problem. The procedure of state courts not only affects the factual basis of the decision by imposing a far more rigorous selection of facts in the first and second stages. It also affects the legal rules themselves and transforms them into rather inflexible substantive rules, divested of the procedural elements they have in village processes of decision making.

In my discussion of the fourth stage, the realization of the decision, I have pointed out that decisions are by no means always executed in the way intended. Compensation is probably rarely fully paid. The common tactical approach seems to be that if it can be avoided the decision should not be carried out. Furthermore, though in the short term a number of decisions seem to be realized, long term realization is rare. An execution in the sense that everything is completely realized in the way intended by state courts is an exception rather than the rule. It seems therefore that in this stage the process is governed more by *adat* principles of procedure than by western procedure.

NOTES

1.   See, for an overview of the Indonesian formal legal system, Damian and Hornick 1972.
2.   *Adat* in its broadest sense means as much as culture. In a more restricted sense it refers to all normative rules governing social life. The term "*adat* law" was a Dutch invention and refers to the legal norms in *adat*. In state courts the terms are used synonymously. See for literature on Minangkabau *adat* law: F. von Benda-Beckmann 1979; K. von Benda-Beckmann 1981, 1982, 1983; Tanner 1969, 1970, 1971; Westenenk 1918; Willinck 1909.
3.   Kato 1982; Nain 1973.

4.   Shortly after the conference in Bellagio, Comaroff and Roberts 1981 appeared, with a fascinating study of the relation between norms and processes in two Tswana chiefdoms. It would require a long discussion to do justice to their highly sophisticated treatment of that relation. Since this volume is meant to be a publication of the conference papers, I shall have to leave such a discussion for a later moment.

5.   My stages somewhat resemble those suggested by van Velsen (1969: 146 ff). For the purpose of this paper I leave out the pre-trial stage, but my model could be easily included in a more comprehensive one, which would have to differentiate the pre-trial stage (cf. Felstiner, Abel, Sarat 1980/81). I include a post-trial stage, which to my knowledge has never been done in an analytical model, although many authors do pay considerable attention to that stage. See also Cochrane 1972; Holleman 1974: 19f.

6.   See for a discussion of the term *mupakat* Koesnoe 1969.

7.   Bukit Hijau is a pseudonym for the village in which I stayed together with my husband Franz von Benda-Beckmann during a 16-month fieldwork period in 1974-75. One of the reasons for choosing that particular village was that a relatively large number of court cases had originated there. For a more comprehensive description of conflict management in a village see K. von Benda-Beckmann 1981.

8.   See for an overview of village institutions K. von Benda-Beckmann 1981:118 f.

9.   Between 1874 and 1935 *adat* councils formally were not recognised as institutions of dispute settlement, although in practice they were never abolished and courts even referred disputes back to elicit a decision from the *adat* court before they would consider them (Guyt 1934; 1936). In 1935 village justice was officially recognized, but as a mediating institution only. Every person who wants to go to the state court directly is entitled to do so. In land disputes this is hardly ever done.

10.   Comaroff and Roberts (1977) speak in this context of a "paradigm of argument". Cf. also above.

11.   Since I have written extensively about evidence elsewhere I shall only give a summary here. K. von Benda-Beckmann 1984; cf. Tanner 1971:196-198.

12.   I have called the courts' use of norms centrifugal, because judges are most interested in the outer boundaries of norms. In contrast, villagers are more interested in the basic meaning of a norm, in its kernel. Therefore I have referred to their approach as centripetal: K. von Benda-Beckmann 1984.

13.   Of all civil disputes 15% end with a settlement, but of these only one third concern lineage land, whereas of the total number of civil disputes two thirds concern lineage land. (In my survey: N = 499; settled cases = 74; land disputes = 332; settled land disputes = 26.). In contrast, of all disputes involving bank loans, in which banks are a party (= 71), 46.5% (= 33) are settled: cf. K. von Benda-Beckmann 1980:4 ff; F. von Benda-Beckmann 1979: 307.

14.   Dutch judgments only mention the means of evidence on which the decision is based. Indonesian judgments therefore provide far more useful information for a researcher than Dutch judgments.

15.   Koesnoe goes so far as to say that *adat* law has no pre- existing substantive rules at all (in this volume). I do not agree with this statement, although the Minangkabau have far fewer rules in the sense of programmatic statements mentioned at the beginning of this paper than for instance Dutch law has. Minangkabau *adat* has far more principles - in the sense Dworkin (1977) uses the term - than rules, but these may come very close to rules: cf. Woodman in this volume. These principles are, however, different from the "basic principles in *adat* by which the functionaries have to abide when they elaborate and create the real form of *adat*", which Koesnoe has in mind. Both principles in the Dworkinian sense and rules can be found in the constitutional, the institutional and the realizational category of Koesnoe's analytical frame-work and they vary greatly in the level of abstraction. It should be noted that, according to our research findings, these categories do not correspond with the Minangkabau folk categories,

whatever merits they may have as analytical tools. Minangkabau *adat* has four categories, all referring to social life; there is no category referring to the laws of nature only. Also, there is no Minangkabau author who differentiates *adat* categories according to the level of abstraction, as Koesnoe does with his three categories. Although he is correct in stating that Minangkabau authors do not agree about the precise meaning of each category, there is a marked agreement that they concern a differentiation according to the source of *adat*. They determine who made the various kinds of *adat* and whether and by whom they may be changed. The *Adat Nan Sabana Adat* is according to all authors the *adat* which always has been with the Minangkabau people and cannot be changed. Only in the last respect do they resemble the laws of nature, which also cannot be changed. Cf. F. and K. von Benda-Beckmann 1977: 29 ff. Cf. also Holleman 1974: 18f.

16.   Korn complained about this change in 1941. He wrote: "The legal rules are ... formulated much more strictly than is necessary or desirable in the mild practice of small societies" (1941: 315).

17.   K. von Benda-Beckmann 1982: 46 f. On a more general level we have discussed the problem of transformation of *adat* rules in F. and K. von Benda-Beckmann 1981.

18.   Some courts do not limit this period, because *adat* law does not have anything comparable with a statute of limitations. It is not uncommon for a court to be required to decide on an alleged illegal act of 50 years ago. The oldest case still pending in 1975 was based on a conflict which had started in 1909 and had come to court for the first time in 1919. As a result of the chaotic political period starting in the early forties and ending in the late sixties, many such cases have been brought to court several times under several regimes (Dutch - Japanese - Dutch - Sukarno - Suharto) without conclusive results. One court often - but not always - follows a decision by the Court of Appeal in Medan and allows compensation for 5 years only. It has thus introduced an element of forfeiture to make up for the lack of a statute of limitation (State Court of Butkittinggi nrs. 1: 1970; 29: 1968; cf. 6: 1974.)

REFERENCES

Abel, R.L.
1970   *Customary laws of wrongs in Kenya: an essay in research method.* Yale Law School Studies in Law and Modernization No.2. Yale.
Benda-Beckmann, F. von
1979   *Property in social continuity and change: the maintenance of property relationships through time in Minangkabau, West Sumatra*, M. Nijhoff, Den Haag.
Benda-Beckmann, K. von
1980   *Traditional values in a non-traditional context: Adat and state courts in West Sumatra*, paper presented at the Seminar on Minangkabau Culture, Society and Literature, September 1980, Bukittinggi.
1981   'Forum shopping and shopping forums: dispute processing in a Minangkabau village', *Journal of Legal Pluralism*, 19: 117-159.
1982   'Traditional values in a non-traditional context: Adat and state courts in West Sumatra', *Indonesia Circle* No.27 (March 1982): 39-50.
1984   'Evidence and legal reasoning in Minangkabau state courts', in K. von Benda-Beckmann, *The Broken Stairways to Consensus: Village Justice and State Courts in Minangkabau*, Foris, Dordrecht, 65-98.
Benda-Beckmann F. and K. von
1977   'Adat Minangkabau en de "Drie Kategorieën van Adat": Een Weerlegging van Koesnoes Hypothese', *Nieuwsbrief-Volksrechtkring Nijmegen* 2 vol. 2 (July 1977): 24-39.

1981   *Transformations and change in Minangkabau Adat*, paper presented at the IUAES Intercongress, Amsterdam, April 1981.

Cochrane, G.
1972   'Legal decisions and processual models of law', *Man* 7: 50-56.

Comaroff, J. and S. Roberts
1977   'The invocation of norms in dispute settlement: the Tswana case', in I. Hamnett (ed.), *Social Anthropology and Law*, A.S.A. Monograph 14, Academic Press, London, New York, San Franciso.
1981   *Rules and processes: the cultural logic of dispute in an African context*, The University of Chicago Press, Chicago and London.

Damian, E. and R.N. Hornick
1972   'Indonesia's formal legal system: an introduction', *AJCL* 20: 492-530.

Dworkin, R.
1977   *Taking rights seriously*, Duckworth. London.

Felstiner, W.L.F., R.L. Abel, A. Sarat
1980/81   'The emergence and transformation of disputes: naming, blaming, claiming, *Law and Society Review* 15:3:4: 631-654.

Gulliver, P.H.
1978   'Process and decision', in P.H. Gulliver (ed.) *Cross Examinations: Essays in Memory of Max Gluckman*, E.J. Brill, Leiden.

Guyt, H.
1934   'Kerapatan-Adat', *Indisch Tijdschrift voor het Recht* 140: 127-235.

Holleman, J.F.
1974   'Indigenous administration of justice', in *Issues in African Law*, Mouton, The Hague.

Kato, T.
1982   *Matriliny and migration: evolving Minangkabau traditions in Indonesia*, Cornell University Press, Ithaca, London.

Koesnoe, M.
1969   *Musyawarah - een Wijze van Volksbesluitvorming volgens Adat recht*, Publikaties over Adatrecht. Vol.I. Instituut voor Volksrecht Universiteit van Nijmegen, Nijmegen.
in this volume

Korn, V.C.
1941   'De vrouwelijke mama' in de Minangkabausche familie', *Bijdragen tot de Taal-, Land- en Volkenkunde* 100: 301-338.

Moore, S.F.
1977   'Individual interests and organizational structures: dispute settlements as "events of articulation"', in I. Hamnett (ed.) *Social Anthropology and Law*, A.S.A. Monograph 14, Academic Press, London, New York, San Francisco.
1978   *Law as Process: An Anthropological Approach*, Routledge & Kegan Paul, London.

Naim, M.
1974   *Marantau: Minangkabau voluntary migration*, University of Singapore, Singapore.

Tanner, N.
1969   'Disputing and dispute settlement in Minangkabau', *Indonesia* 8: 21-67.
1970   'Disputing and the genesis of legal principles: examples from Minangkabau', *SWJA* 26: 375-401.
1971   *Minangkabau disputes*, unpublished PhD Thesis, University of California, Berkeley.

Velsen, J. van
   1969   'Procedural informality, reconciliation and false comparisons', in M. Gluckman
               (ed.) *Ideas and Procedures in African Customary Law*, Oxford University Press for
               the International African Institute, London.
Westenenk, L.G.
   1918   *De Minangkabausche Nagari*, Mededelingen van het Bureau voor de Bestuursza-
               ken der Buitenbezittingen, bewerkt door het Encyclopaedisch Bureau, aflevering
               17, 3d edition.
Willinck, G.D.
   1909   *Het Rechtsleven bij de Minangkabausche Maleïers*, E.J. Brill, Leiden.
Woodman, G.R.
   in this volume.

Evolution of the different regimes of customary law in Ghana within the framework of the principle of *stare decisis*

A.K.P. Kludze

Regular courts have been established by statute and have enforced the customary law in Ghana since the days of colonial rule. These courts have operated within a hierarchy in which the common law principle of *stare decisis* requires the lower courts to apply the rule of law as pronounced by the higher courts. For the customary law, which is not codified, an obvious advantage from the application of the principle of *stare decisis* is the certainty of the rule when enunciated by judicial decision in adversary proceedings. However, the evolution of the customary law (also referred to in this paper as folk law), under the modern judicial system of regular statutory courts has been fraught with problems. These problems are both theoretical and practical. The traditional rules, as originally evolved within the customary judicial process, are being applied in a system of courts based on the English common law, with all the technical rules of procedure, pleading and evidence. In addition, the substantive rules of customary law are being subjected to the onslaught of modernisation as a result of the emergence of a more complex society.

Although modernisation, whether social, economic or political, is desirable in modern Africa, its effect has been a mixed blessing to the evolution of the customary law. At the same time that it tends to promote the uniformity of rules, modernisation also tends to stifle the growth of the rules in the different ethnic groups, and it also poses new problems of its own.

DIFFERENT REGIMES OF CUSTOMARY LAW

The modern states in sub-Saharan Africa were forged out of diverse ethnic communities welded together arbitrarily by the colonial powers. In each state, therefore, there exist different regimes of customary law with limited application to specific communities. The imposition of colonial rule, and of the central authority in the post-colonial era, involved attempts, sometimes consciously but also unconsciously, to evolve a uniform body of customary law within the boundaries of each state. This is in a sense similar to the evolution of the English common law from the diverse customs of the conquering Normans, and of the Angles and the Saxons. The process over the years in Ghana has involved the imposition of new rules, the rejection of others, and the inevitable adaptation of others. The dilemma facing the courts, lawyers and academics, is whether the better known customary-law rule of a dominant ethnic group, or a rule considered to be more equitable, should be declared to be applicable throughout the whole country. Such attempts by the courts have always met with opposition from ethnic minorities who reject them as an imposition of an alien culture and alien values. An example is the tendency of the courts to treat as a general rule of customary law the Akan rule that on death intestate the individual's self-acquired property becomes family property.[1] Although it is respectfully submitted that this rule is not properly applicable to all communities in Ghana, the courts have often upheld it as a general proposition of law for all ethnic groups.

The successive Chieftaincy Acts have provided for the assimilation of suitable rules of customary law into the common law of Ghana, to become applicable throughout Ghana.[2] Such a declaration would be preceded by study and consultation. So far there has been no recourse to the machinery provided for such assimilation.

REJECTION OF FOLK LAW

In both anglophone and francophone Africa, colonial legislation permitted the application of the customary law between natives in such areas as land law, succession, marriage, and chieftaincy. However, there were "repugnancy clauses" in the British possessions which permitted the application of the customary law only when not repugnant to natural justice, equity and good conscience, nor incompatible with any legislation.[3] The notions applied as criteria were English concepts, mainly foreign to the indigenous population. In francophone Africa, the customary law was applicable only if compatible with the principles of French civilisation. These restrictions enabled the courts to strike down rules of which the colonial power did not approve. It must be at the least debatable whether a rule of customary law, which has evolved as the synthesis of centuries of the human experience of a people, can be properly castigated and rejected as unjust by mere judicial fiat, only because it does not satisfy the alien notions of the Judeo-Christian civilisation.

GROWTH STIFLED BY STARE DECISIS

Modernisation has paradoxically also stifled the growth of customary law in Africa. In the colonial courts, African customary law was foreign law in Africa. Therefore, the rule of customary law had to be proved as a fact in every case until by frequent proof it had become so notorious that the courts took judicial notice of it.[4] This had the merit of certainty. However, the flip side of the coin is that, once established as a rule of customary law by judicial declaration, the principle of *stare decisis* applies. The principle generally requires that courts follow previous decisions on a point of law, even if found to be wrong, until the legislature intervenes to alter it. The principle of *stare decisis* is from a different jurisprudential orbit and perhaps unsuited to the customary law, whose redeeming feature is flexibility. In customary law the demands of the justice of the particular case may override the technical rules of law. By reason of *stare decisis* there persist today in Ghana rules supposedly of the customary law, but totally alien. Examples are the rule that the head of family is not accountable to the family for family property,[5] and the erroneous assumption that in every ethnic group the self-acquired property of the individual becomes family property on his death intestate. When the English common law was getting similarly fossilised by reason *inter alia* of the doctrine of *stare decisis*, the rules of equity developed to mitigate the rigours of the common law. There has been no corresponding development in the customary law in Africa, and the doctrinal adherence to previous decisions has resulted in many cases of injustice.

The areas of the impact of modernisation and the effect of the institution of statutory courts are diverse. They include rules relating to land law, family law, family property concepts, and succession to property. Some of these will be examined.

LAND LAW

Traditionally, all lands were owned in Africa by a group, either the family, the stool or the community. The communal nature of African societies and the limited agricultural purposes of land tenure did not require or justify the evolution of detailed rules of private ownership of land. The "usufruct" or right of user was adequate for the individual, and it was an encumbrance or burden on the title of the owning group or authority. Modernisation brought with it the imposition by the colonial powers of a capitalist economy with the individualistic tendencies of property acquisition which are inherent in capitalism. The usufruct, or the individual's right of occupation or user of group-owned land, has, therefore, been transformed into an interest more like an estate in freehold or the fee simple at common law. Such protection has become necessary because of permanent cash crops like cocoa and coffee, and also because of the pressures on arable land attributable to increases in population. The courts have accordingly articulated and even evolved a body of protective rights for the individual occupant of land by a series of decisions which are now legally binding.

THE FAMILY

The family is a central institution in the laws of most African communities. The composition and membership of the African family did not present problems to the indigenous African society. The unit is traced for most purposes unilineally, either patrilineally or matrilineally. Modern analyses have, however, introduced considerable uncertainty in this area by the designation and judical recognition of such units as the wider or trunk family and the nuclear, atomic or immediate family. The result has been considerable confusion to the native mind regarding the characterisation and destination of family property, as the composition of the family unit is being debated in conflicting judicial pronouncements. The principle of *stare decisis* has been of little value, since one is confronted with an ugly spectre of conflicting and generally irreconcilable definitions of the African family.[6]

FIDUCIARY RESPONSIBILITY OF HEAD OF FAMILY

The strict fiduciary principles which ensured the impartial and beneficial administration of family property have been substantially eroded by changing social values and loosened religious prescriptions. Nevertheless, the courts continue to apply the rule that a head of family is not accountable for family property under his management. Misconduct by the head of family is now more common and more tempting, but the judicial customary law has been unable to develop to provide appropriate sanctions and remedies. The reason is that the courts have felt bound to continue paying lip service to declared rules of the customary law which are now devoid of meaning and generally applied out of context because they applied in different social milieux. When the supposed rule was developed, natives were reluctant to drag their chiefs and heads of family to British courts. In any event, the values of properties involved were insignificant. Furthermore, religious or supernatural sanctions were effective deterrents against official misconduct by heads of family and chiefs. All these factors have changed, with Ghanaian courts manned by Ghanaian judges, and with the loosening of fears of supernatural sanctions, while there are increased opportunities to handle substantial stool or family property. Yet the old rule persists.

SALE OF FAMILY PROPERTY

There remains largely unchanged the basic rule of the customary law that family property can only be validly alienated by the head of family, acting with the consent and concurrence of the principal members of the family.[7] However, even this rule has been subjected to attacks from the modern notions of English common law, with some decisions and opinions suggesting that, where the proper consents are lacking, the alienation may be voidable and not void *ab initio*. To most Africans the notion of voidability is foreign: a transaction is either valid or void.

A further problem now emerging is the identity or designation of principal members or elders of the family whose concurrence is necessary for alienation of family property. This problem is often related to the judicial categorisation of wider and immediate families in the context of property ownership, alienation and succession or inheritance. As the courts continue to proffer conflicting definitions of the family, they engender confusion in the determination of the class of persons who are recognized as principal members of the family.

SUCCESSION

It is still largely true that the right of intestate succession is within the family of the decedent. However, the courts in modern times have sought to impose the rule that in all communities succession is not as of right but is at the unfettered discretion of the family.[8] In most patrilineal communities the right of succession is automatic in the sense of being indefeasible, except that the family has the exclusive function of determining the respective portions in the event of a distribution of the intestate estate.

A significant modern development is the emergent right of women to inherit property equally with men. The change has been wrought, not directly by the courts, but by the redefinition of the role of women in modern society as well as the increased opportunities for the acquisition and transmission of wealth, including durable self-acquired property, like jewelry and interests in realty. However, since the existing rules require that the inherited property must remain in the family of the original acquirer, especially in a patrilineal community, the interest of a female successor in the inherited property is generally a life estate which is inalienable and is not transmissible by testamentary disposition to her children if they belong to a different family.[9] One may forecast that within a short time the present restrictions on the interest of the female successor will be removed. In the matrilineal communities the restriction is meaningless, since the female successor's own children belong to her family and are *ipso facto* entitled to inherit from her as from other members of the family.

TESTATION

It seems that the power of testation was not generally recognized in most African communities. There was probably not much occasion for the exercise of such a power, for individual ownership of property was of a limited nature. With encouragement from the common-law and civil-law notions of the will, legal effect is now being given to rudimentary testamentary declarations of deceased persons as to the destination of their properties. Such a declaration was in the past treated with great respect because of a mixture of respect and fear for the dead and would be enforced unless found to be grossly unfair or the product of a sick mind. However, through judicial decisions without any legislative intervention, such a dying declaration has been elevated to the pedestal of an institutionalised form of testation under customary law.[10] This is not necessarily undesirable, since the power of testation is in any event conferred by statutes dealing with wills. However, apparently because the customary law will does not seem to be of ancient vintage, the courts have differed widely in their prescription of the formalities required for a valid customary law will.[11] Moreover, the judicial decisions suggest that the customary law will is valid even in communities which do not recognise it as having a binding legal force.

TRADITIONAL JUDICIAL PROCESS

The traditional judicial process is very different from that inherited from British rule. Not only does the traditional system lack robed judges and uniformed police and law enforcement personnel, but its rules of procedure and of evidence are different. There is considerable flexibility in the rules of the customary law, and the adjudicators, by their decisions, emphasise reconciliation and neighbourliness rather than blind legal justice. The validity and enforceability of an award under the traditional system depends to a considerable degree on the fairness of the decision which must reflect societal values. These values of the folk law are now generally subordinated to the technical rules of the common law system imposed by the reception of English law. Decisions of the courts purportedly applying or enforcing the folk law have, therefore, often produced results surprising to the native mind.

CONCLUSION

Africa is passing through a period of cataclysmic changes which will put to the test the traditional values which butteressed the old rules of the customary law. Changes in the customary law are inevitable. Indeed every system of law that is to survive must be adaptable to change. While certainty is desirable in the law, the problem in modern Africa is to retain the essential qualities of adaptability, flexibility and changeability in the customary law, to enable it to be moulded to serve the needs of a modern society with a complex cash economy which offers greater opportunities for the individual acquisition and freer alienability of property.

Complicating the problem of evolution is the pluralism of the legal system. In the first place, there is the English common law with the doctrines of equity, as well as statutes, which directly or indirectly modify the indigenous law and which co-exist with the indigenous law. On the other hand, we have diverse regimes of indigenous law applicable to different communities within the same State. The task of the future is to evolve a harmonious relationship between the different segments of the plural legal systems while purposefully working toward a unification of the rules.

NOTES

1.   See e.g., *Yawoga* v. *Yowoga* (1958) 3 W.A.L.R. 309, unquestionably a case arising among the patrilineal Ewe. The decision of the court, although it is respectfully submitted to be correct, was based upon the wrong reasons. The court proceeded on the erroneous premise that a child could not challenge his father's right to sell property inherited on intestacy from the father's father, because the property had become family property and the child (grandchild of original acquirer) was not a principal member of the family with a *locus standi*. The correct basis is that the father had inherited the intestate estate with the right of ownership as purchaser in his own right and was consequently unfettered in his right of disposition.
2.   Chieftaincy Act, 1971 (Act 370), ss 45-47.
3.   For instance, there is the obiter dictum in *Ashiemoa* v. *Bani* [1959] G.L.R. 130, that even if the customary law had been proved to exist that private lands which became town lands were encumbered automatically with the right of free access of every native of the town to build a dwelling house thereon, the rule would not be enforced, because allowing such expropriation of private property was repugnant to natural justice, equity, and good conscience. The court did not elaborate nor explain which of the three elements was invocable, because it was not satisfied as to the existence of the customary-law rule. See also the earlier Nigerian case of *Edet* v. *Essien* (1932) 11 N.L.R. 47, rejecting the presumption that the child of a married woman is the husband's child.
4.   *Angu* v. *Attah* (1915) P.C. 1874-1928, 43.
5.   *Pappoe* v. *Kweku* (1924) F.C. 1923-1925, 158; *Fynn* v. *Koom* (1960) unreported, Land Court, Cape Coast; *Abude* v. *Onano* (1946) 12 W.A.C.A. 102; *Krabah* v. *Krakue* [1963] 2 G.L.R. 122; *Amarfio* v. *Ayorkor* (1954) 14 W.A.C.A. 554. See also Bentsi-Enchill 1964: 126, 134, and Ollennu 1962: 137-139. But see also contra Kludze 1973: 91-99.
6.   See, for instance, conflicting dicta in *Serwah* v. *Kesse* [1960] G.L.R. 227, 228; *Amarfio* v. *Ayorkor* (1954) 14 W.A.C.A. 554; *Mills* v. *Addy* (1958) 3 W.A.L.R. 357; and *Re Eburahim* (1958) 3 W.A.L.R. 317. See also Ollennu 1966: 151, and Bentsi-Enchill 1964: 157, 158 et passim. And see also Kludze 1973: 30-38, 75-79.
7.   *Agbloe* v. *Sappor* (1947) 12 W.A.C.A. 187: *Ohimen* v. *Adjei* (1957) 2 W.A.L.R. 275, 280-281.

8.   *Amarfio* v. *Ayorkor* (1954) 14 W.A.C.A. 554; *Makata* v. *Ahorli* (1956) 1 W.A.L.R. 169. See also Ollennu 1966: 153-154, et passim; and Bentsi-Enchill 1964: 126, 134; but see contra Kludze 1973: 261, 269-283.
9.   *Husunukpe* v. *Dzegblor* (1951) D. C. (Land) '48-'51, 393.
10.   See *Summey* v. *Yohuno* [1960] G.L.R. 68 and *Akele* v. *Cofie* [1961] G.L.R. 236. The formalities spelled out in these cases have been doubted by the Supreme Court, but the customary law will has not been doubted.
11.   See the divergent views of the courts in such cases as *Brobbey* v. *Kyere* (1936) 3 W.A.C.A. 106; *Summey* v. *Yohuno* [1960] G.L.R. 68; *Akele* v. *Cofie* [1961] G.L.R. 334; *Abenyewa* v. *Marfo* [1972] 2 G.L.R. 153; *Abadoo* v. *Awotwi* [1973] 1 G.L.R. 393; and *Mama Hausa* v. *Baako Hausa* [1972] 2 G.L.R. 469.

REFERENCES

Bentsi-Enchill K.
  1964   *Ghana Land Law*, London: Sweet and Maxwell.
Kludze A.K.P.
  1973   *Ewe Law of Property*, London: Sweet and Maxwell.
Ollennu N.A.
  1962   *Principles of Customary Land Law in Ghana*, London: Sweet and Maxwell.
  1966   *The Law of Testate and Intestate Succession in Ghana*, London: Sweet and Maxwell.

From folk law towards jurists' law: a critical review of the state courts' practice concerning adat law in Indonesia

Mohammad Koesnoe

[*Editorial Note.* The principal substance of the paper presented under this title at the Bellagio symposium has been published elsewhere. The following summary has been prepared by Keebet von Benda-Beckmann.]

Since pre-colonial times the law governing the indigenous Indonesians has been *adat* law, the Indonesian folk law. Jalaludin, an author who wrote during the Trusan Kingdom in Aceh, explicitly recognized this in his book *Safinatul Hukkaam fi Tahlisil Khasaam* of 1153 H or 1633 A.D., discussing the "ways for dispute settlements by judges according to the Islamic law".

In the earlier part of the colonial period the status of *adat* law was controversial, but in 1928 *adat* law was officially recognized as one of the bodies of law in Indonesia. This was mainly due to the studies and publications of Van Vollenhoven and his followers such as Ter Haar who pleaded for equality of status between *adat* law and western codified law. Since then *adat* law has been applied in the state courts, but this has resulted in the construction of a different kind of *adat* law from the type used in the folk sphere. We can distinguish two types of *adat* law, one with an indigenous structure and one with a western structure, the first being applied in the folk sphere, the second in the state courts. The differences can be summarized as follows.

1. In the folk sphere *adat* law consists of three categories, the constitutional, the institutional and the realizational categories of *adat*. These correspond to the folkcategories of Minangkabau *adat*, reflecting a cosmic philosophy according to which human life must always be in harmony with the universe. Nature is the teacher of social life and natural events are considered the ultimate true *adat*, the *Adat Nan Sabana Adat* (lit.: the *adat* of *adats*). Nature is taken as an example for social life and is always referred to in metaphors when social life is described. The translation of the metaphorical statements into human activity is structured in the *Adat Pusaka Usang, adat* as it is transmitted from generation to generation. This *adat pusaka usang* consists of three categories for which we use indigenous Minangkabau terms, although there is no consistency in the use of these terms among Minangkabau *adat* elders themselves.

For the constitutional category we choose the term *Adat Istiadat,* consisting of theories, teaching, reflections on nature and natural events in connection with social life. In this sphere the *adat* is expressed in poems, sayings, proverbs, etc., presenting the ideal picture and ways of life based on the teachings of nature. These metaphors always consist of two parts, the first stating the natural event meant as an example for human action, the second part being the transportation of this example into human conduct. The second category, the *Adat Nan Teradat,* is the institutional category. Institutions, or *limbago* in the Minangkabau folk terminology, contain metaphorical typologizations through which human social life can be evaluated in view of the idea of living in harmony in the community. The metaphors in which the institutions are expressed possess certain characteristics and it is through these that can be transformed into a concrete form of *adat,* called the *Adat Nan Diadatkan,* the realizational category, expressed in concrete decisions of *adat* functionaries.

By metaphorical formulations I mean the formulations, expressions and phrases which ordinarily refer to concrete and observable events or things, but are used for something not observable in order to suggest a similarity between the two. Some examples may be given. To indicate the just and proper proportion in the rights and duties prevailing for male and female members in the Javanese *adat* community the term *sepikul-segendong* is used. *Sepikul* literally means the manner in which men carry agricultural products with the use of two baskets on a stick balanced on his shoulder. *Segendong* means literally carrying a basket on the back with the use of a long scarf. The observable number of baskets is translated into the proportion of rights and duties for men and women: two against one. This is the usual interpretation given by the state courts. To indicate the legal characteristics of the property acquired by husband and wife during their marriage the term *harta gono gini* is used on Java, literally meaning male-female property, and thus referring to the fact that male and female as a pair form a unity. In Javanese *adat* law it explains the equal rights of husband and wife to that property. The *Kutaragama,* a Lombok law book, states that the words of a leader or king must be *danta* (ivory), *danti* (saliva), *kusuma* (flower) and *wrasa* (rain). The common characteristics of these is that once it goes out it never comes back again in the original form. So must also be the spoken word of a leader or king: once it is spoken it can not be withdrawn again. In the state courts *adat* is seen as a system of unwritten rules. The courts have to discover and clarify these rules, to interpret them for their decisions.

2. In the folk sphere there are no pre-existing substantive rules, ready to be applied by *adat* functionaries. *Adat* functionaries, in contrast, transform the metaphorical expression into concrete decisions by means of *Gestaltungslehre* by giving *Gestalt* (Indonesian: *memberi wujud*) to the teachings through a

creative activity, based on three operational principles, the principle of peaceful social life (Ind.: *kerukunan*), the principle of propriety (Ind.: *kepatutan*), and the principle of harmony in the community (Ind.: *kelarasan*). These basic principles in turn contain more detailed principles, such as the principle giving meaning to the place, time and situation of the case (Balinese: *desa, kala, patra*), the principle of suitability in view of the status of the person concerned (Javanese: *empan papan*), etc. In the state courts the idea of applying pre-existing substantive rules of *adat* law is dominant. It is the task of judges and legal scholars to discover the unwritten legal rules and apply them through the method of interpretation, not through *Gestaltungslehre*.

3. In the folk sphere the work of *adat* functionaries is truly creative. It requires a high and noble personality, a fine feeling of embarrassment (Indonesian: *malu*), a broad experience in dealing with the *adat* of his community, obtained through intensive and long training as an assistant to *adat* elders. Only persons with these qualities will be given the full respect and faith needed for the satisfactory performance of their task. In the state courts the *adat* functionaries are subjected to and therefore restricted by the substantive rules in *adat* law.

4. In the folk sphere every decision is valid for the case for which it was made only, because of the *adat* law principle "every case possesses its own individuality". In state courts the principle prevails that "similar cases are to be dealt with in similar ways", because this is supposed to provide a minimum guarantee for justice and certainty. Hence the doctrine of *constante jurisprudentie* (Dutch) is relevant in the state courts.

5. In the folk sphere the goal of dispute settlement is to restore the broken harmony and peace between the parties and in the community. The decision must be exhaustive for all problems related to the case (Javanese: *tuntas*), i.e. it must try to give an answer to all possible problems concerning the dispute. In the state courts the ultimate goal of settling disputes is to realize law and justice. Hence, court decisions give answers to claims put forward by the parties based on the stipulations of the law governing the problem.

The current state court practice still follows the pattern laid down in the pre-war state practice and so do the planners of developments in national law when dealing with *adat* law. In the theoretical field most scholars still appreciate the pattern as it was laid out in the studies of Ter Haar, but only a few are tracing new ways in the study of *adat* law. This new trend attempts to go back to folk ideas and folk jurisprudence, and uses that as the raw material for the development of a general jurisprudence based on *adat* law.

The subtlety of legal change: a lesson from northern Zambia

Norman J. Singer

The study of customary or traditional law has taken many forms and emphases over the years since the realization developed that the law of a local ethnic group (tribe) had some relevance to the formation of overall social values (Roberts 1979). At first, it was fashionable to learn what the normative rules of application were for various substantive areas of concern (Pospisil 1971). In a sense, this approach is still utilized even though it is masked by the application of various methodologies (Comaroff and Roberts 1981) and analyses (Abel 1973) that provide a broader frame of reference than the rules themselves (Comaroff and Roberts 1977).

A second approach has been to emphasize the role of courts in the overall administration of legal systems (Roberts 1979; Nader 1969). This entails looking at a particular process for the understanding of the system of resolution of disputes (Epstein 1970; Gulliver 1977; Beattie 1957) and analysing the interface between the traditional resolution mechanisms and a style representative of European values (Eckhoff 1967; van Velsen 1969). Emphasis on process can also be utilized for historical purposes showing that the colonial powers were sensitive to the needs of the local populace through the creation of "Native Courts" (Athe 1972; Spaulding 1970). These were set up to apply custom or rules of local usage (Palley 1969). They presumably all supported the continuation of a cultural system in jeopardy of extinction because of the European rule (Colson 1976).

Both of these analytical systems (rule and process orientation) have come together (Gulliver 1979). Often the court system representing the "natives" has been taken for granted. It represents a mechanism through which the traditional social order can be perpetuated. There should be an assumption that the creation of the courts is evidence that traditional law and legal values are supported (Gulliver 1979). As "custom" is supposedly utilized by the court to resolve disputes, the evidence should be "clear" that tradition lives (Strathern 1974). Likewise, as the traditional process, usually some form of conciliation, is utilized, one need not strain to conclude that the local or traditional legal rules and processes form the core of the "local" legal system (Comaroff and Roberts 1981).

In this paper I would like to dispute the above. Some developing country governments have used the development and continuation of the Native

Court system (now usually referred to as Local Courts (Spaulding 1970)) to attempt to make the transition from the traditional rules to those determined by the policy makers to be the most useful for the development process. Those rules formulated after the transition are generally known as "modern" rules of law. This short presentation will show that the Government of Zambia, by utilizing the mechanisms of "Local Courts", has been able to bring about tremendous legal change and to induce the society to define their legal relationships as "traditional" when in fact they have developed a very sophisticated appreciation of the "moden law" that the government would like to utilize for the resolution of conflict.

It is often assumed that, in order to have a modern system of laws, a comprehensive written set of complex legal rules is necessary. This sytematic set of rules would be appropriate for application in specific circumstances. These rules, however, potentially create a static situation with change introduced through interpretation. In fact, it could be argued that change can be more effectively introduced without imposing a written set of rules. The changes, when they take place, become more subtle and persons are less conscious that change is being imposed upon them. Since the ultimate decision in the resolution of any legal dispute is in the hands of the judge (Gulliver 1977), even in cases where the resolution format is called "conciliation" (Fuller 1971), it is imperative to recognize that the policy decisions calling for the creation of a corps of judges who infiltrate society with a new set of legal rules can be significantly more effective than writing a code which people can read, evaluate and then reject.

The primary source of the law as an unwritten system is the local norm as applied by the decision maker. Often he will listen to those local "elders" who are either panel members in a moot, or who speak up during a hearing where they are recognized as "persons knowledgeable in local law". If a tight administrative system is created and the local judges are instructed how to deal with cases, it is likely that locally rendered decisions would be appealed to a higher authority within the Local Courts hierarchy. It is at the appeal level that the authority of the original hearing judges is either undercut or strengthened. Thus, it is possible to bring about significant change in the applicable legal rules by supporting innovative decisions made below. It is also possible to force change by using every opportunity to undercut the "traditional" decisions that a hearing judge renders. A tight administrative framework allows for this kind of activity to take place. This climate allows for the continued application of a set of "modern" rules under the guise of equity. It is precisely this kind of change that goes unnoticed and new rules are simply slipped into place.

In like manner, it is often supposed that the process utilized for the resolution of conflicts should be an adjudicative one if it is to be modern (Koch, Sodergren and Campbell 1976). However, it is perfectly feasible to utilize the traditional, conciliatory, format with subtle procedural changes in order to introduce change. The open "moot" process, where anyone attending might have his say on any point he feels is relevant can be replaced by a more orderly process which includes procedural regularity and evidential rules (Epstein 1974). It is in the process of this change that there is actually a major refocussing taking place (Cutshall 1980). Traditions are undercut in the name of a more modern, orderly and "appropriate" process.

It is my argument that the Government of Zambia has introduced a modern system for the administration of justice while it professes to continue to support the traditional or customary system. If the argument is correct, Zambia may have discovered the most painless and effective method of transforming a legal system without causing a strain among the persons who must use it to resolve their differences. On the one hand, the system as structured is specifically set up to perpetuate the traditional one. On the other, the centralized administration of this formal structure of Local Courts is designed to create a modern workable system of justice which will be compatible with the ideals of long-term Zambian social development (Sarat 1976).

The research under discussion took place in 1980 as part of a larger-scale project to discover the sources of African law.[1] The research team, Professor Rodolfo Sacco, Dr. Alba Negri, Mr. Justin Mulopa and Professor Norman J. Singer, spent 37 days at various field sites in Luapula Province of northern Zambia. Archives were examined, Local Courts were visited where records were analysed and disputes were heard. A substantial portion of time was spent in Lengwe village among the Chishinga of the Munkanta chieftaincy. Observations were made at the Village Headman's court and informal resolution sessions were attended at the Headman's compound, the Chief's residence and various Local Courts. The research substantiated the basic thesis that the system of the administration of justice has been effectively transformed from the "traditional" one to a "modern" counterpart without creating the stresses that the modernization process has been known to produce. It is important, therefore, to examine what has taken place in order to understand this surprising result.

Native Courts were created in Northern Rhodesia (Zambia's colonial forebear) in 1933. The courts were renamed Local Courts in 1964 just after independence (Spaulding 1970: 194-5). The original structure, however, remains in force. Each court was created around a chieftaincy. The Chief did not sit as a member of the Local Court; he had his own independent jurisdiction on appeal from the Village Headman (Gluckman, Barnes & Mitchell 1949). Thus, the Headman operated at the lowest level. The Chief was ready to hear appeals from the Headman's court, but a case could be taken either directly or on appeal to the Local Court. Thus, one could potentially have as many as three levels of hearing before reaching the typical

European system which operated above this "customary" one. The most typical format for the operation of this Local Court system is for the litigant to try to informally resolve the dispute at the village. If that is not successful, appeal is then taken directly to the Local Court. The Chief enters the picture if there is a serious dispute over an issue of tribal politics (Cunnison 1959).

The premise upon which the three-level system was based took into account the traditional format for resolution of disputes. The Local Court, however, was created with sensitivity to the position of the Chief, as he would be the person who would present a list of three candidates from which a government administrator would select one to serve as the Judge. More often than not, the local disputes would be terminated without necessitating the involvement of an authority from the government's "official" system.

Soon after creation this three-level system evolved into a two-level one. Often the chief would be by-passed. This might occur either on appeal, if the litigant was unhappy about the village Headman's decision, or in a case of first instance by petitioning directly to the Local Court. In fact, most petitions were made directly to the Local Court without an initial village hearing. Litigants interviewed indicated that the reason they would go directly to the Court was that they had more chance of a fair decision which considered all their rights.

To preserve his authority, the Headman has been forced to alter the manner in which he processes disputes. A competitive system has emerged. At each of the three levels an attempt has been made to preserve the authority that each perceives he has. The burden has fallen on the village Headman most heavily, as he must work to retain his position as the authority to resolve disputes at the village level (Cunnison 1956). The Chief retains his position because he nominates the persons who are to serve as Local Court judges. Thus, it is generally recognized that the Chief plays a significant role in the operation of the Local Court and for all intents and purposes it is thought that his authority remains intact even though he may not hear or decide any cases.

The Local Court has become the main focus of the masses. Virtually all of their disputes are heard by the Local Courts (either as a consequence of the inability of the Headman to resolve the dispute or as a matter of first impression). The Headman, as noted, has had to re-establish himself as the community leader who plays the significant role in the resolution of local disputes. He has been helped by the creation of the Village Productivity Committee (VPC), of which he is usually elected Chairman. The Committee is responsible as the caretaker of community affairs, which generally includes resolution of disputes. The Headman can also be threatened by the UNIP[2] representative for authority in the village. Obviously, the Headman in many instances is considered the most authoritative person in the village and thus becomes both the Chairman of the Village Productivity Committee and the local UNIP representative. When this happens, the Headman's authority to resolve disputes is usually intact and he is the decisionmaker. However, when the Headman is not UNIP representative, there is generally a great deal of competition and he must actively cultivate the village constituency.

In Lengwe village the Headman, who was chairman of the VPC but not UNIP representative, was under constant pressure to retain his dominance over the UNIP representative. The UNIP representative not only dealt with the business of the political party but tried to assert his authority over all village matters. This resulted in the inability of the Headman to resolve disputes effectively. The UNIP representative would always interfere in case deliberations, provoking the parties to present new demands which undercut the Headman's ability to bring disputes to an end and forced litigants to go to the Local Court.[3]

The relative status of the three dispute-settling institutions (the Headman, the Chief and the Local Court) is reflected in the amount of leverage each must acquire over the local population in order to function. The weakest of the three, the Headman, has been forced to adapt to that which one finds in the courts in order to preserve a semblance of legitimacy. In a setting where one would expect the most relaxed and informal procedure, there is often a stiffness and a formality which is out of place under the mango tree. Using this technique, the Headman has been able to recoup some of his lost authority, as seen by the fact that persons are willing to file petitions with him. This does not eliminate the competition for authority he faces from the UNIP representative who still attends the hearings and provides negative intervention. Thus, the Headman must utilize a more formal "local-Court-like" procedure in order to maintain his position.

The Chief has extricated himself from this competitive situation almost entirely. He will only act as a dispute-settler when he is asked by someone who shows up at his compound and petitions for help by invoking a personal request (Hamnett 1975; Comaroff 1978). In fact, in a number of cases the Chief would suggest that the parties go to the Local Court. In confidence one chief noted that he was not sure he would have been able to resolve the case. He noted he was out of practice as he had not been resolving cases much. He also mentioned that the Local Court judge acted as his representative, since he played the major role in his selection.

The third level, the Local Court, with the legitimation of the government, has set the style for the resolution of disputes. It should be remembered that the Court operates primarily as a court of equity, as there is no written law dictating the outcome of cases. Local customary law is often marginal as well, and equity or fairness predominates.

The courtroom has taken on an appearance similar to any formal court found in Europe or North America. The two Local Court judges sit on an elevated platform, wearing robes, facing two tables at which the parties to the dispute sit. A gallery allowing up to 100 observers is found behind the litigants' table. Observation is encouraged and frequently the courtroom is filled when cases are being heard. In the middle of the court just in front of the judges (but facing them) sits the clerk of the court. It is his function to record a verbatim account of the parties' and witnesses' testimony. He is required to do a simultaneous translation from the language in which the case is presented to English, the language in which the files are maintained. This transcript often becomes the crucial document in the ultimate disposition of the case.

Court houses have been built throughout most of Zambia. However, in some remote districts of Luapula Province there are still locations that have not yet had any buildings constructed. In these locations, the hearing still takes place in the open air, generally under a mango tree. This tends to preserve the sanctity of tradition. The construction of the court house, even though it introduces a style quite different, does not by itself become a symbol of modernity. It is felt that the building in which a hearing takes place is a natural "development". It did not occur to those who were interviewed that the physical environment and the manner in which the building is designed and utilized is one of the primary inducements to change.

There are four factors that can help us understand the orderly move away from traditional law:

1. *The role of the Clerk of the Local Court.*
As mentioned above, the Local Court judges are appointed through a nominating process involving the local Chief. A recommendation is made usually of three individuals to the Provincial Local Courts Officer who reviews the credentials of each nominee and informs the Chief which person the Local Courts Administration approves. The appointee is generally a man of good local standing. He is usually considered intelligent and knowledgeable on traditional issues. In short, he is a person who would be able to apply the traditional values of society. The appointment of such a person to the bench of the Local Courts would not seem to support efforts to introduce change.

Two factors should be noted at this point. First of all, there is a strong influence on the Local Court judge by the Local Courts Administration. Before the judge takes his place on the bench, he goes through a training programme that presents to him (often for the first time) the expectations that the Administration has for him. During the course of his tenure, he will be closely observed by both the Local Courts Officer at the District level and the Provincial Local Courts Officer. This small bureaucracy operates most efficiently. The Local Court judge is also provided with a copy of *The Local Courts Handbook* (1967), which provides answers to many of the questions relating to the manner in which Local Courts operate (see Appendix I).

Secondly, the person who becomes the crucial lever in the operation of the Local Court is the clerk of the Court. He is selected through a process entirely independent of the local Chief. His primary responsibility is to the Local Courts Administration. His loyalty to the judge is necessary, but the judge does not have any influence in his appointment or dismissal. The clerk must also go through an intensive training. He is briefed on the operation of the Local Court. He likewise functions closely with his administrative superiors and constantly utilizes *The Local Courts Handbook*. As noted, it is the clerk who is responsible for keeping the records. His ability to record the evidence is crucial to the ultimate disposition. He acts as a simultaneous translator, listening to the local language of the testimony and making the record in English, the official government language. Often, as the only person who is able to understand English, he controls how the record is utilized for the judges when they would like to have a point clarified, etc. More importantly, when the research team took part in the decisionmaking process with the judges and the clerk in the Chambers, it was observed that it was inevitably the clerk who took the lead in the discussion and the ultimate formulation of a decision. The judge (the person who possesses the authority) announced the decision in the courtroom, but it was the clerk who formulated and developed the theory upon which the decision was based. Space is too short to present a formal analysis of cases, but let it be noted that the more complicated the issue or the more the issue was foreign to the traditional sector, the more likely it was that the clerk took control over the decision formulating process. Even in cases involving traditional issues like witchcraft, it was usual that the clerk would control the process of issue formulation and then ultimately the decision itself. The judges consistently played a secondary role in the process. In fact, they seemed only to play a dominant role in cases that were non-controversial and probably ended up in court because of some issue related to the personality of the parties.

In chambers it was almost inevitable that the discussion would commence with one of the judges asking the clerk for a review of the case. The clerk would refer to his transcript and translate back the testimony with a heavy sprinkling of individual interpretation. When all the facts were presented, a discussion would then ensue among the three principals - the two judges and the clerk. The clerk would usually take the lead in these discussions, formulating a decision when he felt it was appropriate. Almost without exception in the observed situations, the judges would agree with the clerk. The judges would then return to the courtroom and announce "their" decision.

The importance of the clerk can only be understood when placed in the context of his own training. He must be educated to the senior secondary level. He must be able to do the simulataneous translations from the local language to English and to record the testimony by hand as it is being presented. Prior to his appointment (as noted above), he goes through a special course offered by the Judiciary. In addition to the clerical subjects, he must also study some basic courses in law. The law courses do not contain substantive reference to the specific issues of customary law. He is taught his law in the same way that any person might be who is going to be a government employee. His very existence is as an agent of change. His control of the decionmaking process reflects the needs and desires of a modernizing society. He carries out his function most effectively.

2. *Courtroom demeanour.*

Both the process that is used in the court and the demeanour that is expected of individuals represents a radical change from the traditional system. The process, even though it is supposedly conciliatory in nature, has become classically adjudicatory (Cantor 1978). The litigants present their cases, their witnesses are called, and the judges question both the parties and the witnesses. The presentation of the case is done to clarify the facts and issues. During the period of observation, material was never presented in order to influence a compromise to terminate the dispute. Each of the parties clearly attempts to present the evidence in order to show that he or she has the better case, and leaves it to the judges to determine whom they or the law will support. Since there is no written law and it is easier to approach unwritten rules more flexibly, the parties realize they are pleading to the good will of the judges. The notion of equity is ever pervasive. It is clear that the parties themselves realize that a decision will be handed down and that a compromise will not be sought. This same expectation exists at the level of the village Headman. As noted above, pressure is on the Headman to conform stylistically to the process utilized by the Local Court. Now that the Headmen have conformed, they are viewed as adjudicators, not conciliators.

The demeanour in the courtroom also indicates a move away from tradition to modernity. Traditionally, the process was totally informal. Anyone could come or leave as he or she desired, and people observing could make comments as they wished to help clarify issues. This traditional process appeared to be confusing, but in reality there was some order to this apparent chaos. This style no longer exists. A new code of conduct showing "respect for the law" has been introduced. A set of procedural constraints has been imposed on courtroom activity, even though there is no procedural code. These constraints order the process in a more European manner. Individuals know when they can speak and when they must listen. The presentation by the parties is controlled and the place of witnesses is also clear. Persons observing are expected to sit quietly in the gallery and only participate when they are formally required to come forward as witnesses under oath. Any person who enters the courtroom when the judges are on the bench and a session is in progress must bow at the door. This is presumably done to accord respect to the law.

Respect is also shown in other ways. The judges wear robes, as indicated, and when they enter and leave the courtroom all assembled rise. This code of conduct did not exist in earlier times. A judge was an ordinary person who was accorded respect because of his apparent knowledge of the law and ability to resolve disputes. He did not have to hang his acceptance on material presence. Likewise, many of these same rules apply at the village Headman's court.

3. *The village Headman.*

As noted above, there has been a great deal of pressure on the village Headman. He has been affected by the change in his style of decisionmaking and by the creation of a new local-level political framework. His position has been potentially affected by both the Village Productivity Committee and the development of the local-level UNIP organization (Bates 1976). His function appears to have been altered more as a matter of form than substance, as villagers indicated that he was still perceived as their leader. Apparently, the Headman who retains the strongest position is the one who conforms to UNIP principles and adapts himself to the new procedures of the Local Courts. He then can retain his position as leader in both of his former domains.

4. *Substantive law.*

The type of substantive legal issues that the Local Courts and Headmen must face have also changed considerably. The courts are able to hand down decisions without necessitating the reference to tradition in many cases. This does not mean that traditional issues are no longer present in the cases. In fact one of the most pervasive issues in a wide range of cases is the allegation that witchcraft caused the problems that were under dispute. In most situations the courts side-stepped this thorny issue by noting that even though witchcraft might have been one of the alleged root causes, the case could be decided utilizing a set of legal rules that would be applicable in a more modern setting. The courts are able to do this because there is a great amount of migration from Luapula Province to the Copperbelt (Epstein 1954) and many of the disputes that are generated back in this remote northern province actually come about because of the involvement of migrants in the cash economy of the copper mines (Poewe 1978).

An analysis of cases showed that marriage instability is one of the major disputes with which the Local Courts must deal (White 1971; Epstein 1954). Often the marriage split-up is caused by the migration of the husband, who has found another wife on the copperbelt. Complicated issues of child support and custody are often dealt with by the court. Judges utilize an approach that considers the expectations of a person working in a money economy who has discarded many of the traditional values. This is true in other substantive areas as well. The most surprising element, especially in the personal-law cases, is the fact that the decision included a rationale that would be standard in a western court. This was so even though a well-developed body of rules existed for the resolution of these disputes according to traditional law (Cunnison 1954).

CONCLUSION

The purpose of this paper is to consider mechanisms and realities useful for the modernization of law. Often one of the best techniques for the inducement of social change is the low-key approach that has been evident in the area under study. In Luapula Province of northern Zambia it is clear that the local populace are tied to their traditional system. The people interviewed believe that their traditional system of law is in full operation. However, the data collected indicates rather clearly that the traditional system has been substantially undermined by an aggressive set of policies administered by the Local Courts Authority. They have been able to bring about change through an erosion of the traditional conciliatory process for the resolution of disputes and the introduction of new rules of law that are thought to be more appropriate to the developmental stance that Zambia must take. The genius behind the changes that have taken place is the fact that the local villagers believe that the Local Court system is simply a replication of the Native Courts that were established in the 1930s to provide an organized forum for local disputes. The continued involvement of the Chief on the periphery of the selection process for judges has helped perpetuate the credibility of the system. Similarly the continued existence of the Headman's position, even though in some cases he has no function to play, has allowed the kind of flexibility that is so essential to a system of orderly development. It is this set of policy decisions that creates change without anxiety. Needless to say, a tightly structured administrative system must operate simultaneously with this infrastructure.

One of the crucial questions still to be answered is whether the policy-makers who planned the modern Zambian court system were aware of the impact that their decisions would have. One is left with the feeling that even today, the persons administering the local court system from their offices in the High Court in Lusaka, are more involved in insuring that the Local Courts system is functioning smoothly and not necessarily involved in the use of the system as an catalyst for legal change.

APPENDIX. LOCAL COURTS HANDBOOK

CONTENTS
PART ONE: COURT WORK

Appendices
   A   Specimen Criminal Charges.
   B   Abbreviations for use in Case Recording.
   C   Specimen Civil Statements of Claim.
   D   A Dictionary of Legal Words.

NOTES

1.   The research was funded by the research arm of the Italian Government as CNR n. 780171309 Su le fonti del diritto in Africa.
2.   The United National Indepence Party is the single political party of Zambia: see Tordoff 1974; Rasmussen 1969.
3.   The litigants did not go to the UNIP representative. He would have liked that. He indicated in a number of ways that he was at people's disposal, especially with their disputes. It was to no avail as persons simply went to the Local Court as a substitute for the village Headman.

REFERENCES

Abel. R.
   1973   'A comparative theory of dispute institutions in society', *Law and Society Review*
               8:217-347.
Athe, D.O.
   1972   'Administration of the judiciary in Zambia, 1889-1969', *Nigerian Law Journal*
               6:116-129.

Bates, R.H.
1976   *Rural Responses to Industrialization: A Study of Village Zambia*, New Haven: Yale University Press.
Beattie, J.
1957   'Informal judicial activity in Bunyoro', *Journal of African Administration* 9:188-195.
Canter, R.
1978   'Dispute settlement and dispute processing in Zambia: individual choice versus societal constraints', in: *The Disputing Process: Law in Ten Societies*, L. Nader & H. Todd (eds.). New York: Columbia University Press.
Colson, E.
1976   'From Chief's Court to Local Court', in: *Freedom and Constraint: a Memorial Tribute to Max Gluckman*, M.J. Aronoff (ed.), pp. 15-29. Amsterdam: Van Gorcum.
Comaroff, J.L.
1978   'Rule and rulers: political processes in a Tswana chiefdom', *Man (N.S.)* 13:1-20.
Comaroff, J.L. and Roberts, S.
1977   'The Invocation of norms in dispute settlement: the Tswana case', in: *Social Anthropology and Law*, I. Hamnett (ed.), Association of Social Anthropologists Monograph no. 14. San Francisco: Academic Press.
1981   *Rules and Processes: The Cultural Logic of Dispute in an African Context*. Chicago: The University of Chicago Press.
Cunnison, I.
1954   'A note on the Lunda concept of custom', *Rhodes-Livingstone Journal* 14:20-29.
1956   'Headmanship and the ritual of Luapula villages', *Africa* 16:2-19.
1959   *The Luapula Peoples of Northern Rhodesia: Custom and History in Tribal Politics*. Manchester: Manchester University Press.
Cutshall, C.R.
1980   *Conflict, Contradiction and Legal Change among the Ila: A Preliminary Report*, Manuscript from the files of the author.
Eckhoff, T.
1967   'The mediator, the judge and the administrator in conflict resolution', *Acta Sociologica* 10:148-172.
Epstein, A.L.
1954   'Divorce law and the stability of marriage among the Lunda of Kaze be', *Rhodes-Livingstone Journal* 14:1-19.
1970   'Procedure in the study of customary law', *Melanesian Law Journal* 1:51-57.
1974   'Introduction', in: *Contention and Dispute*, A.L. Epstein (ed.), pp. 1-39. Canberra: Australian National University Press.
Fuller, L.L.
1971   'Mediation – its forms and functions', *Southern California Law Review* 44:305-339.
Gluckman, M., Barnes, J.A. and Mitchell, J.C.
1949   'The village headman in British Central Africa', *Africa* 19:89-104.
Gulliver, P.H.
1977   'On mediators', in: *Social Anthropology and Law*, I. Hamnett (ed.), pp. 15-52. Association of Social Anthropologists Monograph No. 14. San Francisco: Academic Press.
1979   *Disputes and Negotiations: A Cross-cultural Perspective*. San Francisco: Academic Press.

Hamnett, I.
1975   *Chieftainship and Legitimacy: An Anthropological Study of Executive Law in Lesotho.* London and Boston: Routledge and Kegan Paul.
Koch, K.F., Sodergren, J.A. and Campbell, S.
1976   'Political and psychological correlates of conflict management: a cross cultural study', *Law and Society Review* 10:442-466.
Nader, L.
1969   'Styles of court procedure: to make the balance', in: *Law in Culture and Society*, L. Nader (ed.), pp. 69-91. Chicago: Aldine.
Palley
1969   'Rethinking the judicial role: the judiciary and good government', *Zambia Law Journal* 1:25-35.
Poewe, K.O.
1978   'Matriliny in the throes of change: kinship, descent and marriage in Luapula; Zambia', *Africa* 48:205-219.
Pospisil, L.
1971   *Anthropology of Law: A Comparative Theory.* New York: Harper & Row.
Rasmussen, T.
1969   'Political competition and one-party dominance in Zambia', *Journal of Modern African Studies* 7:407-424.
Republic of Zambia
1967   *The Local Courts Handbook.* 3rd Edition. Lusaka: The Registrar of the High Court.
Roberts, S.
1979   *Order and Dispute: An Introduction to Legal Anthropology.* Harmondsworth: Penguin Books Ltd.
Sarat. A.
1976   'Alternatives in dispute processing: litigation in a small claims court', *Law and Society Review* 10:339-375.
Spaulding, F.O., Hoover, E.L. and Piper, J.C.
1970   'One nation, one judiciary: the lower courts of Zambia', *Zambia Law Journal* 2:1-289.
Strathern, M.
1974   'Managing information: the problems of a dispute-settler', in: *Contention and Dispute: Aspects of Law and Social Control in Melanesia*, A.L. Epstein (ed.), pp. 271-316. Canberra: Australian National University Press.
Tordoff, W. (ed.)
1974   *Politics in Zambia.* Berkeley: University of California Press.
Velsen, J. van
1969   'Procedural informality, reconciliation and false comparisons', in: *Ideas and Procedures in African Customary Law*, M. Gluckman (ed.). London: Oxford University Press.
White, C.M.N.
1971   'Matrimonial cases in the Local Courts of Zambia', *Journal of African Law* 15:251-265.

Folk law in official courts of Turkey[1]

June Starr

"*Anthropologist*: What, in your opinion, is justice?
Public Prosecutor: "Adalet mülkü temelidir". Justice is the foundation of property - a proverb we learned in law school. . . .
We forget what words like justice mean. We studied about justice at the Law Faculty, but that was long ago. ... Justice comes from the feelings and from the mind of the judge. Is that what you mean?
Judge: There are the civil servants and there is the Law. These are responsible for justice. That is what justice is. ... We try to give just decisions (*adil*). But the point is whether the law itself is just or not. For we must give our decisions in accordance with the existing law. Law is always changing. They try to make a more just Law. For example, working man's laws have recently been changed. ... They are better now.
Public Prosecutor (interrupting). Justice comes from feelings, and thinking, and from law.
Judge: The government now uses law made by judges.
Public Prosecutor: When we read all those books in law school we thought about these things.
Judge: The law is not always just. Sometimes we make a better law to replace the old one. For example, when two people come to court, we look at them, we hear their witnesses, we view disputed land or places where crime takes place, and we try to decide the case in accordance with the law. We try to come near to justice. No decision is wrong, but some are nearer to justice than others."
(Field Notes, Bodrum Court, 16 October 1967).

Clearly the complexity of fitting the official law of Turkey to the folk law[2] of rural villages did not present itself as an interesting legal exercise or as a topic worthy of judicial reasoning in the mid-1960s. Gaps between rural culture and the new norms of the state, between informal and official sanctions, sweeping changes of property law, marriage, divorce, and kinship support systems were not viewed as problematic by the Judge and Public Prosecutor, graduates of one of two law faculties in Turkey. The law they had studied was based on Attaturk's revolutionary reforms of the 1920s. The law used in the four Bodrum Courts was the Turkish Civil Code, adapted from the Swiss Civil Code, and the Turkish Criminal Code, adapted from the Italian Penal Code. This paper examines selected aspects of the ways in which the folk law and the official state law co-mingled in the rural district courts of Bodrum in southwestern Turkey between 1950 and 1966.

When these new codes were introduced in 1926, they superseded Islamic

Family Law (the *Shari'a*), as well as a number of different European codes governing international relations, business, trade, crime control, and other areas of official state control. This meant that courts of the Turkish nation no longer embraced a dual legal system in which Islamic Law, administered in Islamic Courts, governed family relationships (including marriage, divorce, child custody, adoption, inheritance, and partition of property), while secular courts adjudicated matters of the market place, commerce, contracts, and criminality. Now one system of nation-state law, entirely secular, and one system of state courts, also secular, became the official legal system in the new Republic of Turkey.

Given this situation, at least six different relationships between official state law and informal social control or local-level law-ways[3] are possible. These can be viewed as on a continuum. First, state law can supplant local informal social controls, destroying their hegemony by breaking down ideological distinctions through the introduction of new concepts of sale, contract, ownership, evidence, marriage and divorce relationships, and by introducing new "legal" solutions to problems of social life.

Second, at the opposite extreme, local folk law can continue to flourish, with most members of the groups which recognize its authority considering official state law as irrelevant to their lives, too expensive, or too absurdly fashioned to fit local needs and help resolve local issues. In between these polar opposites are a number of possibilities (and we need to remember that local-level law-ways have also given rise to lynch-law justice). For instance, local law-ways and state law may exist coterminously so that, third, disputants can use state law as an *alternative* to folk law. In such cases, disputants choose forums according to their finances, local knowledge, and legal needs. Some researchers have demonstrated how wily disputants can manipulate a system to their own advantage. Fourth, state law can delineate new areas of official social control by law, moving into areas previously unregulated at the local level or which had been decided on an *ad hoc* basis as new situations occurred. Fifth, state law may "codify" previously unwritten social controls or folk law, raising this folk law to the status of official law, and use these new statutes in official courts. And sixth, state law may use people who have "statuses" within the folk law system as "expert witnesses" in official state courts. In such cases, these witnesses provide a "living link" between the informal social control systems and the new state law system of judges, police, courts and administrators. It is the last three relationships between folk law and state law that this paper addresses, first in relation to land transfers, and afterwards in terms of divorce.

I. LAND TRANSFERS

Researchers into land ownership in rural Turkey in the late 1940s and early 1950s reported that many villagers made *ad hoc* arrangements about houses and untitled fields, which continued for one or more generations. These arrangements were flexible adjustments bound neither by the new official Codes nor by local folk law (Stirling 1957:26-7; 1965: 122,273; Yalman 1979). Villagers preferred to work out the redistribution of property informally after a head of household died rather than "to call in officials who will ruthlessly apply the legally correct rules, and force all the permanent and final rearrangements of ownership to be made at once" (Stirling 1957:26-7). In the past this flexibility was useful in allowing patriarchs considerable freedom in deploying resources and people. For example, in a Bodrum village intensively studied (Starr 1978), a father set up his two eldest sons in small businesses in Izmir in the early 1950s and continued to manage his agricultural lands himself with the aid of a son-in-law. Thus, Turkish householders were able to plan for their children and their expanding families by diversifying assets (Starr 1983a; Stirling 1974), a good strategy in the precarious and unpredictable economy of Turkey in the 1940s and 1950s.

By the 1960s the death of a patriarch in the Bodrum region brought all his adult children back to the village for the funeral and resulting land division. This group might include a high school teacher or even a doctor, who now lived in Izmir, Aydin or Ankara, but still was interested in obtaining his share of property. When land division concerned a middle income family and there were many inheritors, the heirs might ask the court to divide the land because of the problems in finding equivalence for different kinds of terrain and plots. In such circumstances expert testimony might be sought from village farmers or even the oral land transfers expert. Which land is infertile and suitable only for grazing? Which is used for spring crops? Is there an irrigated field, and if so, how ought it be divided? Which sibling shall receive the motorized pump used in irrigation? Five or six inheritors was not an unusual number for land division cases heard in court. (Percentages given below).

But clearly by the 1960s the folk law systems of village land distribution were collapsing in much of Turkey. Not only were the official courts used for deciding undisputed land divisions in inheritance cases, but over half the men in Turkish jails were there on murder charges resulting from land disputes (Aktan 1966:324). By the mid-1960s almost half of the reported four million annual court cases in Turkey related directly, and many more indirectly, to land disputes (Aktan 1966:324). We suggest that the collapse of folk law systems as revealed in murder statistics, land disputes, and applications to state courts in non-disputed inheritance cases, lay not in the greater superiority of the official courts. Rather it stemmed from the enormous economic and social transformations taking place in the Turkish countryside as the

Turkish nation shifted from subsistence economies and tax farming land systems to a capitalist mode of production on titled fields used to grow cash-crops (Starr 1983a, 1980, Abel 1979).

In this paper we focus only on one key point of contact between the unwritten folk system of land transfers and the written official system of courts, land titles, Land Records Offices, Cadastre surveys, Notary sales, and so forth. One key village person witnesses all land transactions. For the practice of keeping written records of land transfers smaller than the size of a province came into being only with the modern Turkish state. Written records in Bodrum go back only to the late 1920s owing to a fire in the Courthouse in 1926. In each village, however, there is a person whose memory is extremely good and who has played a role in the folk law system. He witnesses land transfers and may be called upon at a later date to report to interested parties details, including who was present when land was given or sold to another. These oral recorders of land transfers can be summoned as expert witnesses by official courts. They are frequently used when a person wants to gain registered title (*tapu*) to land he has been farming for twenty years or more. Art. 639 of the Civil Code provides for acquisition of land by way of prescription. If land has not been previously registered to someone else in the Land Registry Office, and if the person has occupied and farmed it as if he were the real owner for twenty years without interruption or dispute, the court is empowered to grant him title. In the Bodrum court there were *vekiller* (singular, *vekil* or *dava vekili*) who had knowledge of land law, but were not lawyers (*avukat*), and had not obtained a law degree. These men were hired by plaintiffs to research and argue their cases, and were less expensive than lawyers. The judges frequently summoned tax records as proof of use rights, since someone both farming and paying taxes on a field usually had good claims to it. Likewise, villagers who rented out their land to others, were careful to reclaim it long before twenty years had passed, because they were cognizant of the official rule. The process of changing usufruct rights into legal title is in part covered by the following laws which were described to me in a letter from Professor Tuğrul Ansay, former Dean of Ankara University Law Faculty:

> "Art. 20 of the Law No. 1617 (July 26, 1972), which amended Art. 33 of the Law on Land Registration No. 766 (dated July 12, 1966) required tax records if the size of the land is more than 20 dönüm. Furthermore, if the total size of several pieces of land in one registration area (*tapulma bolgesi*) is more than 50 donum, again tax records are required, for the purpose of proof.[4]

A second role of oral land transaction witnesses is as "expert witnesses" for the court in cases of disputed land. The following are two cases illustrating points of contact between the unofficial folk law system of land transfers at village level and the official courts.

Case No. 1.

A woman plaintiff, whose husband represented her in court, sued the village *muhtar*, who was claiming part of her inherited land as village common land. When the Bodrum judge, his court stenographer, and the court surveyor were driven to the village to view the contested land, hear witnesses, and find a solution, I recorded the viewing and decision on super-eight film (Starr 1968). The deciding factor in the case hinged on expert testimony from the villager who witnessed land transactions. The viewing of the site brought these essential facts to light. The woman held a registered land title through her father, who had registered his farm land in the Bodrum Land Records Office in 1932. The title read in part that her share of the inheritance was all the land between the dirt road and the sea. Now, at the time of the court viewing, a stone wall separated part of her field from the seashore. The village *muhtar* testified that the shoreline had changed since 1932. The receding sea had exposed more shoreline and this newly created coastal land ought to belong to all villagers and not be in private hands. But, the expert witness, and another old man, testified that the shoreline was unchanged since 1932. The only change was the addition of a stone wall, which was not recorded in the deed. Consequently, the judge decided in favor of the woman.

Case No. 2.

Muzaffer, a village man noteworthy for his age and memory of land transfers, was called as expert witness when the judge and his staff came to Mandalinci village to view contested land. The dispute was between two adult married siblings: one a male, Sami, the other a female, Fatma. The expert witness testified that each of the siblings acquired the right to a house and house lot from their father, and that their father was one of three siblings. But this land had never been divided even within the folk system. What had happened was that *ad hoc* arrangements had been made as people needed houses. The house where camel-herder, Sami, had lived for nine years with his wife and child, and where he had built a stall for his pregnant camel, had recently been given by his father to his sister, Fatma. After this happened, Sami had acquired rights to the house and lot adjoining his, where an old aunt was now living. These two houses were on one undivided plot of ground.

In deciding the case the judge affirmed the informal division already worked out between Sami and Fatma, even though Sami was quite opposed to this arrangement and wanted rights to the house in which he lived. Fatma was even angrier and wanted Sami to "move out" of her house immediately. The judge did not attempt to arrange an exchange of properties (although the houses and lots were just about comparable in value, except for the camel stall), but advised Sami that if he wanted to arrange a switch of titles he needed to open a new case.

This case hinged on the fact that neither Sami's father's sibling cohort nor Sami's own sibling cohort had used the folk or the official law systems in allotting property. Now the contested ownership had reached an official court. In finding a resolution to some of the problems in this case, the judge defined as one of his tasks the division of the property for both cohorts. From one perspective the judge merely gave official sanction to already existing informal arrangements. The judge chose to emphasize the limits of his judicial authority by insisting a new case be opened to facilitate the exchange of titles to houses and lots. This was a case of *men'i müdahale* (a suit to stop interference), he said. The resolution of some of the issues might facilitate a property exchange should a disputant wish to exchange properties.

From another perspective the judge may have frozen the ownership of each house and lot by awarding official title. Fatma had a series of grudges against her brother and now she had a powerful weapon to make his life unpleasant. The judge did not recognize "use rights" as constituting a legitimate claim even though the oral land expert had clearly stated that, within the folk system practiced in the village, Sami's nine years of living in the house was recognized as a right. (For more details, see Starr 1978:213-222).

Let us pause for a moment to examine the linkages between the folk system and the official law system. Case No. 1 demonstrates a village headman attempting to manipulate the official legal system to gain valuable sea-side land from a villager, but he was stopped when a folk land expert testified against him. Here the use of the folk land expert served the interest of justice, and made the official system more humane and responsive to individuals' rights. Case No. 2 demonstrated a judge relying on another village folk land expert to provide a solution to the vexing issue of which sibling should own which house. Thus, contrary to assertions that "official law is ruthless" and ignores villagers' solutions to problems, both cases demonstrate that folk law experts are consulted by Bodrum judges in searching for just solutions to land cases.

Within the folk system, there can be conflicting rights, as the latter case demonstrated. It is clear the judge understood the concept that use constituted a valid claim, and in different circumstances would have invoked the principle of usufruct rights as the decisive factor in reaching a decision. In deciding this case, however, the judge gave greater weight to the father's right to give property to the child he chose, and thus title was awarded to his daughter. The oral land expert also would recognize a father's right to re-distribute his property. But, within the folk law system consensus concerning a hierarchy of land claims centered on male rights. Women's access to fields and houses ought to come from husbands and not from fathers (see also

Stirling 1965:123-25). Within the state legal system, Bodrum judges recognized a different hierarchy of rights based on the principle of equality of the sexes.

Thus, the "ruthless" aspect of official law has two aspects: first, that once rights are attributed and recorded, they are difficult to reverse (as compared to the folk system), and secondly, that in opposition to rural attitudes biased in favor of male ownership, women's claims to land constitute valid rights.

The largest land division case I watched in court had 27 parties - all listed as plaintiffs! Inheritance cases (N= 295) made up 16% of all civil cases in the three-year record of cases heard before the Bodrum Lower and High Civil Court in 1965 through 1967, surpassing even "driving with an excessive number of passengers" which had the largest number of arrests in the Criminal Court (Starr and Pool 1974:548). If inheritance and regaining immovable property are counted together they make up 14.1% of all cases in the courts (N= 411 of 3,350). It is probably not a coincidence that law students are taught to link the concept of justice to the concept of property. Property clearly is the most justiciable issue in the Turkish countryside.

II. DIVORCE

1. The Iddet

The *Iddet* is like a triple entendre. It exists in all systems of Islamic family law. In parts of rural Turkey it is recognized in folk-law systems of marriage and divorce but not practised (Striling 1965:210; Starr 1978:68-70). And in the Turkish Civil Code it has been symbolically altered: it has been extended, divided and subjected to inversion.

According to Islamic law, the *iddet* is the time period a woman must wait to remarry after a man has divorced her by pronouncing the words of repudiation in front of two witnesses. (*Idda* means "wait" in Arabic.) Under most Islamic law systems it is a period of 100 days' duration, but if a woman is pregnant under Turkish Islam she ought to wait 40 days after the child is born (Stirling 1965:210) to assure paternity.

With the introduction of the Turkish Civil Code (adopted from the Swiss Code to Turkish needs in a six-month period in 1926), the *iddet* was retained and became a 300-day period in which divorced persons, widows or widowers could not contract a new marriage (Ansay & Wallace 1966:119). In addition a new waiting period was introduced for all persons wishing to marry. 15 days need to elapse between the granting by state officials of the secular certificate permitting marriage and the actual wedding. By the mid-1960s in rural areas a member of the village council of elders, usually the elected village *muhtar*, was allowed to grant the certificate and register the marriage in the village ledger, as was the case in Mandalinci, one of the 30 villages in the Bodrum district (Starr 1978).

At a 1955 Conference on "The Reception of Foreign Law in Turkey", some researchers suggested that the new official law codes, especially the Turkish Civil Code, "left the village informal system totally unsupported, with no means of plugging the gaps at its weak points. Hence the system which the new laws were intended to abolish continues, but in a less orderly form" (Stirling 1957:32). In 1950 villagers in rural Anatolian villages were ignoring the Islamic rules on marriage and divorce, and when a woman separated from her husband the *iddet* did not occur. Nor were informal or formal sanctions brought against a woman who moved from her husband's house into another man's and took up the status of his new wife after the religious rite of *nikah* (marriage) had been performed. Stirling (1965:209-210) states:

"Legitimacy for the villages still rests solely on the *nikah* the religious rite performed by anyone of sufficient religious learning to know the formula. ... I never heard of anyone refraining from marriage because of the *iddet*. When I raised this issue, they asked, 'And who will cook bread and take care of the children while we wait?'".

Other researchers suggest that Turkish villagers were remarrying without going through a civil ceremony or a state recognized divorce, and thus were living in adulterous or bigamous relationships according to the new state law (Timur 1957). Statistics on illegitimate births from the 1950s support this assertion, and further substantiation is given by the fact that the Turkish National Assembly enacted laws legitimizing children of "irregular unions" in 1932, 1933, 1945, 1950, 1956, 1965, 1974 and 1981.[5]

In marked contrast is our evidence of acceptance of the Turkish Civil Code from our mid-1960s study. Our three-year record from the Bodrum Court docket 1965 through 1967 demonstrated 168 cases or 5% of the total (N=3,350) cases asking to waive the 15-day waiting period between civil registry and village wedding (Starr and Pool 1974:548). This suggests that villagers are: (i) aware of the requirements of registering a marriage with the state; (ii) aware that they must wait fifteen days before the village wedding; (iii) aware that to get the 15-day waiting period waived they need to go to court; and (iv) willing to go to court in order to be married in a way which meets official standards. Our data on divorce also sharply contrast with those collected by Stirling in 1950 for a different area (see Stirling 1957, 1965:210, 214-20).

2. Divorce cases in the Bodrum Court docket

Our data differ from Stirling's, in part because we studied different regions, and in part because our data come from court dockets rather than village observations. Without questioning the validity of Stirling's assertions, we offer a different picture of the process of acceptance of the Turkish Civil Code. Here we examine divorce cases processed through the High Civil Court in the district of Bodrum at two critical points in time 16 years apart: 1950 and 1966 (see Figures 1 and 2). Note that 1950 approximates the time period for Stirling's assertion that in two Anatolian villages people did not observe the Civil Code requiremants to officially divorce.

Figure 1. Divorce cases in the Bodrum district court (asliye hukuk)
1950 – Twelve Month Period

Plaintiffs	Granted	Not Granted	Dropped	Must live separately one year	Law 138 and must live separately on holidays	Total
Women	5	5	7	1	0	18
	26.3%	31.2%	46.7%	50%	0%	34%
Men	14	11	8	1	1	35
	73.7%	68.8%	53.3%	50%	100%	66%
Total	19	16	15	2	1	53

Figure 2. Divorce cases in the Bodrum district court (asliye hukuk).
1966 – Twelve Month Period

Plaintiffs	Granted	Not Granted	Dropped	Live separately one year	Suspended judgment	Total
Women	11*	3	2	0	4	20
	42.3%	75%	66.7%	0%	80%	50%
Men	15**	1	1	2	1	20
	57.7%	25%	33.3%	100%	20%	50%
Total	26	4	3	2	5	40

* In five cases the judicial decision included the statement "the woman may remarry whenever she chooses without having to follow the *iddet*" (i.e., 300 day waiting period, sanctioned by Law, under the Turkish Civil Code).

** In one decision, in which adultery was charged because the wife was co-habiting with a different man and was expecting his child, the judicial decision stated that the wife, now divorced, could not remarry for one year.

If we compare litigation rates in the district of Bodrum with other places where comparable data are available (see Figure 3), we see that the 1967 Bodrum civil litigation rates were more than four times as high as those in Kenya for a comparable time period, and more than twice as high as found in Alameda and San Benito, California in 1970.

Thus litigation rates indicate that Bodrum villagers recognized the saliency of Turkish state law by 1966. When we compare the 1966 statistics on court-initiated divorces with those of 1950, we find 40 people seeking divorces in 1966 and 53 people in 1950 (Figures 1 and 2).[6] Clearly 1950 in the Bodrum district is not a time of strong antipathy to the Turkish Civil Code, with strong preference for local customs and law-ways, as claimed by others (Stirling 1957, 1965:209-10, 273; Ulken 1957:52-3; Timur 1957:34-5). In 1950 men outnumber women in seeking divorces almost two to one. A decade and a half later, *half* of the plaintiffs are female, which is an increase of 16% in court-initiated divorces by women. The figures on "Suspended Judgment" in divorce cases indicate that women have found a further use for official courts. By bringing divorce suits to court against husbands who beat them or do not support them, women have found new sanctions in the official law. When they had gained male compliance, the female plaintiffs stopped attending court hearings, which resulted in a judicial decision to suspend judgment, which was duly noted in the docket. Divorce suits originated with a letter from the complainant to the court.

Figure 3. Civil and criminal litigation rates compared across cultures[1]
(Cases per 1,000 people)

	Alameda,[2] California	San Benito,[2] California	Bodrum, Turkey[3]	Chiangmei Thaliand[4]	Kenya[5]
Civil	11	10.2	25.2	0.64–0.87	4.3– 6.2
Criminal	*	*	15.8	2.48–3.78	11.2–26.7

[1] Data taken from Engel (1978:46).
[2] Data from Friedman and Percival (1976:277), for 1970 only.
[3] Calculated for the year 1967. Census data of 26,000 people taken from the 1965 Bodrum Census Records. Bodrum had a population of about 5,137 and the thirty villages a total population of about 21,000. This field data came to light in a box of lost field notes after Starr and Pool (1974) was published. Starr and Pool used national Census material which over-estimated the local population by about 4,000. This means the litigation rate here is even higher than calculated by Engel (1978:46). Court docket data is taken from Starr and Pool (1974:550).
[4] Data from Engel (1978:45-6) for 1965-74.
[5] Data from Abel (1973: Table II) for 1959-69).
* The California study by Friedman and Percival dealt only with civil and not with criminal litigation (Engel 1978:47, ftn. 7).

There has been also a significant increase in the ways women are obtaining results at court by 1966. In 1950, of the 18 women who went to court, 5 or 27.8% obtained divorces, and the same number were denied them. By 1966, 11 out of 20, or 55%, won their suits.

When we compare women's versus men's court-sought divorces, we find that in 1950, 26.3% of the women won divorces, while in 1966 42.3% obtained them (Figure 1). In 1950, 14 out of 35 men, or 40%, obtained a divorce (Figure 1); but by 1966 this percentage rises drastically, as 15 out of 20, or 75%, of the men won their suit (figure 2).[7]

The case dossiers for 1966 revealed that couples were denied a divorce because they had failed to provide enough evidence of incompatibility, or because children were involved and they had not tested their willingness to divorce by living apart, or because the divorce was contested. If they lived apart for a year and re-activated proceedings, divorce was granted regardless of the sex of plaintiff. In one case a women was granted a divorce because her husband took a second wife (an illegal act under the new Code); in another, because he was living in adultery before marriage and refused to leave his common-law wife to make a village wedding. Two other instances of obtaining a civil certificate of marriage, but not celebrating a wedding, were processed as divorce cases in the court, suggesting the extent to which some villagers recognized the authority of the secular marriage license.

If we ask what light these divorce data throw on prevalence of folk law versus acceptance of the Turkish Civil Code, we can suggest that state law has eclipsed local-level law-ways in the divorce arena. When we subjected the data to analysis we found a stronger association between court use and time (holding gender constant) (Figure 4) than between court use and gender (holding time constant) (see Figure 5). The stronger effects of time lead to the conclusion that the better model for explaining divorce court decision-making is one maintaining that court decisions were more sensitive to the ongoing effects of the legal revolution than the way males or females were perceived and treated by the courts.[8]

These data suggest that the earlier assertions of Stirling were partially correct. It is confirmed that the new Civil Code has undermined older folk law and customs. But Stirling's finding that the Code did not replace village local law-ways is disproved by these data. In the area of marriage and divorce we do not see a climate of law-ignoring and law-breaking in villages in the Bodrum district and, in fact, we found an extremely active law court, constantly filled and overflowing with rural people waiting for their cases to be heard. Not only were the official courts recognized as having sovereignty in matters of divorce, but the individuals flocking to them expected to gain relief from intolerable marital situations. These data clearly indicate, I think, that rather than run the risk of fighting, elopement, or bigamous relations, villagers sought official sanction for the breaking of marital relationships no longer manageable within the extended kinship unit.[9]

Figure 4. Court decision on divorce by year, by gender of plaintiff*
Bodrum (*asliye hukuk*)

Women Decision	1950	1966	Total
Granted	5 27.8%	11 68.8%	16
Not granted	5 27.8%	3 18.7%	8
Dropped	7 38.9%	2 12.5%	9
Live separately	1 5.5%	0 0%	1
Total	18 100%	16 100%	34

Men Decision	1950	1966	Total
Granted	14 41.2%	15 78.9%	29
Not granted	11 32.4%	1 5.3%	12
Dropped	8 23.5%	1 5.3%	9
Live separately	1 2.9%	2 10.5%	3
Total	34 100%	19 100%	53

* To compute the χ^2 statistic we dropped the one 1950 case concerning Law # 138 and the 1966 category Suspended Judgment. This allowed us to compare the court decision categories in an unbiased sense.

Figure 5. Divorce decisions in court by gender and by time

Year 1950 Decision	Women	Men	Total
Granted	5 / 27.8%	14 / 41.2%	19
Not granted	5 / 27.8%	11 / 32.4%	16
Dropped	7 / 38.9%	8 / 23.5%	15
Live separately one year	1 / 5.5%	1 / 2.9%	2
Total	18 / 100%	34 / 100%	52 / 100%

Year 1966 Decision	Women	Men	Total
Granted	11 / 68.8%	15 / 78.9%	26
Not granted	3 / 18.7%	1 / 5.3%	4
Dropped	2 / 12.5%	1 / 5.3%	3
Live separately one year	0 / 0%	2 / 10.5%	2
Total	16 / 100%	19 / 100%	35 / 100%

CONCLUSION

Let us use as our metaphor for acceptance of a radically different Civil Code the following chemical experiment. Suppose several drops of clear water are dropped into a rectangular glass container of yellow oil. The water is heavier than the oil and has a tendency to form droplets which partially adhere to each other. Water does not spread smoothly in layers through oil; nor does it diffuse in a uniform cloud. What it does is fall slowly towards the bottom, leaving lighter concentrations of water which diffuse in droplets slowly from specific points through the liquid oil. If the drops are small and the container big, and if the water is dropped into the left side, it may take a long time to reach the right side. If we want to speed up the process, we might project tear-drops of water into both the left and right sides of our rectangular container, or we could, of course, drop in more water. Moving from the metaphor, let us admit that this may be the process of acceptance of the Civil Code in Turkey: no uniform acceptance; spots incorporated into official law; other areas comparatively unaffected, still other areas using some and not all aspects of the official system.

Bates, an anthropologist also familiar with rural Turkey in the 1960s, reports an administrative centre with villagers using a bustling court and pursuing remedies both at court and in the district governor's office (1980:673-4):

> "...litigation and disputing through the local apparatus of the national court
> system are common. Conflict over land, debts, inheritances and contracts are
> just a few of the reasons why the courthouse is one of the busiest public buildings
> in any Turkish provincial center, and one thronged with villagers. A visit to the
> district governor's office, the *kaymakamlik*, where business is conducted quite
> openly, also reveals the extent to which villagers attempt to make use of the
> power of the state in solving local problems or, conversely, attempt to limit
> intervention where it threatens local interests. Presenting either village or indivi-
> dual concerns, men crowd the offices and hallways: to file complaints against
> each other or against officials, to protest the use of water by other villages,
> demand road maintenance, and the like. Very frequently, villagers pursue feud
> and interpersonal grievance by filling criminal or civil charges against their
> enemies.".

Since Bates' Turkish research took place in south eastern Turkey, we assume that is the general area of the *kaymakamlik* with which he is most familiar, which suggests state law has taken a firm hold there also.

There is good reason why the officials in Ankara would have wanted to keep the Bodrum region pacified, economically productive, and indoctrina-ted into the values of nation-statehood. Bodrum is much too accessible to the Greek islands to let it remain a backwater, illustrating the failure of the nation to maintain a western democratic outlook. Likewise, it is understandable that parts of eastern Turkey, such as the Lake Van region, which used to be linked to the Syrian city of Aleppo before the Versailles Peace Treaty, would be left alone and not developed. (Here the army keeps the area under surveillance, while Kurdish nomads are said to practise transhumance, migrating each spring and fall between eastern Turkey and Azarbaijan in western Iran. This area has been prohibited to researchers since the mid-1960s so we have almost no knowledge of the interrelations among official and folk law systems).

To prove that the Bodrum district represents a sucessful case of peaceful acceptance of the Turkish Civil Code by Moslem citizens, we have provided evidence on the *iddet*, on divorce, and on linkages between folk and state law in the Bodrum courts. We have used data on court-sought divorces in 1950 and 1966 which demonstrate that more people sought divorce in 1950 than in 1966, and that by 1966 an equal number of women and men were plaintiffs. Also, it appears that by 1966 plaintiffs had learned about legal definitions of evidence and more divorces were granted; the use of more substantial evidence is also apparent in the 53 in-depth divorce cases, from 1966 to August 1967, analysed in Starr (n.d.). We used our divorce data to show that in 1950 only 5 of the 18 women who went to court (27.8%) obtained divorces, while the same number were denied them. By 1966, 11 out of 20 (or 55%) won their suits. A comparison of women's versus men's divorce suits revealed that, in 1950, 26.3% of the women as compared to men won them, but women gained considerably by 1966 when 42.3% obtained their freedom. For men the figure drops off drastically: 14 out of 19 men (or 73.7%) won divorces in 1950, while only 15 out of 26 (or 67.7%) obtained them in 1966. The fact that three persons in 1966 used the court to obtain a divorce, even though neither a village wedding nor a religious rite had been performed, suggests that knowledge of state requirements had penetrated the awareness of most villagers.

When parties had been living apart for a year and the divorce was uncontested, they were the most successful in obtaining a divorce decree. When a civil marriage was not consummated by a village wedding (*dugun*) or a male was impotent, or the parties had been living apart for six or more months, the judge usually added in writing to the divorce decree that the woman was free to marry at any time - thus striking down the *iddet*, the secular adaptation of former Islamic law restricting remarriage, which had become a statutory provision in the Turkish Civil Code.

In discussing the points at which folk law and state law meet, we also reviewed the role of witnesses to oral land transactions, noting their role as expert witnesses in court in two important ways: in giving title where none has existed previously, and in attributing unwritten rights to land in contested cases.

Several theorists have criticized the data on acceptance of the Turkish Civil

Code in the Bodrum district as "too district-specific", saying the village of Mandalinci is a special case, or the Bodrum district is not representative of any other part of Turkey (Abel 1979; Bates 1980). Elsewhere I have explained at length the ways Bodrum's history links up with and is similar to that of Aegean Turkey on the one hand, and the Turkish Mediterranean coastal plains and mountains on the other (Starr 1981, 1983a). This paper is a further demonstration, along with Starr and Pool (1974), that the Bodrum district provides a case-study of a region where a Moslem population sucessfully accepted a radical change in nation-state law. As such, this study of social control in the Bodrum district can be compared with other case-studies of radical law change, such as that by Massell (1968, 1974), which portrays attempts by the Russian Marxist government in the period 1920-1929 to bring official secular law to the largely illiterate Moslem populations of Soviet Central Asia.

The reason for Bodrum's peaceful acceptance of secular law by 1966 is that economic change, regional development and secular ideology accompanied penetration by national law (Starr 1983b). In the Bodrum region we find also that folk law has become useful to judges as one source of legal norms, but in certain domains, such as the new laws concerning equality for women, folk law has not been adaptive. Although males with statuses in the oral law tradition are sometimes used as expert witnesses in official state courts, their evidence is not accorded highest priority when it conflicts with new legal precepts. Thus, in contrast to folk law, the Civil Code is able to provide authoritative, flexible and adaptive solutions to interpersonal conflict which have not been resolvable at the level.

NOTES

1.   Research for this paper was conducted for 16 months in 1966-68, sponsored by an NIMH pre-doctoral Fellowship and Grant. I wish to thank Rick Abel and Scott Meadow for their useful comments on this paper.
2.   The IUAES definition of "folk law" is used throughout this paper in the following meanings: the social processes, procedures and legally relevant behaviour recognized by members of a socially interacting group as embodied in their ideology, institutions, and behavioral repertoires. At the first level of contrast, folk law is the informal social controls of a social group. At the second level of contrast, the term folk law refers to all legally relevant behaviour which is not official state law. I reserve the term "customary law" to refer to fully developed indigenous (i.e. non-contact) law systems of which there has only been a finite number throughout human life. Within the last eighty years less than a dozen intact indigenous systems have been recorded. Examples are the customary law of the Bedouin of the Sinai (but not the Bedouin of the Negev), and the customary law which developed among the feuding mountain Ghegs of Albania. Hence, unwritten law, law-ways, and folk law are terms referring to all other non-state local level, or "tribal" law systems which evolved in part or in whole through contact with a more developed legal system. I would place the Barotse (Gluckman 1955) and the Tiv (Bohannan 1957) in this latter category. Tiv moots may have developed as an indigenous folk system.

3.   I use the term "law-ways" in the way in which Llewellyn and Hoebel did (1941). Hence "law-ways refers to the regularized processes by which a socially interacting group air, handle, and sometimes resolve disputes and interpersonal problems". It also refers to the ways a social group might try to curb the behaviour of troublesome people. By dispute I mean nothing more than a social relationship which contains elements of conflict, which elements become the focal point for disagreement (Abel 1974:226-7; Starr & Yngvesson 1975).

4.   Personal communication: Tugrul Ansay, Professor of Law, Ankara Universitesi, Hukuk Falkultesi, 14 December 1980.

5.   *Ibid.* These laws are effective only for several years, and therefore are enacted periodically, all with similar texts.

6.   Data include handwritten copies of court dossiers on all divorce cases heard by the Bodrum Court for the 20 month period January 1966 to August 1, 1967. These will be analysed more fully later (Starr n.d.). There may be slight discrepancies among these data and those analysed in Starr and Pool (1974), for those data on divorce came from the court docket (not the dossiers). Although in both instances the anthropologist was also scribe, errors may have occurred when data were transferred onto computer sheets, coded onto cards, or put into the computer.

7.   When we examined the way divorce court decisions changed over time, controlling for the plaintiff's gender, we found that $\chi^2 = 17.16$ (χ.90 on df3 $= 0.584$). When we examined the way court decisions varied across gender while controlling for the effects of time, the $\chi^2 = 5.5$ (χ^2.90 on df3 $= 0.584$). Therefore, the better model for explaining divorce court decision-making is one that maintains that court decisions affecting men and women were more sensitive to the ongoing effects of the Civil Code than the way males or females were perceived by the court. These contrast with findings in Starr & Pool (1974) because of closer and more sophisticated examination of the data.

8.   See note 7.

9.   Some researchers suggest that strong incentives to record marriages and divorces with the state were given by Turkish participation in the Korean War in the late 1950s. Wives and widows in irregular unions were not sent soldiers' pay checks or widows' benefits. The 1950s Bodrum court docket suggests that such sanctions were unnecessary in the Bodrum region, where many had already applied to courts for divorce.

REFERENCES

Abel, Richard L.
  1973   'Why go to court: a historical and comparative study of patterns of local court use in Kenya'. Unpublished working draft.
  1974   'A comparative theory of dispute institutions in society', *Law & Society Review* 8(2):217-347.
  1979   'The rise of capitalism and the transformation of disputing: from confrontation over honor to competition for property', *UCLA Law Review* 27(1):223-255.
Aktan, Resat
  1966   'Problems of land reform in Turkey', *Middle East Journal* 20:317.
Ansay, Tugul and Don Wallace, Jr.
  1966   *Introduction to Turkish Law*, Ankara:Gizel Instanbul Matbaasi.
Bates, Daniel
  1980   Review of *Dispute and Settlement in Rural Turkey: An Ethnography of Law* by June Starr, *American Anthropologist* 82:673-675.
Bodrum Census Bureau
  1965   *Bodrum Ilcesinin 1965 Yilina ait Genel Nüfus Sayimi* [1965 Bodrum Census], Bodrum Census Bureau: Bodrum, Turkey.

Bohannan, Paul
1957   *Justice and Judgment Among the Tiv*, London: Oxford University Press.
Engel, David M.
1978   *Code and Custom in a Thai Provincial Court: the Interaction of Formal and Informal Systems of Justice*, Tucson, Arizona: University of Arizona Press.
Friedman, Laurence M. and R.V. Percival
1976   'A tale of two courts: litigation in Alameda and San Benito Counties', *Law & Society Review* 10(2): 267-301.
Gluckman, Max
1955   *The Judicial Process Among the Barotse of Northern Rhodesia*, Manchester: Manchester University Press.
Gutkind, P.C.W. and I Wallerstein (eds.)
1976   'Introduction', in: *The Political Economy of Contemporary Africa*, Beverly Hills and London: Sage.
Hasluck, Margaret
1954   *The Unwritten Law in Albania*, Cambridge: Cambridge University Press.
Llewellyn, K.N. and E.A. Hoebel
1941   *The Cheyenne Way: Conflict and Case Law in Primitive Jurisprudence*, Norman: University of Oklahoma Press.
Massell, G.
1968   'Law as an instrument of revolutionary change in a traditional milieu: the case of Soviet Central Asia', *Law & Society Review* 2:179-228.
1974   *The Surrogate Proletariat - Moslem Women and Revolutionary Strategies in Soviet Central Asia, 1919-1929*, Princeton, N.J.: Princeton University Press.
Starr, June
1968   *Adliye: The Ethnography of a Turkish Rural District Court*, 37-minute colour, Super-8 film and film script: on file with the author.
1978   *Dispute and Settlement in Rural Turkey: An Ethnography of Law*, Leiden, Holland: E.J. Brill.
1980   'First thoughts on Western law in Islam: its effect on Aegean Turkey', *American Legal Studies Association Forum* 4(3):23-31.
1981   'Strengths of the anthropological method in the study of law', *UCLA Law Review* 28(3):591-604.
1983a   'The legal and social transformation of rural women in Aegean Turkey', in: Renee Hirschon (ed.), *Women and Property/Women as Property*, London: Croom Helm.
1983b   'Secularization of the law in Turkey: rural perspectives', in: Daisy Dwyer (ed.), *The Politics of Middle Eastern Law*, New York: Columbia University Press.
n.d.   From Renunciation to Divorce by Mutual Consent: Legal Evolution and Turkish Culture. Unpublished paper on file with the author.
Starr, June and Jonathan Pool
1974   'The impact of a legal revolution in rural Turkey', *Law & Society Review* 8(4):533-560.
Starr, June and Barbara Yingvesson
1975   'Scarcity and disputing: zeroing-in on compromise decisions', *American Ethnologist* 2(3):533-566.
Stirling, Paul
1957   'Land, marriage, and the law in Turkish villages. The reception of foreign law in Turkey', *International Social Bulletin* 9:21-33.
1965   *Turkish Village*, London: Weidenfeld & Nicolson.
1974   'Cause, knowledge and change: Turkish village revisited', in: J. Davis (ed.), *Choice and Change: Essays in Honour of Lucy Mair*, pp.191-229, London: Athlone Press.

Timur, H.
1957   'Civil marriage in Turkey: difficulties, causes and remedies. The reception of
            foreign law in Turkey', *International Social Science Bulletin* 9:34-36.
Ulken, H.Z.
1957   'The new Civil Code and the traditional customary law. The reception of foreign
            law in Turkey', *International Social Science Bulletin* 9:51-53.
Yalman, Nur
1979   'Land disputes in Eastern Turkey', *Research in Economic Anthropology* 2:269-
            302.

Customary law, state courts, and the notion of institutionalization of norms in Ghana and Nigeria

Gordon R. Woodman

This paper examines one aspect of the interaction between folk law and modern state law. It seeks to demonstrate some consequences of the precept, frequently found in state law, that portions of folk law be enforced by state courts and thereby incorporated into state law. To secure relatively precise and conclusive arguments I focus on the two similar legal systems of Ghana and Nigeria. In accordance with usage in those states, and with my own preference, the term "customary law" will be used instead of "folk law". Objections to the term, and the possibility that it carries different, conflicting meanings, will be mentioned later.

I. THE LEGISLATIVE DIRECTIVE TO STATE COURTS TO APPLY CUSTOMARY LAW

Between 1874 and 1876 a legal structure of government was established by the imperial power in the Colony of the Gold Coast and Lagos. The British were aware that the inhabitants were governed in their ordinary affairs by bodies of social norms regarded popularly as binding. The British wished to establish a system of courts, using British judges trained in the common law. These courts would apply common law[1] and local legislation to those activities which were regarded as obviously vital to the maintenance of the colonial state's power: acts designated as crimes affecting public order, the establishment of the organs of the colonial state, the acquisition of property for governmental purposes, taxation, and dealings by or involving Europeans. It was necessary to determine what should be done about the indigenous customary law.

The government might have instructed its courts to hear all cases which complainants wished to bring, and to apply only the common law. This would have constituted an attempt to suppress immediately all contrary social norms. This, it was realised, would be impracticable. The government could alternatively have restricted the jurisdiction of its new courts to certain types of cases, to be decided by common law, leaving other issues to be determined by customary law according to customary processes. It partially adopted this policy. It recognised existing "native tribunals", whose members were customarily responsible for the resolution of disputes. They were conceded jurisdiction in large numbers of cases, and required to apply "native law and custom" (Allott 1960: Chap. 5; Ollennu 1966a: Chap. 2). But the British government was not prepared to exclude from the jurisdiction of its new courts all those cases which it considered should be governed by customary law. Consequently the ordinance constituting the new Supreme Court, having provided that the court was to apply common law, proceeded: proceeded:

> "Nothing in this Ordinance shall deprive the Supreme Court of the right to observe and enforce the observance, or shall deprive any person of the benefit, of any law or custom existing in the said Colony and Territories subject to its jurisdiction ..." (Supreme Court Ordinance, 1876 (No. 4), s. 19)

When further areas came under colonial control in subsequent decades, and the original single colony was divided, the policy was extended to the new entities. In both Ghana and Nigeria all subsequent courts statutes have continued to require the superior courts to apply "any existing law or custom", now generally referred to as customary law.[2] Later the government determined to exercise more control over the traditional courts, and replaced the "native tribunals" with "native courts", which legally were established, not merely recognised, by the colonial regime (Allott 1960: Chap. 5; Ollennu 1966a: Chap. 2). The experience with native courts was not adjudged successful, for reasons not here relevant, and since independence, occurring in 1957 in Ghana and 1960 in Nigeria, they have in most areas been abolished, or superseded by "customary courts" whose judges frequently do not hold traditional offices requiring a special knowledge of traditional social norms. Thus originally the application of customary law by courts not of the traditional type was relatively rare, although significant; today it has become general.

Because of this development the history of the relationship between common law and customary law has a different pattern for the legal profession, concerned primarily with the work of the superior courts, from that which has appeared over the years to most of society. For Ghanaian and Nigerian society in general the historical process has been: originally, social control by traditional social norms; then the imposition of common law and state legislation, both of which grew steadily in importance during most of the colonial period, with perhaps a slight reversion towards customary law shortly before independence; since then, a period of co-existence in which the overall trends are difficult to determine, except for a marked growth in statutory law. The superior courts, on the other hand, started with the common law. They received it in written form, and from the earliest period members of the profession learnt it during their training. They have gradually added to it a growing volume of customary law. Thus the procedure by which the courts establish customary law should be viewed as a mode of incremental development of state law, adding to the body of established common law. This pattern of development may explain why common-law methods and ideas have often been used in the courts' development of customary law. But the pattern is not that of general social development in Ghana and Nigeria. It results from the rapid and forcible imposition of an alien law at the end of the last century.

It might have been supposed that a strong case could have been made, from the viewpoint of the colonial regime, for limiting its courts to those cases deemed suitable for the application of common law or state legislation. But instead the regime delimited its courts' jurisdiction primarily in terms of the value of the subject-matter of causes. I know of no explicit contemporaneous discussion of the question. The Supreme Court Ordinance was a redrafting of earlier provisions and of enactments in other colonies. It would seem that the regime considered that the exercise of authority over "private" spheres of activity was self-evidently necessary to its interests, or (perhaps) to its supposed "civilising" mission (cf Adinkrah 1980). Moreover, the subsequent trend was for the lawmakers repeatedly to extend the jurisdiction of the state courts, applying all types of law in force, at the expense of those courts which applied exclusively or predominantly customary law - another instance of the modern state's expansionism. (Cf. Griffiths 1977: 108; and, on substantive law as distinct from courts, Diamond 1971, advancing the notion of state law's tendency to "cannibalise" custom.)

II. THE PERCEIVED NEED TO "ESTABLISH" THE CONTENT OF CUSTOMARY LAW: ALLOCATION OF THE FUNCTION TO STATE COURTS

The decision that state courts were to apply customary law caused a further problem. This arose from the almost total ignorance, on the part of the British judges, of this law: an ignorance far greater than the often-alleged ignorance of British judges of the practices and beliefs of the ordinary British citizen. While the problem has become less acute in modern times with the appointment of Ghanaian and Nigerian judges, it has by no means disappeared. A judge today will have some personal acquaintance with customary law, but this will not normally extend beyond the customary law of the ethnic group into which he was born, and will be reasonably reliable only of his own sub-group within that wider group.

Any investigation *de novo* of an aspect of customary law is lengthy and costly. The need for efficiency therefore posed a need for customary law to be established. *Establishment* of a norm in this context means its articulation in a pronouncement which is (a) accessible to the courts, and (b) of sufficient legal authority to justify the judicial application of that norm. In other words, the Supreme Court Ordinance having determined that existing customary norms were to constitute a legal source of Ghanaian and Nigerian law, these norms were now to be incorporated into a different legal source. "Establishment" is a type of institutionalization, but is a precisely delineated type. (Cf. Bohannan 1965, 1968, discussed below.)

The task of establishing customary law in this sense was relegated to the courts, and has remained with them, with few and insignificant exceptions. Norms could have been made accessible and authoritative by, for example, a legislative conferment of authority on specified statements of customary law. There are various ways in which legislative power can be used to confer authority on statements of norms. At one extreme is the code embodied in a principal statute. There are various possibilities of delegating legislative power. And at the other extreme is the publication of declarations such as restatements, which courts may be required to consider, without being bound to follow them. The lawmakers rejected, impliedly and quite possibly by default, these various alternative modes of establishing legal norms.

Thus the legislature's contribution to the establishment of customary law has been slight. Moreover, there has been no increase in activity over the years. Legislative abolition of portions of customary law has been more significant, but that is not relevant here. It may be asked why the legislature did so little to foster the establishment of the law which it had decided should be applied in the courts which it had instituted.

A reading of official sources such as Legislative Council debates suggests that one possible explanation may be rejected. Common lawyers have in other contexts sometimes urged legislative restraint, particularly in respect of codification, on the ground that judicial development of the law was to be preferred.[3] I have found no evidence that this view has prevented the legislative establishment of customary law. Had it done so, it is likely that there would be evidence of argument on the point, since the view would have been used to resist pressure towards legislative action. There is no evidence that such pressure existed.

There could develop explicit opposition to legislative action. It will be suggested in the next section that the courts have adopted a system of establishing customary law through precedent. As the case-law develops, those who consider it to be successful may express opposition to any other system, if only to anticipate changes by legislation. One of the outstanding British practitioners of incremental development by case-law, Lord Mansfield, was an opponent of legislative reform of the common law (Holdsworth 1923-1956, V: 550-551). There is some evidence that Mr. Justice Ollennu, who played a leading role in the development of customary-law case-law, has similarly some antipathy (not, however, unqualified) to reform by legislation of customary law (Ollennu 1962: 68-69: 1971: 143-145, 165-167; but ibid. 168-169). Nevertheless, while such opposition could now be developing as a result of the experience of development by case-law, it does not seem to have been influential in earlier times. The choice in favour of judicial establishment of customary law was not, it seems, a result of a decision preferring the inherent advantages of that mode.

The question is essentially one for the political historian. It concerns the problem why certain organs of state chose not to exercise functions which were legally within their competence. It may be suggested that the lack of activity reflects the scarcity of the requisite technical skills and the relatively low priority given to the task.

The effect of the decision was to place the expense of establishing customary law on the litigant who sought to rely on it, rather than on the taxpayer, local or British. One wonders how far this reflected sympathy for the taxpayer, antipathy for the litigant, or lack of conscious thought. Whatever the cause of this non-development, it augurs ill for current proposals for legislative reform of the customary law.

III. THE ESTABLISHMENT OF CUSTOMARY LAW - THE JUDICIAL PROCESS

Before observing the process which the courts adopted for the establishment of customary law, we should notice the manner in which a customary-law norm is initially communicated to a court.

The early courts had perforce to treat questions as to the content of customary law as questions of fact, a view which produced the unfortunate remark in an early Ghanaian case that customary law was "foreign law".[4] The modes of proof, which have been described elsewhere (Woodman 1969:131-136), were originally: the evidence of expert witnesses; accounts in authoritative textbooks; opinions of native courts; advice of expert assessors; and reports of referees. In addition the courts came to rely upon sources of information which were not so explicitly acknowledged. These were: previous decisions of the superior courts on questions of customary law; personal knowledge of the judges; judges' opinions of what was reasonable; and assertions by litigants when not effectively challenged. In using most of these forms of proof and sources of information the judges tended to presume a widespread uniformity in customary law, taking the proven practices of one ethnic group to be reliable evidence of those of another group closely - and sometimes not at all closely - related. These modes of proof continue, with greater use being made today of judges' personal knowledge and their opinions of what is reasonable.

Proof of a norm in one case for the purposes of that case is merely the preliminary to establishment. The principal stage of the process is stated in the "rule in *Angu* v *Attah*", which provides: "All customary law ... has to be proved in the first instance ... until the particular customs have, by frequent proof in the courts, become so notorious that the courts will take judicial notice of them" ((1916) P.C. '74-'28, 43). The practical application of the rule has already been documented (Woodman 1969: 136-139). There has been a trend towards the acceptance of a single previous decision as not only constituting evidence of customary law, but as rendering it "notorious", and so constituting authority which justifies a subsequent decision. Thus the conclusion which the courts have almost, if not finally reached, is that decisions on customary law constitute precedents in the same way as decisions on common law. This enables the creation of a body of case-law setting out the content of customary law. Since my earlier documentation of the trend it appears to have continued.[5]

This development also has been extended, at least in Ghana, by the assumption of uniformity of customary laws of different communities. A decision on a point of customary law made in a case concerning one community is liable to be treated as authority in a case concerning another.

Broadly we may summarise thus the answer which has been given to the question, by what mode is customary law to be established: it is established by converting it into case-law. By this process state law apparently incorporates customary social norms. The legal source of customary law becomes precedent, while social practice becomes a historical source.[6] Customary law acquires a character very similar to common law, since the judges declare it from their own knowledge, and their decisions thereon become authorities in the same hierarchy of precedent.

The implications of this process may be revealed more clearly by a consideration of the reasons why it was chosen. Given that the task of establishing customary law had been relegated to the courts, there were nevertheless other processes which could have been adopted.

The modes of initial proof adopted by the courts are none likely to be entirely reliable. As a result the courts have probably on occasion reached mistaken conclusions on the content of social norms (Woodman 1969). The possibility of error is perhaps greatest when judges rely on their personal knowledge or sense of reasonableness and when they assume extensive uniformity of customary law. They could have chosen to insist on strict proof by more reliable methods, such as evidence by numerous, impartial, genuinely expert witnesses, perhaps secured by reference to carefully selected boards of referees, in every case. Why did they not?

The most obvious ground for the adoption of the current modes of proof is their relative convenience. Convenience need not have been regarded as absolutely more important than accuracy. The courts were balancing two incompatible ideals, trying to achieve each in limited measure. They perhaps assumed that, if they did usually ascertain the social norms correctly, they could accept the risk of a limited number of errors in order to avoid tedious and expensive hearings over every issue.

However, although the courts have never acknowledged this, the argument against unreliable modes of proof was strengthened when it became apparent that decisions were influential, or even determinative, in subsequent cases. Any tendency to follow past decisions multiplies the deleterious consequences of a wrong decision, while reducing the cost which would be incurred over a period by more elaborate methods of initial proof.

The courts' reliance on their own knowledge may perhaps have been induced less by arguments on the merits of this method than by their established practice of relying on their own knowledge of other, closely similar facts. They explicitly take judicial notice of well-known facts, and, beyond this, in deciding all cases inevitably make use of their own knowledge of scientific laws, of human nature, and of their societies. There is a large area for intriguing research into the sources of judges' opinions on these frequently uncertain matters in different juridictions. It is at least debatable whether such facts are in a different class from the social norms referred to in determining the content of customary law.[7] If there is no difference, it is hardly surprising that the judges have used their own knowledge in both instances. Moreover, even if the distinction can be drawn, it is not necessarily reflected in differences in reliability of judicial knowledge of the two classes of phenomena. The judges may therefore have commenced to rely on their own knowledge of customary law in pursuance of an established usage, from which they saw no reason to depart in this instance. If they considered the process critically, they may have concluded that it provided reliable indicators of social practice, and perhaps some limited occasions for inserting their own policy preferences into the law. In view of the total lack of judicial discussion of the issue, the common-law usage appears the most tenable explanation.

We need to ask also why the courts have concluded that earlier decisions may be treated not merely as evidence but as precedent, or that customary law should be established through the medium of case-law. Here again I suggest that there were both arguments on the merits and established usages, and that the latter may well have been decisive.

Given that efficiency necessitated the establishment of customary law, and legislation to this end was not to be forthcoming, the courts could have developed other modes of establishment. The dictum in *Angu* v. *Attah* contemplated establishment through "frequent proof in the courts". There were further possibilities. For example, the judges could have devised a procedure whereby from time to time they collectively made formal declarations of the norms of customary law in particular areas. An analogy for this is the "practice statement", by which important principles have been established in some common-law countries. In Britain it was by this eans, not by a judgment, that the House of Lords abolished the rule that it was bound by its own decisions ([1966] 3 All E.R. 77). If used in West Africa, of course, such a device could have developed its own characteristics. Why, then, did the courts come to treat customary law as just another body of case law?[8]

The most obvious argument for the system is that it is likely to produce certainty, and to do so more rapidly than any other method, because the techniques of interpreting and applying precedents are well known to common lawyers. This argument in its general aspect would emphasise the value of a legal system in which people can choose their actions with a knowledge of their legal effects. However, the weakness of the argument is that case-law provides certainty only for those who have access to the requisite legal information, and principally those who are seriously contemplating litigation. In third-world states knowledge of state law is probably very restricted (Seidman 1978: Chap. 7). However, the type of certainty which judges are most likely to seek is certainty by lawyers about the outcomes of contemplated litigation. The argument of certainty in the establishment of customary law says that, even if the law is unsatisfactory in some respects, it is better that it be certain, than that it be left uncertain in a search for perfection.

The system was fostered by individual judges who were concerned to produce certainty while giving authority to particular comprehensive views of areas of the customary law. Mr. Justice Jackson attempted this in Ghana in the 1940s and '50s.[9] He was not greatly successful in obtaining general acceptance for his ideas, partly because they were controversial on some matters, and partly because his judgments were not reported at a time when they could have had their strongest impact on the profession. More influential has been Mr. Justice Ollennu. He gave a notable series of judgments during his tenure of office from 1956 to 1969, in which he set out a comprehensive and detailed view of many areas of customary law. He appears in many instances to have deliberately exploited the opportunities furnished by the cases. In some, for example, instead of disposing of the case on one or two issues, he took every one of the issues raised by the parties, and sometimes some others raised by himself, and gave a full account of the law on each.[10] The success of some of his work was shown in 1961 when the Privy Council accepted his views as constituting the customary land law in important respects.[11]

However, his development of the law was strictly within the context of a case-law system, and was limited by the rules of that system. Until he moved to the Supreme Court in 1962, he decided most of his cases sitting alone in the High Court, so that his judgments did not visibly enjoy the benefit of prior discussion with colleagues. His judgments in the High Court were of limited authority in the hierarchy of precedent. And this mode of establishing authority meant that he was able to lay down rules only on questions which could be held relevant to litigation, and only in the haphazard order in which they arose.[12] Finally, he himself contributed to the strictness of the system by insisting on the binding effect of his own decisions.[13]

The argument for certainty appears to have prevailed over two objections to the system. First, and more commonly, it has been said that it produces a divergence between customary social norms in practice and norms enforced by the courts under the name of customary law (Kludze 1973. For evidence of the common nature of this objection I rely principally on the reactions of Ghanaians with whom I have discussed the customary-law case-law.) There can be little doubt that the divergence exists, and that it arises inevitably from the system (Woodman 1969; Kludze 1972, 1973, in this volume). The objection is not solely that it is misleading to call the case-law norms "customary law" if they are not in fact regarded customarily as binding. The primary objection is not to the name but to the content of the judicial norms. Socially accepted norms are, almost by definition, those which people expect to be enforced, and consider ought to be enforced. For the courts to enforce contrary norms defeats people's expectations and violates their sense of justice. One cause of the divergence is the unreliability of the modes of proof. However, if the system of case-law had not been developed, initial erroneous findings could have been corrected.

Secondly, it has been objected that the method produces an inflexible body of norms. Once a norm has been judicially declared in a binding precedent to be customary law, it cannot be changed except by legislation. Social norms, on the other hand, are constantly changing. Thus a social norm may change after the courts have established the customary law on that subject, and the case-law system could prevent a corresponding change in the law. However, it is possible that a litigant would be permitted to argue, and bring evidence to show that the change had occurred. While writers have discussed the possibility (Hannigan 1958: 114-115; Allott 1960: 89-90; Bennion 1962: 424-426), there is no record of a litigant attempting this, so one cannot predict how receptive the courts would be. It is quite possible, in any case, that the judges have not thought of case-law as inflexible. Common-law judges in many jurisdictions have demonstrated repeatedly that norms stated in precedents can be restricted, extended, reformulated, or swept away, when they considered that social change so required. Thus the arguments of inflexibility, if considered, may have appeared weaker than the arguments for certainty.

Apart from these merits and demerits of case-law, it is possible that the common-law culture of the legal profession may have predisposed the judges to favour this mode of establishment. They have all been trained primarily in the common law, which they have been applying daily in the determination of other issues simultaneously with their establishment of customary law. Thus when John Mensah Sarbah wrote the first book by a lawyer on customary law (Sarbah 1897), it seemed natural to him to contribute to the development of the customary law by compiling a substantial appendix consisting of reports of cases.

Furthermore, the experience of other jurisdictions shows that, when common-law judges are faced with the need to incorporate a new body of norms into the main body of the law, they normally do this by methods similar to those of the Ghanaian and Nigerian judges. This observation is supported by the practice of many other common-law African jurisdictions in establishing customary law in the same way (Allott 1970: Chap. 8). It is illustrated also by the initial establishment of the principles of the common law in the English royal courts,[14] and by the absorption of the norms of commercial custom into the English common law in the time of Lord Mansfield.[15] A judicial tendency to follow precedent is probably universal. What is noteworthy is the tendency of common-law courts to apply their own brand of case-law, and to extend its hegemony, to any new area which is seen to need development.

The presumption of uniformity of customary law, influential both in its initial proof and in its establishment through case-law, may likewise have been accepted on the grounds of efficiency in initial decision-making and of subsequent certainty of the law, already mentioned. There could have been additional, special grounds. It has sometimes been argued that a multitude of differing customary laws would be undesirable in a developing nation where local rivalries and prejudices might be barriers to necessary change.[16] However, it could have been argued, on the contrary, that the imposition on one ethnic group of the social norms of another might provoke inter-ethnic antagonism. This view could be a reason for the Nigerian courts' rejection of the presumption in recent years, although the only reason given has been the inaccuracy of the presumption.

IV. THE NEW CONTENT OF LAWYERS' CUSTOMARY LAW

The process just discussed has resulted in a body of norms which are applied in the state courts, and referred to, at least in those courts, as customary law. These bodies of norms, built up over a century, are now of impressive extent. A full analysis of the implications of the process would require a detailed consideration of the content of these norms. While that is not possible here, some brief observations can be supported on less evidence. This section discusses some implications for legal systems such as those of Ghana and Nigeria. The next, and concluding section will suggest some wider implications.

The most obvious and dramatic aspect of the results is the divergence between the content of those norms applied as customary law in the state courts, and the content of the customary law which is socially recognised outside. The foregoing sections have attempted to show not only or primarily that the mode of establishment entailed this result, but rather why this mode was nonetheless adopted. It is now necessary to refine our terminology to distinguish between the divergent varieties of customary law. I shall retain the term "customary law" for both, while distinguishing between sociologists' customary law and lawyers' customary law. It may be objected that sociologists' customary law is not law (Diamond 1971: 45), and that lawyers' customary law is not customary (Allott 1960: 89; 1970: 278). Such definitional disputes have been discussed elsewhere (Woodman 1969), and may now be passed over.[17]

A less obvious but more important observation on the divergence is that it is pervasive and inevitable. It does not arise solely from mistaken findings on the content of sociologists' customary law. Even if no such mistakes ever occurred, divergence would arise from two other causes, at least one of which renders it unavoidable and indeed necessary.

The first of these other causes is that the courts sometimes have to reach conclusions on the content of customary law when sociologists' customary law is in a state of change. Lawyers' customary law must determine all cases to which it is required to be applied, and therefore must be fixed and consistent. Sociologists' customary law has these characteristics generally, but in particular respects it may be transient or contradictory. An example may be given from the Ghanaian Akan law of inheritance. It is well established that a man's property in general passes on his death intestate to his matrilineage, which does not include his children. It is likely that a century ago his children would have been entitled to nothing beyond a few, specific, minor items, such as the tools of his trade. In the present century social change led to an intense popular debate as to whether his wife and children ought to have recognised rights to a share of his estate. When cases on this reached the courts in the 1960s it was unclear whether sociologists' customary law had developed such rights. In 1963 the Supreme Court heard a case in which children claimed rights in an estate. State courts do not have the option of declining to decide issues. The decision in this case established the lawyers' customary law in the issue.[18] This ground of divergence seems contingent. It is conceivable that a body of sociologists' customary law might be as fixed and consistent throughout as lawyers' customary law needs to be.

Second, divergence occurs also because state courts have a peculiar character which demands in every case an answer to a question which sociologists' customary law has never had to answer, and cannot answer. This cause is necessary. It ought to be taken as the most fundamental premise in any study of the relationship between lawyers' customary law and society, and yet it is frequently overlooked. It can be established in general terms by a simple, almost formal argument. In any case before a state court the essential question, to the answering of which all other questions are directed, is invariably, how ought this court to exercise its power with regard to this case? State courts are not subjects of non-state, sociologists' customary law.

Therefore sociologists' customary law never answers the question before the court, and hence lawyers' law, which does, must have a different content.

The argument may be put in more particular terms, with some examples. The outcome of a case in a state court is the grant or refusal of a *remedy*. In practice the courts of Ghana and Nigeria have taken their law of remedies from the common law, even for customary-law cases, so that they grant, for example, damages for trespass to land according to the rules of the old English common-law courts, or orders for accounts according to the doctrines of the court of Chancery.[19] Even had they sought to avoid following common-law authorities, it is difficult to see how they could have developed any greatly different remedies. But to give damages for slander or adultery, or an order for accounts against the administrator of family property, is not to reproduce the consequences which would have confronted a wrongdoer in the absence of state courts.[20] Those courts cannot, by their nature, reproduce those consequences. This factor also requires the state courts to distinguish between those social norms which are legal and those which are not. The distinction is not clearly drawn in social practice outside the state courts (Woodman 1975: 6-8).

The decision as to a remedy follows from the application of one or more *rules*. Sociologists' customary law contains many rules. Could not some of these become part of lawyers' customary law without change? This is doubtful, because every rule employed by a court must, if it is to be relevant, be directed towards the final conclusion of the grant or refusal of a (peculiar, state court's) remedy. No rule of sociologists' customary law adverts to these remedies, and so no such rule can say anything about their applicability. Such law may, for example, say whether a head of family ought to account to certain members of his family in certain conditions on certain occasions, and may state the duties of various other persons on the head's default. But such rules about the "accountability" of the head cannot answer any question for a state court, and so will provide no answer for a state court seeking to decide whether to issue an order for accounts. Again, sociologists' customary law may contain rules stating what ought to be done with a person's property on his death. They may be subtle and detailed, indicating how various individuals, including traditional office-holders, ought to behave in the event of a dispute, usually with the object of restoring social harmony. They may confer rights, which will be enforceable in the sense conveyed in the context of the social norms. But none of them, either singly or in combination with others, will indicate what a state court ought to do in the event of a dispute, nor can it confer a right to a state court's order.

While the two types of law diverge as to remedies and rules, could they coincide as to *concepts*? Are not terms such as "family", "marriage" and "title" capable of carrying the same meaning, even if they appear in different types of rules? In theory they could. In practice it is unlikely because of the difficulty of giving a precise meaning to any legal concept independently of its function in the expression of a body of legal rules. The three terms mentioned could perhaps be defined in terms apt for both sociologists' and lawyers' customary law, but each definition would be vague. Thus a family could be defined as a unilineal descent group. This would not indicate the persons who constituted the family of X for any particular purpose, because it would not indicate which ancester of X should be taken as the common ancestor of members. Once a purpose was specified, a definition of a family for that purpose could be provided. However, the purpose would either be activity of a state court or be some other form of activity. The definition would be limited to the context of a rule which would either be part of lawyers' customary law or belong to sociologists' customary law. Similar arguments could be developed for the other terms mentioned, and for any others. (On "marriage", see Woodman 1977: 129-130).

It seems more likely that some *principles* of the two systems of customary law may coincide, although not all. The term is used here in Dworkin's (1977a) sense. Principles of law, like rules of law, are legal standards, but unlike a rule, a principle relevant in any given case "argues in one direction, but does not necessitate a particular decision", and carries weight, requiring that it be taken into account in reaching a decision, without being binding in "all-or-nothing fashion". (Dworkin 1977a: 22-28 and generally Chap. 2.) Principles generally prescribe less specific acts than rules (Christie 1968; Raz 1972), and lie behind rules, providing common justifications for groups of rules (Dworkin 1977a: 66, Chap. 4.) [21] ("Norm" is used throughout this paper to include both rules and principles.) I suggest that a principle of both systems of customary law in both Ghana and Nigeria is that a person who develops land ought to be secured the fruits of his investment. Another is that individuals who belong to the same social group ought to behave towards each other in a manner which will promote the social cohesion of the group. On the other hand it is doubtful whether there are in sociologists' customary law principles advancing the authority of the state, national integration, and national economic development, while there probably are in state law, including lawyers' customary law. Moreover, even when principles with the same content are found in both systems, it is likely that their weights will differ. This will be partly because principles will frequently justify statutory rules as well as customary-law rules (Dworkin 1977a: 116-117), and partly because principles are functions of theories about social objectives (Dworkin 1977a: 105, referring to "political" theories), which differ to some degree between state law and sociologists' customary law.

It therefore appears that the divergence between lawyers' customary law and sociologists' customary law, which was earlier demonstrated to exist, must be seen as not a consequence of unfortunate, remediable defects in the process of establishing lawyers' customary law, but as a necessary, irremovable phenomenon in the enforcement of customary law by state courts. This has consequences for both evaluative and descriptive discussion of customary law in state courts.

It follows that it is erroneous to regret or criticise the divergence, if this is to imply that it would be possible for lawyers' customary law to have the same content as sociologists' customary law (Kludze 1972; 1973: 278; in this volume; cf. Bentsi-Enchill 1972: 123). For the same reason the notion of a restatement of customary law needs reconsideration. (Cf. Allott 1968-73.) A revision of terminology is required also. It is not possible for state courts to incorporate, adopt, apply, enforce, administer, observe, absorb, receive or have transferred to them sociologists' customary law (Supreme Court Ordinance, 1876, s. 19, quoted above; Allott 1960: Chap. 4; 1977: 11; Ollennu 1971: 133-135; Kludze in this volume). Perhaps state law may "cannibalize" sociologists' customary law (Diamond 1971), but not if that means the consumption of like by like: accuracy would be increased, although the shock effect reduced, if we spoke instead of "devouring".

If we can avoid the mistaken propositions and misleading terms, an intriguing prospect for investigation opens. For although there cannot be an identity of sociologists' customary law and lawyers' customary law, there is obviously a relationship. Acceptance of the misleading notion of incorporation has prevented students from starting to analyse this relationship. My argument suggests that the state courts are engaged in a creative function, establishing as lawyers' customary law norms which have not previously existed. They use the norms of sociologists' customary law as principal factors. It seems likely that policies affect the process, lawyers' customary law being directed rather more than sociologists' customary law towards the values of the modern, bourgeois economy, a possibility hinted at in some recent writing (Snyder 1980: 777-778). It may be, however, that a more influential factor is the goal of forming norms which will function coherently and efficiently within the state court system. The driving force in the process of creation may be this technical requirement (which may itself, of course, be formed partly by ideology).

In place of the existing schemes and terminology, which must be discarded if my argument is correct, it may be helpful to use provisionally the notion of institutionalization promoted by Bohannan (1965; 1968). A principal objection to this term is that it is vague. It indicates only that the objects in question - in this case norms - are changed in some unspecified way to function as part of an institution - in this case state courts. The nature of the change is in no way indicated. But provided it is noticed that the change may be considerable, the term at least is not misleading.[22]

V. GENERAL CONCLUSIONS

It is not to be assumed that the example of Ghana and Nigeria will be followed elsewhere. However, the examination above of the grounds for the various stages in the development, from the legislature's directive to the state courts to the courts' creation of a body of case-law, suggests that it arose from factors which are not unusual.[23]

The example may assist an understanding of general issues concerning the possibility of incorporating other bodies of norms into legal systems, and the consequences of attempting to do so. The example suggests that there is great difficulty in any such enterprise, and that we must expect any attempt to result in the creation of new norms, institutionalising those which were intended to be incorporated. In the case of sociologists' customary law, even if a legislature were to attempt the process of incorporation itself, by means of, say, a code or restatement, the same basic difficulties would be encountered as when the function was passed to the courts. The question is sometimes discussed whether state law should incorporate the norms of positive morality. Perhaps the question does not arise, because the process is impossible. Member states of the European Communities are supposedly incorporating bodies of community law into their municipal state laws: is this possible? Perhaps all forms of legal transfers (transplants) are impossible, not because transferred norms would perform different social functions in their new environments (Seidman 1978: Chap. 2) (which is an argument that transfers are inadvisable, not impossible), but because the norms cannot retain their original content as components of a different system. Changes in the bases of traditional courts may effectively convert them into different institutions, in which case they cannot continue to apply the same law, which will need to be institutionalised to fit the new courts and legal system of which they are a part.

All such instances may be usefully studied, not in the expectation that norms can be incorporated into new systems, but as illustrations of a special class of influences on judicial law-making. The recognition of judicial creativity need not lead to an assumption of unfettered, strong discretion. It may well be that judges understand themselves to be bound by principles which indicate fairly precisely the right answer to any case in which a new rule of lawyers' customary law needs to be made.[24]

Bohannan's notion of institutionalization features in his proposed description of the origins of law (1965, 1968). The development of lawyers' customary law may assist an assessment of his scheme. Bohannan draws a distinction between custom and law. Human activity is either institutionalised or random. Custom is a form of institutionalised norm, in that it prescribes a form of behaviour necessary if a social institution is to achieve its purposes. A legal institution is distinguished by the fact that "by means of [it] the people of a society settle disputes that arise between one another and counteract any gross and flagrant abuse of the rules of the other [i.e. nonlegal] institutions of society". Law arises when the norms of custom are institutionalised again, this second institutionalization entailing their restatement "in order to make [them] amenable to the activities of the legal institutions ... The law rests on the basis of this double institutionalization". (1968: 74-75) This could cover the process discussed in this paper, but it is doubtful whether Bohannan means that the second institutionalization occurs in modern state courts, although he is not specific. He probably refers to the traditional courts which existed before the advent of the modern state, and which frequently continued for a time with state endorsement afterwards.[25] Not all the peoples of Ghana and Nigeria have had such courts (Fortes 1940: 271; Tait 1958: 186-187). For court-less societies the advent of state law including lawyers' customary law may perhaps have produced a second institutionalization. But for those societies which had courts (Rattray 1929; Nadel 1942) lawyers' customary law must have emerged as a result of, at least, a third institutionalization. In any case, this counting-up may involve oversimplification, since it assumes that these metamorphoses have been the only elements of change in the development of laws. Courts and other institutions constantly undergo change. A norm which has been institutionalized into a court system in one form may need to be reformed if that system changes, so that becomes "amenable" to the changed activities of the changed court. Bohannan' simple picture cannot be retained. The notion of institutionalization, however, still seems revealing. The type of investigation suggested above might usefully be pursued with the object of elucidating the process of institutionalization.

Diamond has disputed the Bohannan explanation of law, suggesting that a conflict perspective should be substituted. Double institutionalization, he argues, is not the major source of law, much of which is unprecedented, and opposed to the customary law. Law being symptomatic of the emergence of the state, it promotes interests which are opposed to those which previously prevailed, and has constrasting characteristics. Whereas custom is typically spontaneous, traditional, personal, commonly known, corporate and relatively unchanging, law tends to have opposite qualities. The development of law is not a simple passage of custom into law, but neither do all laws in an emergent state overtly contradict custom. State laws may appear to reinforce custom by, for example, codifying it or sharpening its punitive character. In this case, however, law is in truth cannibalising custom, appropriating the authority which previously ensured and was confirmed by compliance with the custom (Diamond 1971. The principal illustration is the "proto-state" of Dahomey before the colonial period.)

In so far as Bohannan proposes an account of the genesis of all law, Diamond's criticism must be well-founded. A great deal of state law is not reformed custom or sociologists' customary law, and is not illuminated by attempting to analyse it as such. However, the concern of this paper has been with an area in which state law has appeared to accept and reinforce what these writers call custom.[26] Neither appears greatly interested in the law of the modern state, and each perhaps attempts excessively wide generalisations. However, each provides insights into the process which has been discussed. Having argued that the process was not incorporation of norms into state law, I have suggested that Bohannan's notion of institutionalization may assist an understanding. But I have also suggested that the new norms of lawyers' customary law probably meet the claims prominent in a modern economy to a greater extent than did the old norms of sociologists' customary law. Diamond's notion of the state enforcing traditional norms for tactical reasons could help to explain the origins and persistence of the requirement that state courts enforce customary law, and an understanding of this motive may assist an analysis of the judicial creation of the new content of lawyers' customary law.

NOTES

1.   In the present context "common law", when referred to as applicable in Ghana and Nigeria, comprises the case-law of law and equity, and certain English statutes.
2.   In Nigeria subsequent courts legislation has continued in redrafted form the provision quoted. In Ghana it was remodelled in 1960, but customary law has continued to be part of the laws of the state: Constitution, 1960, art. 40; Constitution, 1969, art. 126; Constitution, 1979, art. 4.
3.   See generally the summary of Savigny's and Austin's arguments in Pound 1959: III, 728-732. See also Campbell 1874: III, 275-276, on the mode of development of commercial law in the time of Lord Mansfield, a process comparable to the establishment of customary law.
4.   *Hughes v Davies* (1909) Renner 550.
5.   See e.g.: *Fiaklu v Adjiani* [1972] 2 G.L.R. 209: 212; *In re armah: Awotwi v Abadoo* [1975] 1 G.L.R. 374: 378; *Foli v Agya-Atta* [1976] 1 G.L.R. 194: 201; *Amissah-Abadoo v Daniels* [1979] G.L.R. 509.
6.   On legal as compared with historical sources, see Allen 1964: 1, 269; Fitzgerald 1966: 109-112. It is accepted that the dichotomy is not complete, in that courts may feel some degree of compulsion to accept the norms contained in historical sources.
7.   Cf. Hannigan 1958: 112-113, commenting on Allott 1957: 259, where a distinction was drawn between customs and habits which are admittedly judicially recognised as fact, and customary law, which is judicially recognised only as law. The distinction is particularly difficult to apply to rebuttable presumptions, which are based on observations of what is typical in fact, but are themselves legal norms. Thus Hannigan (1958: 102) refers to the "custom" that among the Akan land is held generally by the family, which at that time was also a legal presumption. The West African courts have not drawn a clear dividing line between the types of facts "noticed", although there is obviously a distinction between the effects of noticing them. In the present discussion I am concerned with the possibility of distinguishing between the types of facts noticed. The distinction is that drawn by anthropologists between law and other social facts. It is doubtful whether they have been successful. The work of Gluckman (1965) suggests

that the various types of facts on which judges draw for their decisions may not be clearly distinct.

8.   There is considerable discussion in the literature of the advantages and disadvantages, and reasons for the continuance of the case-law system in general. See e.g. Dias 1976: 170-176.

9.   Especially in his voluminous judgment in *Kokomlemle Consolidated Cases*, reported in abridged form (1951) D.C. (Land) '48-'51, 301. His Findings as Stool Lands Boundaries Settlement Commissioner, published in the *Gazette* in the 1950s are also noteworthy.

10.   See e.g.: *Thompson* v *Mensah* (1957) 3 W.A.L.R. 240; *Yaotey* v *Quaye* [1961] 2 G.L.R. 573; *Total Oil Products* v *Obeng* [1962] 1 G.L.R. 228.

11.   *Kotei* v *Asere Stool* [1961] G.L.R. 492, the court noting that it had "been referred to a series of decisions in the Land Court [i.e., the Lands Division of the High Court, to which Ollennu had frequently been assigned] in recent years, affirmed on occasions by the Court of Appeal".

12.   He never encountered cases which raised directly, and so enabled him to lay down clear decisions on, certain controversial points on which he had strong opinions. His extra-judicial writings provide more orderly surveys of the law, and discuss these questions, e.g. 1962: 53-54; 1971: 137-139. The difficulty was mitigated, but not solved, by the fact that, being assigned (as Jackson before him) to sit in the Lands Division, he heard disproportionately large numbers of customary-law issues.

13.   See e.g.: *Wutoh* v *Gyebi* (1959) C.L.L.G. 193; but cf. his judgment in *Krabah* v *Krakue* [1963] 2 G.L.R. 122.

14.   See Blackstone 1765-1769: I, 74-75; Pollock and Maitland 1968: 166, 183-184, 224-225; Holdworth 1923-1956: III, 654-656; Allen 1964: 126-129; Milsom 1969: x, on the process whereby "customs ... turn into reasoned law".

15.   See: Holdsworth 1923-1956: XII, 524-526; Fifoot 1936: 86-88, 104-115.

16.   *Biei* v *Akomea* (1956) 1 W.A.L.R. 174, 176.

17.   Ehrlich 1936, writing on German law, draws a similar distiction between "living law" and "positive law". Allott 1970: 278; 1977: 11, on African law, followed by Kludze 1972; 1973, on Ghanaian law, distinguished between "popular" or "practised customary law" and "judicial customary law".

18.   *Manu* v *Kuma* [1963] 1 G.L.R. 464. The decision was in favour of the children. But even had it been against them it would have established a lawyers' customary law where there was no corresponding sociologists' customary law. On this example, see further Woodman 1975:29. For other examples, see Woodman 1977: 119-120, 135.

19.   See e.g.: Kodilinye 1982: Chap. 8 (where many of the cases cited were disputes over customary-law titles to land).

20.   On slander, see e.g. *Attiase* v *Abobbtey* (1969) C.C. 149, discussed Date-Bah 1970. On adultery, see e.g. *Billa* v *Salifu* [1971] 2 G.L.R. 87, discussed Date-Bah 1972. See generally on the issue Woodman 1975: 4, 20; 1977: 134-135.

21.   Cf. Stone 1981: 228-233, referring to Pound 1959: II, 104-133. But for the present purpose Dworkin's distinction is adequate and convenient.

22.   A discussion of a possible institutionalization of sociologists' customary law (in this case, constitutional law) into state law, considering in particular its practicability and desirability, is contained in Goldschmidt 1981. Generally this fully recognises the impossibility of direct incorporation, although occasionally that terminology is used, e.g. 197, 202.

23.   It is not appropriate here to survey the considerable literature which might be used to show similar tendencies elsewhere. But it is noteworthy that Gluckman suggested the widespread appearance of one aspect of the development discussed above: "It may be that whenever courts become established, they will tend to enforce customs, breaches of which in themselves did not provoke in the past a forceful reaction", Gluckman 1961-62: 446.

24.   Cf. Dworkin's "right answer thesis" (Dworkin 1977a: Chap. 4; 1977b).

25.   This was the type of court which he studied in his fieldwork among the Tiv: Bohannan 1957.
26.   The term "custom", which normally includes many facts in addition to norms, is not appropriate for these writers' purpose (cf. above note (7)), unless the reader is careful to note its special meaning. Cf. Dworkin 1977a: 29-30. The same failure to distinguish between norm and fact in the case of custom appears in Hart 1961: 230.

REFERENCES

Adinkrah, Kofi O.
1980   'Ghana's Marriage Ordinance: an inquiry into a legal transplant for social change', *African Law Studies* 18:1-42.
Allen, Carlton K.
1964   *Law in the Making* (7th ed.), Oxford: Clarendon Press.
Allott, Antony N.
1957   'The judicial ascertainment of customary law in British Africa', *Modern Law Review* 20:244-263.
1960   *Essays in African Law*, London: Butterworths.
1968-73   'Introduction', in *Restatement of African Law*, London: Sweet & Maxwell.
1970   *New Essays in African Law*, London: Butterworths.
1977   'The people as law-makers: custom, practice and public opinion as sources of law in Africa and England', *Journal of African Law* 21:1-23.
Bennion, Francis A.R.
1962   *The Constitutional Law of Ghana*, London: Butterworths.
Bentsi-Enchill, Kwamena
1972   'Intestate succession revisited I', *University of Ghana Law Journal* 9:123-134.
Blackstone, William
1765-1769   *Commentaries on the Laws of England*, Oxford: Clarendon Press.
Bohannan, Paul
1957   *Justice and Judgment Among the Tiv*, London: International African Institute.
1965   'The differing realms of the law', *American Anthropologist* 67 (6, Part 2, Special Publication): 33-42; and in P. Bohannan (ed.), *Law and Warfare* (1967), pp. 43-56.
1968   'Law: Law and Legal Institutions', in: L. Sills (ed.), *International Encyclopeadia of the Social Sciences* 9, pp. 72-78.
Campbell, John
1874   *Lives of the Chief Justices of England* (3rd ed), London: John Murray.
Christie, George C.
1968   'The model of principles', *Duke Law Journal* 649-669.
Date-Bah, S.K.
1970   'A restatement of the application of the customary law of slander', *Review of Ghana Law* 2:150-152.
1972   'The rights of cuckolds in Dagomba customary law', *Review of Ghana Law* 4:221-226.
Diamond, Stanley
1971   'Law and custom', *Social Research* 38:42-72.
Dias, R.W.M.
1976   *Jurisprudence* (4th ed.), London: Butterworths.

Dworkin, Ronald
  1977a   *Taking Rights Seriously*, London: Duckworth.
  1977b   'No right answer?', in: P.M.S. Hacker and J. Raz (eds.), *Law, Morality and Society*, Oxford: Clarendon Press.
Ehrlich, E.
  1936   *Fundamental Principles of the Sociology of Law* (trans. Moll), Cambridge: Harvard University Press.
Fifoot, C.H.S.
  1936   *Lord Mansfield*, Oxford: Oxford University Press.
Fitzgerald
  1966   *Salmond on Jurisprudence* (12th ed.), London: Sweet & Maxwell.
Fortes, Meyer
  1940   'The political system of the Tallensi of the Northern Territories of the Gold Coast', in: M. Fortes and E.E. Evans-Pritchard (eds.), *African Political Systems* Oxford: Oxford University Press, pp. 239-271.
Gluckman, Max
  1961-62   'African jurisprudence', *Advancement of Science* 18:439-454.
  1965   *The Ideas in Barotse Jurisprudence*, New Haven: Yale University Press.
Goldschmidt, Jenny E.
  1981   *National and Indigenous Constitutional Law in Ghana*, Doctoral Dissertation, University of Leiden.
Griffiths, John
  1977   'E.A.B. van Rouveroy van Nieuwaal, A la Recherche de la Justice', *African Law Studies* 15:100-117.
Hannigan, A. St. J.J.
  1958   'Native law, its similarity to English conventional custom, and its mode of proof', *Journal of African Law* 2:101-115.
Hart, H.L.A.
  1963   *The Concept of Law*, Oxford: Clarendon Press.
Holdsworth, William S.
  1923-1956   *A History of English Law*, London: Methuen.
Kludze, A.K.P.
  1972   'Problems of intestate succession in Ghana', *University of Ghana Law Journal* 9:89-122.
  1973   *Ewe Law of Property*, London: Sweet & Maxwell.
Kodilinye, Gilbert
  1982   *The Nigerian Law of Torts*, London: Sweet & Maxwell.
Milsom, S.F.C.
  1969   *Historical Foundations of the Common Law*, London: Butterworths.
Nadel, S.F.
  1942   *A Black Byzantium*, Oxford: Oxford University Press.
Ollennu, Nii A.
  1962   *Principles of Customary Land Law in Ghana*, London: Sweet & Maxwell.
  1966a   *The Law of Testate and Intestate Succession in Ghana*, London: Sweet & Maxwell.
  1966b   'Judicial precedent in Ghana', *University of Ghana Law Journal* 3:139-164.
  1971   'The changing law and law reform in Ghana', *Journal of African Law* 15:132-181.
Pollock, Frederick and Frederick W. Maitland
  1968   *The History of English Law* (3rd ed., ed. Milson), Cambridge: Cambridge University Press.
Pound, Roscoe
  1959   *Jurisprudence*, St Paul, Minnesota: West Publishing.

Rattray, R.S.
1929   *Ashanti Law and Constitution*, London: Oxford University Press.
Raz, Joseph
1972   'Legal principles and the limits of law', *Yale Law Journal* 81:823-854.
Sarbah, John M.
1897   *Fanti Customary Laws*, London: Methuen.
Seidman, Robert B.
1978   *The State, Law and Development*, London: Croom Helm.
Snyder, Francis G.
1980   'Law and development in the light of dependency theory', *Law and Society Review* 14:723.
Stone, Julius
1981   'From principles to principles', *Law Quarterly Review* 97:224-253.
Tait, David
1958   'The territorial pattern and lineage system of Konkomba', in: John Middleton and David Tait (eds.), *Tribes Without Rulers*, London: Routledge and Kegan Paul, pp. 167-202.
Woodman, Gordon R.
1969   'Some realism about customary law - the West African experience', *Wisconsin Law Review* 128-152.
1975   'The family as a corporation in Ghanaian and Nigerian law', *African Law Studies* 11:1-35.
1977   'Judicial development of customary law: the case of marriage law in Ghana and Nigeria', *University of Ghana Law Journal* 14:115-136.

Part III
Competition between state and unofficial law

Introduction

Peter Fitzpatrick

COMMENTS ON THE PAPERS

The papers divide most sharply between a concern with the difference and hostility between the two types of legal order and a concern with their companionable fusion. The former concern tends to the upholding of unofficial law; the latter tends to the perspective of the state.

The oppositional concern is strongest in Baxi's graphic, rich and moving account of a particular legal case and its ramifications for a popular grouping of people from "tribal communities" in Gujarat with their people's court, the *Lok Adalat*. It is a case not just of issues affecting its immediate parties and those closely related to them but it is also something of considerable historical significance, particularly if one values popular history. In moral, political and effectual terms, Baxi finds the unofficial legal order to be comprehensively superior, in contrast to the state-favouring stance at least implicit in most work on legal plurality in the third world. Indeed Baxi shows state legal procedures here to be utterly decadent and quite subordinated to political manipulation - in particular, manipulation aimed at inhibiting or perhaps destroying the popular grouping which is seen by those in the official sphere as a threat to them. In the struggle he recounts, state law becomes vividly, almost transparently a locus for particularist assertions of power. Indeed the whole idea of state law is brought into the fray and used as a weapon of particularist political struggle. In dramatic contrast, the popular grouping itself tends to be presented in terms of pristine integrity. The Lok Adalat is also presented in terms that are surely ideal, even though doubtless reflecting a significant reality. But what is particularly illuminating about Baxi's conflictual approach is that the Lok Adalat becomes a site for "intensified social solidarity" in people's struggles against state-centered oppressions and in this it performs functions ranging well beyond dispute settlement such as checking on state action and providing assistance in the assertion of legal rights. This involves promoting "access to beneficent aspects of state law and administration". How the "beneficent" can be operatively separated and how it can be pursued without a compromising containment in the state system are questions that Baxi does not raise.

The oppositional strand is central if not as vivid in Schott's paper. Informing the whole of his account is the belief that traditional views are operatively more "just" than much state law and hence they should not be ignored or suppressed. He instances a neo-traditional authority of chiefs which persisted in the face of post-colonial prohibition on their continuing to act in this way; the modernizing alternatives provided by Nkrumah *e tutti quanti* were not found popularly acceptable or effective, it seems.

Thus far the oppositional strand has been frankly evaluative. It sees unofficial law as a site of justice or of popular political expression, usually in sharp opposition to state law. There is also a coolly analytical element in the oppositional strand in Griffiths' innovative and elegant analysis of competition between dispute-settling bodies, entailing a mix of organizational effects and of conditions necessary for the persistence of a competing plurality of dispute-settling bodies, some of which could be state-run. In exploring these conditions, Griffiths' paper is the only one that directly confronts the explanation of legal pluralism.

As Griffiths shows, competition between legal orders imports elements of convergence. Other papers take this theme further to the point where there is some operative fusion of legal orders; specifically, to the point where unofficial law lodges in the belly of the state. Chiba provides the most comprehensive account. His fascinating analysis operates on two levels. First, the paper is informed in the perspective that unofficial and official law must be understood as interactive phenomena; that is, each in significant ways takes meaning from the other. Second, and quantitatively the main concern of his paper, he describes various channels, various mechanisms, through which, in Japan, this interaction is effected. Examples are the qualified recognition of custom and customary law in the Civil Code and the implicit incorporation of these things through general clauses adopting "public policy or good morals". What seems especially significant here is that unofficial law, when incorporated through these channels, is not to be understood as something peripherally and occasionally used for the purpose of official law. Rather, unofficial law and its underlying "values" and "postulates" enter into the operative constitution of state law itself. That is, distinctive and basic elements of state law depend on unofficial law and its underlying "values" and "postulates".

To return to Schott's paper, in its revealing blend of acute emic perspectives and the accommodation of forces introduced with colonization it takes account of legal traditions originating in Africa and in Europe which, in modes of interaction and mutual shaping, resulted in distinct legal forms and processes. Thus, the chiefs' authority which I mentioned earlier involved the promotion by the colonist of chiefs - ostensibly a traditional mode - as dispute settlers in instances where, in pre-colonial times, neither the chiefs nor any mode could assuredly have handled the dispute.

Finally, von Benda-Beckmann's paper provides a particular and a sophisticated application of the theme of fusion. He brings out the significance of the precise location where jurisdictional boundaries are drawn between state law and unofficial law. More specifically, and referring to Abel's work in Kenya and his own in West Sumatra, he finds that state dispute-settling bodies are markedly more effective if they, as it were, take over "the top level of the former indigenous system" than if they are based on modern court systems. There is a close and compact working of the data for each of the instances he considers and it amounts in all to a formidable argument.

DISCUSSION

The main focus of discussion was the distinction between official and unofficial law. There was some, but very little, concern with how the distinction could be drawn. The prime questions were whether the distinction was significant or whether it was operatively maintainable at all. Some saw official law as but a small part of a totality comprising official and unofficial orders, with the official being utterly dependent on and subordinate to the unofficial. Official law was left with only a peripheral distinctness and with no area of necessary dominance. Without going this far, others were concerned at least to prick the pretentions of official law by instancing how it relies considerably on unofficial inputs effected through varieties of lay participation and through working concepts that integrate unofficial values and rationalities into the "official" process.

A somewhat opposed line of argument challenged the reliance on a certain integrity of such legal spheres as the "traditional". Does it make any sense now to talk of traditional law or traditional dispute settlement given the extent of official or state penetration? The practical, if implicit, line of division here was between a concern with the setting of the First World and a concern with the setting of the Third. For the First World, people were concerned to cut state law down to size, as it were, and in this they adopted an ultra-pluralist position. Several people took a more unitary view in the Third World setting, seeing much so-called traditional or customary law as but a manifestation of state action. Such baiting of the anthropologists was countered with the argument that, where traditional law is organizationally re-channelled or even displaced, traditional values have an operative persistence. "Traditional" here, it was often stressed, should not be seen as something static but as a dynamic, even burgeoning element capable of absorbing and even subordinating aspects of the official. It was, as well, suggested that categories such as "traditional" and "indigenous" are too reified and had to be "unpacked" to get at the realities of law's operation in the Third World.

Understandably, these wide-ranging issues were illuminated rather than resolved. An attempt at resolution would require an exploration of the conditions necessary for the constitution, operation and varied interaction of different types of law. The discussion did not follow such a potentially divisive course. However, the issue of criteria for judging different legal orders in moral and political terms was raised. This was not pursued either. But this issue did provoke a brief exchange on the salience of modes of dispute settlement in effecting social change. On the one hand, it was felt that here dispute settlement was peripheral and that it made more strategic sense to concentrate on effecting change in such areas as production, housing, health and education. On the other hand, it was argued that for a group to take over a mode of dispute settlement had great symbolical value and served to inform and legitimate wider struggles for change, as Baxi's paper instanced.

A more extensive, if fitful debate was also left inconclusive in the absence of agreed conditions for the constitution and operation of law. Many people asserted that state law had an autonomous and strong effectiveness in marking and maintaining the jurisdiction of courts and these assertions had strong links with the argument of von Benda-Beckmann's paper. The contrary argument, which was illustrated in the use of fictions by judges, had it that such state law would be re-shaped or undermined in response to contrary social change.

Several people argued that it is not sufficient or correct to adopt an institutional perpective on dispute settlement; they advocated a "consumer perspective". It was said that this approach would reveal how people used and manipulated institutions of dispute settlement. The institutionalist response was to absorb this position by according it an unexceptional validity in illustrating a dynamic of the institutional perspective. Griffith's institutional "law of inside washing of dirty linen", for example, was bolstered by the observation that "consumers", in a strategic forcing of their claims within the group, would threaten to take disputes to an outside forum.

Popular justice, participatory development and power politics: *The Lok Adalat* in turmoil[1]

Upendra Baxi

I

On July 5, 1978, a historic event occurred in Bhakha, near Naswadi in Baroda district of Gujarat. At a mass meeting thousands of *adivasis* (tribals) and villagers subscribed by acclamation to a resolution which, in part, read:

> "It is our democratic right to operate the *Lok Adalat*. All kinds of questions and problems concerning us arise. It is the foundation of people's government for us to have the power to deal with them and solve them. We shall brook no interference in the matter. We do not interfere with the social organization or the 'lifestyle' of the 'advanced' classes. Similarly, they should not interfere with our social organization which has traditions going back to many centuries. We shall not tolerate any interference".

Two days later, a much bigger mass meeting at Dhanpuri village also solemnly reiterated this right to self-determination.

The event is historic because it is for the first time in Independent India that a group of historically and contemporaneously disadvantaged and depressed people assembled together to assert their "democratic right" to preserve and protect their own system of adjudication and self-government. Significantly, they did this in the title of democracy in terms of "people's government" whose prime function it is to preserve the autonomy of group life, its legal culture and traditions. The claim for self-determination was also supported by a plea for equality. They asserted that they did not presume to interfere in the manner in which the higher strata of Indian society dealt with its disputes and conflicts through a legal system of their making and choice. They demanded reciprocity: an equal respect for their autonomy to maintain a legal system of their own choice and making, without any interference. They went further to serve notice on the "other side": the institutions of the formal policy, administration and adjudication. The message was clear and simple: "We shall not tolerate any interference with our social organization".

What made this miracle possible? For, it is nothing short of a miracle for thousands of illiterate, poor, and depressed people to assert such a unique right. The answer generally lies in their commitment to the survival of the institution known as *Lok Adalat* (People's Court) which has been functioning in and around Rangpur for well over the last quarter century under the leadership of a stalwart Sarvodaya worker, Harivallabh Parekh (popularly known as Bhai) who is India's foremost practising Ghandhian.

The *Lok Adalat* is primarily a community dispute institution, covering roughly about one thousand villages, which has settled a very large number of diverse disputes among people with their own participation. It is difficult to ascertain the exact number of disputes handled by the Lok Adalat owing to the lack of an adequate record; but the available record places them in the range of 20,000 to 25,000.

The *Lok Adalat* is only an aspect of a large-scale effort at the mobilization of rural poor for the task of socio-economic development of the region. The *Lok Adalat* is as much a forum for processing disputes and conflicts as it is for generating people's participation, and self reliance, in non-governmental processes of social and economic development. This latter includes agrarian reforms through *Gramdan* and *Bhoodan*, the organization of credit cooperatives, minor irrigation work, adult literacy and formal education, farm mechanization, and animal husbandry programmes among others. The base of all activities is the *Ashram* at Rangpur, the most notable of whose achievements is the elimination of exploitative patterns of revenue and forest administration inherited from the British, and a constant struggle, continuing even now, to protect the people against the tyrannies of the law enforcement officials and *sahukars*. Naturally, the *Ashram* has become through this process a significant political force in the state of Gujarat; and many victories at the polls have depended on patronage and support by the *Ashram* and its leadership. In many ways, the Rangpur *Ashram* has become over time the centre of government of about 1000 villages in this area. This has happened, over a period of a quarter century, under the indefatigable and charismatic leadership of Bhai, which has attracted the support of many voluntary, non-governmental agencies throughout the world. (See, for a detailed analysis of some of these aspects, Baxi 1976: 53; Avadh Prasad 1977).

No doubt in the course of its evolution the Rangpur *Ashram* has confronted many clusters of dominant structures of power in the region and the state. But it had not faced so far a crisis of the magnitude which brought forth this anguished but resilient declaration of self-determination. Never before in its history had the leader of the *Ashram* (who is regarded by many people as their saviour) been charged with a serious criminal offence. Never before had he been arrested by the police. Never before were any moves made to restrict his travel overseas by an attempt at impounding his passport on the ground that a criminal prosecution was pending against him. Never before in the history of the region had the state and law retaliated so massively against this centre of parallel government. Thousands of people who pledged themselves to the declaration were struggling to keep alive an institution which had done so much for them against a state which had betrayed them for so long.

The cause of confrontation lay in the death of an eighteen-year-old girl named Gharki. Gharki was found dead in the fields of Vankala village on the morning of 13 April 1978. In her death lay the genesis of the crises which engulfed the people of the *Lok Adalat*. The crises continue. Let us follow a little closely the tragic story of Gharki in her life and upon her death.

II

Gharki was married to Bijala Suria in the neighbouring village of Palahdi. But within 15 days of her marriage, she was turned out by her in-laws. On payment of compensation (in accordance with custom in matrimonial matters) Gharki was "divorced" from Bijala. Gharki developed intimacy with a young man, Mohansingh Palia (hereafter called MP) who happened to be her close relative and neighbour. Their friendship was well known in the village and it was even suggested that she was 5 months pregnant at the time of her death. Gharki went out on the evening of 12 April 1978, ostensibly to attend a religious programme of devotional songs (*bhajans*). She went out at 8 p.m. with her father's consent; her father asked her on her return to pick *mahuva* flowers from the tree in the field. That is where she was found dead the following morning. In consultation with relatives and elders in the village, Gharki was cremated according to customary rites the same day. The relevant village official (*talati*) was notified of Gharki's death which was entered in the register of deaths. The cause of her death was given as epilepsy (*fefru*), a disease from which she was said to have been suffering for a long time. The police made a routine investigation and apparently closed the matter around 4 May 1978 as a case of accidental death. There the matter should have ordinarily ended. But it does not, at any rate in India's villages. Gharki's father Sobhan was in trouble, both with the father of MP and the police. The boy's father, worried about allegations of MP's involvement with the girl and possible involvement in her death, insisted that Sobhan make some amends to him by cash compensation. He apparently needed some money to pay to the police who allegedly threatened him with a murder case against his son, despite the case having been already formally closed. The police, Sobhan was to allege, had already collected a sum of 300 rupees, presumably in return for not proceeding further in the matter.

The twofold pressures on Sobhan seem to have continued; demands for more money made him desperate. Where was a father, just bereaved, to turn? About three weeks after Gharki's death, the harassed Sobhan decided to bring the matter to the *Lok Adalat*. On 4 June he complained to Bhai that he was harrassed by the police *patel* (village police functionary) in his own village as well as by the *fozdar* (a police official) of Naswadi. The complaint was processed in the usual manner and notices to all parties, including the police, were sent. The matter was heard at the sitting of the *Lok Adalat* (with about 200 people present and participating) on 10 June, 1978. A police *patel* from Wankla, present with his "village", said at the meeting that "Naswadi *fozdar* recovered Rs. 3000/- from the father of the boy and Rs. 300/- from the father of the girl in lieu of suppressing the matter" by filing a report of death due to accident. It was also mentioned in the proceedings that Sobhan and some others were locked up and beaten soon after the complaint was filed with the *Lok Adalat*. Sobhan was to later elaborate this charge in newspaper interviews. For example, he is reported to have said to *Sandesh* (6 July 1978) that he was threatened with imprisonment; and that he was "picked up by the police and kept in detention for 48 hours, given food only once and was dropped back to his place by a milk van". He was also asked for an additional sum of Rs. 300/- on pain of further detention.

Apparently, the corruption and torture aspects, so common to people's life in the region, were left to be dealt with by Bhai by the people. They knew that Bhai was fearless in his exposés. On 14 June, Bhai wrote to the Naswadi *fozdar* asking him to see him at once; on the same day he also sent a message to the Wankala *patel* to come to Rangpur on 20 June and to help him "together to find a path of peace". Should he not do so, Bhai warned, "it will be clear that you are reversing a unanimous decision of *panchas* before the presence of your village" which would bring him discredit. Bhai further said, quoting a Gujarati saying, that it would be unjust (if the charges of corruption were true) to allow a state of affairs where "the thief punishes the custodians of law and order" (*Chor Kotwal ne dande*). There was a charming irony in the use of this phrase: for the reference here was to the thief (corrupt officials) punishing people (custodians of the law).

The addressee of this communication had apparently sound second thoughts; he did not respond. Bhai also wrote letters to the Deputy Superintendent of Police but to no avail.

Instead, on 18 June 1978, about nine weeks after the event, the First Information Report was filed stating that Gharki was in fact murdered by her paramour; that her body bore marks of multiple wounds; and that Sobhan and others were accessories after the fact. They were also charged with destruction of evidence (the body and blood-stained clothes). Bhai was also charged separately as accessory after the fact on the allegation that he had concealed the information about murder of Gharki brought to him on the *Lok Adalat* sitting on 10 June.

At that sitting, in addition to the corruption issue, the entire case of Gharki appears to have been discussed. The boy MP made some statements concerning his relationship with Gharki, his grief at her death and a possible altercation with her on that fateful night. But he insisted that he had not murdered her; nor did he intend to. He expressed his sorrow that all this should ever have happened. Since it was felt by the people assembled at the Court that some compensation was due to Gharki's father Sobhan for the boy having maintained illicit relations with her, the *panchas* (selected adjudicators from both sides) initially awarded a compensation of Rs. 10,000. The assembly, the affected parties and Bhai all felt that the amount was excessive. Interestingly, the *panchas* explained the high award by reference to the state law; they said that when a girl in their village was run over by a speeding truck, the compensation awarded by the state tribunal was in the range of 13,000/- rupees. They pointed out that the fatally injured girl was only 13 years and unmarried. Gharki was eighteen years when she died and was pregnant. Even so they felt that, under the circumstances of the case, the award they had proposed was appropriate and met the ends of justice. After much discussion in which MP's father pointed out that he had already paid a large sum to the police - Rs. 3000 - Bhai's suggestion that half the proposed amount be accepted as compensation by the *Lok Adalat* as reasonable was also found to be unacceptable. The question of compensation (*valtar*) was then deferred; the *more* important point was that there should be no vendetta and peace must be restored in the affected communities. It was generally felt that, if there was further strife on this issue in the village, the major beneficiaries would be the agents of the state legal system and not the people, who might find themselves in an even worse situation. Two *karar-khats* (literally, deeds embodying consensual agreement) were agreed upon. One *karar-khat* was signed by MP beseeching forgiveness of the people for what had happened and accepting moral responsibility for the events. Another *karar-khat* was signed by leaders of Vankala village, and others, assuring that no further events disturbing peace of the village, centred on the present incident, would take place. Contrary to the usual practice, the *karar- khats* were not signed at the conclusion of the hearing since the *Lok Adalat* meeting continued till late in the evening.

It was on this basis that Bhai's complicity in murder was alleged! Bhai was requested to go to Kavant police station on 24 June, where he was placed under arrest. He was asked to sign a personal bond which he refused to do until late afternoon. The news of Bhai's arrest spread like wildfire and vast crowds assembled outside the police station in peaceful protest. Special contingents of reserved police were summoned to deal with any contingencies. Parleys continued by phone with the police chief in Baroda and many friends and advisors of Bhai, including political leaders of the Congress (I) party. He was reluctant to sign a personal bond but was advised by the latter to do so, on the ground that the government in daring to arrest him had begun a war of attrition where his presence was needed outside the jail. Reluctantly, he signed the bond.

There was incomprehension as well as anger among the followers and people in the area. For many the very arrest of Bhai was an indication that the "oppressors" would stop short of nothing; to many others it was simply a sacrilege, and the cause for which he was arrested was equally outrageous for them: how could an orderly, expeditious, just and participative outcome in *Lok Adalat* proceedings ever be "illegal"? What was wrong, they asked, in what had been decided by collective wisdom? Above all, the most incomprehensible thing to them was the fact that, instead of the corrupt officials being brought to book, their own leader, who had helped them expose the injustice of the system, should have been arrested.

Something had to be done. The young *adivasis*, who had been born and brought up in the new consciousness of right and justice in the *Ashram* schools and workplaces, were restive; and they were beginning to question the peaceful direct action method of Bhai. Violence of any kind by his supporters was just what his opponents wanted. A true Gandhian, he decided to hold mass rallies of public protest. In the past such direct action tactics had paid dividends, even in matters involving corrupt and rapacious police and revenue officers. Two large mass rallies were planned for a week later; energies were diverted in spreading the information, from village to village, concerning the schedule and venue of the meetings: one was to be held in Naswadi, and the other in the district town of Chottaudepur.

The Government reacted promptly. A day before the first rally the carrying of arms or "lethal" weapons was prohibited by an order lasting for about a week. Prohibitory orders banning congregations of five or more people were issued, causing massive difficulties for the organizers. The venues had to be shifted 12 to 16 miles from the originally announced venues in a great hurry; yet the turnout was massive. Equally massive was the turnout of the police. According to a press report, on 5 July 1978, the day of the first rally, there were 1000 special police, 1000 ordinary police, 45 sub-inspectors, 4 deputy superintendents, 2 superintendents and one inspector general of police retained for those two events (*Jai Hind*: "Police Raj in Naswadi", 5 July 1978). In addition, civilian forces (*gram rakskas*) were also deployed in large numbers. There were reports of summary arrests and irksome diversions of people who had wanted to join the rallies.

The rallies took place with discipline and peace. The authorities had no cause for complaint, except for the fact that they were held at all and they went off so peacefully! Alternatively, they could always take the credit for elaborate *bandobast* (arrangements) which prevented the otherwise imminent violence. But the law was still to be used if possible against the movement.

And yet, on all accounts, the turnout was massive and even spectacular. It was in these circumstances that the declaration of democratic right to popular adjudication was resoundingly made. Gharki, through her death, had made history.

III

The death of Gharki, and the involvement of the *Lok Adalat* and its leader in
criminal proceedings, provided ample scope for the political opponents of
Bhai to denigrate and if possible destroy him and his work among the
adivasis. The attack was led by local political leaders. It took three forms.
First, there was an attack on the system of popular justice through the *Lok
Adalat* itself. Secondly, there was criticism of the Rangpur *Ashram* as catering
only to the interests of a few and not of the whole *adivasi* population. The
third form of attack was on the direct involvement of the Congress (I) with
the *Ashram* activities.

The first line of attack was made explicit in a statement by Manohar
Acharaya, leader of Janata Party (Baroda, East) who asserted that *the
constitution of India and the law of the land were brought into ridicule and
contempt by the Lok Adalat*. The *Lok Adalat* eroded people's confidence in
the national legal order. The "cruel denigration" of the legal system, he
urged, must be stopped henceforth. He demanded a full-scale enquiry into
the functioning of the *Lok Adalat* by the national Central Bureau of Investigation (*Sandesh*: 7 July 1978). This view was shared by many Janata Party
people in Baroda district; indeed, according to my information, a delegation
of Janata workers met the Gujarat Chief Minister to press for such an
enquiry and ensure that criminal prosecutions would be launched expedi-
tiously against Bhai. The statement of the Chief Minister was that "proper
action will be taken against Bhai upon an enquiry" (*Vadodara Samachar*: 26
June 1978). One result of political pressures was the launching of an investigation on 18 June, nearly seven weeks after the death of Gharki; it is certain
that the police at Baroda were constrained to lodge a prosecution despite
highly improbable prospects of success. The arrest of Bhai too must have had
the concurrence of the government at Gandhinager (the capital of Gujarat).
Nor would the elaborate security arrangements at the rallies have been
possible without the very active support of the party headquaters and the
government. If the rallies had not proved so overwhelmingly successful, an
enquiry of some kind would most probably have been launched into the
working of the *Lok Adalat*, as urged by Acharya.

The second type of criticism, heard probably for the first time in the
region, was that the *Ashram*'s activities resulted in an exploitation of *adivasis*
in the region. Gharki's death was somehow linked with the theme of organized exploitation of the people in the region. The *Lok Adalat* was itself
identified as a means of exploitation. No further details were given in support
of this fantastic charge; we call it "fantastic" because, whatever may be said
about *Lok Adalat*'s shortcomings (see Baxi 1976: 53) calling it a "means of
exploitation" of *adivasis* flies in the face of known realities. Many opponents
of the *Lok Adalat* attempted to demonstrate their thesis that only a few

adivasis were beneficiaries of the *Ashram* activities, who in turn dominated and exploited the masses, by issuing a call to hold counter rallies, and to boycott the rallies convened by the *Ashrama* (see *Loksatta*: 21 June 1978). Their contention was disproved by events. Their appeal for boycotting of rallies by the "exploited" *adivasis* failed spectacularly. Nor were they able to organize a rally opposed to the *Ashram*'s. Even the Chairman of the Naswadi unit of Janata Party, the very area in which the first rally was held, was unsuccessful in organizing a rival rally. Anti-*Lok Adalat* public opinion was hard to foster in the area, even in the wake of the tragic and dramatic turn of events surrounding and following the death of Gharki.

The third form of political attack was at the level of party politics. It was alleged that the Congress (I) was consolidating its position in the region by supporting the *Ashram* activities; and that this itself showed that something must be really wrong with all the activities, including *Lok Adalat*, of the *Ashram*. The first part of this allegation was most certainly true. Although Bhai himself scrupulousy refrained from a call to support Congress (I) at the mass rallies, or any other political grouping, he shared platforms at both the rallies with the stalwarts of Congress (I) including Jinabhai and Sanat Mehta. Many ex-ministers and ex-*sarpanchas* (heads of village *panchayat*) and important holders of positions in the party hierarchy, including the ex-Chief Minister Madhavasingh Solanki, were prominently associated with the rallies. These Congress (I) leaders who spoke at the rallies made sharp political attacks on the Janata Party at the Centre and in the State, laced with rhetoric concerning the uplift of the downtrodden and expoited masses.

Bhai himself did not join these attacks. He only mentioned the fact that many legislative measures were "stayed" in their implementation in Gujarat. He made much of the non-implementation of the Gujarat Debt Relief Act, 1976. He quoted the views of the Janata Party president, Chandrashekhar, that the legislation affecting the poor had been weakened in implementation. He exhorted people to understand the simple fact that "unless we generate and harness *Lokshakti* (People's power) ... there is no salvation for the poor and the exploited people".

But Congress (I)'s presence and participation in the events following the death of Gharki were massively conspicuous. This more than anything else caused genuine apprehension in the minds of the Janata Party people. The *panchayati raj* institutions elections were imminent in Gujarat; and the elections to the state legislative assembly were scheduled for early 1980. Experience indicated that they might be advanced to late 1979. This theme was explicit, for example, in the speech of Congress (I) leader Shri Sanat Mehta, an ex-minister in the government, when he said that if the party in power wanted, through political attacks against the *Ashram*, "to annihilate out of existence, the poor people, we will defeat them by vote-bullets" in the forthcoming state elections (*Sandesh*: 7 July 1978).

when events disprove it concretely in the future, one would not be surprised at all if some people in the party become critical of Bhai's political role and repeat the very words, and actions, which are now being used by the people to whom they are currently opposed. The Congress (I) politicians are involved not so much because the *Ashram* needs them but rather because they need the *Ashram's* support in regaining political power. Of course, there are people, in all political parties, committed to social changes on the lines advocated and championed by Bhai. But the bulk of the *Ashram's* political supporters are not known or proven votaries of redistributive change just as the bulk of *Ashram* detractors are not committed to it. In 1979, during the heyday of the Janata regime as many as 90% of returned candidates for local selfgovernment from the Rangpur area (in Panchayati institutions) were Congress (I) candidates. This must indicate that support for the *Ashram* activities, and visible association within it, has considerable electoral payoffs.

Independent India has recurrently witnessed this kind of dramatic, and often destructive, tension between social entrepreneurs and professional politicians. Both these groups ultimately manage to retain some amount of power through conflict and accommodation; but the former wields it readily and visibly for the service of the people while the latter group increasingly appears to be involved in the power struggle for its own sake. Sometimes the consequence of protracted conflict between the two groups entails the collapse of a social movement led by the social entrepreneurs without any genuine substitution of worthwhile innovative activity by political parties and governments. The Rangpur *Ashram* is more than ever before caught in this vortex of conflict. The electoral fray is not in any event going to lessen the tensions; the war of attrition that began in 1977 reached its median point in the events attending the death of Gharki; the tensions have yet to reach their nadir. One hopes that the people of the area will not be the ultimate losers.

IV

The trial of MP for the alleged murder of Gharki ended on 31 March, 1979 when the Additional Sessions Judge acquitted him and all his co-accused. The prosecution case was that the accused had murdered Gharki, "confessed" his crime at the *Lok Adalat* on 10 June 1978, and agreed to abide by an alleged "decision" of the *Lok Adalat* to pay a "compensation of Rs. 5000/-" to Sobhan. The case was investigated by the police on the complaint of Sobhan on 18 June 1978 on the orders of the deputy superintendent of police (Dy. S. P.) Baroda. The investigation was completed on 19 August 1978, when the case was filed.

The fact that the orders for investigation emanated from a higher police official is significant as it indicates that the case had acquired a distinct

Interestingly, both the rallies were called under the auspices of the All India *Khet Mazdoor Kishan Parishad* (i.e. All India Farm Labourers' and Farmers' Conference - hereafter KMKP)[2]. This signified the determination to give in form a non-partisan character to the events following the death of Gharki. But in substance the preponderant support of the Congress (I) could not be avoided. This support was manifested not just in political speeches but through concrete action. A deputation of Congress (I) leaders waited on the deputy superintendent of police at Baroda in the wake of Bhai's arrest. They condemned in their statements Bhai's arrest as "political mischief" (*rajkiya kinnakhori*) and as "political tyranny" (*Vadodara Samachar*: 26 June 1978). Harubhat Mehta, a supporter of the Communist Party of India (CPI) and an active Congress (I) worker, himself a practising lawyer, announced in the wake of Bhai's arrest that 101 lawyers of the Gujarat High Court would form a panel of legal assistance for the *Ashram* in the hour of its need (*Sandesh*: 9 July 1978; *Vadodara Samachar*: 10 July 1978). Indeed, Mehta and a group of young lawyers have since been the main source of legal support for Bhai and the *Ashram* during this crisis. They also coordinate, generally, the legal services programme of the *Ashram* both in the region and up to the High Court level at Ahmedabad. It is true that most lawyers thus associated with the *Ashram* owe allegiance to Congress (I). But many lawyers, of different political persuasion, seem also to be involved, as they find in the *Ashram* activities scope for idealism which everyday experience at the Bar unfortunately denies them.[3]

It is natural that the Janata Party workers and leaders see the heavy hand of Congress (I) in whatever the *Ashram* does or tries to do. Some of them find the political situation so desperate, in terms of their prospects, as even to suggest (as noted) that the *Ashram* activities thus organized with the support of the Congress (I) actually result in the exploitation of the *adivasis*. The pressures and tensions of electoral politics are very great, and palpably so, in the region. There is therefore no possibility of any balanced political critique of the *Lok Adalat* and *Ashram* emerging in Gujarat. But it must be said that much of the political evaluation has been substantially influenced by the dominant interests in the region opposing the redistributive thrust of the *Ashram*'s social welfare activities. Politicians have, generally, failed to perceive that legitimation for the *Ashram* emanates not from politicians but from the *people*. The record of the *Ashram's* achievements in all-round development of the region, including popular adjudication, is more tangible and real to the people in the region than the alluring promises and the now not-so seductive rhetoric of politicians.

This failure to understand the politics of the *Ashram* is not distinctive to the ruling party in Gujarat.[4] The Congress (I) too is likely to misdiagnose Bhai's present need for support as a permanent one, leading to a distinctly viable political alliance. In the nature of things, this is a vain assumption; and political complexion. This order for investigation was not accompanied by any similar order for enquiry against police officials who had allegedly taken bribes. This too is significant, as between the 10 June sitting of the *Lok Adalat* and the orders for investigation issued on 18 June, the *Lok Adalat* leader and other people were agitating for a proper enquiry into the matter. Clearly, the use of discretion to investigate and prosecute was partly self- defensive; it was also partly influenced by the overall political contexts in which the Indian police have to function.

What makes this prosecutorial vigour even more interesting is the fact that the Dy. S.P. Baroda had received as early as 4 May 1978 an anonymous report alleging that Gharki had been murdered by certain named people. The report stated that Gharki was five months pregnant when she was killed, that certain named people were aware of the crime and were liable to be prosecuted for having concealed this information from the police. The Court had before it a copy of this document and agreed with counsel for the accused that it should be treated as the first information report and not the report filed as late as 18 June, on which the prosecution was based. The Court has not pursued the question as to why the very first report was not investigated. Nor has it passed any strictures on this default. But the fact that the Court itself acknowledges that no action was taken from 4 May to 18 June, is, objectively, a good enough indictment of the way in which the police work.

The prosecution clearly was an afterthought, compelled by directions from above and the necessity to protect the organization from exposure. Further, there was no evidence on the basis of which it could reasonably be argued that the crime had been probably committed. Gharki was cremated and with her the alleged blood-stained clothes. The only two pieces of evidence offered to make the charge even prima facie plausible were charred bones and an ornament (*kandora*). The charred bones were collected from the crematorium on 7 July 1978, 85 days after the death of Gharki. The Professor of Anatomy at the medical college in Baroda testified that the bones were totally charred, and that it was not even possible for him to say whether they were bones of a man or woman or even of a human being or animal! The other piece of evidence, an ornament, was supposed to have been discovered as a result of the interrogation of the accused; but Sobhan disclaimed that his girl wore the ornament and the judge ruled that in any case it was found in a wide open space, accessible to everyone.

It is thus clear that the principal plank of the prosecution was the alleged "extra-judicial confession" by the accused at the *Lok Adalat*; some of the *panchas* were made co-accused. However, even here the prosecution faced difficulties; it had to seek permission of the Court to cross-examine the bulk of its own witnesses, on the plea that they were "hostile" witnesses. A permission of this kind was asked for, and denied, even as respects the testimony of Bhai who deposed that the accused never made any confession of the crime before him in the *Lok Adalat* and that *panchas* did not, to his memory, adjudicate this issue at all. The two *kararkhats* were drawn up by him much later, relying on his recollection of events at that long sitting and were signed also subsequently and not before the *Lok Adalat*. The Court believed the testimony of Bhai; thus the prosecution lost on all counts. Naturally, no appeal has been preferred against the verdict. This verdict also weakens to the point of its demise the related allegation against Bhai in a separate criminal proceeding, that he concealed information regarding the commission of murder from the police.

Thus although we have learnt many important things from this narration, the finding on the central question as to whether Gharki died a natural or a contrived death (and if the latter, who caused her death) remains indeterminate. It is significant that the death of the young girl, which brought about all these developments, remains still shrouded in mystery. Clearly, the state legal system failed to detect the crime and punish the criminal. But the people's legal system, with participative communitarian justice, failed equally to do so.[5]

However, as compared with the state legal system, the system of popular adjudication did raise and settle the question of moral responsibility for Gharki's death; it did produce a sense of remorse in MP for his wayward behaviour; it also produced pledges to maintain the public peace in the village and for immunity from vendetta. In this last respect, the *Lok Adalat* intensified social solidarity and the collective conscience of the community. At the same time it enabled the people to be collectively self-reliant in their fight against unscrupulous elements and aspects of the law enforcement authorities. None of such types of gain can reasonably be expected from the state legal order.

What is equally significant is that the Lok Adalat's focus was prominently on deviant police behaviour, primarily the alleged extortion of money from the already long suffering *adivasis* (an aspect which did not enter at all in the trial of MP). This transformed a family's bereavement into a manifestation of community solidarity against, as it seemed to them, the perpetual abuse of authority, and thus injustice, by the organs of the state. Bhai's arrest in this very context seemed the acme of the process of the state as a dispenser of *injustice*. The issue was thus transformed to wider dimensions. It was not any more the question of everyday excesses of authority by holders of public power, nor even the specific excess of power in the events surrounding the death of Gharki. The issue now was nothing short of the very survival of the collective organization of the people, and their unique culture, against the predatory aggressions by the external 'system' of power politics. To this issue, the answer of hundreds of people in the area was the battle cry of self-determination reproduced at the beginning of this paper. The battle cry was foreshadowed in the handbills widely distributed to people urging them to attend.

They make interesting reading. They are entitled: "Our *Lokadalat* is Under Attack by Agents of Litigation" (*Apani Lokadalat Uppar Kijiyadao no Humlo*).[6] The leaflets maintain that the present events constitute a frontal attack on "people's democratic right to conduct *Lok Adalat*", which is but a "manifestation of people's power". It explains that just as *swaraj* (freedom, self-rule) means a social order where "people rule themselves", so also it means that "people settle their own questions in their own way". The latter is an activity which sustains (gives life to) the people. It condemns the source of attack on the *Lok Adalat* as *kajiadalals*, and "corrupt officials". A telling Gujarati saying is used: "*chor ni ma ne ajwaloo na game*"; the mother of the thief does not prefer broad daylight. The leaflet exhorts people to participate in the rally despite inclement weather and work in the fields to demonstrate their strength and solidarity and to communicate to officialdom, through a "peaceful and disciplined" protest, that "we are citizens of a free country and that we shall meet with all our might anyone who attacks our rights". The purpose of the rallies, as stated, is to maximize the autonomy of the people and their traditions: "to demonstrate that we shall not allow others to interfere with our social and economic life".

The battle has been won by the people's organization. But the war remains to be won.

V

The Rangpur experience can be viewed from several perspectives (see Baxi 1979). We conclude this presentation, however, with reference to only one perspective, namely, the use of law and legal resources in the mobilization of the rural poor for self-reliant development. In the context of Rangpur the term "law" embraces both the people's law and the law of the state. Rangpur provides us with a rather unique insight. It is that the needs-centered, participatory, self-reliant model of development entails the growth of a body of norms and practices as well as institutions of the people's law. In other words, the need to deal with social conflicts at a collective level, within the milieux of the group's cultural and social traditions, emerges in the Rangpur experience as a felt human need, integral to its notion of "development". People's law is thus a real political resource itself for the Rangpur communities. If dispute handling and conflict management are generally regarded as governmental functions, then the Rangpur experience suggests that the political dimension of self-reliant development is the recognition of self-government. If law is to be identified wholly with state law, and politics and government only with the formal constitutional polity and government, then (at least in the case under study) there is no possibility of self-reliant, participatory development.

Recognition of people's law does not necessarily mean denial of state law but rather an acceptance of a plurality of legal systems and the underlying systems of power and authority. The Rangpur experience shows that people's law and people's power can be used to reinforce the positive (for the people) values of state law as well as to combat its negative aspects. The involvement of the *Lok Adalat* in fighting corruption and exploitation demonstrates the latter aspect; the *Ashram* activities in support of the debt relief legislation demonstrates the former. In both respects, people's law and people's power are used for fostering the values of self-reliant development of the rural poor. In both situations, the existence of a people's court, or more aptly a people's adjudicatory forum, plays a very vital role.

The *Lok Adalat* certainly performs several functions in addition to conflict management and dispensation of justice. As regards deviance by government functionaries, it performs an ombudsman function, manifest in the case of Gharki and in other situations (see Baxi 1976). It performs powerful invigilatory functions in regard to the grievances of the people in the area against public functionaries. It provides a focal point for efforts at mobilization against injustice and strategies of direct action to combat it.

The *Lok Adalat* also performs, as our earlier study of it shows (Baxi 1976), the additional and crucial task of providing for legal literacy and legal services. Its officials help people to prepare representations against authorities. It gives people procedural advice to enable them to exercise their rights against various dominant groups. It offers unerring guidance to people in regard to their rights over land and revenue records, which are open to manipulation in favour of the literate and the economically and politically powerful. The service aspect also involves access to beneficent aspects of state law and administration. This aspect includes the provision of sureties for loans from nationalized banks for agricultural inputs, guidance concerning execution of instruments for credit and mortgage, formation of cooperative societies, and access to other services such as crops, seeds, fertilizers, irrigation, etc. In all these diverse fields, there is involvement of state law and bureaucracy; the *Lok Adalat* secretariat makes available the necessary information, skills and competences for maximizing access. The *Lok Adalat* also performs an ancillary, but no less important, recordkeeping function. It provides for registration of marriages and divorces, alimony and custody, loan and other transactions, and land records. Though far from perfect, this recordkeeping is an important device, in a basically illiterate society, often used tellingly against the prevarications of moneylenders and some governmental departments.

In the ongoing struggle between people's law and state law, there are increasing signs that, as the state uses its legal processes and institutions as a part of its strategy to contain the reach of the *Lok Adalat* and to question the bases of its legitimation, so also the *Lok Adalat* activates courts both in self-defence and pre-emptively. Indeed, the Rangpur communities have now developed a fully-fledged salaried lawyers' legal aid scheme, which is, generally, used to manipulate the state court system to reinforce the legitimacy of *Lok Adalat*, and the people's law.

If one were to adapt the framework of a recent ICLD (1979) analysis, we could say that this mobilization is made possible by the autonomous pursuit in Rangpur of "human needs-centred means and ends". The experience of Rangpur has undoubtedly shown that it has pursued such needs as civic education (defined as "developing functional knowledge of ... rights", to claim "resources essential to well-being"), "collective advocacy" (defined as "developing means of asserting these claims by challenging public agencies" and other dominant interests such as landlords, and setting up "... structures to provide resources ... or resolve problems shared within the group"), and finally "political participation" (defined as "developing new means of influencing governmental policy making in the more remote areas of decision-making"). In addition, demands for autonomy, self-rule and even self-determination in the domain of socio-cultural traditions forms the "essence of development" in the Rangpur experience.

NOTES

1. This paper is a revised version of a paper by the same title prepared as a part of series of studies of participatory organizations of the rural poor in India. The earlier unpublished version (July, 1979) deals also with other aspects of the crises surrounding the *Lok Adalat* and Rangpur communities. This paper was presented to the Bellagio Symposium of the IUAES Commission on Contemporary Folk Law with a hope that it would direct attention to the relations of complementarity and conflict between state legal systems and the people's law and the impact of these relations on the aspiration and achievement of social development.
2. The multi-party Parishad was constituted in 1976; Harivallabh Parekh played a key role in its formation and functioning.
3. For example, a lawyer elected to the Baroda Municipal Corporation on the Janata Party ticket, and who is the Chairman of the party unit in the city, has undertaken to defend Bhai in the criminal matter now pending.
4. This failing is not peculiar to the present party in power. When Bhai supported the socialist movement in the Naswadi area in the 1954-56 period, those people in the Congress who claimed to be or were Gandhians sharply criticized him for collaborating with "leftists" and thus being "un-Ghandhian". Bhai also assisted the Praja Samajvadi Party's (PSP) movement during 1953-57 in Paradi satyagraha; at that time too he was criticized by several political leaders in the area and the state for betraying *sarvodaya* by associating with socialists. Some of his critics have now joined Congress (I) and others have joined the Janata Party. It is understandable that Bhai's "eclecticism" constantly creates problems of politically "rational" comprehension all round. On the other hand, it seems ironical that single-minded dedication to the cause of the poor should in the first place be called "eclecticism" and in the second should remain politically incomprehensible to the very group of people who repeatedly pledge themselves to remove poverty!
5. Interestingly, the *Lok Adalat* seems to have taken account of a number of special features

of the case in absolving MP of the charge of murdering Gharki. The facts which appear to have weighed with the *panchas* were that she was a patient of epilepsy, and might have fallen from the tree because of a sudden fit; alternatively, she might have committed suicide out of the problematic relationship, and exasperation at altercations, with MP. (Both were consistent with the posture in which the corpse was found.) There was then no evidence for the *panchas* to infer that Gharki was killed. The Court might have reasoned the same way, although its decision does not reflect any of these reasons. In this respect too the *Lok Adalat* processes are more public than those of the state judicial process.

6.   "Agents of Litigation" is a poor translation for the Gujarati word *kajiadalal*. The suffix *dalal* is a word of opprobrium for unscrupulous bargainers and agents; the word *kajia* literally means quarrel and litigation but in the context it may be read to connote "agents of the State Law".

GLOSSARY OF INDIAN TERMS USED

Adivasis	Tribal communities, usually Scheduled Tribes under the Indian Constitution.
Ashram	Hermitage, a religious retreat for colony of disciples.
Bhoodan	Gift of land.
Fozdar	Police constable.
Gramdan	Gift of village.
Lok Adalat	People's Court.
Mahuva tree	Maple tree.
Sahukars	Moneylenders.

REFERENCES

Avadh Prashad
    1977   *Lok Adalat*, Sterling (in Hindi).
Baxi, U.
    1976   "From Takrar to Karar: the Lok Adalat at Rangpur - a Preliminary Study", *J. of Constitutional and Parliamentary Studies*, 10, 53.
    1979   "People's law, development, justice", *Verfassung und Recht in Ubersee*, 12, 97-114.
I.C.L.D.
    1979   *Law and Legal Resources in the Mobilization of the Rural Poor for Self-Reliant Development*, New York: International Center for Law in Development (mimeo).

Some comparative generalizations about the differential use of state and folk institutions of dispute settlement

Franz von Benda-Beckmann

INTRODUCTION

In my paper I wish to make some comparative generalizations about the differential use disputants (excluding the administrative agencies of the state) make of the various folk and state institutions of dispute settlement. My analysis is confined to situations in those, mainly Third-World, states where indigenous politico-legal systems have been superseded by and incorporated into a colonial/national state. The study of this topic forms only one part of a more general inquiry into the relative social significance of different laws and institutions in a pluralistic legal system. It gives us an important indication of the social significance of institutions of dispute settlement, of the laws upon which they are based and of the laws which they use to rationalize and justify their decisions.[1] The patterns observed in these domains may, of course, vary from patterns of law use and/or from the significance of folk and state institutions in activities other than dispute management; they therefore must not be taken to indicate the general social significance of folk-law/institutions and state-law/institutions.

Folk and state institutions and processes of dispute management have been studied by anthropologists and jurists, but systematic studies of the topics dealt with in my paper are rare. Jurists tend to view the problems and facts involved through the eyes of the official colonial/state law and its legal science. Here, state law is given the status of "dominant law", whereas folk law is treated as "servient law" (Hooker 1975:4). Studies of the actual use of institutions of dispute settlement by jurists are usually carried out in the narrow context of those institutions which are officially constituted or recognized by state law. Here, state law may indeed turn out to be the dominant law in practice. However, the practice of these courts may merely form an insignificant part of the comprehensive pattern of the differential use of institutions of dispute settlement. Legal anthropologists, on the other hand, who have studied the practice of dispute management usually have confined their attention to dispute processing on the local level and by folk institutions, and their main interest has been the style of dispute processing rather than the effectiveness of such proceedings. Only in recent years have anthropologists begun to turn to intra-societal comparisons of dispute settlement.[2]

The comparative study of the differential use of dispute institutions and of the effectiveness of their decisions is a difficult enterprise as it requires intra- and inter-societal comparison. Reliable data for intra-societal comparison are scarce; this lack of data weighs even heavier in inter-societal comparisons. Moreover there is no adequate methodological basis upon which they proceed.[3] In the attempt to evolve general theoretical propositions we are usually caught between superficial general observations without much theoretical value and the historical and morphological idiosyncrasies of concrete situations in concrete societies which do not lend themselves to easy generalization. Theoretical propositions to a large extent have to work on the basis of "all other things being equal". But looking at the immense variety of indigenous political organizations, colonial policies, content of legal rules and principles, both of state and folk law, types of conflict loaded issues etc., one is apt to conclude that almost all other things are unequal. Furthermore, we have to deal with situations in different historical periods, with different phases in the history of co-existence of indigenous and state institutions within one inclusive political system. Our basic problem thus is to "equalize things", to categorize varieties of social phenomena and to specify in their terms the conditions under which the general propositions are supposed to work. Part of my paper therefore necessarily is concerned with these methodological problems. In the other part I shall present some comparative generalizations about the differential use of dispute institutions.

SOME METHODOLOGICAL AND CONCEPTUAL ISSUES

The methodological problems already begin when we are speaking about the different *types of institutions* the differential use of which we intend to study. As a starting point we may perhaps speak of two basic types of institutions as is usually done in the literature, folk (traditional) and state (western) institutions; that is, institutions of dispute settlement which owe their existence and normative validity to the pre-colonial political and legal system irrespective of what the official legal system may say about them (folk/indigenous institutions), and institutions which owe their existence and normative validity to the political and legal system of the state. However, in all colonial systems hybrid institutions have come into existence which comprise elements of both political and legal systems: institutions officially recognized or fully constituted by colonial/national law but based upon pre-existing indigenous institutions. Prototypes of such institutions were the Native Authority Courts in the Former British colonies, but this type of institution was and still is found elsewhere, e.g. in Indonesia. In the following I shall call these institutions "neo-traditional" (cf. F. von Benda-Beckmann 1981: 170). Due to differences in colonial policies concerning indigenous political organizations, we find situations where the indigenous institutions, or at least the top layers, have been incorporated more or less wholesale into the colonial system where they continue, albeit with transformed functions, to represent the whole of indigenous institutions as a bloc in contrast to the state institutions. In other societies, on the other hand, pre-colonial institutions have only been partially incorporated.

Depending on the type of incorporation and on the perspective of the observer, neo-traditional institutions are described as "traditional" and contrasted with "state institutions" (cf. Roberts 1972, 1979 for the situation in Botswana), or as "western courts" which are then contrasted with "traditional" institutions of "informal arbitration" (cf. Abel 1970: 76, 1979). To make things even more complicated, colonial policy may, by functionally and institutionally differentiating the powers left to traditional institutions, have created a variety of neo-traditional institutions in place of a single pre-colonial institution (cf. Holleman 1979 on the situation in Shonaland, Zimbabwe). When making diachronic intra-societal or inter-societal comparisons of the differential use of folk and state institutions, we therefore must be careful to distinguish at least three types of institutions: a) state institutions not based upon the indigenous political organization; b) state imposed institutions based upon the indigenous political organization; and c) indigenous institutions not incorporated into the colonial/national governmental system. Otherwise, we are not talking about the same things.[4]

The notion of "the use" of an institution is rather unproblematic. However, we must take care to distinguish at least two types of use when we speak about the differential use of state and folk institutions: cases in which disputants have brought their dispute directly to a state institution, and cases in which disputants do so after having exhausted folk institutions before, briefly, whether state institutions are used *instead of* folk institutions or *in addition to* them. Whereas in the literature the questions asking about the differential use of institutions and the answers supplied by general propositions seem to envisage the first situation, the actual data are usually of the second type-situation. The choices perceived and made by disputants usually concern the question whether they go to state institutions after they have exhausted the hierarchy of indigenous/neo-traditional institutions, or they involve the choice between the highest-level indigenous/neo-traditional and the state institution.

Besides, another question relevant for any generalisation about use and effectiveness of different institutions has often not been asked or answered in the literature: where do parties stop with their disputes, or, in other words, by which institutions are the disputes *contained?* This concerns, on the one hand, the behaviour of the disputants, and thus forms an element of the differential use of institutions of dispute-management. On the other hand, it is one aspect of the effectiveness of the institutions' decisionmaking activities. I shall speak of "effectiveness" if the disputants behave according to the decision or if the decision is executed, or if the disputants, though not behaving according to the decision, do not publicly continue their dispute. "Successful containment" of a dispute by an institution is one aspect of, but not identical with the institution's effectiveness; it indicates that the decision is at least effective in the sense that it is not appealed to a higher/more inclusive institution.

The differential use of institutions of dispute-settlement, the institutions' capacity to contain disputes and the effectiveness of their decisions are closely interrelated aspects of dispute-processing. Once the choice of an institution has been made, the problem is whether the institution can contain the dispute and whether its decision is effective. These three aspects together give us an indication of the actual social significance of the indigenous, neo-traditional and state institution of the laws upon which they are based and of laws which they use in decisionmaking. Yet they express three different issues and each of them tells us different things about the larger issue of the social significance of institutions of dispute-settlement. In the following, I shall confine my discussion to the problems of differential use and containment of decisions.[5]

STRUCTURAL VARIATION AS THEORETICAL FOCUS

The idea which I wish to pursue in my paper is that the topic of the differential use of institutions of dispute-settlement in colonial and ex-colonial systems must be studied as part of the overall socio-political system in which it occurs, and that any comparative generalization must take into account the nature and specific structural features of these systems. Although I am, of course, not concerned with or looking for monocausal explanations, I suggest that variation in these structural features accounts for some significant differences in the use and effectiveness of indigenous, neo-traditional and state institutions. In particular, I shall single out 1) variation in the legal structures of indigenous political organizations and the way in which they have been affected by their incorporation into the colonial states, and 2) variation in the socio-spatial location of state-imposed institutions (state or neo-traditional) and their jurisdictions in relation to the (pre-colonial) sociopolitical system.

This focus brings with it a new perspective upon the comparative study of pluralistic systems of dispute-settlement. Usually, the perspective has been to ask whether or not folk institutions have been recognized by/incorporated into the official colonial/national legal system and what the effects of such recognition/non-recognition or of increasing incorporation ("westernization") were on the functioning of the institutions. I suggest that it is more fruitful to examine the situation the other way around and ask whether or not state/neo-traditional institutions have been placed within or outside the indigenous political system and the socio-spatial jurisdictions of its institutions.

The view taken in most anthropological analyses has usually been narrower. Anthropological discussions of dispute-management which take account of the pluralistic situation at all have usually been concerned with the analysis of the factors determining the choice of (one type of) an institution and with the style of dispute-management within institutions. These factors, though often called structural as well,[6] have been seen primarily in the nature of the concrete relationships of the disputants and between the disputants and the institutions, their concrete social, political and economic status or their concrete emotions and intentions (cf. Gluckman 1955, Kuper 1971, Abel 1973, 1979, cf. Black 1976). The best known and probably most basic proposition is that disputants related to each other by permanent many-stranded (multiplex) relationships tend to bring their disputes to folk (mediating, arbitrating) institutions, whereas disputants not so related rather tend to go to state institutions (adjudicative, legalistic); and that variation in the style of dispute-management in (all) institutions co-varies with the type of relationships or "relational distance": many-stranded relationships being associated with a mediating, conciliatory style, single-stranded relationships with an adjudicative, legalistic style (Gluckman 1955; Abel 1973, 1979; Black 1976). This proposition has been the point of departure against which other variables identified as contributing to a better understanding of the differential use of dispute settlement institutions have been measured: the nature of the relationships between the parties and the institutions (Kuper 1971, Rothenberger 1978); the disputants' social, economic and political status and actual strength (Rothenberger 1978); the subject-matter of the dispute (Abel 1973, Starr 1978, Starr and Yngvesson 1975, Nader 1974, Collier 1973); the goal of the disputants (Lowy 1978); and the degree to which inter-individual disputes are transformed into inter-group or inter-faction disputes (Rothenberger 1978, K. von Benda-Beckmann 1981).These correlations between the differential use of institutions of dispute-settlement and the variables mentioned and the explanatory value given to them in anthropological analyses are quite plausible. But as most studies were primarily conducted with the aim to explain the situation *within* a given society, the structural features of the society have generally not been considered systematically as independent explanatory factors. Most of the explanations given are relative to the particular systems. Even when they have general cross-cultural validity, they can only explain the same type of correlations in different societies, but they cannot - as will be shown - explain the differences between societies and are therefore of limited value for comparative generalizations. As I hope to demonstrate, it is the variation in the structural features mentioned which provides an explanatory context which sets boundaries for, and gives meaning to the explanatory value of the other variables.

THE CHOICE OF INSTITUTIONS - LAW AS AN EXPLANATORY FACTOR

As analyses of the differential use of institutions of dispute-settlement have focused upon actual relationships rather than on structural features of the overall socio-political system, law, the legal dimension of these features, has rarely been systematically regarded as an independent explanatory factor. The law in question here is generally called constitutional or administrative law. If we consider e.g., the topic of the disputants' first choice of an institution and observe that persons related by permanent multiplex relationships tend to go to low-level mediating institutions, we get the impression of an empirical pattern of behaviour which is explained by the proposition focusing upon the nature of the relationships. But it may well be, as, e.g., in the case of the Minangkabau and probably in many other societies, that the indigenous or the state law about dispute-processing prescribes that disputants *must* go to this institution before they may move up a hierarchy. And this may influence the disputants' behaviour also if their relationships are *not* multiplex and permanent. In indigenous societies such law typically ties group membership to the use of a given institution of dispute-settlement; with more inclusive groups we get institutions with more inclusive jurisdictions. The institutions are typically joined in a hierarchy. Non-group members (of whichever size) usually go, and usually *have to go* according to the law, to that institution whose jurisdiction is so inclusive that it comprises the less inclusive group and the non-group member.

This factor, law, plays a role in all spheres of the overall socio-political organisation. Take, as the next step, the question whether disputants choose between folk institutions and state courts, to which the general anthropological proposition usually is extended. The law, here often state law, may prescribe that the dispute has to be dealt with by folk institutions, or at least by the top-level folk institutions, before the state court is going to deal with it. This factor will influence the disputants' behaviour and the behaviour of the courts, independently of the actual nature of the disputants' relationship or of the eventual competitive behaviour of folk and state institutions. If we wish to make comparative generalizations about the differential use of folk and state institutions, the existence or non-existence of such law is at least one crucial factor to be considered. It may help to explain differences or similarities which are unexplainable by the propositions based upon concrete relationships and concrete behaviour.

The explanatory power of the concrete nature of the disputants' relationships therefore loses much of its original force. The legal dimension of the socio-political structure is, of course, to a large extent the consequence of patterned relationships and behaviour patterns. If we look for propositions to explain this type of law, these relationships and the concrete behaviour would qualify as explanatory factors. But in our present inquiry we are concerned with the explanation of *behaviour*. Here the concrete relationships may fit the structural pattern, but this pattern and its legal dimension exist independently of and prior to the relationship between individual disputants.[7]

I wish to emhasize that this does not deny the explanatory value of the propositions relying on the actual relationships between disputants; it only puts them in their proper place. Firstly, the structures and their legal dimension usually leave room for options and choices within the structures; the proposition based upon actual behaviour or relationships may well be crucial for the understanding/explanation of that behaviour. Secondly, as is the case with all law, disputants or institutions do not necessarily behave in accordance with it. The "actual relationship"-proposition may explain why disputants deviate from the law; or why, if new patterns develop in a legal system, new structures and new law come into being.

In the anthropological literature we find a curious difference in the treatment of the legal-structural factors. Whereas the legal dimension of social and political structures is usually not systematically analysed on the local level of dispute-management and explanatory propositions focus more or less exclusively on the nature of concrete relationships and concrete behaviour, exactly the opposite is true as far as state institutions are concerned. The law laying down state court hierarchies, possibilities and chains of appeal, etc., are usually taken for granted. As in addition the whole set of state institutions is usually set into opposition to folk institutions, hardly any attention is given to the concrete relationships and the concrete behaviour within these structures. Therefore little attention is given to competition between state courts, e.g. stte courts of first instance and high(er) level courts; little attention is given to differing rates of containment, e.g. to appeal rates. Here again law – though of course not as the single explanatory factor - may significantly influence disputants' and institutions' behaviour, e.g. by allowing or prohibiting appeals. Generally, these elements of the laws about courts are rather effective and generally adhered to, but this should not be taken for granted. Higher courts may compete for cases by manipulating procedural and appeal rules in the same way as folk institutions do with folk law rules. In an approach which professes to view disputing behaviour in the context of the overall socio-political context in which it occurs, the structures and the behaviour within the state court domain theoretically are equally important as in the folk law domain. Only its systematic inclusion into an inquiry allows us to make comparative generalizations about the relative social significance of the different institutions and, in particular, about the social significance of folk and state law in one legal domain: the domain of constitutional law and the law pertaining to the procedures of dispute-management.

The use of folk institutions as a starting point for processing disputes thus must be seen and be explained by structural *and* social factors. The social factors, the (changing) nature of the concrete relationships between the disputants and the (changing) actual authority wielded by indigenous/neo-traditional institutions constitute the major social forces which keep the disputants' behaviour within, or force it outside, the channels laid down in the indigenous legal system, and they may remain in force, or even become dominant after the indigenous system and its jurisdictions have been superseded by the colonial system. On account of the nature of their relationships, disputants may continue to go first to folk institutions even if the indigenous law of jurisdiction has lost most of its force and if the indigenous authorities have lost much of their authority to enforce directly or indirectly adherence to the indigenous law of dispute-management. The introduction of the colonial court system as such has, as far as we can gather, nowhere seriously affected the authority of indigenous/neo-traditional leaders to induce the use of indigenous/neo-traditional institutions. If only one strand of the power-relationships between them and the other members of society - the formal authority to decide or settle disputes - is duplicated or replaced by the colonial system, the other strands and bases of their power (kinship, economics, religion, etc.) may still be strong enough to prevent disputants from disregarding their indigenous institutions, gladly or not, when it comes to the settlement of disputes (cf. K. von Benda-Beckmann 1981:143). Rather than through official recognition/non-recognition, their authority is negatively affected if multifunctional state institutions are introduced which duplicate all their political functions, or if their other power bases, e.g. the economic, are affected by changes in the economy (see for an impressive example Pospisil 1981). As has been mentioned, their authority may also be strengthened externally by the state law, or by the state courts' procedures e.g. by requiring that indigenous institutions must be approached before any dispute is brought before the state courts (cf. K. von Benda-Beckmann 1981, Roberts 1979).

USE AND CONTAINMENT - THE SOCIO-SPATIAL LOCATION OF DISPUTE THRESHOLDS

So far, my discussion bears primarily upon the question of whether and why disputants use indigenous institutions at all and as a matter of first choice. I have not dealt with the question of where they go afterwards and where they stop their disputing, and where and why disputes are contained. In all societies we can observe certain patterns of use of the different institutions. Taking the absolute number of disputes as a basis, these patterns will show one - or more - thresholds at which the number of disputes being processed suddenly shows a radical decrease. These "dispute thresholds" indicate the institutional level at which disputes are relatively successfully contained. A more differentiated analysis of the single institutions then gives us the data about the containment rate of the individual institutions on either side of the dispute threshold. By comparing ratios of processed disputes in two or more institutions and by comparing relative containment rates we can form an impression about the differential use of institutions and their effectiveness in containing disputes. These ratios and containment rates then form the basic material upon which comparative generalizations must rest.

A comprehensive analysis of the differential use of institutions as envisaged above is more or less impossible for lack of data. We have mainly to work with the number of cases being processed in the top level indigenous institutions, neo-traditional institutions and primary state courts. We are lucky if appeal data are given at all. We have - understandably - no hard data about the absolute number of disputes and hardly any statistical information about lower level indigenous institutions. Still, it is interesting to take a closer look at the available data. When comparing litigation rates in primary state courts and top-level indigenous and neo-traditional dispute institutions across societies, we encounter some striking differences. Primary (Local, Magistrates') courts in former British African colonies have a comparatively very high average of one case to 100-300 persons, per year.[8] Van Rouveroy van Nieuwaal (1975) reportsd an average of 1:2,700 for the Juge de Paix (State Court) in Northern Togo and of 1:360-540 for the chief's unofficial court, Roberts (1979:40) an average of 1:3,000 for the District Magistrate and of 1:720 for the official court of the Kgatla chief in Botswana.[9] In West Sumatra we find a very low average of 1:10,000 for primary state courts alone, or 1:5.000 if the case load of the Religious Court is added. The average for the neo-traditional village council is 1:892.[10] For some societies we construct the ratio of litigation rates in state courts and indigenous/neo-traditional institutions [11], but even these ratios are of little use for generalizations about the differential use of state v. folk institutions unless we know the total number of disputes being processed and the containment rates of lower-level indigenous institutions.

To look at our extreme cases: Are African tribes simply more litigious than the Minangkabau as the primary court data suggests; or do the Minangkabau start processing as many disputes, the greater part of which, however, is contained below the top level of the indigenous and neo-traditional village institutions, whereas in Africa more or less all disputes are processed up to the primary state courts? Our own impression while doing research in a Minangkabau village was, indeed, that there were but few persons or sublineages not currently involved in one or more disputes which were handled by lineage heads and neo-traditional functionaries in their capacity of institutions of dispute-settlement; and that these institutions were very succesful in containing (though not solving) the disputes (cf. K. von Benda-Beckmann 1981; Tanner 1969 for state courts).[12] On the other hand, descriptions of African dispute-management do certainly not convey the impression that "all" disputes are processed up to the primary court level, and frequently the dispute-settlement activities of tribal elders and councils are mentioned (Canter 1978, Abel 1970: 75 ff). Do we have to conclude that these indigenous institutions have broken down completely? If not, how do we explain the tremendous case loads of primary courts? If we turn to the propositions discussed in the earlier sections, we can see that they help us understand the pattern of differential use *in* the various societies. They explain similar patterns of differential use. Thus the correlation between less permanent/less many-stranded relationships and increasing use of state courts holds true for African situations (Canter 1978: 278, Abel 1970, 1979) as well as for the Minangkabau situation (F. von Benda-Beckmann 1979: 307 f.). This holds true for other variables as well. Both among the Lenje in Zambia and the Minangkabau the people conceive and use the range of remedy agents by which they can process their disputes as a hierarchy, an order established and maintained by the remedy agents themselves who insist on hierarchical dispute-processing. The state courts uphold the boundaries of the lower level corporate groups and the hierarchy associated with them, inter alia by calling lower-level remedy agents as expert-witnesses.[13] However, the explanatory value of these variables is relative to the societies studied. They in no way provide us with an explanation for the enormous inter-societal differences in litigation rates. Of all the variables mentioned, only two appear to correlate significantly with inter-societal differences in primary state court use: the duration of the process and the costs involved. In West Sumatra, where the litigation rate in state courts is very low, the court processes take much more time (one to two years) and are much more expensive than in the other countries (compare Van Rouveroy van Nieuwaal 1976, Abel 1979, Canter 1978, Lowy 1978).

Yet these variables fail us if we consider the use of the next higher institutional level, the use of appeal courts, and the striking differences we find there. The length and costs of appeal proceedings in West Sumatra again are much longer and higher, yet the average appeal rate in African primary courts is more or less zero (Van Rouveroy van Nieuwaal), about 1% (in Ghana, see Lowy 1978: 191; in Kenya, see Abel 1970: 62), or, if "high", about 3-4% (Lenje/Zambia, see Canter 1978: 256). In West Sumatra, on the other hand, the appeal rate is 54%, and even the rate of reviews to the Supreme Court in Jakarta is 18% of the appeal decisions - thus about 10% of all primary court cases (F. von Benda-Beckmann 1979: 308).

Thus, in the African examples, the primary state courts are frequently used by disputants and can contain the disputes. Do the attributes of state courts (enforceable judgment, etc.) show their strength, whereas in West Sumatra the primary state courts cannot successfully contain disputes and the disputants are relatively unimpressed by the authority of the primary state court decision? Are African disputants content once they have reached a state institution, whereas Minangkabau disputants, once they have reached a state institution, want to go all the way up to the top? Unless we consider structural features of the political system as independent variables, we shall never be able to extricate ourselves from the idiosyncrasies of the individual cases.

It seems to me that the location of state courts in relation to the indigenous politico-legal jurisdictions is such a variable. My hypothesis is that disputes are (relatively) succesfully contained within the indigenous jurisdictions and that the dispute threshold coincides with the boundary of the highest folk jurisdiction. It thus makes hardly any difference for the containment of disputes within the indigenous jurisdiction whether indigenous, and/or neo-traditional and/or state courts operate within/at the top of the indigenous jurisdiction.[14] But depending on the variable, different general patterns of differential use of the state institutions will follow. If primary state courts are located below or at the top level of the indigenous jurisdiction, they are (in inter-societal comparison) used relatively frequently, and can contain disputes effectively. However, if primary state courts are placed outside the indigenous political jurisdictions, they are relatively infrequently used; and, if used, they are relatively unsuccessful in containing disputes. In one case, they have a high case-load and there are low appeal rates, whereas in the second case they have fewer cases and there are high appeal rates.

Thus, for the question of use and containment rates of state institutions, the importance of their "state" or "folk" characteristics, their degree of "westernization", etc., are only of secondary importance if compared with the structural location of these institutions. Therefore it is structural, rather than social or territorial, distance between the disputants and the institutions which explains the differential use of institutions of dispute-settlement. We could elaborate our hypotheses as follow. In the one case, neo-traditional or state institutions are incorporated or adapted to the indigenous system/hierarchy. Even if, as generally is the case, they are new (state courts) or transformed (neo-traditional) elements, adaptation is easy as it occurs within the indigenous jurisdictional boundaries. Primary state courts in this case form the apex of the adapted system and appeal would bring with it the necessity for boundary crossing. In the other case, primary state courts are outside the indigenous system and they form the bottom of this outside hierarchy. As their use involves boundary-crossing, they are not frequently used, but once disputants operate within the new or outside system, appeals are easy as no further boundary-crossing is involved.

For the proper working of our proposition the location of neo-traditional/state courts may not be seen statically but in historical perspective. It will make a difference whether new institutions are directly placed outside the indigenous system or whether they have been gradually removed from the indigenous system. The latter has been the case in some African countries, where neo-traditional (Native Authority) courts were gradually pushed up, or beyond, the original tribal hierarchy (e.g. by creating paramount chiefs of tribes the sections of which had formerly been autonomous, cf. Moore 1978), thereby reducing the number of officially recognized courts, and/or by creating state courts in their place. In this case we could speak of "apex extension": the new courts, though placed outside the original jurisdictions, are not conceived of as at the bottom of a new hierarchy but as the extended apex of the traditional hierarchy. In such circumstances the original hypothesis holds true, though possibly in a weaker form, for the comparison of "extended apex-institutions" with neo-traditional or state courts directly placed outside the system, whereas, in relation to courts placed within the indigenous jurisdiction, we would expect a relatively lower court use.

The strength of our variable would further presumably vary with the "permeability" of the boundary or boundary strength of the indigenous system. Variation in "boundary strength" is of course the result of many factors such as the original strength of the indigenous boundaries, state law, etc., which cannot all be discussed in this paper. By comparing court use in the Turkish situation (described by Starr 1978) and the Lebanese situation (Rothenberger 1978) we can get support for our hypotheses. The Lebanese village has a rather definite corporate structure; here 91% of all disputes were contained in the village (Rothenberger 1978: 166). The Turkish village described by Starr has no corporate identity (1978: 126 f.); here only 66% of the disputes were contained in the village (1978: 124). The activity of dispute settlement agencies itself can of course be one mechanism of boundary maintenance (see Canter 1978). According to our hypothesis we would expect institutions (state or folk) acting within the border to be more strongly engaged in boundary maintenance than institutions placed outside. This a.o. means that such institutions would tend to uphold the traditional hierarchies of dispute settlement and not engage in competition for cases with them. Vice versa we would conclude that, if state courts are working within the system, there would be less competition for cases by lower level folk institutions that in cases where state courts are placed outside. [15]

STATE COURTS AND TRADITIONAL JURISDICTIONS IN KENYA

All data from the societies discussed above - the striking differences in state court use and appeal rates - support these hypotheses. Their more general value will be more plausible if we apply it to a body of data which were not considered when the hypothesis was formed. In the next section I shall use them to re-analyse the statistical data on state court use in Kenya provided by Abel (1970, 1979). As will be seen, the introduction of my hypotheses contributes a fuller understanding of the data, partly in addition to, partly at variance with, Abel's interpretation The tests are carried out at three levels: the national, district and tribal level. Due to the restrictions imposed by the data, the tests are crude and limited.

1. The national level: the decline of civil litigation rates in Kenya primary state courts

The average civil litigation rates in Kenya have dropped during the period between 1931 and 1971 from 9.1 cases per 1000 population in 1948 to 4.4 in 1969 and to 2.9 in 1971 (Abel 1979: 181). During the period between 1943 and 1969 the number of primary courts in the districts mentioned in the different tables dropped from 127 to 91 (table 10.1) or from 119 to 86 (table 10.2). These primary courts had originally been adapted from indigenous, traditional councils of elders in accordance with the principles of indirect rule embodied in the Native Tribunals Ordinance of 1930. In 1944, the courts were reorganized, more in the direction of western courts, but still on the basis of native authorities. In 1967-1969 the primary courts became Magistrates' Courts, even more westernized in form and were no longer staffed by traditional or neo-traditional authorities (1979: 176).

Our hypothesis is perfectly consistent with these data. We would expect more/relatively higher litigation rates in situations where the neo-traditional/state courts' jurisdictions coincide with the indigenous/neo-traditional jurisdictions. Thus, if the number of courts is reduced, this would mean that the new courts' jurisdictions comprise more than one former indigenous-/neo-traditional jurisdiction; in other words, that the courts have been placed outside the indigenous jurisdictions. Given the reduction of the number of courts in Kenya, we therefore would expect, independently of other factors, a decline in the overall litigation rates.

This alone does not "prove" that my variable is more important than the factors mentioned by Abel, e.g. the increasing "westernization" of the courts or increasing population density or decreasing social (tribal) homogeneity. But if we follow Abel to the district level, we get a clearer idea of its importance.

2. The district level

If we relate my variable to the litigation rates of the districts [16] - excepting for the time being the extremely urbanized areas of Nairobi and Mombasa - we see that it correlates much better than the variables, population density and tribal homogeneity, selected by Abel. Abel's selection was based upon the assumption that low litigation rates would be the consequence (among others) of a high degree of tribal homogeneity and a low population density, whereas a high degree of heterogeneity of the population and a high population density would result in high litigation rates; the borders between high/ low being (more/less than) 100 persons per km2 for population density (see Abel 1979: 182) and (more/less than) 85% population of the largest tribe as a percentage of the district's population.[17]

Abel's material makes it possible to compare my variable with the variables "tribal homogeneity" and "population density" in 19 districts. Of these 10 have a higher than average litigation rate, 9 a lower litigation rate. In the *high litigation districts*, in 6 districts the number of courts has remained equal or has been increased, whereas it has been decreased in 4 districts. My variable thus shows a positive 6:4 correlation with high(er) litigation. *Tribal homogeneity*, on the other hand, was low only in 3 and high in 7 districts, thus nearly contradicting Abel's hypothesis that there will be less litigation in homogeneous societies. *Population density* was high in 2, low in 8 districts, again rather contradicting Abel's suggestion that there will be high litigation rates in densely populated areas. My positive correlation-record of 6:4 thus compares quite favourably with the negative scores of 3:7 (tribal homogeneity) and 2:8 (population density). In the *low litigation districts*, my variable shows a positive 8:1 correlation. *Population density* scores equally well, but *tribal homogeneity* looks bad again. Only in 2 districts was tribal homogeneity (according to Abel's hypothesis) high, whereas, contrary to that hypothesis, it was low in 7 districts. Even if we would add those districts with low litigation rates and high homogeneity for which Abel gives no data about the decrease/increase of courts, the correlation reaches a mere 7:7.

The overall correlation score thus is 14:5 for my variable, 10:9 for population density and 5(9):14 for tribal homogeneity. The admittedly crude experiment in my view clearly demonstrates the explanatory power of my propositions. In particular it suggests that the court structure as related to the tribal structure of jurisdictions (our structural variable) is more important than the degree of homogeneity, taking homogeneity as an indicator of rather multiplex than simplex relationships. The fact that highly urbanized areas have the highest litigation rates and the lowest rates of homogeneity (Abel 1979: 184) does not contradict this contention. The very fact that in urban areas the correlation pattern is radically different (clearly positive in contrast to clearly negative) from rural areas suggests that homogeneity as such is not the decisive variable, but rather the type of indigenous jurisdictions in relation to the court structure. As our test has demonstrated, this is an independent variable. Heterogeneity as such does not "imply that there will be neither traditional institutions nor traditional norms to resolve

conflicts" as Abel suggests (1979: 184), although it may, of course, contribute
to a development in that direction.

3. The tribal level

We can also make our hypothesis work at the tribal level. Here, too, it can
provide additional explanations for questions as yet unanswered, as the
following (admittedly very restricted) experiment shows. The question left
unexplained in Abel's analysis is why some Kenyan tribes are more litigious
than others and why in particular there are notable differences between
sections of tribes, e.g. the Luo, living in different districts (Abel 1970: 48 ff.).
This question is particularly interesting as - contrary to Abel's expectation -
the "traditionalist" Luo in the district of South Nyanza are much more
litigious than their "more modern counterparts" in Central Nyanza (1970:
48). In his analysis, Abel notes that the inversion in the ranking of tribes or
tribal sections between the degree of modernization/westernization and
frequent court use "may be due to the persistent vitality of indigenous
institutions for the settlement of disputes" (1970: 48, Note 191, 75 ff.). While
this - in principle - is a plausible expectation, it is difficult to see how it could
explain the intra-tribal differences in litigation among the Luo. For we would
expect that in the much more densely populated district of Central Nyanza,
which nearly has twice the population per court as the southern Nyanza
district (1979: 178) and which is inhabited by the more modern Luo, the
chances for the persistent vitality of indigenous institutions would rather be
lower than higher, and the litigation rates therefore rather higher than lower.
Yet the opposite is the case. The litigation rate of the central district Luo is
one third lower than of the southern district Luo (per case 338 v. 228 persons
per year).

But if we apply our hypothesis to the question it fits the data very well. We
would expect more litigation in the district in which the number of courts has
remained equal, and less litigation where the number of courts has been
reduced. And indeed, in the modern densely populated Central Nyanza
district the number of courts was reduced from 9 to 6, whereas in the less
densely populated traditionalist southern Nyanza district the number of
courts has been even increased from 8 to 9. According to our hypothesis we
would therefore expect higher litigation rates in the southern district.

CONCLUSIONS

In my paper I have drawn attention to variations in the politico-legal
structure as explanatory factors for different patterns of differential use of
indigenous, neo-traditional and state institutions in ex-colonial countries. I

have suggested that structural features of the overall jurisdictional system - the laws about jurisdictions and the location of newly introduced institutions in relation to indigenous jurisdictions - are independent variables of considerable explanatory value. My experiments have shown that their significance may be greater than of factors such as "westernization of courts", "modernization of society" or the nature of the relationships between individual disputants.

I would also like to draw attention to the *practical* implications of my hypotheses for legal policy in third world countries. They suggest that the discussion about judicial reform should free itself from the opposition/alternative "folk - state" institutions. Full restoration of judicial autonomy to traditional communities being no realistic alternative, the discussion should shift its focus to the most appropriate place of state institutions in the politico-legal system. My analysis has shown that state institutions of dispute settlement are frequently used and work effectively (in the restricted sense of containing disputes) if they are located at the top level of the former indigenous system. The African Local Court model, if considered in inter-societal comparison, functions excellently and has a much greater social significance (in the positive sense) than, e.g., state courts in West Sumatra and probably in Indonesia in general. Besides, they work faster and cheaper. Even if one takes into account that a policy following this suggestion in many countries would mean a considerable extension of the number of courts and judicial personnel, the overall financial costs may well be lower and the political gain (better acceptance of state courts by the population, more effective working of state institutions) may be considerable.

NOTES

1.   But the social significance of dispute management institutions may also be much higher than the frequency of their use by disputants may suggest, as Galanter (1981) has suggested. For an illustration, see K. von Benda-Beckmann 1981.
2.   See the studies in Nader and Todd (eds.) 1978; Moore 1973, 1977; Starr and Yngvesson 1975; Collier 1973; Holleman 1979; Roberts 1979; K. von Benda-Beckmann 1981; Van Rouveroy van Nieuwaal 1975; Gessner 1977.
3.   Abel's comparative theory about dispute institutions in society (1973) provides a useful framework but does not offer explanations for the kind of data we have to deal with in intersocietal comparison.
4.   Abel (1979) for example analyses the historical development of the use of "western courts" in Kenya. During the period analysed, these courts changed from "neo-traditional" to "state imposed beside ex-neo traditional courts", a change not systematically taken into account in the analysis.
5.   For some preliminary hypotheses concerning the relative effectiveness of institutions' decisions in a colonial pluralistic system of dispute institutions, see F. von Benda-Beckmann 1981.

6.   See e.g. in Abel 1979. Authors tend to confuse or fuse the culturally and statistically dominant pattern of relationships with the actual nature of the relationships between disputants. Pospisil's distinction between social structure and societal structure (1979: 129) is helpful here. In Pospisil's terms I am concerned with societal-structural variations.

7.   For a more detailed explication of my understanding of law and its dialectical relationship with behaviour see F. von Benda-Beckmann 1979: 18 ff., and n.d.

8.   Canter (1978) for Zambia (Lenje); Lowy 1978: 191 for Ghana; Abel 1970: 48, 1979 for Kenya; F. von Benda-Beckmann 1970: 70 and Chimango 1977: 48 for Malawi.

9.   The average is 360 for both civil and criminal cases. From Roberts's break up of the case load I conclude that no more than 50% should be classified as "civil" for comparative purposes.

10.   K. von Benda-Beckmann 1981.

11.   In Botswana the ratio is 4.3: 1 (chief: district magistrate); in Northern Togo it is 5: 1 (chief: juge de paix); in Lebanon 9.8: 1 (village institutions: village external institutions); in Minangkabau 5.5: 1 (neo-traditional village council: state courts plus religious courts).

12.   Besides, many would-be court disputants (women, individual lineage members in general) cannot succesfully file a suit over lineage property - the object of most property disputes (K. von Benda-Beckmann 1981: 143 ff.).

13.   Canter 1978: 276 ff., K. von Benda-Beckmann 1981: 144; for Kenya compare Abel 1970: 75 ff.

14.   However, different constellations of institutions *within* the boundaries of the indigenous jurisdiction will lead to different patterns of differential use within the boundaries. An analysis of these variations is beyond the scope of this paper.

15.   This does not exhaust the topic of inter-institutional competition: see below; but so far this derived hypothesis would be supported by the African and Minangkabau data (see Canter 1978 and K. von Benda-Beckmann 1981).

16.   Unfortunately, only synchronic data on litigation rates are given for the districts.

17.   In his essay, Abel does not set a border between "high" and "low" homogeneity but only gives a ranking of districts. So my setting of the border at 85% is, of course, arbitrary. The same experiment can of course be made if the border is set higher or lower than 85%.

REFERENCES

Abel, R.L.
    1970   *Customary laws of wrongs in Kenya: an essay in research method*, Yale Law School Studies in Law and Modernization No. 2. Yale.
    1973   "A comparative theory of dispute institutions in society". *Law and Society Review*, 1973, 217-347.
    1979   "Western courts in non-western settings: patterns of court use in colonial and neo-colonial Africa", in: S.B. Burman and B.E. Harrell-Bond (eds.) *The imposition of law*, Academic Press, New York, London, Toronto, Sydney, San Francisco.
Benda-Beckmann, F. von
    1970   *Rechtspluralismus in Malawi; Geschichtliche Entwicklung und heutige Problematik des pluralistischen Rechtssystems eines ehemals britischen Kolonialgebiets*, Ifo-Institut für Wirtschaftsforschung, Afrika-Studien no. 56, München, Weltforum Verlag.
    1979   *Property in social continuity; continuity and change in the maintenance of property relationships through time in Minangkabau, West Sumatra*, M. Nijhoff, den Haag.

1981   "Some comments on the problems of comparing the relationship between tradi-
               tional and state systems of administration of justice in Africa and Indonesia",
               Journal of Legal Pluralism 19: 165-175.
n.d.   *A concept of law for legal anthropology.*
Benda-Beckmann, K. von
1981   "Forum shopping and shopping forums; dispute processing in a Minangkabau
               village in West Sumatra, Indonesia", *Journal of Legal Pluralism* 19: 117-159.
Black, D.
1976   *The behaviour of law,* Academic Press. New York, San Fransisco, London.
Canter, R.S.
1978   "Dispute settlement and dispute processing in Zambia: individual choice and
               societal constraints", in: L. Nader and H.F, Todd Jr. (eds.) *The disputing process
               - law in ten societies,* Columbia University Press, New York.
Chimango, L.J.
1977   Tradition and the traditional Courts in Malawi, X *CILSA* 1977, 39-66.
Collier, J.F.
1973   *Law and social change in Zinacantan.* Stanford: University Press.
Galanter, M.
1981   "Justice in many rooms", *Journal of Legal Pluralism* 19: 1-47.
Gessner, V.
1976   *Recht und Konflikt,* Beiträge zum Ausländischen und Internationalen Priva-
               trecht, herausgegeben vom Max-Planck-Institut für Ausländisches und Interna-
               tionales Privatrecht 40, J.C.B. Mohr (Paul Siebeck), Tübingen.
Gluckman, M.
1955   *The judicial process among the Barotse of Northern Rhodesia,* University Press for
               the Rhodes-Livingstone Institute, Manchester.
Hooker, M.B.
1975   *Legal pluralism; an introduction to colonial and neo-colonial law,* Clarendon Press,
               Oxford.
Holleman, J.F.
1979   "Disparities and uncertainties in African law and judicial authority: a Rhodesian
               case study". *ALS* 17: 1-35.
Lowy, M.
1978   "A good name is worth more than money; strategies of court use in urban
               Ghana", in: L. Nader and H.F. Todd Jr. (eds.) *The disputing process - law in ten
               societies,* Columbia University Press.
Moore, S.F.
1977   "Individual interests and organisational structures; dispute settlements as
               'Events of Articulation'", in: I. Hamnett (ed.), *Social anthropology and law,* ASA
               Monograph 14, Academic Press, London, New York, San Fransisco.
1978   "Politics, procedures, and norms in changing Chagga law", in: S.F. Moore, *Law
               as process; an anthropological approach,* Routledge & Kegan Paul, London,
               Henley and Boston.
Nader, L.
1964   *Talea and Juquila: A comparison of Zapotec social organization,* University of
               California Publications in American Archeology and Ethnography 48(3): 195-
               296.
Nader, L. and H.F. Todd Jr. (eds.)
1978   *The disputing process - law in ten societies,* Columbia University Press.
Pospisil, L.
1979   "Legally induced culture change in New Guinea", in: S.B. Burman and B.E.
               Harrell-Bond (eds.) *The imposition of law,* New York, Academic Press.

1981 "Modern and traditional administration of justice in New Guinea", *Journal of Legal Pluralism* 19: 93-116.

Roberts, S.
1979 "Tradition and change at Mochudi; competing jurisdictions in Botswana", *ALS* 17: 37-51.

Rothenberger, J.E.
1978 "The social dynamics of dispute settlement in a Sunni Muslim village in Lebanon", in L. Nader and H.F. Todd Jr. (eds.) *The disputing process - law in ten societies*, Columbia University Press.

Rouveroy van Nieuwaal, E.A.B. van
1976 *Vrouw, Vorst, Vrederechter; Aspekten van het huwelijksrecht, de traditionele en moderne volksrechtspraak bij de Anufom in Noord-Togo*, Afrika-Studiecentrum, Leiden.

Starr, J.O.
1978 "Turkish village disputing behavior", in: L. Nader and H.F. Todd Jr. (eds.) *The disputing process - law in ten societies*, Columbia University Press.

Starr, J.O. and B. Yngvesson
1975 "Scarcity and disputing; zeroing-in on compromise decisions", *American Ethnologist* 2(3): 533-566.

Tanner, N.M.
1969 "Disputing and dispute settlement in Minangkabau", *Indonesia* 8: 21-67.

Witty, C.J.
1978 "Disputing issues in Shehaam, a multireligious village in Lebanon", in: L. Nader and H.F. Todd Jr. (eds.), *The disputing process - law in ten societies*, Columbia University Press.

The channel of official law to unofficial law in Japan

Masaji Chiba

1. The "Present state of information on the substance of the various papers" reported in the Newsletter IV of the IUAES Commission on Contemporary Folk Law, 1981 (pp. 8, 14) is, though a small collection of brief mentions, of much informative value on the problems to be pursued in contemporary folk law in the world. One of the basic problems found among them is the interaction between folk law and state law, whether positive or negative.[1] The interaction has been never duly dealt with in scientific research, for the anthropology of law has generally tended to concentrate itself on folk law with rare regard to state law, while the sociology of law mainly concentrated on the function of state law.

The first task in order to advance the analysis of the interaction is clearly to identify concrete channels of the interaction. Some of them are suggested in the above-referred mentions (see note 1). Among others, Woodman focuses on this issue in his outlines "1. Legislative decision on the judicial recognition of customary law .... The rejection of codification and restatement. The delegation of the establishment of customary law to the court. 2. The judicial mode of establishing customary law ((a) the adoption of a system of precedent, (b) the rejection of a system of precedent, (c) reasons for the above). 3. Implications for legal theory". But his discussion seems to be based on data from a common law colonial country. As to civil law countries, the argument of George Krzeczunowicz on Ethiopia (cited in Hooker 1975: 400-402) seems to be more applicable. According to him, the Ethiopian Civil Code is first provided with four "outlets for custom" to recognize folk law: (a) "incorporation" for "putting into code form ... some general customs which relate primarily to personal and family law", (b) "references to custom" in the Civil Code concerning various aspects of betrothal, marriage, maintenance, as well as such property law as rights of way and servitudes, transfer of rights in land, lease of land, damages, (c) "filling Code vacuums" though with rare examples, and (d) "judicial interpretation". He enumerates in addition three "para-legal outlets for custom", such as 1. "the vesting of a discretionary jurisdiction in the customary 'family arbitrators'", 2. "the contract of compromise ... under which the parties are absolutely bound and which the Code considers *res judicata* and not subject to appeal", and 3. "the possibility of indigenous groups ... being recognized as 'associations' under the Code", however remote they may be.

My paper aims to present some data on the channels of interaction between state law and folk law in Japan for comparison with other countries as means of a contribution to formulating a general hypothesis.

As to the terminology, I here prefer "official law" and "unofficial law" to that of "state law" and "folk law" respectively. The term "folk law" is truly useful when paying special attention to law other than state law. But it may be often adopted into state law even with reformulation, sometimes as public institutions like the *Tenno* system of Japan. As far as these cases are concerned, the term "folk law" obscures the boundary between both laws. In addition, we can truly extend our scope to observe the legal life of a people by using "folk law" instead of "state law". But it is still not enough to cover the whole legal life of a people, which may be regulated by other types of law not clearly classified into either of the two laws, such as the case of canon law. In consideration of those problems, it would be wise for operational purposes to adopt the terms of "official law"[2] and "unofficial law"[3] with the possibility of further elaboration. In Japan, however, official law being in reality occupied by state law with no co-existing other kinds, official law and state law may be interchangeably used.

2. The main channel by which Japanese state law may positively interact with unofficial law is to adopt it into official law in various forms through deliberation, choice and reformulation on the part of official law.

The fundamental form is individually to incorporate originally unofficial rights and institutions into the provisions of enacted law. Among remarkable examples are the *Tenno* system in the Constitution and related Acts; *nengo* or *gengo* (name of an era under the reign of a *Tenno* like Meiji or Showa), and national holidays in special Acts; traditional practices regarding marriage and the family such as *naien* (*de facto* marriage), divorce by consent, privileged inheritance of family memorials of ancestors in the Civil Code; *inkan* or *hanko* (seals and their impressions) in place of signatures and *noren* (goodwill) in the Commercial Code; the well-known conciliation of civil and domestic affairs in special Acts; and so on.

Another form is the general clause as to the specific authorization to adopt "custom" or "customary law" in place of official provisions. There are two basic provisions of this kind. One is Article 2 of the Law concerning the Application of Laws in General, sanctioning certain customs as official law.[4] The other is Article 92 of the Civil Code, allowing the parties to rely upon customs.[5] There are still other provisions of limited application. A notable one is Article 263 and 294 of the Civil Code to sanction the customs of common land as official rights.[6] Others are the similar provisions of customary rights in various adjoining relationships in the Civil Code. Still another one is, as may be theoretically more significant, Article 1 of the Commercial Code, applying commercial customary law prior to the Civil Code in the absence of commercial provisions concerned.[7]

In comparison with the above provisions which overtly aim to allow the adoption of unofficial law into official law,[8] there are also found other kinds of provision which allow unofficial law covertly to creep into official law though without an express provision for this. This is by another kind of general clause to be applied for diffused purposes, above all the principle of "public policy or good morals" (Civil Code, Article 90).[9] Here we find room for the substantial adoption of unofficial law even without manifest reference to its label, unless it is disapproved as contrary to public policy or good morals. A similar function may be performed by the constitutional principle of private freedom, in so far as it is left to the volition of a person to choose a specific pattern of behavior, including one conforming to unofficial law. [10]

Whether or not these general clauses and the private freedom principle may in reality cause the adoption of unofficial law into official law depends upon the final decision of the judge in court. And it goes without saying that the judge is empowered and obligated to make such a decision in accordance with his own discretion unless otherwise provided by enacted law. In general, as in other countries, judicial decisions form an important channel of official law to unofficial law other than the above-mentioned enacted law. The channelling capacity of judicial decisions may be further-reaching than that of the above provisions, for what is adopted is not limited to unofficial law and the adoption may be often done without being specifically so mentioned.

Discretion is also exercised by administrative authorities with regard to the matters within their jurisdiction. Among numerous discretionary cases, some are decided by consideration of the prevalence of unofficial law, on whatever grounds they may be formally rationalized. For example, local governments ordinarily entrust self-regulated town-block associations prevailing in Japanese society with some official business in order to facilitate direct contact with their citizens; prosecutors are as a rule reluctant to prosecute persons who commit misdemeanours for the first time. Established administrative practices as a result of discretion thus function as if official law, including cases substantially adopting unofficial law.

In sum, unofficial law in Japan may be channelled to official law either by being identified as "custom" or "customary law" overtly sanctioned in enacted law, or through the authorized discretion of legal agents, or else indirectly by the volitional choice of persons based upon constitutional right to private freedom. Except through these limited channels, Japanese official law appears to be empowered definitively to reject unofficial law. Certainly, there are many cases which exemplify such definitive rejection. For instance, official law orders the punishment of criminal behaviour, even when the behaviour is justified by the unofficial law prevailing in deviant groups like gangster organizations[11] (cf. Iwai 1974); official law invalidates some decisions of a village community, like an agreement to vote a specific candidate into office in a public election, regardless of whether it may have been based on village autonomy, a typical unofficial law; official decisions may not approve of government commitment, central or local, to any religious activities, however firmly local Shinto shrines may be supported by people bound by traditional practices as an unofficial law and however eagerly official agents personally want to worship shrines. The channels of official law to unofficial law in these examples appear to be irresistibly established.

3. On the other hand, the appearance cannot be generalized as it is, because many cases are in reality to be found, on which unofficial laws exert strong influences along with official law and in which the validity of official law is substantially competed with and very often undermined by the significant function of unofficial law. In this function, however, unofficial law is more conspicuous in its ideal than behavioural elements. Giving the ideal elements the label of "unofficial jural postulates"[12] in consideration of the usage of E. Adamson Hoebel (1954), their influential function is indicated below.

First, when a ceremony for commencing construction of a municipal gymnasium held by a city government in a traditional *Shinto* rite was objected by citizens on the ground of its violation of the constitutional principle of the separation of government from religion, the Supreme Court of Japan, reversing the decision of a High Court in favour of the citizens, ruled that the ceremony was constitutional because it was based upon a "popular custom" and not a "religious rite" (cf. Tanaka 1976: 735-737). As a result, the official law rejected to approve the religious rite by formal logic, while it approved in substance the rite and supporting unofficial jural postulate of *Shinto* God worship. In this way of interpretation, there is found a peculiar but authorized compromise between official law and unofficial law, or an official jural postulate and an unofficial one. A similar compromise is seen in the official interpretation which insists upon the constitutionality of visits of Cabinet Ministers to the Yasukuni Shrine, the central Shinto shrine for the war dead, and to the Ise Shrine, originally the Shinto shrine of the *Tenno* family, on the ground that the visits are carried out "not officially but personally though with official positions." Remarkably enough, in this kind of rationalization unofficial laws and jural postulates, *Shinto* God worship and *Tenno* adoration (which are, strictly speaking, incompatible with official law) are covertly adopted, while they are overtly rationalized as having been rejected.

Secondly, when a man and a women enter into matrimony, they are entitled to choose either of their family names for the family name of the new couple. Most of the cases, though not so many, where the woman's family name is chosen are those where the man intends to succeed to the hereditary status of the head of the woman's family according to the traditional postulate of "family idea". The postulate also works when all of the children except one decline to inherit property, so as to allow the one child to inherit the whole, and in other cases. Thirdly, there is an ordinance (a form of enacted law) which allows, exceptionally, the use of units of about 1.818 metres, 3.3. square metres, or 1.8 litres under the official metric system. Those odd units are adopted in reality so as to sanction the use of the traditional units of 1 *ken* for length, 1 *tsubo* for square measure, and 1 *sho* for volume respectively, all of which are still widely prevailing as special usages forming an unofficial law. The official law in the above examples does not overtly adopt unofficial laws and jural postulates, but in reality covertly sanctions those which may be in substance incompatible with, and therefore able to undermine, the official law. There are other cases where unofficial laws and jural postulates are adopted, though without being overtly so declared.

Fourthly, *giri*,[13] one of the best-known cultural features of Japanese behaviour, should be mentioned in this connexion. Being a Japanese version of the reciprocity principle, *giri* obliges a person to reward someone who gave him particular gifts or services by reason of a special relationship between them, such as co-members of a community, lineage or status, respectively supported by such postulates as "community spirit", "lineage principle", or "status order".[14] It presents the main justification for such frequent gift exchanges among Japanese (cf. Befu 1974). Legal issues were often provoked when public servants received gifts in relation to their official duties from persons in special relationship, for instance, administrators from dealers, or teachers from pupils' parents. If the Penal Code is rigidly applied, even the smallest gift received forms a ground for the receiving public servant to be accused of bribery. But judicial decisions have left such cases unchallenged when the gift is rated as reasonable according to "the common sense of society", as against challenged cases where the value exceeds the limit. *Giri*, an unofficial jural postulate, and *giri* relations, an unofficial law, are here also covertly adopted in the name of the "the common sense of society".

Such ways of interpretation and practices in the administration of law in Japan are from a formal viewpoint explained as a natural result of the authorized discretion of legal agents or volitional choice of persons in exercise of their private freedom in accordance with overt provisions or supporting jural postulates of the official law. On the other hand, the result seen from the substantial viewpoint cannot be disregarded, because unofficial laws and jural postulates which may in substance undermine official law are adopted in disguise. The Japanese system of official law includes, as a matter of fact, the mechanism which bring forth such results. This mechanism is a variation of the "challenge- absorbing mechanism"[15] of official law found characteristically in Japan and comparable with similar variations in other countries.

4. The above challenge-absorbing mechanism of Japanese law is worth

examining for its importance in the analysis of the unofficial jural postulate in Japan.

First of all, the family idea, community spirit, lineage principle, status order, *Tenno* adoration, and *Shinto* God worship as referred to above are the main existing unofficial jural postulates.[16] Their essence was protected by the official legal system under the former constitution for the *Tenno* monopoly regime before World War II and was invalidated by the present Constitution since 1947, faithful to the western type of democracy. If these postulates are openly mentioned in official legal cases with their proper appellations, they should have to be rejected with no consideration given to them. But they are in fact accepted by official law with no reference to their effect. From the substantial point of view, such a disguised acceptance of these postulates is criticized by those who wish to be faithful to the present constitutional postulates. Government and the majority of the people, however, have favoured an official interpretation which is satisfied with the formal rationalization. This fact shows that the challenge-absorbing mechanism covers a domain where some unofficial jural postulates, which, strictly speaking, are incompatible with official law, are accommodated as if there were no conflicts between both systems. Here one must hypothesize another basic jural postulate functioning ambivalently overtly to support the formal logic of official law as well as covertly to approve the prevailing postulates of unofficial law, let alone the problem whether the latter is of a constitutional nature or not. Its ambivalence makes it possible, however curious it may sound, that apparently incompatible official law and unofficial law co-exist whether understood to be in conflict or harmony. I would tentatively call this postulate an "amoeba-like way of thinking and behaviour" or briefly "amoeba-like behaviour", meaning "a postulate to enable people to behave as flexibly as possible to adapt themselves to varying circumstances as well as to maintain their individuality". With this postulate presupposed, such well-known Japanese attitudes toward law can be reasonably understood as respecting "living law", which inspires in Japanese a reluctance to resort to official law (cf. Noda 1976: 39, 160) or "harmony", which leads Japanese to prefer reconciliation of conflict to judicial decision (cf. Kawashima 1963: 44, 50). Rooted diffusedly in the cultural pattern of Japanese behaviour, the amoeba-like behaviour functions specifically to influence the validity and effectivity of official law by accommodating its conflicts with unofficial law, however overtly rejected. It thus forms a basic unofficial jural postulate, and might be seen to function as a latent official jural postulate for its substantial effects.

The conflicts between both systems of law accommodated by the amoeba-like behaviour may be taken, on the other hand, as ones between received law and indigenous law in Japan. However, some indigenous laws are overtly adopted in enacted provisions or may be adopted through the discretion of legal agents and the private freedom of persons, by choice or reformulation.

They formally constitute part of official law. For this reason, the interaction between received law and indigenous law, whether in mutual assimilation or conflict, comes about in a wider domain than that between official law and unofficial law. Although analysis of the interaction has yet to be made, one thing is clear, that the Japanese reception of western law has resulted not in an exact copy of their models but in an assimilation with indigenous law to a greater degree than usually recognized by scholars. This fact may suggest a reasonable ground for an attempt to examine the Japanese reception of foreign law from the viewpoint of how indigenous law accepted or rejected foreign law in the process of interaction, and what indigenous jural postulates justified the process. Here one must hypothesize that some basic indigenous postulate was functioning. I would call it the "identity postulate of indigenous law", meaning "the indigenous jural postulate which functions as the criterion for evaluating or devaluing foreign law in order to decide how to accept or reject it so as to keep the cultural identity of a people in the whole structure of their law". The amoeba-like way of thinking and behaviour is thought also to function as such a postulate, when we cannot fail to observe that Japanese people have been so flexible in receiving foreign law but so rigid in keeping their cultural identity in their whole structure of law.

I know that the postulate of the "amoeba-like behaviour" is rather a naive black-box concept not yet satisfactorily elaborated for use in scientific operations, and that exploration of its substance may not be successful immediately. The reason why I would put forward the identity postulate of indigenous law in disregard of those facts is that various basic indigenous jural postulates which play the role of the identity postulates are reported in foreign countries by many scholars. To mention a few examples: similar basic postulates are working in countries under more or less influence of Indian culture such as *dharma* for Hindu law (Derrett and Iyer 1975) and *thammasat* for Thai law (Hooker 1975: 372-373); *shariah* is well-known by its comprehensive regulation of Muslim behaviour (Afchar 1975); *chilot* is suspected of having worked as such a postulate in Ethiopia (Hooker 1975: 396-398); "the conception of the universe as the basis of the conception of law" is found in China, which "remains China throughout all these changes" by recent revolution (Noda 1975: 125, 129). When compared with such examples, the Japanese amoeba-like behaviour may raise a theoretical problem of examining the identity postulate of indigenous law as a universal legal postulate. My putting forward of this hypothesis is intended to pay due respect to cultural identity in the whole structure of law of a people. Naturally this respect should not go as far as an ethnocentric adherence to a culture, but should be accompanied by respect for other cultures, consistent with the endeavour to develop mutual understanding among cultures.

When the identity postulate of indigenous law is affirmatively examined, the official law of Japan will be found to interact with unofficial law by the channel of the amoeba-like way of thinking and behaviour, that is, a basic unofficial jural postulate, in addition to official provisions, authorized discretion and private freedom.

NOTES

1.   Presupposing "the conflictual or antagonistic aspects of [the] interaction" (Baxi), many try to analyse the modes of the interaction. Some of them pay attention to the nature of folk law as "a source ... and modifier of law" (Allott), "social control from below" (Black and Baumgartner), and thus "a theory of competition" (Griffiths) or "the way ... 'folk law' ... interweaves traditional conceptions with newer court methods" (Schott). Many others lay stress on the positive response of state law to folk law in various conceptions such as "recognition" (Abel, Kirby, Maddock, Yusef), "ascertainment" (Kludze), "integration" (Fitzpatrick), "the change" of folk law (Koesnoe), "relation" (Galanter), "relationship" (F. von Benda-Beckmann), or "interaction" (McGuillis).
2.   Defined as "state law and the legal systems which are sanctioned by the authorities other than the state and which are officially authorized by the state itself".
3.   Defined as "social norms customarily sanctioned by a certain circle of people in popular conceptions and actual behaviour patterns with the function of supplementing, competing with, modifying or undermining official law including state law".
4.   "Customs which are not contrary to public policy shall have the same force as law in so far as they are recognized by the provision of a law or an ordinance or relate to matters which are not provided for laws or ordinances".
5.   "If, in cases where there exists a custom which differs from any provisions of laws or ordinances which are not concerned with public policy, it is to be considered that the parties to a juristic act have intended to conform to such custom, that custom shall prevail".
6.   Article 263 reads: "With regard to commonage which has the nature of co-ownership, the provisions of this section (co-ownership) shall apply subject to the custom of each locality". Article 294: "With regard to commonage not partaking of the nature of co-ownership, the provisions of this section (servitudes) shall apply *mutatis mutandis*, subject to the custom of each locality".
7.   "As to a commercial matter, the commercial customary law shall apply if there are no provisions in this Code; and the Civil Code shall apply, if there is no such law".
8.   Generally speaking in disregard of minor exceptions, there is found a difference in "references to custom" between Ethiopia by individual provisions and Japan by general clauses.
9.   "A juristic act which has for its object such matters as are contrary to public policy or good morals is null and void".
10.   Here is another difference between Ethiopia and Japan concerning the "para-legal outlets for custom". In Japan, some social agents supposedly corresponding to "family arbitrators" in Ethiopia have been found, but their role may be said to have been transferred to the official Conciliation Commitee so depriving the traditional custom of the nature of unofficial law. A similar transfer is found in the Japanese practice corresponding to the Ethiopian "contract of compromise". A most remarkable difference is found in the third outlet. In Ethiopia, indigenous groups such as age-grades or kin-groups may be recognized as "associations" under the Civil Code. In Japan, by contrast, the indigenous groups seem to be of a greater variety and to enjoy the constitutional freedom of association in general. For instance, religious groups are particularly protected as religious corporations by a special Act, leaving their internal regulation to their autonomy which forms an unofficial law. Another kind of indigenous group is one founded on the system of *iemoto* (main family with subordinate branch

families, or the leading master with training disciples) for the tea-ceremony, flower- arrangement, *no*-play, old military arts, *sumo* (Japanese wrestling), and so on (cf. Hsu 1975). Regulated by their own unofficial law, they may also take on official forms of foundations, corporations, or companies.

11.   Some might raise an objection to such a classification of deviant social regulation as law, however unofficial it may be. I do not deny the possibility. From the viewpoint of the members of the group concerned, however, the regulation forms their valid social norm, often more authoritative and effective than competing official law. It is not only possible but also necessary to regard it as an unofficial law in order to assess the validity and effectivity of official law.

12.   Jural postulates are defined as "specific principles, values, ideals or authority so firmly established as to influence application of social norms and legal rules". Among them, official ones are those specifically relevant to official law, such as justice, equity, natural law, reasonableness, human rights, private freedom, and so on in western law, while unofficial ones relevant to unofficial law come under various labels.

13.   Defined as "a category of Japanese obligations" (Benedict 1954: 317) or "the manner of behaviour required of one person to others in consequence of his social status" (Noda 1976: 175).

14.   "Community" is here used for *buraku* in Japanese, meaning originally "a village community with the orientation of group solidarity" , and fictitiously "any social group with a similar orientation", which is widely applicable even to some modern enterprises. "Lineage" translates *dozoku*, meaning originally "an extended family with a main family and branch ones ordered in a genealogical hierarchy" and fictitiously "any social group founded on the principle", like *iemoto* groups, Buddhist sects. "Status" translates *mibun*, meaning originally "social status in a hierarchy", and fictitiously "the hierarchical social position of a person".

15.   The term "challenge-absorbing mechanism" is used to conceptualize a special mechanism inherent in the system of official law, above all, modern western law. It serves to maintain the self-consistent normative structure of an official legal system, when it is faced with challenges arising from varying and changing social realities, by absorbing some of the challenges into the system. Examples are the elaborate system of inclusive rules, definite but highly abstract concepts of rights and duties, legal ideas complementing rights and duties, alternatives of principal and exceptional rules, and so on. The function is supplemented by another, the "challenge-rejecting mechanism", which rejects challenges dangerous to the legal system, as exemplified by the principle of separation between norm and fact, politics and religion, law and ethics, and so on. (For details, see Chiba forthcoming.)

16.   Found in my report to be included in the joint study mentioned in Chiba 1979: 293.

REFERENCES

Afchar, H.
1975   "The Muslim conception of law", in *International Encyclopedia of Comparative Law*, Vol. 2, Chap. 1, The Hague: Mouton.
Befu, Harumi
1974   "Gift-giving in modernizing Japan", in T.S. Lebra & W.P. Lebra (eds.), *Japanese Culture and Behavior*, Honolulu: University Press of Hawaii.
Benedict, Ruth
1954   *The chrysanthemum and the sword: patterns of Japanese culture*, Tokyo: Charles E. Tuttle.
Chiba, Masaji
1979   "Three-level structure of law in a world of many cultures", in *Law and the Future of Society*, ARSP Beiheft, Nr. 11, Wiesbaden, BRD: Franz Steiner.

forthcoming   "Cultural universality and particularity of jurisprudence", in M.L. Marasinghe & W.E. Conclin (eds.), *Essays on Third World Perspectives in Jurisprudence*, Kuala Lumpur: Malaysian Law Journal.

Derrett, J.D.M., & T.K.K. Iyer
1975   "The Hindu conception of law", in *International Encyclopedia of Comparative Law*, Vol. 2, Chap. 1, The Hague: Mouton.

Hoebel, E. Adamson
1954   *The law of primitive man.* Cambridge, Mass.: Harvard University Press.

Hooker, M.B.
1975   *Legal pluralism: an introduction to colonial and neo-colonial laws*, Oxford: Clarendon Press.

Hsu, Francis L.K.
1975   *Iemoto: the heart of Japan*, New York: Halsted Press.

Iwai, Hiroaki
1974   "Delinquent groups and organized crimes", in T.S. Lebra & W.P. Lebra (eds.), *Japanese culture and behavior*, Honolulu: University Press of Hawaii.

Kawashima, Takeyoshi
1963   "Dispute resolution in contemporary Japan", in Arthur T. von Mehren (ed.), *Law in Japan*, Cambridge, Mass.: Harvard University Press.

Noda, Yoshiyuki
1975   "The far eastern conception of law", in *International Encyclopedia of Comparative Law*, Vol. 2, Chap. 1, The Hague: Mouton.

1976   *Introduction to Japanese law*, Tokyo: Tokyo University Press.

Tanaka, Hideo
1976   *The Japanese legal system*, Tokyo: Tokyo University Press.

Four laws of interaction in circumstances of legal pluralism: first steps towards an explanatory theory

J. Griffiths

What follows is not a "paper", let alone an "essay", but only four propositions, encumbered with just enough commentary to make them provocative and to make their intended meaning reasonably clear. The idea is to stimulate a critical discussion to the end of seeing whether the sort of approach here attempted has anything to recommend it.

These four propositions are meant as a tentative first step toward unifying and organizing a certain (not very extensive) body of information and theoretical notions concerning the sort of institutional interaction which takes place in circumstances of legal pluralism. The focus here is upon that aspect of a full theory of litigation which deals with the institutional structure within which litigation takes place, rather than upon concrete litigation behavior or upon what Black calls the "behavior of social control" (Black 1976; see generally Griffiths 1984b).[1]

What is the situation to which these propositions are supposed to be applicable? - what is "legal pluralism"? I have (tentatively) dealt with that question at length elsewhere (Griffiths n.d.; see also Galanter 1981). For present purposes it will have to suffice to define legal pluralism as the (variably frequent) presence within a social group of multiple legal orders, where the existence of a separate legal order entails the existence of a distinct rule of recognition: that is, "separate" legal orders are not reducible the one to the other. And a "legal" order is any normative order which includes secondary rules: that is, exhibits division of labor in any of its aspects, is to any extent institutionalized (see Griffiths 1984a).[2] The four propositions involved in the discussion which follows, however, concern only litigation institutions, so for practical purposes the scope of the discussion here is limited to situations of multiple legal orders which have that sort of institutional specialization. When more than one such legal order is present in a social group, the litigation institutions inevitably interact with one another, at least to some extent. The pretention of the following propositions is to describe and explain the interaction which takes place.

The four propositions with which I will deal are as follows: (1) The law of inside washing of dirty linen. (2) The law of maximization of litigation profit. (3) The law of equal return on social control energy. (4) The law of convergence (and divergence) of norms.

1. THE LAW OF INSIDE WASHING OF DIRTY LINEN

This law states that every social group ("semi-autonomous social field") strives to process disputes between its members internally: it seeks to make its internal processes attractive and to punish the use of external processes. The classic description of this law in operation is Gulliver's *Social Control in an African Society* (1963); the underlying theory of group dynamics is set forth in Olson's *The Logic of Collective Action* (1965).

Any group which regularly permits its members to carry their disputing outside is on the way to disintegration. In this connection, it is important to distinguish between groups of different "life-space inclusiveness" (Galanter 1974: 133). Every group is a "public" with its own "public issues" (Smith 1974), but the range of sorts of issues which it reckons to be its "public issues", and as to which it seeks to affect a monopoly on dispute processing, varies widely. That is, groups vary in what they deem "their" dirty linen. For the family, virtually any dispute between members is a family dispute; for businessmen, the relevant dirty linen consists of contractual and related disputes, but not interpersonal, political, and other sorts of disputes (see Macaulay 1963; Moore 1973). Groups do, of course, tend to be imperialistic in this respect: to gather to them dirty linen which is not really "theirs".

For purposes of this law, groups can stand in varying relations to one another, defined by the degree of overlap in membership. Groups with little or no overlap can be said to be "parallel" to each other (the structure of a larger group which subsumes them is then "segmentary"), whereas groups with considerable overlap stand in a relationship of "inclusiveness" - and if one is smaller than and subsumed within the other, it is a "lesser included group" in relation to the other. The distinction is important in understanding the application of the law. The law applies with the greatest force to the case of parallel groups: members of one group virtually never take their litigation to (institutions of) another group of which they are not both members (the exceptional situations in which this may occur should be particularly interesting and, presumably, short-lived); this case is, for most practical purposes, unimportant. On the other hand, the law is of no application to the situation in which members of an inclusive group take their litigation to a lesser included group of which both are members, since no outside washing of the inclusive group's dirty linen takes place. There may well be competitive relations between the litigation institutions concerned, but it is the second law (maximization of litigation profit) which applies to that situation.

The important application of the law is to litigation between members of a lesser included group. This should not be taken to an inclusive group of which both are also members. For in such an inclusive group will be members of other groups, before whom the "dirty linen" of the disputants' group would then be washed - and it is precisely this state of affairs which the law forbids. The greater the degree to which an inclusive group's structure is segmentary - the less the overlap in the membership of its subsumed sub-groups - the greater the force with which the law applies. It is worse for internal conflicts of a sect or a family to be aired in public, than for those of a business group or (in many cases) a village.

The law can be rephrased, as it is by Gulliver (see also van Rouveroy van Nieuwåal 1976: 70-71), in choice-of-forum terms: litigation should occur in (institutions of) the smallest group of which both parties are members. The law explains, thus, the common observation that litigation in specialized tribunals (e.g., of the state) tends to be between otherwise unrelated parties: if they were otherwise related, there would be a lesser included group within which they should do their litigating. Furthermore, the larger the smallest group of which both are members - the more attenuated their social bonds, the greater the "relational distance" between them - the more likely that its litigation institutions will be differentiated and specialized ones, and that litigation will be "legal" in character (see Griffiths 1984a and Abel 1973) - thus the first law also explains the often noted association between forma-lism/legalism and "relational distance".

2. THE LAW OF MAXIMIZATION OF LITIGATION PROFIT

The first law deals with relationships between social groups in relation to litigation. The second law deals with relations between litigation institutions (generally of groups which stand in a relation of inclusiveness to each other). The second law states that every litigation institution competes with others to maximize its institutional profit from the handling of cases. I must emphasize that this is a proposition explanatory of the behavior of institutions as such and therefore of the structure with which individual actors are confronted and within which their behavior takes place. The law is not, however, proposed as explanatory of individual behavior, as such.

The second law is of little interest in the case of institutions belonging to groups standing in a parallel relationship to each other. Because of the strength of the first law in such a case, there is little opportunity for competi-tion. The second law applies to competitive relations among the various institutions of the various groups of which the disputants are both members - it applies, that is, to institutions of groups in a relation of inclusiveness to each other.

What are, in general, the costs and benefits of litigation for a litigation institution? The benefits are often straightforward: cash, in the form of fines, fees, forfeitures and the like. Each additional case may also, in a slightly less direct sense, represent profit to an institution, to the extent that its position within the institutional structure to which it belongs depends upon its caseload. The benefits of litigation to an institution are often, however, less straightforward. Processing cases seems in itself to render returns in terms of general political power, it gives opportunities for direct exercise of social control, and it affords important access to information.[3] The costs of litigation to a litigation institution are mostly concrete: time, energy, staff, and the like. There is also the opposite side of the power coin to consider: for solving problems for others can bring not only power, but also criticism and attack, and hence (if one is vulnerable), weakness.

The ultimate conclusion of the above line of thought is this: every additional case of a particular sort brings with it, for any given litigation institution, a net profit or loss. Whether the institution acts to aquire such a case, or to pass it along to another institution (or into limbo, that is, "lumping it" or "exit"), depends (in general - I am not talking about individual decisions) upon the state of the balance sheet.

So much for the independent variable side of the second law; what about the dependent variable? What is the competition behavior which it is supposed to explain? What sort of positive or negative reactions to cases and litigants can litigation institutions exhibit? Positive competition for cases is generally of three sorts, well known from the commercial counterpart of the litigation market: one can make one's product more attractive than the alternative to the consumer/litigant, one can monopolize the market, or one can bind consumer/litigants to one with various sorts of product-binding techniques. Monopolization is accomplished either by complete success with the other competitive strategies, or by main force. While it is possible to drive particular competitors out of the market, lasting and complete monopoly is rarely if ever achieved. The modern state makes the most extravagant claims in this regard for its litigation institutions, the (empirical) falsity of which is a matter of considerable current interest (see Griffiths n.d.; Galanter 1981).

How do litigation institutions make their services more attractive to potential litigants? They can *lower the cost*, to begin with - the court fees and associated costs (e.g. of counsel, which as a last resort can be excluded altogether), the costs in time (e.g. delay) and distance, and the social and psychological costs (e.g. formality, symbolic dress and behavior, language - cf. Danet 1980: 451, on the "plain English" movement). This strategy manifests itself in such otherwise diverse institutional settings as African local courts (Abel 1979), family and juvenile courts, Cuban Popular Tribunals (Berman 1969), "access to justice" proposals (see Galanter 1981), small claims courts, in-house arbitration, etc. In the second place, a litigation institution can make its services more attractive by *improving the quality*. This consists of such things as the magnitude and predictability of the risks of litigation, the effectiveness of the enforcement possibilities, and the substance of the rules which the institution applies. Especially that last sort of possible adjustment to a situation of competition has received explicit attention in the recent literature - the results of which are summarized in law four - but armchair reflection suggests many other examples of institutional attention to the quality of the service offered, examples which it would be fascinating to attempt to explain in terms of (threatening) competition. Should the last hundred years of streamlining of civil procedure be seen (partly) in this light? Does the quality of service in "indigenous" tribunals (Galanter 1981) improve with the advent of competition from the state? Should the relative quality of medieval English royal justice (see Pollock and Maitland 1968: 202-203) be seen as a competitive strategy? *Advertising* can accompany or take the place of actual changes in the quality of litigation service. An improved system of administrative appeals designed (from our present point of view) to improve the competitive position of the "official" legal system against its political alternatives ("patronage") can be accompanied by an information campaign intended to make potential litigants aware of its existence (research concerning the Dutch example here referred to is described in Griffiths 1984b). But a great deal of advertising of litigation institutions is better described as "product differentiation advertising" (in political discourse often called "propaganda"). In the case of the modern state, for instance, considerable energy is invested in convincing the public that, by contrast with the competition, its litigation institutions are "modern", treat all comers "equally" and "fairly", exemplify the "rule of law", etc. (cf. Thompson 1975; Balbus 1973). Competing institutions are publicly denounced as "primitive", "barbaric", "feudal", etc. (see e.g. van den Bergh 1980).

If it would cost too much or is otherwise unfeasible to make one's institution more attractive to litigants, one can discourage use of available alternatives by product-binding. The technique is simple, if one happens to offer another product or service which potential litigants need and cannot obtain elsewhere: one makes access to the latter dependent on use of the institution in question (or, at least, non-use of the alternatives). When the institution concerned belongs to a group which stands in a lesser included relationship to the group of the alternative institution, this sort of product-binding is simply a special case of the application of the first law: the included group as a whole, and its litigation institutions in particular, attach negative sanctions (among them, denial of access to other services afforded by the group and its institutions) to those who wash their dirty linen in 'public" (see e.g. K. von Benda-Beckmann 1981; cf. also Macaulay 1963; Moore 1973).

When (particular sorts of) cases entail losses rather than profits, there are many strategies available for avoiding or getting rid of them, or for reducing unit cost. Cost reduction can be accomplished with a variety of measures designed to improve the bureaucratic efficiency of an institution's procedures without losing cases to other forums, of which some are simple and straightforward while others may entail radical changes in the normative structure of the disputes concerned (e.g. "no fault" divorce and tort litigation[4]). If efficiency measures are not feasible, then it is preferable to divert cases into more or less controlled sub-institutions than to lose them to competitors (hence, perhaps, the doctrine of "exhaustion of administrative remedies", the "diversion" of criminal cases and judicial toleration and encouragement of "plea bargaining", the requirement of representation by the *mamak* which effectively refers cases to him - see K. von Benda-Beckmann 1981 - etc.). In all of these and other "supervised settlement" processes - what Galanter (1974: 127) calls "'appended' dispute-settlement systems" - the supervising institution manages to keep at least some control over litigation on which it itself expends little or no effort. And since, as Galanter (1981) argues, the power which courts have resides to a large extent in the influence which the messages they project into society can have (among other things, on bargaining between litigants and on litigation in other forums), rather than in the direct influence of their decisions, wise attention to the effectiveness of such messages can preserve to a litigation institution some of the profit even of litigation with which it never has any direct contact.

3. THE LAW OF EQUAL RETURN ON SOCIAL CONTROL ENERGY

It is often supposed that, in a situation of competition between alternative litigation institutions, one will be "more effective" than another. It is hard to see what could be meant by this other than the notion that, for a given investment of social control energy, some institutions accomplish more social control than others. (For the concept of social control involved here, see Griffiths 1984a) The usual supposition seems to be that the institutions which thus get more bang for their buck are, generally speaking, those which are relatively small, intimate, "internal" in relation to their public (see Kidder 1979), informal (cf. Schwartz 1954), etc.

The third law of interaction between litigation institutions states that, on the contrary, given equal input, social control outputs are equal. Except that it is superficially counter-intuitive, there is nothing really remarkable about this, and the phenomena which are usually accounted for as if the law of conservation of energy did not apply to social control can be shown to be consequences of this law, not violations of it.

The reason why social control in the family is so "effective" is not because the family (by comparison with the state and its institutions) gets something for little or nothing, but because the family invests proportionally vastly much more energy in social control than the state does. The "informal" control of the communistic *kvutza* was not more effective than the "formal" control of the individualistic *moshav* (see Schwartz 1954); there simply was much more of it. The thing to explain, in short, is not the superior "effectiveness" of small-scale, informal social control, but the ability of some social fields to generate so much more control energy than other social fields. It is no use saying that people are more dependent on each other in small-scale, intimate social fields. Of course they are, but interdependence is not a natural state: it is the result of the investment of energy. Why can't larger social fields, and in particular the state, succeed in creating the same degree of dependency? That is the *question* (not the answer).

This is not the place to seek to answer such questions deriving from the propositions being formulated. But it will not hurt to state that in my opinion one ought to begin by subjecting - here as elsewhere in the economics of production - the notion of "economies of scale" to a good lot of sceptical acid. In the case of social control labour, I think the concept of "diseconomies of scale" will prove more fruitful. The larger the field a source of social control energy must control, and the farther removed it is (where "distance" summarizes several different dimensions) from the behavior to be controlled, the greater the degree of concentration and specialization - that is, the greater the division of social control labour (hence the relationship between "relational distance" and the division of social control labour - see Griffiths 1984a). Specialized social control labour tends to *look* relatively expensive; or, rather, it has to be paid for (in several senses) on a distinct budget line. A state official can raise his eyebrows as easily as the next person, but you have to pay him to do it. In daily life, in intimate social fields like the family, all this sort of thing gets done for "nothing". That is why families and *kvutzas* can afford to do so much of it.

"Ineffective" social control - that is, *expensive* social control - is a result of those social forces which generate social fields characterized by high relational distance and therefore by a high degree of division of social control labour, or what I have elsewhere called relatively "legal" social control (see Griffiths 1984a).[5] The third law denies that "law" is less "effective" than other social control, and by doing so directs research and theory to two other questions: why is social control effort harder to afford for some social fields than for others? and what factors explain the development (nevertheless) of the more expensive sorts of societal entities (and the resulting decline in social control)?

4. THE LAW OF CONVERGENCE (AND DIVERGENCE) OF NORMS

This is not a real law, but (to the extent that it holds at all) merely a derivative of the first, second and third laws. It is given independent status here because of the prominence it has received in some recent literature, and the need, therefore, to formulate more precisely than has been done to date the conditions (derivative of the first three laws) in which it holds.

The basic idea is simple (and analogous to observations that have been made with regard to other sorts of competitive relationships, e.g. two-party politics): when two litigation institutions are competing for the same business, there is a tendency for the substantive law they apply to converge. Neither can afford that the other appear to offer a higher quality product, for fear of loss of potential cases. The differences in substantive law which remain can be explained as a function of bargaining advantages in terms other than substantive law (e.g., costs, product-binding, etc.). The common limit which both approach is the normative preference, as expressed in litigation behavior, of the majority of the population for which the two institutions are competing.

Many observations have been made of this sort of convergence. The grounds for annulment in American Roman Catholic tribunals have been shown to converge toward the grounds for divorce in the civil courts (Donahue 1977). The court of the paramount chief of the Anufòm of Northern Togo has adjusted its case-law on "divorce" (that is, the right of a woman to reject an arranged marriage) and the return of marriage prestations in the direction of the rules applied by the local *Tribunal Coutumier de Première Instance* (van Rouveroy van Nieuwaal 1975). Local Indian political leaders in Zinacantan "have altered the types of solutions they offer disputants so that disputants who might expect to benefit from appealing to the Mestizo authorities can obtain some of the benefit of codified law without sacrificing the advantages of a conciliatory settlement" (Collier 1976: 149). The observed tendency for the internal law of various sorts of associations to conform to the basic legal principles of the state's law (see Selznick 1969; Ehrlich 1936: 150-152) need not be explained in terms of the values immanent in the state's law or in terms of the need of the overall society for uniformity; the fourth law of interaction between litigation institutions - the consequences of competitive relations between litigation institutions - will suffice.

The fourth law is, however, subject to some important conditions. In the first place, as a derivate of the second law, it applies only where that law applies - that is, to litigation institutions of the same group or of groups which stand in a relationship of inclusiveness to each other. Furthermore, an institution will generally only adjust its law in the direction of that of a competing institution if a substantial portion of its potential population has access to (and the possible inclination to use) the competition: one does not compete by rule change for a small group of litigants at the risk of losing a larger part of one's public. Thus the chief of the Anufòm can move in the direction of Togolese national law, but the *Tribunal Coutumier* cannot move in the direction of Anufò law. The fourth law also only applies in the positive direction when litigation is profitable - unprofitable cases can be shuffled off into other institutions by adopting (or retaining) an unattractively divergent substantive law (this being an instance of the negative direction of the law -

the Law of Divergence of Norms). The law of convergence only applies (at least in the simple way which its formulation suggests) to the situation of two competitors: the more extra competitors there are, the more each one of them can appeal to its own small segment of the litigation market. And finally, the law only applies to the extent that other, cheaper means of competition are not available. As Collier (1976) indicates, so long as an institution offers better service at a lower cost, litigants will continue to use it even if it does not give them quite what they want.

The first and third laws also limit the scope of the fourth law's applicability. Groups which invest relatively heavily in social control can maintain deviant norms even in highly competitive situations. By the same token, creation of a new deviation requires a relatively heavy commitment to social control. Since, as we have seen, it is generally smaller groups with low relational distance which can devote substantial resources to social control labor, such groups will in general be more capable of maintaining their deviant norms against the competition of an inclusive group (e.g., the state) than a larger group would be, and it is also in such contexts that divergence of norms is to be expected: Chinese-American and Orthodox Jewish communities were able to sustain their "indigenous law" (Galanter 1981) with respect to a wide scope of issues for a remarkably long time against the larger American society (Doo 1973; Columbia Journal 1970). The deviant law of such groups disappears only when the groups themselves are no longer viable, cannot enforce the first law, whereas groups plagued by diseconomies of scale, such as the Catholic Church (Donahue 1977), regularly have to cede ground to the secular competition.

NOTES

1.   The same phenomenon of competition is considered from the point of view of litigant behaviour by Tanner (1970) and from that of overall social control output by Abel (1979), both dealing with the competition between national and indigenous tribunals in Africa.

2.   A "semi-autonomous social field" (Moore 1973) may or not have a "legal" order, in this sense.

3.   It is dangerous, of course, to the explanatory power of the second law, to expand the concept of benefit in this way: the danger is that of tautology - whatever positively associates with institutional efforts to maintain or increase caseload being treated as by definition "beneficial". Whether it is possible to avoid the problem of tautology in operationalizing the law - a general problem in the economic analysis of institutional and individual behaviour - I am not sure. But even if tautological, the law is not entirely empty: in such a case it explains nothing, but stands nevertheless as a model for explanatory theory: the behavior of litigation institutions in relation to their caseload is to be seen (partly) under the rubric of a theory of (self- interested) choice.

4.   But cf. Engel 1980 and Whitford 1968 respectively for analyses suggestive of a different interpretation of these changes as quality improvements required to avoid a loss of cases.

5.   There must be a natural limit on the concentration of social control labor which can thus be effected: that is, at some point the required control becomes so expensive that it can no longer be afforded at the level required for group coherence.

REFERENCES

Abel, R.L.
    1973   'A comparative theory of dispute institutions in society', *Law & Society Rev.*, 8, 217-347.
    1979   'Western courts in non-western settings: patterns of court use in colonial and neo-colonial Africa', in: S.B. Burman and B.E. Harrell-Bond, *The Imposition of Law*, 167-200, New York: Academic Press.
Balbus, I.D.
    1973   *The Dialectics of Legal Repression*, New York: Russell Sage.
Benda-Beckmann, K. von
    1981   'Forum shopping and shopping forums: dispute settlement in a Minangkabau village in West Sumatra', *J. of Legal Pluralism*, 19, 117-159.
Bergh, G. van den
    1980   *Staphorst en zijn Gerichten*, Amsterdam: Boom.
Berman, J.
    1969   'The Cuban Popular Tribunals', *Columbia Law Rev.*, 69, 1317-1354.
Black, D.
    1976   *The Behavior of Law*, New York: Academic Press.
Collier, J.F.
    1976   'Political leadership and legal change in Zinacantan', *Law & Society Rev.*, 11, 11-163.
Columbia Journal
    1970   'Rabbinical courts: modern day solomons', *Columbia J. of Law and Social Problems*, 6, 49-75.
Danet, B.
    1980   'Language in the legal process', *Law & Society Rev.*, 14, 445-564.
Donahue, C.
    1977   'Comparative reflections on the "New Matrimonial Jurisprudence" of the Roman Catholic Church', *Michigan Law Rev.*, 75, 994-1020.
Doo, L.-W.
    1973   'Dispute settlement in Chinese-American communities', *American J. of Comparative Law*, 21, 627-663.
Ehrlich, E.
    1936   *Fundamental Principles of the Sociology of Law* (trans. W.L. Moll), Cambridge: Harvard Univ. Press.
Engel, D.M.
    1980   'Legal pluralism in an American community: perspectives on a civil trial court', *American Bar Foundation Research J.*, 425-454.
Galanter, M.
    1974   'Why the "Haves" come out ahead: speculations on the limits of legal change', *Law & Society Rev.*, 9, 95-160.
    1981   'Justice in many rooms: courts, private ordering, and indigenous law', *J. of Legal Pluralism*, 19, 1-47.

Griffiths, J.
1984a   'The division of labor in social control: a reformulation of the relationship between law and social control', forthcoming in: D. Black, *Toward a General Theory of Social Control*, New York: Academic Press.
1984b   'The general theory of litigation – a first step', *Zeitschrift für Rechtssoziologie* 5: 145.
n.d.   'What is legal Pluralism?', unpublished paper delivered at the 1981 meeting of the Law and Society Association.
Gulliver, P.
1963   *Social Control in an African Society*, London: Routledge & Kegan Paul.
Kidder, R.
1979   'Towards an integrated theory of imposed law', in: S.B. Burman and B.E. Harrell-Bond, *The Imposition of Law*, 289-306, New York: Academic Press.
Macaulay, S.
1963   'Non-contractual relations in business: a preliminary study', *American Sociological Rev.*, 28, 55-67.
Moore, S.F.
1973   'Law and social change: the semi-autonomous field as an appropriate subject of study', *Law & Society Rev.*, 7, 719-746.
Olsen, M.
1965   *The Logic of Collective Action*, Cambridge: Harvard Univ. Press.
Pollock, F., and F.W. Maitland
1968   *The History of English Law* (2nd ed., rev. S.F.C. Milsom) Vol. I, Cambridge: Cambridge Univ. Press.
Rouveroy van Nieuwaal, E. and E. van
1975   'To claim or not to claim: changing views about the restitution of marriage prestations among the Anufòm of northern Togo', *African Law Studies* 12, 102-128.
Rouveroy van Nieuwaal, E. van
1976   *A la Recherche de la Justice: Quelques aspects du Droit Matrimonial et de la Justice du Juge de Paix et du Chef Superieur des Anufòm a Mango dans le Nord du Togo*, Leiden: Afrika Studiecentrum.
Schwartz, R.
1954   'Social factors in the development of legal control: a case study of two Israeli settlements', *Yale Law J.*, 63, 471-491.
Selznick, P.
1969   *Law, Society and Industrial Justice*, New York: Russell Sage.
Smith, M.G.
1974   'A structural aproach to comparative politics', in: M.G. Smith, *Corporations and Society*, Chicago: Aldine Publishing Co.
Tanner, R.E.S.
1970   'The selective use of legal systems in East Africa', in: R.E.S. Tanner, *Three Studies in East African Criminology*, Uppsala: Scandinavian Institute of African Studies.
Thompson, E.P.
1975   *Whigs and Hunters*, New York: Pantheon.
Whitford, W.C.
1968   'Strict products liability and the automobile industry: much ado about nothing', *Wisconsin Law Rev.*, 83-171.

Justice against the law: traditional and modern jurisdiction in northern Ghana

Rüdiger Schott

[*Editorial Note.* The paper presented under this title at the Bellagio symposium has been published elsewhere. The following summary has been prepared by Anthony Allott.]

The Bulsa people are an ethnic group of about 60,000 in Northern Ghana. The paper contrasts the administration of justice in pre-colonial times, during British colonisation, and in independent Ghana as it affects the Bulsa.

PRE-COLONIAL

The Bulsa were segmentary, there being no authority higher than the clan sections or maximal lineages. Although there were chiefs, they did not exercise judicial authority; they did however sometimes act as arbitrators. Within the clan sections or local group the "elders", "house-owners" or *yie-nyam* (sing. *yeri-nyono*) had religious and hence legal authority. They had the legal right to apply physical force against wrongdoers, even to expelling or killing them. Elders, living and dead (ancestors), derived their authority from sacred tradition; there was no sharp separation between the living and the dead elders in this respect.

The second source of legal authority was the "Earth". Among the Bulsa it was venerated in special shrines; those who quarrelled or offended were advised to resort to earth-shrines (*teng-gbana*) for purification and settlement of their disputes. Failure to propitiate the Earth was held to lead to the Earth itself pursuing anyone violating her commands, by death. The concept of "spoiling the Earth" is central to an understanding of Bulsa religion, law and justice. Deviation from customary norms of behaviour was felt to spoil the land.

Where there were disputes between several compounds, it was the duty of the *yeri-nyono* ("owner of the compound") to settle them in conjunction with the elders and in the presence of the Earth-priest or *teng-nyono* (lit. "owner of the Earth"). Where disputes between unrelated clan sections could not be settled peaceably by these means, they were settled by feud or self-help.

COLONIAL

The advent of British colonial rule had several important consequences. First, it brought peace, abolished the power of life and death of the elders, and suppressed feuds. Mutual killing stopped; but at the same time respect for the authority of the elders diminished. Similarly, people ceased to come together and make sacrifices to the Earth, or resort to the Earth-shrine in the case of disputes. This had the effect of strengthening conflicts in compounds and within sections, thus leading to fragmentation of them.

Secondly, the British colonial power created new chiefs and strengthened the position of the old ones. They were given numerous legal and administrative functions, the most significant of which was the creation of "Native Courts". The procedure followed in such courts was largely English, but their judgments corresponded in part with traditional African legal conceptions. But these native courts, and the chiefs who sat in them, were largely the creation of the British, and had no traditional sanctions behind them.

INDEPENDENT

Ghana received its independence in 1957. The government of Kwame Nkrumah first restricted, and then abolished, the powers of chiefs to collect court fees and fines, and eventually to adjudicate in cases. Even arbitration by the chiefs was forbidden. However, the problem for a central government of administering justice in remote areas such as that of the Bulsa is insuperable, with the result that the chiefs continue, illegally, to try cases, especially "woman cases". A villager will normally go to his chief first in order to obtain justice, "his" justice. This is because (1) legal proceedings in the state magistrates' courts are carried on in English, which most Bulsa do not speak; (2) the atmosphere of such courts is totally foreign to them; (3) such courts are often far distant, and travel to them is difficult; (4) the costs involved are often excessive; (5) the most important point, the concepts of law and justice prevailing in magistrates' courts differ essentially from the traditional concepts of the Bulsa. Bulsa may find themselves forced to distort their own customary law (e.g. in regard to marriage payments, which - exceptionally among the Bulsa - are low) in order to conform to the courts' expectations.

Chiefs continue (at least in 1974) to try cases. In one case, concerning title to some donkeys, the parties had previously been referred to a diviner. The Paramount Chief, to whom the case eventually came, refused to try it, referring the parties back to the elders of the village. The parties could not consult a diviner of their own motion without being authorised by their seniors, thus exemplifying the all-pervading notion of seniority, with rights and duties graded according to age and status.

The *yeri-nyono* still acts as arbitrator of domestic conflicts, e.g. between co-wives or between half-brothers of polygynous marriages.

Interestingly enough, some modern procedures, notably the written recording of claims, have now entered into "traditional" proceedings. Contrariwise, use may be made in state courts of traditional means of adducing evidence (e.g. by way of oaths). Marriage and family matters are of particular concern to the unofficial courts, in which the relevant customary law is still followed.

CONCLUSION

Bulsa unofficial courts follow the "living law" (Ehrlich), which is now a blend of traditional and western elements. The village chief, in dealing with cases, is not concerned with abstract concepts such as "law", "justice", "custom" or "customary law", but with regulating the everyday affairs of villagers in the light of traditional ideas of how to behave. The "justice" of such unofficial courts opposes itself to the formal "law" of Ghana, according to which traditional authorities should not try cases according to the customary law of the people. The significance of this conflict should not be brushed aside. The concept of law in the life of a great portion of the rural African population is more than just the state legislation and judicial procedure, to a great extent modelled on foreign examples; while the local customary "law" corresponds to the traditional social structures and religious views of the population.

Some preliminary notes to a socio-legal documentary film: "In Search of Justice: different levels of dispute settlement among the Anufom in North Togo"

E.A.B. van Rouveroy van Nieuwaal

Ever since the film camera was invented, it has been used by anthropologists as a technical means of conducting research into human behaviour. They have understood its power both as a teaching tool and as a technique of recording swiftly changing cultures (Mead 1963; Collier 1967).

Since the beginning there has also been doubt as to whether this method of research, when used for the publication of data, is not more subjective than the traditional ways of reporting. However, the particular question of film as a mode of publication seems to me uninteresting. I would argue that it is not the technical means of presentation that makes research data scientific or otherwise.

More fundamental is the question of film as a mode of understanding and analysis. Experience with film shows convincingly that it gives enormous possibilities to manipulate time, that is, to shorten time, to make it seem longer, to reverse it, and even to make a new mixture of elements from the past, the present and the future (Eaton 1979). Film may thus create a new time, that is opposed to what we may call the real time (Gerbrands 1981). However, as the Belgian anthropologist and filmmaker De Heusch pointed out in the 60s, in anthropology for a film to be considered scientific, film time and real time must be equal, or almost so, or at least as much as possible so (De Heusch 1962). Despite this, as every anthropologist-filmmaker knows from his own experience, what happens in practice is that film time is nearly always a condensation of real time. This would appear to be the basis of the critical question, is film science or not? Whatever answer is ultimately given to this general question, the fact is that, within limits such as these, film has proven an invaluable tool for research into human behaviour, including in my opinion socio-legal behaviour (Hockings 1975).

In watching anthropological film of dispute settlement, one of the main topics of folk law, the viewer or spectator has to realize that in almost every case the registration of the dispute process which is shown is not complete or integral. A selection has necessarily been made. We may discern: a selection made during the filming itself; and a selection made after the shooting during the cutting, and taking place in a completely different atmosphere from that of the filming (Mercken-Spaas 1980).

In the first selection the methodological and theoretical reflections of the filmmaker as to the relevance of particular moments play an important, usually decisive role. As a result of a long period of fieldwork the researcher comes to know the process in all its details. Although this requires much time, it has become one of the basic principles in visual anthropology that fruitful scientific film-registration requires very detailed research by means of a long period of active and passive participation (Husmann 1981). This means also that any anthropological filming, and particularly socio-legal filming, is an expensive mode of reporting.

Further practical considerations exert their influence. For instance, in almost every situation the anthropologist-filmer has only one single camera, directed by himself, while the sound must be taped in a simple, and sometimes almost an amateurish way (Heider 1977). More often than not the anthropological filmer has to do everything by himself, which is of course absurd, for human behaviour is so complex and varied that it is impossible to catch it with one pair of hands, even if the action takes place in the restricted area of a courtroom.

The second selection, that of the cutting, is also based on the theoretical reflections of the filmer. However, these will have been refined since the original filming by the re-reading of his fieldnotes, changed by conversations with his colleagues, and so on. We may perhaps ask whether this process of selection is really different from that conducted by his colleagues in preparing a book or an article. Even if there is no difference on this ground, there are other determining factors peculiar to the medium of film, such as the technical or aesthetic quality of the images, techniques used during the cutting, etc.

In general any anthropological film contains a huge volume of information which is visually communicated to the viewer. Nevertheless a film dealing with an anthropological subject suffers from a serious drawback as compared with a film of equal length dealing with a subject taken from the viewer's own culture (Gerbrands 1981). An anthropological film is nearly always too short to communicate all the information necessary for the viewer to understand fully the meaning of what is shown. For this he needs additional information explaining the cultural background of the data that are only visually communicated to him. The viewer needs a spoken or written explanation to go with the images and together with them to form an *anthropological unit of information* (Le Roy 1981).

Although the portable 16 mm camera came into use among social scientists some decades ago, it is striking that little attention has been paid, as far as I know, to what I call socio-legal behaviour. Only a few legal anthropologists have included filmmaking in their socio-legal research. Among these are

Laura Nader and James Gibbs, the first among the Zapotec Indians of Middle America, the other among the Kpelle in Liberia, West Africa.

Nader sees folk law dispute processing as involving eleven elements, of which the most important is "the goal to have parties compromise their differences; the so called minimax principle (give a little, get a little) rather than the zero-sum game (win or lose) prevails" (Nader 1969:88). Nader's own film "Making the Balance" naturally focuses on these eleven elements. It would be interesting to know how far other legal anthropologists, using film as a tool of research, adopted them.

Gibbs puts the emphasis in the process of folk-law dispute-settlement on the principles of *psycho-analytic theory* which underlie psychotherapy, whatever that may be. He distinguishes between *formal adjudicators*, such as the head of a district, the paramount chief, and *informal adjudicators*, or moots, groupings such as church councils or cooperative workgroups. Gibbs states that formal courts are particularly inapt for the numerous matrimonial disputes, because their harsh tone tends to drive parties further apart rather than to reconcile them. The moot, in contrast, is more effective in handling such cases. The Kpelle moot is an informal airing of a dispute before an assembled group which includes kinsmen of the litigants and neighbours from the ward where the case is being heard. It is a completely *ad hoc* group varying greatly in composition from case to case.

One of the most important differences between a court and a moot is that in the former the solution is, by and large, imposed by the adjudicator, whereas in the latter the solution is more consensual. The coercive tone of the courtroom hearing limits the court's effectiveness in dealing with matrimonial disputes, and especially in effecting reconciliation. The moot, on the other hand, is particularly effective in bringing about reconciliation between husband and wife. This is because the moot is not only conciliatory, but *therapeutic*, that is, it re-educates the parties through a type of social learning in a specially structured, interpersonal setting (Gibbs 1967:284).

In my film "In Search of Justice" the same difference between formal and informal adjudicators is made, while it is appreciated that terms such as "formal" and "informal", "modern" and "traditional" are somewhat relative and depend upon the user's own interpretation (von Benda-Beckmann 1979). The emphasis is on the one hand on the paramount chief, the highest traditional authority in the area and the principal representative of the Anufò folk law adjudication; and on the other hand, on his "modern" and newly introduced counterpart, the Justice of the Peace, a primary state court (van Rouveroy van Nieuwaal 1976, 1977). Both are required in principle to settle disputes on the basis of the same legal principles, those of the Anufò people of West Africa. Their interpretation, however, is often very different, owing to their different backgrounds, training, and, as far as concerns the Justice of the Peace, the instructions he receives from the central government.

The most crucial and fundamental difference between the two adjudicators lies in the fact that all chiefs, or headmen if preferred, base their process of dispute-settlement on the principle of first repairing the broken social relationship between the parties (E.A. and E.A.B. van Rouveroy van Nieuwaal 1981). Relations in the society in which the film was shot have - as anywhere else - an important survival value, and practically all rights and duties are based on these relations. The only way for the litigants to be wholly re-invested in their rights is to re-establish their relationship. This is achieved by a judicial process under the authority of a chief, in which:

- parties get satisfaction by stating their cases in public in as much detail as they wish without being interrupted by members of the court;
- having the right to speak and be heard without interruption is of great importance, not only to the audience which gets thereby a balanced view of the facts and the emotions of the litigants, but also to the parties themselves who get satisfaction by showing openly their grievances. The Anufòm compare a judicial process with a ring fight in which both parties show their intellectual muscle (van Rouveroy van Nieuwaal 1977);
- thirdly, the behaviour of the parties is weighed against the rules and norms. In a long discussion the shortcomings and misconduct of the parties are exposed and they are confronted with models of correct and incorrect behaviour;
- after the recognition of the norms the relation is re-established through the parties showing mutual respect by offering each other their apologies, indicating also thereby that they desire to continue their social relationship;
- generally a ceremony takes place at the lineage level to cement the repaired relationship (Gibbs 1967:283; E.A. and E.A.B. van Rouveroy van Nieuwaal 1981).

The adjudication of the Justice of the peace also is required, according to the national law, to reconcile the parties. We wonder, however, if he is able to do so, because certain practical handicaps constitute serious impediments to achieving reconciliation. In most cases the Justice of the Peace does not understand a single word of the proceedings. Therefore he needs an interpreter, who himself has often a limited understanding of his function and sometimes such a limited linguistic skill also that he is unable to translate accurately the local language into French. Furthermore this Judge does not form part of the social network to which the parties belong. Thus he lacks the extensive fore-knowledge enjoyed by his traditional counterpart, the paramount chief, of not only the facts but also the kinship ties, and the economic and political status of the parties. Another handicap seems to be his legal education, which hitherto has been based almost exclusively on the French civil code (van Rouveroy van Niewaal 1977:231). In this system the requirement to maintain an infringed norm prevails over the objective of first repairing the broken social ties. Thus, by upholding rules - in the film the well-known rule that a woman has the right to choose her husband freely - the Justice of the Peace tends to break relations rather than to mend them. In our opinion the Judge has not in practice the same startingpoint as the Anufò chief, which is that the only way to uphold the law, is first to repair social relations.

REFERENCES

Benda-Beckmann, F. von
1979   'Modernes Recht und traditionelle Gesellschaften', *Verfassung und Recht in Uebersee*, 12 (4), 337-353.
Collier, J.
1967   *Visual Anthropology; Photography as a Research Method*, New York: Holt, Rinehart and Winston.
Eaton, M.
1979   *Anthropology, Reality, Cinema; the Films of Jean Rouch*, London: British Film Institute.
Gerbrands, A.A.
1981   'Male: Forward; Female: Sideways, or the Red Bowman'; paper presented at the Symposium on Visual Anthropology, IUAES, 23-25 April, Amsterdam.
Gibbs, J.
1967   'The Kpelle Moot', in: P. Bohannan (ed.), *Law and Warfare; Studies in the Anthropology of Conflict*, New York, Natural History Press, pp. 227-291.
Heider, K.G.
1977   *Films for Anthropological Teaching*, American Anthropological Association, No. 9.
Heusch, L. de
1962   *The Cinema and Social Sciences*, Paris, UNESCO.
Hockings, P.
1975   *Principles of Visual Anthropology*, The Hague: Mouton.
Husmann, R.
1981   'Film and Fieldwork; Some Problems Reconsidered', paper presented at the Symposium on Visual Anthropology, IUAES, 23-25 April, Amsterdam.
Mead, M.
1963   'Anthropology and the Camera', in: W.D. Morgan (ed.), *The Encyclopaedia of Photography*, Vol. 1, New York: Greystone Press, pp. 166-84.
Mercken-Spaas, L.
1980   'Le Texte et la Loi; Van Rouveroy van Nieuwaal au Togo', paper presented at the Séminaire sur le Documentaire Socio-Scientifique en Afrique Francophone, 9-12 December, Amsterdam.
Nader, L.
1969   'Styles of Court Procedure; to Make the Balance', in: L. Nader (ed.), *Law in Culture and Society*, Chicago: Aldine Press, pp. 69-92.
Rouveroy van Nieuwaal, E.A.B. van
1976   'La Justice Coutumière au Togo', *Recueil Penant*, 751, 35-70.
1977   *A la Recherche de la Justice; Quelques Aspects du Droit Matrimonial et de la Justice Coutumière au Nord-Togo*, Leiden: Africa Study Center.

1980   'L'Anthopologue, le Cinéaste et la Réalité Sociale', paper presented at the
            Séminaire sur le Documentaire Socio-Scientifique en Afrique Francophone,
            9-12 December, Amsterdam.
Rouveroy van Nieuwaal, E.A.B. van, and E.A. van Rouveroy van Nieuwaal-Baerends
1976   *Ti Anufo, un Coup d'Oeil sur la Societe des Anufom au Nord-Togo*, Leiden: Africa
            Study Center.
1981   'Het Mogelijke en Onmogelijke in Verzoening Bij de Anufom in Noord-Togo,
            West-Afrika', *Sociologische Gids*, 4, 305-27, to be published in English, 'Recon-
            ciliation among the Anufòm in Northern Togo'.
Roy, E. le
1981   'Le Séminaire sur le Documentaire Socio-Scientifique en Afrique Francophone;
            un Nouveau Regard et de Nouvelles Exigences', *Politique Africaine, Chronique
            Scientifique*, 2.

Part IV
Neo-Marxist interpretations of folk law in pluralistic legal systems

Introduction

Franz von Benda-Beckmann

I.

In trying to write a report on the session which I chaired at the Bellagio symposium I feel in an uncomfortable situation. In my introduction of the three papers I thought it useful to point to some empirical, conceptual and theoretical problems which had been raised in the papers or which had not, at least in my view, been dealt with clearly enough. Rather than presenting an objective summary of the papers' contents, I took a rather subjective and personal stroll through the papers and aired my own questions and criticisms, hoping that these and other questions would be taken up during the discussion. As it turned out I could call myself happy that at least I had had my say. For the discussion which followed was an utterly disappointing and frustrating experience. Hardly any point raised in the papers or my introduction was discussed, if at all, at a level of sophistication which could have been expected. Most of the time was filled with exchanges of statements of belief and feelings and with labelling ("I am no Marxist, in fact I am anti-Marxist", "you are no real Marxists, you should not call yourselves Marxists", "I am not calling myself a Marxist").

So in this report I can do little else than repeat the questions I singled out in my introduction and insert here and there the few relevant bits of the discussion, hoping to place my questions on the agenda of some future discussion of the relative value of neo-Marxist interpretations for the study of law in pluralistic legal systems.

II.

At Bellagio we definitely missed a good chance to have such a discussion. This was not the authors' fault. The three papers in their theoretical assumptions and scientific terminology were all strictly informed by underdevelopment theories and neo-Marxist theories about socio-economic and political change in colonial and post-colonial societies. Upon this broad common basis they varied in the scope of their empirical referents and in their more specific theoretical persuasions. The theoretical variation is obvious from the different characterizations of the conditions in third-world countries, and of the processes producing these conditions. In general terms the conditions have resulted from the gradual incorporation of indigenous socio-political and economic systems into colonial and later independent states, and from the increasing contacts and relations of these indigenous and state systems with the world market economy.

Fitzpatrick develops the articulation of modes of production approach, extending it to the description and analysis of the interaction of legal forms in plural legal systems and to the new forms of law, which he calls *combined law*, resulting from this interaction. Drawing upon a wide range of ethnographic data, he shows that and how combined law is formed both in the local (traditional) and the national (state law) sphere. Le Roy's paper is the topically and empirically most restricted and concrete analysis of the three papers. Referring to his researches in Senegal, he analyses the emergence of *local law* - which would qualify as a type of combined law in Fitzpatrick's sense - in the field of land law. This local law was created partly through the introduction in 1964 of a French-style law on landed property which transformed the indigenous land rights of Senegalese peasants, and partly through the establishment at a later stage of administrative councils to administer the law and control land allocations and exchanges. In focussing upon combined law and local law, however, both Fitzpatrick and Le Roy give little or no attention to the indigenous legal rules and concepts operated by the people outside the context of state or state-transformed neo-traditional administrative institutions.

Snyder, and less explicitly Le Roy, see the historical process as "transitions" from one historically dominant mode of production to another, in the Senegalese case from the pre-capitalist tributary mode of production to the capitalist mode. In his critical analysis of the articulation of modes of production approach, Snyder elaborates his argument for holding that the historical process is more adequately described as "subsumption" of formerly non- or pre-capitalist societies under the dominant system of world capitalism. These different approaches in the papers are due to, or perhaps result in different meanings being attributed to the concept of the mode of production. In Snyder's conceptual system mode of production denotes a mode dominant in a specific historical epoch. Patterns of productive relations and processes which do not correspond to the dominant mode (such as the forms of petty commodity production and tributary relations of production existing in contemporary Senegal) are characterized as "forms of immediate production". On the other hand, in Fitzpatrick's conceptual scheme these patterns and processes appear as more or less the articulating modes of production.

III.

From both the empirical and theoretical points of view the three papers thus offered a multifacetted Marxist perspective on legal pluralism which could have been discussed. In the discussion which took place, most exchanges were directed at Snyder's conceptualization of law. As he made clear when pleading not quilty to accusations of non-Marxist thinking and incomprehensibility, he felt himself engaged in a two-front war. This was on the one hand against the classical legal anthropologists with their exclusive focus on dispute settlement processes. As they hardly give attention to legal rules and principles, those of state law in particular, they provide much too narrow a framework for adequate analysis and explanation of the changes which have occurred in the law of local communities. On the other hand, Snyder found himself engaged with those Marxists, older Marxists in particular, who refused to recognize the normative systems of primitive pre- capitalist societies as law on the ground that law was a function of the capitalist bourgeois state - a vision evidently too narrow for Snyder and the other authors.

Snyder therefore formulates a conception of law characterized by two related aspects. The first is a *simple concept* of law denoting "those forms of social consciousness or institutionalized social relations that have as their generic function the expression, regulation and maintenance of the dominant social relations within a social formation". As a general, ahistorical notion it establishes the general preconditions of law, but does not define the concrete forms that characterize and thus distinguish the particular modes of production. Second, the *concrete legal forms* are an integral part of the relations of production. They do not belong to a metaphorical superstructure. They are historically specific in character in that (a) they only exist within particular modes of production, or (b) although not necessarily limited to a single mode of production, they form parts of specific combinations of legal forms as concrete concepts in particular historical periods.

Though some participants expressed delight that Marxists had finally come to recognize law in non-capitalist socio-economic systems, it was just these ideas which were most heavily criticized by others. Thus some castigated Snyder for being fundamentally un-Marxist in his conceptualization of law, arguing that in Marx's thinking law was, and could not be otherwise than, a function of the state and by necessity a historical phenomenon. Scientists conceptualizing law as an ahistorical phenomen - an idea which, they suggested, would make Marx and Engels rotate in their graves - had foregone the right to claim to be Marxist. Unfortunately the discussion about Snyder's conceptualization of law did not transcend these and similar statements.

In my view, Snyder's conceptualization is an understandable departure from classical Marxist thought about law in the light of contemporary knowledge about non-capitalist societies. It does not, however, work out the full implications of the initial stance. If law is to be the subject of synchronic and diachronic comparison, the resultant generalizations must be based upon an analytical concept of law which incorporates properties of social phenomena, modes of production, and political organization, while allowing for variation in its empirical manifestations in time and space, but which does not define any specific empirical form of law. Such a concept comes close to Snyder's simple concept of law, although he seems to treat law in this sense as phenomenon. The varying empirical manifestations of law would then be those phenomena which exhibited the properties indicated by the analytical concept. They more or less correspond to Snyder's concrete legal forms. However, I would not agree that these concepts should be defined as necessarily connected to specific modes of production. How they relate to the modes of production and the processes of immediate production is an empirical question. Theoretical propositions should, of course, be addressed to this question. But it cannot be answered by dogmatic and apodictical definitive statements.

Regarding the reproach that Snyder's conceptualization should not be called Marxist, I have less difficulty. Marx and Engels requiescant in pace or not, nobody should be reproached for trying to re(de)fine their concepts in the light of contemporary ethnographic and theoretical knowledge. Snyder's reformulation of law can remain essentially embedded in Marxist general theory in the same way as most contemporary anthropological conceptualizations and definitions of law (such as those of Hoebel, Pospisil and Hart) have remained essentially Austinian despite having in appearance dramatically replaced Austin's command-issuing sovereign by pro tanto officials privileged to sanction deviant behaviour, or by "secondary" rules which control the discovery, interpretation, application and change of "primary" rules.

IV.

What I find more disturbing in the analytical apparatus offered by neo-Marxist interpretations of law is its failure, in my view, to provide any account of the way in which law, either as simple concept or as concrete legal forms, relates to the concepts of social formation, mode of production, relations of production or process of immediate production. In common with most neo-Marxist writers, Snyder, Le Roy and Fitzpatrick have abandoned the classical distinction between base and superstructure. Law is made an integral part of the relations of production. However, it is nowhere made clear what its relation may be to the other relations of production. On the one hand Snyder explicitly rejects the conception of different and relatively autonomous levels of the economic, political and legal-ideological. On the other hand, Snyder's and Le Roy's papers clearly regard law (legal rules, principles and concepts) as an aspect or part of a social formation and/or mode of production which operates according to different laws of motion from the other parts or aspects. Thus Snyder and Le Roy show that changes in legal form occur independently of changes in the relations of production or the processes of immediate production. The emergence of Le Roy's local law and Fitzpatrick's combined law, for example, may be solely or predominantly due to the establishment of state institutions which interpret, apply, and in the process transform the concepts, rules and principles of indigenous laws. The capitalist logic of law may penetrate folk systems if the institutions of dispute settlement and adjudication and the legal reasoning of the functionaries operating within them are taken from or modelled upon the processes and reasoning of the institutions of capitalist politico-economic systems. Such change, and the resultant emergence of droit local or combined law, can thus occur in a situation where the capitalist mode of production has not otherwise affected the communities. In short: we know from the empirical reality of non-western societies that changes in the economy (economic variables) and the political organization (political variables) can differentially contribute to changes in law.

The papers in my view contain no coherent analytical model or theoretical propositions which could deal effectively with this set of questions. The problem which most clearly illustrates these difficulties is posed by the situation where continuity of legal concepts and rules accompanies significant changes in the processes of immediate production (Snyder) or the mode of production (Fitzpatrick). Here at least neo-Marxist theory needs to deal with the relation between law, conceived of as (further specified) phenomena in the realm of objectified meaning (rules, principles, standards, concepts etc.), on the one hand, and behaviour on the other - in other words, with the relation between the behaviour of production and reproduction and the normative rules pertaining to it.

As we can see from the descriptions Snyder has given in the paper addressed to the symposium[1] as well as in other publications, in the Senegalese case there have been changes in the processes of production, yet a significant part of the law has not changed. There Snyder has stated that there has been a continuity of simple legal concepts concealing a profound transformation of legal forms. If meant as a description, this statement is rather ambiguous. As I understand him, he refers, under the label of legal form, to unchanged rules plus changed behaviour (in the processes of production), or rather, to differential change in law *and* behaviour. By subsuming both elements under the label of legal form, attempts to explain this situation are frustrated. This form of expression reveals Snyder's implicit structuralist-idealist notion of law: legal rules are in principle tied to a pattern of behaviour with a specific economic significance or "meaning". Changes in this meaning are seen as profound changes in legal form; changes in this meaning unaccompanied by rule change are therefore characterized as "concealment". This does not take into account the fact that law always refers to open, broad categories of conduct, within which there can be quite significant changes in behaviour. There is nothing to be concealed. All this makes the distinction between rules and behaviour all the more important.

When neo-Marxist thought abandoned the base-superstructure distinction, which included the law-behaviour distinction but which was not identical with it, they also threw out of their conceptual and theoretical apparatus the distinction between law and behaviour. Therefore they no longer focus upon the analytical relation between the two, nor on theoretical propositions which would explain their empirical relation in concrete historical situations and processes. It is therefore understandable, but all the more regrettable, that Renner's approach to legal and economic change is rejected. In my view, Renner's conceptualization offers more opportunities for adequately analysing the problems of legal and economic change, and I find that Snyder, in the original paper presented to the symposium,[1] treated him somewhat unjustly. When Snyder stated that Renner stressed changes in the economy rather than the emergence of the state, we must remember that Renner had good reasons for this: in the historical period he analysed, the state had already emerged. And it can hardly be said that Renner excluded legal change from his study. On the contrary, one of his key concepts, "change of norms", refers precisely to that situation where changes in the economic and political domain (if you wish: incorporation and capitalist penetration) lead to changes in legal rules, concepts, and principles - as opposed to "change of function", where considerable changes in the economic significance of legal norms (changes in economic behaviour) co-exist with unchanged legal norms.

I do not wish to argue that the complexity of legal, economic and political change should be analysed exclusively in terms of Renner's two key concepts. But the advantage of Renner's scheme, and his lasting contribution to the sociology of law, is that it explicitly recognized the distinction between legal norms and social, political and economic behaviour, and focussed analysis upon the mechanisms of change in both spheres, this conceptualization being based on the empirically justified assumption that the changes are due to different laws of motion.

V.

All the papers in this volume, whatever the scope of the empirical situation they discuss, and whatever their analytical and theoretical intensity, are set in the same overall situation. This is characterized by (a) a plurality of - depending on the terminology - modes of production or forms of immediate production (subsistence, tributary, petty commodity, capitalist) which interact, co-exist or articulate, but which are in any case united at least in so far as they are tied into a single exchange network, the circulation of commodities; (b) a plurality of co-existing and interacting legal forms, both as continuities and as newly emerging forms; and (c) structures of political organization wherein each institution is the potential author of new law. The three papers in this section address themselves to the analytical and theoretical problems involved in this complex situation on a more general level and with more ambitious claims than most of the other papers. Fitzpatrick's paper is mainly and most comprehensively concerned with the morphology of these pluralities of law and their (structural, functional and causal) relations to the plural relations of production. Le Roy and Snyder show and assert that there are crucial correlations between the new forms of the contemporary state, the legal structures, and the extension of capital. Our discussion should have attempted to secure a clearer analysis of the types of correlations and to formulate a body of hypotheses aimed at explaining specific historical constellations on a broad comparative basis. We could have tried to determine whether a Marxist approach to law, as exemplified by the papers, could in fact provide us with a deeper understanding of law and legal change in relation to social, economic, and political change, or whether it merely restates the obvious on a very general level in a different terminology and leaves us as wise or ignorant as we are with the models of non-Marxist sociology and anthropology of law.

It is a pity we did not do so.

NOTE

1.   This passage has been omitted in Snyder's revised version in this volume.

Underdevelopment and the plurality of law

Peter Fitzpatrick

[*Editorial Note*. The paper presented under this title at the Bellagio symposium has been subsequently published: Fitzpatrick 1983. The following introduction to the paper's argument has been prepared by the author.]

The argument of this paper centered on the plurality of semi-autonomous orders in society. Each of these could be seen as having its own constitutive legal element. The concern here was not, however, so much with legal pluralism in this immediate, banal sense. If legal pluralism is ever to transcend the perpetual surprise at its own re-discovery, it must confront structuring elements of unity, or at least cohesion, beyond the diversity it reflects. Yet is has to do this without, as is so often done, subordinating diversity to some abrupt totality - usually conceived in the literature as a formal or a functional dominance of the state.

In the spirit of that credo, the immediate inspiration for this paper was Foucault's "rule of double conditioning", set in a project exploring the nature of power in modern society. This "rule" has it that no specific and localized exercise of power can be effective without its being incorporated into an overall or general "strategy" of power and, conversely, the strategy cannot work unless supported by specific and localized exercises of power. These two elements are integral but not homogeneous. One cannot be reduced to the other (Foucault 1979: 99-100). Given the profound concern of some symposium participants at Bellagio with the nature of Marxism, it may be as well to ground this guiding perspective more securely in the Marxist tradition by reference to Lukács of the *Ontology*, where "individual constituents" in a totality are accorded a relative autonomy but "can only be understood from their concrete interaction within the complex of being involved, whilst it would be futile for us to try theoretically to reconstruct the complex of being itself from its constituents" (translated in Varga 1981:163).

Such formulations are set against what the paper sees as explicit or implicit totalities or premature imperatives such as, for example, Althusserian Marxism or the recent critical concern in the U.S. with "informal justice" which in functionalist terms would subject the particular in some grand design. This is not to deny the value of such exercises. For example, much of the work done on popular justice has been deeply demystifying in showing the dependence of "informal" elements on wider universalist strategies of power (see now Abel ed. 1982). Yet such broad critiques should not deny the vitality, the persistence of particularist sites of power (the paper takes the family as an egregious example) that have their own histories and that cannot be reduced in easy totalities of capitalism, modernism, state domination and such.

It is in this light that the paper offered theories of the articulation of modes of production as a vital perspective on law and society in the third world. That is, law and society were not to be understood as part of or as effects of a (capitalist) mode of production but of an articulation of modes, capitalist and pre-capitalist. Not that the outcome immediately reflects a duality - as an immediate existential matter it probably could not, and last. Rather, the result is more a "reciprocal interaction" and "synthesis" of modes as Marx perceived (Marx 1973:97).

The paper does not claim that theories of articulation provide ultimate or total answers. Their approach is inherently provisional. They contribute no independent dynamic. They provide an arena for the working-out in complex interaction of different dynamic elements. They provide an opening, an alternative to the staggering simplicities of theories which view the third world in terms of a programmatic modernization or of a symptomatic backwardness. Theories of articulation have the virtue of reponsiveness to the diversity and specificity of pre-capitalist elements but also to the diversity of types of capitalist penetration. The operative combination will vary markedly in different social formations.

Yet the most adventurous claim of the paper is that, despite this diversity, the articulation of pre-capitalist and capitalist relations characterizes the third world in general. The particular point of emphasis here is that pre-capitalist relations do not comprise a static, residual element in the articulation of modes. Rather, they retain some dynamic independent of the capitalist mode and in this they adapt and develop in the cause, as it were, of their own survival. But, before getting to the essence, I must stress and repeat even in a summary that I am dealing with tendencies and forces the relevance of which will vary in different societies. This is not a total theory about the third world or some such.

The essence historically is that the very maintenance of the capitalist mode of production in the third world required the conservation in some integrity of pre-capitalist modes of production. These modes serve to subsidize hugely the provision of labour for capitalist enterprises and they come as well to bear much of the costs of peasant commodity production. Politically, the conservation of pre-capitalist modes maintains ethnic and communal division and thus counters a capitalist class organization that would undermine a weakly-based colonial and post-colonial rule.

The essence academically is that theories of the articulation of modes of production set themselves against general theories of underdevelopment based in the causal efficacy of the capitalist mode of production. When such theories confront the issue of the articulation of modes, pre-capitalist elements are relegated to "forms" or "appearances" or to "household" production (e.g. Banaji 1977; Bernstein 1977; Snyder 1981. Compare Fitzpatrick 1980: ch. 1, and 1983). Where do these forms and appearances come from? Clearly they are not mere irrational survivals at most only marginally modifying capitalist relations. The answer that these accounts provide is that the forms are based in their relation to or utility for the capitalist mode of production. Doubtless the nature of these forms and the changes in them will owe much to this relation. Indeed, the very reason why the forms are supportive of the capitalist mode of production is because they are different to and, in a sense, apart from it. Subordination, these accounts tell us, stops short of full proletarianization leaving some integral economy apart from the capitalist mode (even if one reduced to a "household") that meets costs of producing commodities, including labour-power, costs which would otherwise have to be met within the capitalist mode. What this gloss amounts to is that some continuing identity and distinctness of pre-capitalist forms can be based in their relation to the capitalist mode. But to so base this identity and distinctness is to stretch the terms form and appearance impossibly to accommodate that element of integral economy which meets costs of producing commodities. Another way of looking at this issue is to observe historically that the capitalist mode's side of the relation has been and is served by an enormous diversity of forms. The concrete forms vary greatly and cannot simply be deduced from or reduced to their relation to the capitalist mode, taking even the broadest conception of that mode (*cf.* Wolpe 1980). That is, the specificity of the forms cannot be based in this relation.

Having explored a necessary plurality in the constitution of third world societies, the bulk of the paper then pursues the implications of this for the state and for law in the third world. In a situation of articulation, the state is found to have a central, integrative role. Law's part in this is seen to be particularly explicit and prominent. Here it assumes a necessarily universalist character. Yet, with the persistence of pre-capitalist elements, it is subject to the constant invasion of particularist orders which shape and serve to constitute state law itself. The maintenance of particularist orders is a condition of a universalist state law. That is, if fundamental conflicts of interest were not contained at particularist levels, the necessarily universalist stance of state law could not be maintained. State law, in turn, constitutively acts on and reacts back on these particularist orders. In all, there result certain combined forms and syntheses which typify law in the third world - forms and syntheses that cannot be reduced to capitalist or to pre-capitalist elements.

REFERENCES

Abel, R.L. (ed.)
1982   *The Politics of Informal Justice, Vol. 1; The American Experience. Vol. 2; Comparative Perspectives*, New York: Academic Press.

Banaji, J.
1977   'Modes of production in a materialist conception of history', *Capital and Class*, 3, 1-44.

Bernstein, H.
1977   'Notes on capital and peasantry', *Review of African Political Economy*, 10, 60-73.

Fitzpatrick, P.
1980   *Law and State in Papua New Guinea*, London and New York: Academic Press.
1983   'Law, plurality and underdevelopment', in D. Sugarman (ed.), *Legality, Ideology and the State*, London and New York: Academic Press, pp. 159-182.

Foucault, M.
1979   *The History of Sexuality, Vol. 1; An Introduction*, London: Allen Lane.

Marx, K.
1973   *Grundrisse; Foundations of the Critique of Political Economy*, Harmondsworth: Penguin.

Snyder, F.G.
1981   *Capitalism and Legal Change; An African Transformation*, New York: Academic Press.

Varga, Cs.,
1981   'Towards a sociological concept of law; an analysis of Lukács' ontology', *International Journal of the Sociology of law*, 9, 159-176.

Wolpe, H.
1980   'Introduction', in H. Wolpe (ed.), *The Articulation of Modes of Production: Essays from Economy and Society*, London: Routledge and Kegan Paul, pp. 1-43.

Local law in black Africa: contemporary experiences of folk law facing state and capital in Senegal and some other countries

Etienne Le Roy

What are the new expressions of folk law in contemporary Black Africa? Transformations of the contemporary state and the introduction of capital in the peasantry imply novations of the legal framework. In Senegal we may observe with especial clarity one of these adaptations, namely, where the folk law generates a new legal system: local law. If by folk law we mean all the instances of "non-state laws", local law appears to differ from other folk laws - traditional law, customary law, and so on - as well as from state law.

How does this new law arise? What are its links with state and capital? In this paper we start our analysis by summarising the legal reforms and their institutions observed in Senegal (Part I). Then we shall explain the structure of local law and its relations with state and capital (Part II). In conclusion we shall attempt to measure this innovation and to clarify the consequences of this research.

I. LEGAL REFORMS AND THE RISE OF LOCAL LAW IN SENEGAL

It is impossible here to summarise some of my earlier studies between 1976 and 1981 investigating, analysing and interpreting material concerning case studies and legal norms in Senegal collected during field research in 1976 and 1979 (Le Roy 1978, 1979, 1980a and b, Le Roy and Wane 1982). Nonetheless, it is necessary to summarise the process of legal reform to understand the specificity of contemporary experiences of "communautés rurales" in rural areas, and to understand why we refer to certain transformations through the land reform of 1964 and the administrative reform of 1972 as the rise of local law instead of the administrative law that was envisaged by the French legal model (see République du Sénégal 1965, 1972).

1. Historical Summary

Senegal was the oldest French colony in Africa, and it was also the first to furnish France, its "mother country", with supplies of slaves (from the 16th to the 18th centuries), peanuts (in the 19th and the 20th centuries) and, last but not least, black immigrant workers (from 1945 to the present). Exports of labour power or farm produce entailed several problems or disfunctions which were considered, at the time of political independence (1960), to be crucial obstacles to national unity and community development (Lebret 1961, M. Dia 1961).

But the ideology of Developmentalism, linked to the theory of modernisation, and a liberal legalism (Snyder 1980: 727-734) justified the idea of (and the belief in) Law as the only means of adaptation. And that idea implied of course Law on French patterns and not along the traditional lines. This choice was formally discussed initially at State level (d'Arboussier 1965) and the option of law on a foreign pattern was explicitly justified on technical and political grounds, but not ideologically (M'Baye 1966:146-148).

This set of ideas and options explains a policy of legal codes, in which Senegal is a champion among the new African states. Among these legal codes, which concern fishing, hunting, investments and family law, for example, the land reform promulgated by the "Loi sur le domaine national" (No. 64-46 of June 17, 1964) was one of the main works of Senghor's two decades, and a test of political success for his liberal and capitalist way of development. This law was initiated during the 1957-1959 period of internal autonomy and formulated by a "comité interministériel d'études pour une réforme foncière" whose place was taken, in 1960, by a "commission de réforme foncière" within the "comité d'études économiques" (see especially CINAM SERESA 1960).

In a very interesting paper, Grosmaire (1960) identified three possible policies of reform: renewing the "pre-colonial" model; extending the Torrens' system of registration; and nationalising the customary claims to land, with respect to legal claims on registered tenures. For political and ideological reasons, the first and second ways were excluded (see, for examples, Le Roy 1980b) and, after much debate, the new law of 1964 identified three categories of land tenure: land tenure with legal claims by registration, state property, and national property (in French: *domaine national*). Only the third, those holdings or estates on the "domaine national", were organised by this law and will be discussed here.

The law gives the state a right of "trusteeship" in respect to national property (Le Roy 1970:243-244). Indeed, the nationalisation may only concern primary estates, those denoted by the colonial rulers as "droits éminents" of "chefs de terre". Peasants and their secondary estates on plots ("droits de culture") were maintained with their claims, at least till the time of local application of the new legal framework. Enforcement of the law was initially delayed on the grounds of the social and economic difficulties of application.

After dividing the national property into four areas (*zones urbaines, zones classées, zones pionnières* and *zones de terroirs*), the reform mainly organised the last, the most important area spatially and economically. Indeed the "zones de terroirs" (including 58% of the national territory) is the area where lands are normally used for agricultural and pastoral activities (see article 7.2 of Law 64-46 and Diao 1976:144). There estates are administered under the authority of the state by new councils named "Conseils de communauté rurale", the members of which are "elected" among peasants of the local area ("terroir") gathering together from twenty to eighty villages and about 10,000 people. If peasants were, in effect, maintained on their lands, their customary claims were (theoretically) abrogated, and a new claim ("droit d'usage") was identified with "usus" and "fructus" protected only by continued work on the land. Abusus was forbidden, and transfers of land were only possible by allocation through the "conseils de communauté rurale".

The organisation of councils and the procedures of allocation would be, after 1972, the focus of the transformation of an administrative law into a local law. But in 1964 new choices were necessary to complete the legal framework.

2. The new choices between 1965 and 1972: the future of the "communautés rurales" linked to an administrative view and a territorial reform

In 1965 an interdepartmental commitee ("le comité interministériel d'application de la loi sur le domaine national") had to choose between two policies: an African socialism or the French administrative pattern. The first appealed to Senghor's ideology of "negritude" and the second to the senghorian way of development, seeking economic efficiency in liberalism. Thus, with a common reference to President Senghor, a democratic process by community development was opposed to a hierarchical pattern in which orders would be sent out by the centre to the outlying districts and to the local communities.

In the first period, from 1965 to 1970, the ideological criteria triumphed over administrative and economic arguments. Experimental studies were entrusted to the agency of National Development ("Aménagement du territoire") connected with the Ministry of Plan and Development (Senegal 1965). But, with too few means, researchers were concerned with overly large problems. They hoped to "cover" seven experimental areas ("terroirs") by gathering all demographic, ecological, economic, historical and sociological data. They hoped to discover new ways to African socialism and a specifically Senegalese approach to domestic economic problems. In consequence they were too slow in collecting empirical results and also posed a danger to the local leaders of political factions within the Union Progressiste Sénégalaise, the dominant party.

In August 1970, after conflicts at central and local levels, the Ministry of the Interior was entrusted with the application of the law with a view to administrative reform. In order to establish hierarchical and centralised relations, the territorial reform made provision for powers of the councils of "Communautés rurales". By articles 24 to 30 of Law no. 72-25 of February 2, 1972, these powers were limited to voting on land tenure allocations, electing to the upper (in hierarchy) "conseil d'arrondissement", advising on local development, and expressing their wishes on villages' common rights. The exercise of all these powers was subjected to the authorisation of administrative authorities ("sous-préfet", "Préfet" and "gouverneur de région"). The "sous-préfet" was the only administrative officer competent to enforce decisions.

It is therefore possible to affirm that the Senegalese state operated a very timorous decentralisation following the French model of reform.

Why does a "classical administrative framework" give rise to a local law?

3. How folk law infiltrates through the loopholes of the reforms; the consequences of this

The legal framework of land reform (1964) and administrative reform (1972) entailed certain difficulties in ensuring the transformation of conceptions and technical behaviour. It was not possible to avoid a period of transition, during which all matters continued to be affected by the previously existing legal organisation.

But, in some aspects, the new legal framework is empty, and here folk law emerges, instead of modern law, to generate local law. What are the "empty spaces", or loopholes, of the reforms? In other studies, I have detected three main "empty spaces" (especially Le Roy 1980b:27-35).

First, the selection of councillors for the "conseils de communautés rurales" is founded on political criteria and on factional competition (see above). The dependency of the new "Parti socialiste sénégalais" (taking the place of the Union Progressiste sénégalaise) on the class of traditional notables and the recruitment of candidates from the peasantry results in the selection of councillors oriented to upholding the permanence or continuity of local (or ethnic) behaviour and its values in opposition to the spirit of a "modern" law. These councillors cannot belong to the Senegalese bureaucratic "bourgeoisie" nor hope to enter the middle class. But they become a new class differing from the colonial rural "notables" including Islamic clerics, or marabouts. They are too close to traditional law to understand the complexity of the new law. But their interests (in both the ideological and economic senses) lead the councillors to play the new game. For these reasons, they have to situate themselves against both customary law and modern law and are "obliged" to innovate in local law.

Second, the settlement of conflicts concerning land tenure allocation is organised only in matters of jurisdiction and appeal and not in relation to deliberation and writing of decisions. After having respected modern jurisdictional rules for the proceedings, councils can employ traditional law in judgment. Indeed, "Equity" is the leading criterion of the decision and finds here the possibility of being incorporated in the development of the new local law (Le Roy 1980a:128-133).

Third, the institutional framework in dispute settlement may be "got round" or evaded by all interested persons, including the administrative officers, the councillors and the parties. Conflicts may be conciliated by administrative or traditional extra-jural procedures, and in practice seldom follow the official pattern.

Although the allocation of land tenure is within the exclusive jurisdiction of councils, in fact procedures are not enforced nor considered as forever binding on all parties. Councillors have to operate procedures which are credible yet different from other procedures. Local law is a solution to this problem also.

In these Senegalese cases, folk law is, theoretically, an explosive mixture including traditional law, Islamic law, customary law and some aspects of modern law. If folk law has turned into local law, this is due to the particular context of the Senegalese state and its relations with the world market.

II. LOCAL LAW, STATE AND CAPITAL: AN ATTEMPT AT GENERALISATION

We have seen that in the Senegalese experience, local law is not customary nor traditional law, nor a real administrative decentralisation. Local law represents an original attempt to balance the convergence of central and local general needs. What are its forms, and what are the needs?

1. The Legal Form of Local Law

We have seen that local law is organised and legitimated by state regulations while procedures are determined by councils in the direction of modernization but not always in the spirit of the reforms.

Local law is not an initiative "from the bottom up" nor a true folk law. But it may attach the greatest importance to specific criteria such as ecological considerations, social relations or peasant organisation (Le Roy 1980a:134-135). The local issues of the decisions are founded on the endeavour to avoid "battle" and ensure "peace" inside the village, as a councillor said to me in 1976 (Le Roy 1978:15).

In another study (Le Roy and Wane 1982:384), comparing experiences in Sénégal, Bénin and the République Populaire du Congo where some attempts at local law are developing, I drew these conclusions:

- Local law arises with the organisation of new administrative (in Senegal) or judicial (Benin and Congo) jurisdictions taking the place of customary law in local dispute settlement.
- Competence is limited to minor matters such as land tenure (Senegal) or private claims (Benin).
- If procedures for dispute settlement are adaptive to local customs for enquiry and judgment, hierarchical control becomes patent, and the interventions often meddlesome.
- Decisions are not founded on case-law or an established "jurisprudence". In each case the mention of legal texts is stylistic, and judgments are very near to the customary law in the French colonial style (that is, argumentation is founded on "facts", not "in law"). If we note exceptions in judgments (for example, Le Roy 1980a:135), this is due, in our Senegalese example, to the desire to "cover" many different situations and to ensure the success of the new legal framework and the new class of local "brokers" (Perry 1977) which sustains it.

On this view, the local law corresponds to a new form of state penetration into local communities. In according a semblance of autonomy, the State introduces new patterns by using available means: administrative bureaucracy, political clientele and legal procedures. Local law is a point of intersection between central advances and local customs, and exists to meet general needs. What are these general needs?

2. The New Needs

We may distinguish three levels (local, national and international).

At the local level, the new social patterns introduced by colonialism (and linked with migrations, legal individualism, commodity relations, conversions to Christianity or Islam, and so on) make it impossible to ensure that all dispute settlement occurs inside the village or the family. New jurisdictions are inevitable, and only the state may act nationally to establish procedures and enforce judgments.

What are the preferences of the peasantry? They are compelled to call on state law, permitting the introduction of new agencies and new ideas. African countries meet the same problems and follow the same path as European local communities during the Middle Ages. At the end of the road is the absolute and centralised State that is the model of the French colonial state inherited at political independence in the 1960s.

At the national level, the obligation to administer the state and its agencies without the ideas that in Europe legitimate the central power or ensure the full meaning of the manifestations of state intervention (Alliot 1980:84, on the partial reception of State values) implies both authoritarianism (on the

Bonapartist model) and forced submission of local communities to observance of state regulation.

With the increase of the administrative bureaucracy and public development corporations, African states infiltrate in all matters and concern themselves with all national subjects, such as agricultural production, mining and so on, introducing foreign patterns in politics, economics and administration. As intermediaries (or "brokers" - see above) between producers and international agencies or firms, African states are linked by Western standards. And the local law expresses this in administrative matters. Legal reforms also express the need for the state to legitimate itself in relation to its subjects.

At the international level, the character of exchanges between African countries and other states is determined by the world market and the capitalist system. It would be out of place to discuss here the various theses concerning "the overdeveloped postcolonial state', "law and modernisation theory" or "peripheral capitalism" (Snyder 1980:770-772). For present purposes, and only in relation to the peasantry, we must underline a "new deal" for capital. Following the supervision of exchanges (as in the slave trade) and the organisation of exports (from the 1880s to the 1940s), the new capitalist needs entail the direct control of the producer and of the means of production (standards, rates and so on). There is thus a fundamental transformation from the historical roles of merchant and industrial capital. This entails the introduction of both class relations (especially for the local brokers, see above) and new relations of production (Le Roy 1979). Like Bernstein, I consider that: "peasants have to be located in their relations with capital and the state, in other words, within capitalist relations of production mediated through forms of household production which are the site of a struggle for effective possession and control between the producers and capital/state" (1977, quoted in Snyder 1980:778-779).

The local law joins in this new deal where "the state promotes the extension and intensification of commodity relations" (Snyder 1980:779) through the supervision of local regulations. It is thereby linked to the propagation of transnational capital from African towns to bush communities, and from merchants to producers.

CONCLUSIONS

As Luckham shows concerning the Ghana legal profession (1978: 201-243), it is possible to explore the meanings of the new framework as the basis for the position and role of the state, classes and capital in Black Africa.

But for our purposes, I want here to define the position and role of local law in the African transition from precapitalist to capitalist patterns. It is difficult to suggest a parallel between modes of production in Terray's (1972) conception and legal forms while still avoiding an evolutionary interpretation or reliance on formal Weberian ideal types. Our concepts are too poor or weak. But there are crucial correlations between the new forms of the contemporary state, the legal structure (especially for the local law) and the extension of capital. Similarly, there were other evident correlations between the introduction of a new model of the state, the insertion of capitalist patterns, and the customary law of the colonial era.

Envisaging the central role of the state in relation to law and capital in these two cases, it is interesting to consider, as F.G. Snyder suggests (personal communication), traditional law, customary law, local law and national law as being characteristic, at each level, of different phases in the development of capitalist relations of production in conjunction with the state and its institutional framework. Thus, the local law now developing in French-speaking Africa should appear in other countries given the same state and the same extension of capitalist relations of production. Is this occurring?

REFERENCES

Alliot, M.
1980   'Le miroir noir, images réfléchies de l'état et du droit français', *Bulletin de Liaison de l'Equipe de Recherche en Anthropologie Juridique*, Paris, LAJP, Université de Paris 1, Juin, 2, 77-86.
Arbousier, G. d'
1965   'L'évolution de la législation dans les pays africains d'expression française et à Madagascar', in: H. and L. Kuper (eds.), *African Law: Adaptation and Development*, Berkeley: University of California Press.
Bernstein, H.
1977   'Notes on capital and peasantry', *Review of African Political Economy*, 60.
CINAM SERESA
1960   *Rapport Général sur les Perspectives de Développement au Sénégal*, Parts 1, 2, Dakar, Ministère du Plan.
Dia, M.
1961   *Réflexions sur l'Economie d'Afrique Noire*, Paris, Présence Africaine.
Diao, M.
1976   'Réforme du système foncier traditionnel et développement rural dans le bassin arachidier au Sénégal', doctoral thesis EHESS, Paris 3me cycle.
Grosmaire
1960   *Eléments d'une Documentation pour une Réforme Agraire*, Dakar, Mars.
Lebret, Père L.J.
1961   'Etude générale préliminaire au développement du Sénégal', *Europe-France-Outre-Mer*, 376.
Le Roy, E.
1970   'Système foncier et développement rural. Essai d'anthropologie juridique sur la répartition des terres chez les Wolof ruraux de la zone arachidière nord Sénégal', doctoral thesis, F.D.S.E., Paris.

1978   'Concepts recteurs et pratique juridique dans le droit foncier local en zone arachidière nord Sénégal', paper for the first meeting of the UNESCO IADL African network, Paris.

1979   'Réforme foncière et stratégie de développement. Réflexions à partir de l'exemple sénégalais', *African Perspectives,* 1, 67-82.

1980a   'l'émergence d'un droit foncier local au Sénégal', in: G. Conac (e.), *Dynamiques et Finalités des Droits Africains,* Economica Collection Recherches, Pantheon Sorbonne Série Sciences Juridiques, Paris, pp. 109-140.

1980b   "Le sous-préfet, le président de communauté rurale et les paysans. Limitations de la compétence judiciaire et adaptations du contentieux administratif dans le réglement de conflits fonciers au Sénégal, in: *Fonction de Juger et Pouvoir Judiciaire, Transformations et Déplacements,* Brussels: Publications des Facultés Universitaires Saint Louis, pp. 551-579.

Le Roy, E., and M. Wane
1982   'La formation des droits non étatiques', in: *Encyclopédie Juridique de l'Afrique,* Vol. 1, *L'Etat et le Droit,* Dakar: N.E.A., pp. 353-91.

Luckham, R.
1978   'Imperialism, law and structural dependence: the Ghana legal profession', *Development and Change,* 9, 201-243.

M'Baye, K.
1966   'Droit et développement en Afrique francophone de l'ouest', in: *Les Aspects Juridiques du Développement Economique,* Paris: UNESCO, Dalloz.

Perry, J.A.G.
1977   'Law-codes and brokerage in a Lesotho village', in: I. Hamnet (ed.), *Social Anthropology and Law* ASA Monographs 14, London: Academic Press, pp. 187-226.

Sénégal, République du
1965   *Loi, Décrets, Arrêtés et Circulaires Concernant le Domaine National,* Dakar: Ministère du Plan et de l'Industrie (2nd ed. 1970), roneo.

1972   *La Réforme de l'Administration Territoriale,* Dakar: Ministère de l'Intérieur, ronéo.

Snyder, F.G.
1980   'Law and development in the light of dependency theory', *Law and Society Review,* 14 (3), 723-804.

Terray, E.
1972   'Le marxisme devant les sociétés primitives. Deux études', Paris: François Maspero, Collection Théorie, 95-173.

'Folk law' and historical transitions: some conceptual issues

Francis G. Snyder

I. INTRODUCTION

Among the central features of recent world history is the development of capitalism as a mode of production, originating in western Europe and subsequently expanding throughout most of the world. This historical transition is often considered to embody and symbolise the triumph of state law over other, more localised forms of social regulation. Such a perception is at best only partially correct, but nevertheless it has provided the basis for a substantial literature on the implications of capitalism for legal ideologies, institutions and processes, at least in Europe. Concerning third world countries, however, scholars have begun only recently to try to understand the relations between the development of capitalism and law. Despite the impression which might be conveyed by the burgeoning, often perceptive literature on law in underdeveloped countries (see Fitzpatrick 1980; Greenberg 1980; Snyder 1980, 1981a), relatively little direct, sustained attention has in fact been devoted to broad historical interpretation. Most of the macro-sociological generalisations which have thus far been advanced actually derive from detailed empirical studies, oriented mainly towards more specific aims. In relation to these studies, the general propositions concerning the historical transformation of forms of social regulation in the third world represent by-products, largely unintended.

Legal scholars, including those interested in Africa, Asia and Latin America, have traditionally been preoccupied primarily with the analysis of legal doctrine. Even those who took a broader view of law were (and many still remain) beguiled by the chimera of modernisation (see Snyder 1982). Elaborated after World War II, the theories of the modernisation of law assumed a teleological and ahistorical conception of social change, which envisaged development as an evolutionary movement from an original state of underdevelopment to an idealised version of western capitalist countries. Their implicit assumptions concerning history and politics precluded any serious analysis of the relation between processes of legal change and the development of capitalism. In the past decade, however, research on law by scholars in several disciplines has tended increasingly to focus on the historical expansion and contemporary dynamics of capitalism as a specific socio-economic form (albeit with many variants), while at the same time analysing in detail the particular characteristics of African, Asian or Latin American countries. This convergence of research lays the foundation of a political economy of law (see Ghai, Luckham and Snyder 1984), which accords sufficient importance to social and cultural diversity yet places the form of law in third world countries within a general theoretical framework to explain its historical transformation.

In third world countries, the historical transition which is broadly analogous to that in Europe from feudalism to capitalism comprised, in fact, different transitions to capitalism from specific, precapitalist modes of production. Almost nowhere did these changes result in the mere replacement of local forms of social regulation by the forms of law characteristic of European and American capitalism. What theoretical frameworks are useful in analysing the place of 'folk law' in these recent, and often still continuing transitions? How can we explain both the profound changes in and the sometimes fragmentary persistence of 'folk law'? In this paper, I hope to raise for discussion some of the theoretical and conceptual issues involved in such a macro-sociological analysis.

This paper is based on a long-term study of the social formation of the Banjal in southwestern Senegal. The Banjal are wet-rice farmers who belong to the congeries of peoples which today compose the 300,000 Diola in the Lower Casamance area between The Gambia and Guinea Bissau. They number about 5000 people occupying ten villages at a population density of approximately 40 persons per km^2. I have elsewhere examined in detail the principal economic and legal changes which occurred as the Banjal were drawn into the world capitalist economy between 1900 and 1975 (see Snyder 1977, 1978, 1981b, 1981c, 1981d). There I was concerned with two general questions. First, what changes in legal forms accompanied the subsumption of precapitalist social formations into the world capitalist economy? Second, what relationships obtained between economic changes and legal ideas during this transition period? My purpose was to analyse legal changes in the context of the gradually widening division of labour, which marked the entire range of productive processes of which the Banjal were increasingly a part. The analysis was designed to show the emergence or combination of particular legal forms in specific historical circumstances, and also to demonstrate that such legal changes formed part of a more general transformation.

Here, in contrast, I am concerned with the overall structure of my theoretical argument. I discuss the presuppositions and concepts which underlie my explanation of the changes in Banjal legal ideas since the beginning of the century. In fact, the history of the Banjal includes two major transitions. One, which occurred in the late 18th or early 19th century, involved the formation of a weakly centralised rain priesthood or divine kingship which can provisionally be considered to be a form of precapitalist state. The other, which occurred in the 20th century, was the subsumption of the Banjal within capitalist relations of production and the creation of a Banjal peasantry within the contemporary social formation of Senegal. In this paper I concentrate on the later transition, but I hope that the discussion will help to clarify basic concepts and assess their usefulness for a subsequent analysis of the first major shift.

II. PRESUPPOSITIONS

In order to advance even tentative answers to general questions concerning historical transitions, it is necessary to aim for conceptual rigour and economy of explanation. This requires, in turn, that one's methodological and theoretical presuppositions should be stated explicitly rather than being left implicit. Similarly, basic theoretical concepts and the ways in which they are interconnected in a coherent theoretical explanation should be defined as clearly as possible. This section outlines two basic presuppositions, while the following section discusses several concepts.

My first presupposition is that any analysis of the historical transformation of legal ideas in Africa should be based upon a combination of emic ethnographic description and etic theoretical explanation. This operation, viewed logically, consists of three different phases. (a) The ideas, rules and processes being studied should, so far as possible, be apprehended in the terms and through the language in which they are expressed by the people concerned. (b) The distinctive logic, terms and connotations of African forms of social regulation, far from remaining raw material to be dissected, must be taken into account in formulating the theoretical concepts; western historical experience and its particular logic have no monopoly of appropriate theoretical concepts and forms of explanation. (c) Nevertheless, the conceptions and rationality of the actors cannot, by themselves, necessarily determine either the form or the content of a theoretical explanation. Indeed, it is unlikely that they would ever do so, especially in the macro- sociological study of major historical changes.

Secondly, the method of successive approximation (see Sweezy 1968: 11-20) provides the most fruitful means of analysing detailed ethnographic and historical material. In my study, I isolated the most abstract concrete categories, such as the commodity called labour power, and used these to identify processes of change. Such a method made it possible to integrate the different levels of abstraction which together, in my view, constitute an explanation for historical change. This does not, however, imply that propositions at different levels of abstraction can be derived from each other by simple deduction. Instead, the logical role of more general levels of abstraction is to limit, not determine, the range of variation in progressively less general levels of abstraction. Clearly, the analysis of empirical material and the formulation of a theoretical interpretation go necessarily hand- in-hand. This analytic method helped me to reconcile two potentially conflicting purposes: to reconstruct the ways in which, during the course of a century, empirically distinct legal forms changed and developed at different rates and in different periods; and also to show the interconnections and coherence of these changes within a more general theoretical framework.

III. CONCEPTS

The questions with which a study begins invariably embody theoretical concepts. In turn, such concepts, revised if necessary, are essential in formulating answers and proposing explanations. My basic concepts were drawn from the marxist tradition. Today, however, marxist scholarship is extremely heterogeneous, so that commonly agreed definitions of basic concepts can no longer be assumed. For my particular purposes, the most important concepts were those of mode of production, relations of production, social formation, law and subsumption. Derived after several preliminary drafts of my study, they delimited the temporal and social boundaries of the unit of analysis; identified more precisely the aspects of social relations on which I focussed; and expressed my conception of the general nature of historical changes during the period.

The concepts of mode of production and social formation are related by certain common definitional elements, but they differ fundamentally in their levels of abstraction and theoretical purpose. I employ the concept of mode of production in an expressly historical sense: it refers to "epochs of production", "historical organisation of production", or "social forms of production" (Marx 1973:85, 105; 1974:36; see also Banaji 1977:4-5). A mode of production embraces the relations and forces of production and their laws of motion. Of these elements, the most important is the relations of production: the unity of production, distribution, consumption and exchange. "The conclusion we reach is not that production, distribution, exchange, and consumption are identical, but that they all form the members of a totality, distinctions within a unity. ... A definite production thus determines a definite consumption, distribution and exchange as well as *definite relations between these different moments.* ... " (Marx 1973: 99, emphasis in original.)

Although this definition of a mode of production resembles Wolpe's (1980:7, 36) extended concept of a mode of production, it has two further, important implications. It is not defined solely at the level of the labour process or only as a means for the extraction of surplus labour. To do so would reduce the mode of production to what Marx (1973:100-108) called a simple abstraction, because particular labour processes or modes of exploitation are not necessarily exclusive to specific historical periods. In addition, this definition presumes the unity, rather than the separation, of production and reproduction. As Marx (1967:566) wrote, "[a] society can no more cease to produce than it can cease to consume. When viewed, therefore, as a connected whole, and as flowing on with incessant renewal, every social process of production is, at the same time, a process of reproduction". This conception avoids the separation, which is inherent in demographic notions of reproduction, between the perpetuation or transformation of social relations and the process of production as a whole.

Whereas the concept of mode of production provides a way of distinguishing the essential feature of different historical periods, the concept of social formation furnishes a conception of the social totality. Without accepting any theory of societal evolution or necessary stages of development, I use the term to denote "the relations of production in their totality [which] constitute what are called the social relations, society, and, specifically, a society at a definite stage of [its] historical development" (Marx 1968:80, original emphasis omitted). The social formation comprises and thus derives its basic, skeletal form from the relations of production. As a social whole, it constitutes a complex of totality of social relations which may be isolated for purposes of analysis, but whose boundaries must be determined in each set of specific historical circumstances. Hence, there is no necessary permanence or fixity to a social formation.

This heuristic concept of a social formation is consistent with my conception of reproduction as integral to the process of production and also with my historical definition of mode of production. It implies, however, that two other conceptions of social totality frequently used by marxist writers need to be abandoned. The first is the representation of the social formation by a crude spatial metaphor, which distinguishes between an economic base and a political and ideological superstructure, the latter merely reflecting the former. The second is the Althusserian conception of the social formation as comprising three relatively autonomous levels: an economic level, which is determinant in the last instance, and a political-legal level and an ideological level, both remote from the process of production. Moreover, it follows from these definitions of social formation and mode of production that there is no necessary congruence between a social formation and a mode (or modes) of production. Social formations do not necessarily circumscribe modes of production, and modes of production cannot necessarily be 'mapped' or 'located' within social formations. These concepts have different theoretical purposes and are defined at different levels of abstraction.

Capitalism, as the term is used in my study, refers to an historically specific mode of production which has two central features. One is generalised commodity production: "being a commodity is the dominant and determining characteristic of its products". The other is that "the production of surplus-value [is] the direct aim and determining motive of production" (Marx 1974:879-880; see also Mandel 1971:97-99). Both labour power and the means of commodity production take the form of commodities, therefore, if capitalist relations of production are considered as a whole. This definition of capitalism as an historical mode of production does not, however, exclude the existence within a particular social formation of other forms of immediate production. Nor does it deny the possibility that direct producers may have legal claims and some control of the means of production, though formally they are subordinated to capital. These might be thought to follow from the definition of the capitalist mode at its most abstract level. But, as already noted, such statements at more general levels of abstraction limit, rather than determine, those which are possible at less general levels of abstraction. Even in Europe and America the continued existence of noncapitalist forms has proved compatible with the capitalist mode of production.

Marxist analysis of law, as is well known, has often assumed law to be specific to capitalism, associated with the development of opposed social classes and the state. For my purpose, however, this is not a very useful point of departure. Here my concern lies primarily with relations of production at the level of the household, not the state; and with the ideas, norms and institutions pertinent to an African social formation during its subsumption within capitalist relations of production, not with the legal forms of an established capitalist society. I therefore make use of the contributions of four writers who were specifically concerned with precapitalist, rather than solely capitalist, social formations. Stanley Diamond (1971), Karl Renner (1949), E.B. Pashukanis (1978) and Richard Kinsey (1978) represent different strands in the marxist analysis of precapitalist legal forms. Taken together, they emphasise the importance of Marx's distinction between simple and concrete abstractions for the analysis of law.

Marx distinguished between two types of abstractions: simple abstractions, which were valid for all epochs of production, and concrete abstractions, which were historically specific. He used the examples of possession, money and labour to show "strikingly how even the most abstract categories, despite their validity - precisely because of the abstractness - for all epochs, are nevertheless, in the specific [concrete] character of this abstraction, themselves likewise a product of historical relations, and possess their full validity only for and within these relations" (Marx 1973:105). This distinction was elaborated particularly by Pashukanis. His argument that law is a specifically capitalist category is based on an historical method which reconstructs the past by looking backward from the present, and to that extent is not useful for my purposes. But his emphasis on Marx's distinction between simple and concrete categories is of fundamental importance, and this distinction underlies my conception of law.

Accepting Marx's (1973:88) point that "every form of production creates its own legal relations", I consider a conception of law to be more useful than a strict definition. For my purposes, an adequate conception of law consists of two interrelated, yet distinct aspects. The first is a simple concept of law, which establishes the general preconditions of law and is basically ahistorical. Law, in this sense, may be defined as those forms of social consciousness or institutionalised social relations which have as their generic function the expression, regulation or maintenance of the dominant social relations within a social formation. I adopt this concept directly from Sumner (1979:272; see also Marx 1974:793). Unlike Sumner, however, I consider it to be only one aspect - the simple concept - of a conception of law. Although essential, it is limited, in that it does not define the specific forms which characterise and thus distinguish particular modes of production. These historically specific, or concrete, legal forms are the second, and more important, aspect of law. Either they exist only within particular modes of production; or while not necessarily limited (as simple concepts) to a single mode of production, nevertheless they form part of specific combinations of legal forms as concrete concepts in particular historical periods. These legal forms are therefore to be defined in conjunction with specific modes of production. They form an integral part of the relations of production.

It follows from this conception of law that law, as a simple concept, is not limited to any particular mode of production. Yet, in the analysis of historical transitions the simple concept of law is of much less importance than concrete legal forms, since only the latter exist solely or are combined in specific ways in particular historic forms of production. Thus, while recognising abstractly the continuity of (simple) legal forms, I draw a sharp distinction between historically specific (concrete) legal forms according to the mode of production that characterises the social formation of which these legal forms are a part.

The history of the Banjal since the mid-19th century may, in my view, be succinctly described as the subsumption of formerly precapitalist producers within capitalist relations of production. At the most abstract level, this shift may be expressed as a transition from a precapitalist to the capitalist mode of production. This does not, however, necessarily imply that the Banjal produce rice by capitalist methods, or that Banjal communities are split by a class division between bourgeoisie and proletariat. Rather, the Banjal are now integrated into the social formation of Senegal, in which the relations of production, as previously defined, are basically capitalist: the predominant form of production is not for use but for exchange, and it involves the production of surplus value. The Banjal are incorporated into these relations by simple commodity production, by the reproduction and sale of labour power as a commodity and by their fundamental dependence upon the production and circulation of commodities for their own social reproduction.

This same transition may also be described, much more concretely, as the conjunction of a number of fundamental changes in Banjal economic and legal forms; it is with the latter that I am primarily concerned. One may discern three different types of legal change. The first comprises changes in particular legal ideas. For example, the pledge of land often amounts to a sale; a new concept concerning the renting of peanut land has developed during the past several decades; and a concept referring to certain exchange transactions has widened in scope. A second type of change is a shift in the relationships between different legal forms. Thus, for example, the transmutation of labour power into a commodity form, together with the increased role of the nuclear family as the means of its reproduction, have undermined the Banjal notion of homogeneous inheritance. The third type of legal change is a transformation of the logic and position of Banjal legal ideas viewed as a whole. Formerly, Banjal legal ideas were given a distinctive logic by an abstract, symbolic parallel between the annual production cycle and human reproduction. Today, however, the central thread running through Banjal legal concepts is the production of rural labour power as an urban commodity, as is dramatically demonstrated in the transformation of the notion of *gamoen* or childwealth (see Snyder 1981d).

In order to elaborate a theoretical framework in which to analyse these changes, I use the concept of subsumption. As defined by Galeski (1975:22), subsumption

> "signifies the subordination of some forms of economic activity in the economic system to principles determining the functioning of the system as a whole. The peasant farm, under the conditions of a capitalist economic order, is usually cited as an example of a subsumed system. This implies that (1) the peasant farm lacks the basic characteristics of a capitalist enterprise, (2) changes in the mode of peasant farming are determined by the laws governing the functioning of the capitalist economy system as a whole, and (3) the peasant farm is acquiring certain features specific to the capitalist enterprise".

Thus defined, the concept of subsumption is less abstract than, but entirely consistent with, my historical definition of mode of production. The ideas of subsumption, mode of production, relations of production, and law are central to my conclusion that, among the Banjal, the continuity of numerous simple legal concepts masks the transformation of concrete legal forms.

The conjunction of these concepts in a coherent theoretical statement captures the position of the Banjal within the contemporary Senegalese political economy more accurately, in my view, than would a notion of the articulation of modes of production. In other words, the former, not the latter, fits the facts concerning the specific historical processes which I seek to explain. In this particular instance, therefore, the uneven extent and historical forms of the subordination of peasants to capital provide a more concise and more convincing explanation of the changes in Banjal legal ideas than would a conception of the simultaneous conservation and dissolution of a precapitalist mode.

Theories of articulation have the advantage that they appear, by their terms, both to recognise the linkages between precapitalist producers and capitalist production and to grant a substantial degree of economic and political autonomy to subordinate (putatively precapitalist) groups. Clearly, both elements are in fact important, and the latter is also tactically useful from the standpoint of populist politics. Yet these gains, worthwhile as they may be, are obtained by articulation theory only at a considerable price. It is useful to develop this point briefly.

Articulation theories typically suffer from certain conceptual difficulties.

> "One is that it makes little sense to talk of the 'conservation' of modes of production whose conditions of reproduction ... have been destroyed by capitalism even if the forms of production have not been completely transformed. Second, theories of articulation tend to be functionalist in the sense that the degree and the forms of 'dissolution/conservation' are held to be determined by what is functional for capital. Third, in these theories precapitalist modes of production and the capitalist mode 'meet' essentially at the level of exchange ..." (Bernstein 1977:69).

Even though these objections, particularly the first, may be rather overstated, nevertheless they seem to be basically correct.

In addition, articulation theories often reproduce, albeit in other terms and in a sophisticated manner, the dualism which was inherent in the now largely abandoned dichotomous distinction between tradition and modernity. This dualism has two unfortunate consequences. On the one hand, it vitiates any attempt at holistic analysis. A partial exception may be made in cases in which either market exchange or the state is assigned the role of insuring social cohesion, since then an adequate analysis of either requires some view of the social formation, or other unit of analysis, as a whole. On the other hand, it tends towards the misconception that ethnic groups are essential rather than contingent. Even today, such groups are frequently considered to represent distinct social formations, instead of being understood as integral to the weave of social relations and ideologies in peripheral capitalist social formations structured by the state. Ethnic groups are sometimes viewed, therefore, as the locus of particular, precapitalist modes of production, articulated to a separate capitalist mode.

Such a conception of an ethnic group as a social formation, embodying a mode of production, is related to a central weakness in articulation theory, namely the failure to define clearly the concept of mode of production. It is perhaps surprising that a theory of the articulation of modes of production should lack a satisfactory definition of its basic concept. That the expression 'mode of production' refers generally to the economic level, or to the way in which surplus is extracted, or to a particular labour process is often assumed, without discussion. Despite the number of stimulating studies in which the concept has been used, the notion of mode of production tends frequently to be employed in an evocative, rhetorical manner, like the notion of social control. In such instances its precise meaning and its relation to law remain unclear. As a consequence, perhaps, it is sometimes considered that the notion of a particular mode of production provides a basis from which to deduce the existence, or the logical necessity, of particular legal ideas, forms of work or other social relations; or, conversely, that specific legal ideas necessarily imply the existence of a particular mode of production. Yet, with the exception of the ideas of private property, contract and legal personality in relation to the capitalist mode of production, these presumptions have rarely, if ever, been supported by cogent argument.

There is no reason, however, to assume that the concept of a mode of production can explain all social relations, that law is isomorphic with a mode of production, or that particular types of social relations are necessarily exclusive to a particular mode of production. To do so is to fall victim to both an historical misconception and a logical fallacy. The former is that any mode of production, including capitalism, is monolithic; the latter, that the particular can be explained by the general. Both neglect the crucial distinction between levels of abstraction. For example, the capitalist mode of production may be said, at its most abstract level, to generate two general classes; but even Marx recognised that, empirically speaking, the number of classes was actually far greater. Similarly, the capitalist mode may be thought to require certain general legal concepts. But it is also consistent with a wide range of more specific ideas, rules and practices which might be considered, in the abstract, to be inimical to its operation.

IV. CONCLUSION

The creation and diversity of 'folk law' in third world countries can be explained by a holistic method, which uses a broad historical conception of modes of production. It is necessary, however, to distinguish and show the connections between law and different aspects of the relations of production, namely production, distribution, exchange and consumption. It is also essential to distinguish carefully between different levels of abstraction, both in analysis and explanation. In this way, it is possible to bring Marx's research hypothesis, his 'production theory' of society (see Carver 1982) to bear on the study of changing, pluralistic forms of social regulation.

So far as the Banjal of Senegal are concerned, the major historical shift which occurred between 1900 and 1975 was not simply economic. It also embraced a series of fundamental changes in the social meaning of a range of legal concepts. These symbolised, expressed, reflected or were conditioned by changes in the social relations of production. In analysing these changes, my purpose is not, of course, to suggest that all of social life may be reduced to the economic element, which would clearly be nonsensical. Nor am I concerned here to delimit the scope of relatively independent political action potentially available to Banjal; this would require a separate study. Instead, I aim to illustrate the ways in which the integration of the Banjal into the world capitalist economy has altered profoundly many of their basic ideas, even though these ideas are often expressed today in what seem to be the same terms as in the past. Thus, I stress the interconnections between legal ideas and the relations of production, and I emphasise the extent of historical rupture rather than that of continuity. In these respects, the Banjal exemplify the recent history of many third world communities, providing a case study of the changes in 'folk law' during an historical transition.

REFERENCES

Banaji, J.
1977   'Modes of production in a materialist conception of history', *Capital and Class*,
            3, Autumn, 1-44.
Bernstein, H.
1977   'Notes on capital and peasantry', *Review of African Political Economy*, 10, 60-73.
Carver, T.
1982   *Marx's Social Theory*, Oxford: Oxford University Press.
Diamond, S.
1971   'The rule of law versus the order of custom', in: R.P. Wolff (ed.) *The Rule of Law*,
            pp. 115-144, New York: Simon and Schuster.
Fitzpatrick, P.
1980   'Law, modernization and mystification', in: S. Spitzer (ed.) *Research in Law and
            Sociology; A Research Annual*, Vol. 3, pp. 168-178, Greenwich, Connecticut: Jai
            Press.
Galeski, B.
1972   *Basic Concepts of Rural Sociology*, ed. T. Shanin and P. Worsley, trans. H.C.
            Stevens, Manchester: Manchester University Press.
Ghai, Y.P., A.R. Luckham and F.G. Snyder
1984   *The Political Economy of Law; A Third World Reader*, London: Heinemann,
            forthcoming.
Greenberg, D.
1980   'Law and development in light of dependency theory', in: S. Spitzer (ed.)
            Research in Law and Sociology: A Research Annual, Vol. 3, pp. 129-159, Green-
            wich, Connecticut: Jai Press.
Kinsey, R.
1978   'Marxism and the law: preliminary analyses', *British Journal of Law and Society*,
            5, Winter, 202-227.

Mandel, E.
1971   *The Formation of the Economic Thought of Karl Marx: 1843 to Capital* (trans. B.
          Pearce), London: Monthly Review Press.

Marx, K.
1967   *Capital: A Critique of Political Economy*, Vol. 1 (ed. F. Engels, trans. S. Moore
          and E. Aveling), New York: International Publishers.
1968   'Wage labour and capital', in: K. Marx and F. Engels, *Selected Works in One
          Volume*, London: Lawrence and Wishart.
1973   *Grundrisse; Foundations of the Critique of Political Economy* (Rough Draft) trans.
          M. Nicolaus Harmondsworth: Penguin Books
1974   *Capital: A Critique of Political Economy*, Vol. 3 ed. F. Engels London: Lawrence
          and Wishart.

Pashukanis, E.B.
1978   *Law and Marxism; A General Theory* (ed. C. Arthur, trans. B. Einhorn), London:
          Ink Links.

Renner, K.
1949   *The Institutions of Private Law and Their Social Functions* (ed. O. Kahn-Freund),
          London: Routledge and Kegan Paul.

Snyder, F.G.
1977   'Land law and economic change in rural Senegal: Diola pledge transactions and
          disputes', in: I. Hamnett (ed.), *Social Anthropology and Law*, pp. 113-157,
          London and New York: Academic Press.
1978   'Legal innovation and social change in a peasant community: a Senegalese
          village police', *Africa*, 48, 3, 231-247.
1980   'Law and development in the light of dependency theory', *Law and Society
          Review*, 14, 3, 723-804.
1980a   'Anthropology, dispute processes and law: a critical introduction', *British Jour-
          nal of Law and Society*, 8, 2, 1-40.
1981b   *Capitalism and Legal Change; An African Transformation*, New York and Lon-
          don: Academic Press.
1981c   'Colonialism and legal form: the creation of "customary law" in Senegal', in: C.
          Sumner (ed.), *Crime, Justice and Underdevelopment*, pp. 90-121, London: Heine-
          mann Educational Books.
1981d   'Labour power and legal transformation in Senegal', *Review of African Political
          Economy*, 21, 26-43.
1982   'The failure of "Law and Development"', *Wisconsin Law Review*, 3, 373-396.

Sumner, C.
1979   *Reading Ideologies; An Investigation into the Marxist Theory of Ideology and Law*,
          London: Academic Press.

Sweezy, P.M.
1968   *The Theory of Capitalist Development; Principles of Marxian Political Economy*,
          London: Monthly Review Press.

Wolpe, H.
1980   'Introduction', in: H. Wolpe (ed.), *The Articulation of Modes of Production;
          Essays from Economy and Society*, London: Routledge and Kegan Paul.

Part V
Legal policies

Introduction

G.R. Woodman

The debate which began in the papers printed below and was continued in the discussion of them at Bellagio, started on relatively familiar territory with the issue: Are folk law and institutions (or "informal institutions", "aboriginal customs", "aboriginal customary law", "bush justice", "traditional measures", and suchlike terms) to be approved in preference to state law and institutions? It progressed to challenge the assumptions inherent in that question.

All but one of the authors wrote favourably of folk law, at least to the extent of regretting its partial replacement by state law in their areas of experience. Three write of the experience of minority ethnic groups faced by the power of the first-world states into which they have been politically incorporated: Bayly and Finkler on the northern peoples of Canada; Conn on the natives of Alaska. Strijbosch considers the comparable situation of a people in a third-world state, Indonesia, finding their traditional culture faced by the power of the new nation state. In contrast with their concern at the encroachment of modern state law on the spheres of activity hitherto the object of folk law the main theme of Abel's paper is scepticism about the claims of "informal" dispute-settlement mechanisms. The difference in view is quite possibly related to a difference in subject matter. Abel writes of the experience of newly-developed "informal alternatives" to state courts in the first world - alternatives often created or fostered by the state. (The paper by the Australian Law Reform Commission reported investigations and discussions in progress, and did not take a stance on the controversial issues mentioned here.)

These contrasting judgments of folk law and institutions are based on valuable accounts of observed social facts. However, such judgments can be formed only by the application to such facts of criteria derived from value-systems. It is noteworthy that the judgments unfavourable to state law are mainly based upon criteria associated with, and quite possibly derived from state law. Bayly finds state law and institutions wanting in terms of the satisfaction of existing social interests, and he emphasises that the social scientist needs to act within a state constitutional framework. Conn finds state institutions wanting in terms of the securing of due process, the value which the state itself explicitly holds out. The villagers, he says, wish simply an end to violence. Finkler judges the observed facts in terms of effectiveness in arresting conduct likely to cause social friction, and notes a growing anger among native communities at the state's failure to achieve this. Strijbosch judges in terms of efficient, cheap or predictable settlement of disputes according to socially approved rules. Abel, again in contrast to the others, sets against the preservation of the status quo the value of social development.

The use of criteria from state law was justified in the discussion on the ground that, since state law failed by its own criteria, it must obviously be defective, and so it was hardly necessary to devise other criteria. However, while this may have been sufficient in the cases of the examples set out in the papers, it does not provide an adequate general theory for the criticism of various types of law in circumstances of legal pluralism. One participant pointed out that the ideologies of state law and folk law generally differed, and there was no prima facie justification for basing critique on one to the exclusion of the other. Another argued forcefully that the criteria likely to be adopted, and which had been adopted, were those of the Western states, and their adoption thus fostered external interference in the internal affairs of Third-World states. I return to the issue of Western ethnocentrism below.

The discussion of policy criteria went no further than this point. It could be that participants saw no possibility of making common progress on such a fundamental and controversial issue. There were also suggestions that, even if criteria were settled, they could not be applied to non-Western societies until we had developed a far more extensive and sympathetic understanding of those societies. It was not explained how in the mean time we were to reach decisions forced upon us by circumstances.

Regarding the "folk law v. state law" issue, several participants commented on the crudity of the question formulated thus. It made no sense to imagine that we could universally opt for one side over the other. There might, for example, be instances where folk law generally should be preserved, but where at the same time state law needed to be employed deliberately to attack particular evils within folk law, such as the oppression of women. (Hesitancy in forming criteria for fear of ethnocentrism or of lack of sympathetic understanding can inhibit necessary attacks on injustice, on this view.) Again, the issue needed to be formulated with more precision: if in some circumstances we compared the ideals of the two systems, state law might well be preferred, but if we considered the realities of the systems in operation, an equally strong preference for folk law might be justified. The most fully-argued rejection of the contrast appears in Abel's paper. He argues in respect of dispute settlement institutions that the vital issue is not between the formal and the informal, but between legal and "political" modes of conflict.

A further challenge to the assumptions of the question is inherent in reports of failed attempts at social engineering. What, one may ask, is the use of passing judgment if we cannot follow it with effective action? On this occasion, as always when socio-legal students are gathered together, accounts of failures were exchanged. Several participants emphasised that in practice state law and folk law always intertwined, and argued that in consequence it was not a practical policy simply to foster one in preference to the other. Strijbosch's meticulous account of a deeply intricate series of processes, although it generally adopts the distinction, demonstrates this impossibility of separation in the design of the policy. As participants remarked, any attempt to suppress folk courts would result in people rapidly developing alternative institutions. Conversely it made no practical sense to follow a simplistic slogan "informal justice good, state law bad". More radically and depressingly it might be concluded from studies such as Bayly's that activity by the state, even when benign in intent, was likely to cause harm to societies dependent upon state law, not very different from instances such as that described by Conn, where the state motives were far from benign. This last observation, as Abel pointed out, confirms his scepticism about the desirability of extending the reach of state legal dispute-settlement institutions, whether formal or informal.

The consideration of these questions led to the issue as to whether the legal anthropologist could and should become involved in political discussion. The general opinion seemed to be that, if value-judgments were to be made at all (as all the papers supposed), it would necessarily follow that we should try to influence policy decisions. The Australian Law Reform Commission had commented in its paper that "it must get on with the job of completing its enquiry, delivering its report and drafting any legislation it proposes". Conn clearly considers that political involvement is called for when investigation reveals extensive, institutionalised injustice. However, participants had several reports of social scientists being excluded from influential discussions of policy, their work being subject to licensing controls, and their projects being restricted by lack of funds. While there could be various reasons for these limitations, one participant suggested that they might arise partly from the perception that the conclusions drawn in much anthropological research had been unscientific.

Since several papers focussed on ethnic minorities part of the discussion was concerned with their particular situation. The argument that ethnic minorities should be predominantly involved in making and enforcing their own laws appears in the papers of Conn, Bayly, Finkler and Strijbosch. Moreover, all these writers, and especially Conn and Finkler, complain that state agencies at present fail adequately to involve members of local communities in these processes. However, Bayly points to a serious obstacle to progress: the development of laws adapted to the needs of ethnic minorities requires a differentiation between them and other categories of citizens of the nation-state, a differentiation which would run contrary to the philosophies and policies generally avowed by those states. The problem of the ethnic minority concerned participants to the extent that it was given prominence in the plans for the next conference of the Commission on Folk Law and Legal Pluralism.

Perhaps the most critical challenge to the "folk law v. state law" question was that which doubted the possibility of generalisation, at least in our present state of knowledge. The difficulty of justifying general propositions was demonstrated when a participant suggested that several of Abel's statements were contrary to his own experience. Abel countered by indicating scientific, published research which supported those particular propositions. However, most social scientists will have had the experience of being told that their findings are not true of some other particular society. The participant who suggested that the failings of anthropologists might be a part cause of their exclusion from influential policy discussion argued that most of their work in sensitive areas had been deeply ethnocentric, and that their wider conclusions had been ahistorical, seeking cross-cultural generalisations without regard to fundamental differences in economic structure.

Such warnings, while justified, should not entirely prevent legal anthropologists from moving towards the formulation of value-judgments of state and folk law. As seen, there is a pressing need for specific judgments in particular circumstances for practical purposes. It ought to be possible for collaboration between students of widely differing cultures to assist such judgments by providing evidence, arguments and insights. The Bellagio papers, by pointing to some lines of development, especially in the refinement and particularisation of the questions asked, while not providing proven, clear answers, achieve progress.

Informal alternatives to courts as a mode of legalizing conflict

Richard L. Abel

[*Editorial Note*. The paper presented under this title at the Bellagio symposium has been subsequently published in an amended form: Abel 1981. The following summary has been prepared by Gordon Woodman.]

Legal scholars and social scientists are currently preoccupied with informal alternatives to courts. The ideology of informalism includes a number of discrete and often inconsistent claims and promises. The alleged advantages of informal alternatives to courts, in cost, access, processual variables, lay participation, and potential for suppressing violence and crime, averting social disintegration, and altering patterns of disputing, are not proven. The ideology being naive, vague and inconsistent, it cannot offer a foundation for understanding the social phenomenon it has inspired.

A more satisfactory analytic framework may be developed by constructing two ideal-typical models of conflict. Legal conflict, which encompasses both formal courts and informal alternatives, is homeostatic, repetitive, and preserves the status quo. Political conflict is disequilibrating, transformative, and contributes to structural social change.

Participants in legal conflict carry the advantages and disadvantages of characteristics which they bear in the larger society, such as class, socio-economic status, education, gender, age and ethnicity. Political conflict produces organisation of the hitherto disorganised and leads to forms of struggle which may invert prior advantage, as where a highly integrated corporation or state becomes vulnerable to activity which dislocates a small but vital part of its functioning. Adversaries in legal conflict are frequently unequal, as when an individual disputes with the state. The practices associated with the ideology of liberal legalism, promising equal justice for all, simultaneously encourage the weak to invoke their legal rights against the strong, and legitimate the coercion exercised by powerful corporations and the state over individuals. Political conflict generally does not occur unless adversaries are approximately equal.

In legal conflict a single, exhaustive, internally consistent normative order is appealed to by both parties. In political conflict the inconsistent demands of the parties are justified by norms that are wholly antagonistic. Legal conflict displays a high degree of role differentiation in respect of the third parties, their subordinates, and the disputants' own structuring in hierarchies and representation by professionals. Political conflict displays none of this role differentiation. Legal conflict is contained within clear, rigid boundaries of time, place, institution, permitted strategy and language. Political conflict is subject to no such boundaries, being waged in all arenas and being concerned with both normative evaluation of the past and the determination of the future. In legal conflict the outcome is paternalistically imposed in a form which perpetuates the status quo. Political conflict results in outcomes that affect equally everyone in each camp, thereby strengthening the camps' corporate characters, altering the balance of power, and contributing to social structural change.

Actual conflicts are located on the continuum between these ideal types and are constantly pushed back and forth by social forces. In capitalist society the dominant classes benefit from, and so seek to promote the legalization of conflict, while the oppressed classes seek to politicize it. Thus the history of conflict between labour and capital in the nineteenth and twentieth centuries can be read as the progressive transformation of political conflict into highly legalized conflict. Simultaneously class conflict is constantly re-politicized by the efforts of labour. This has happened, for example, in recent controversies over health and safety at work, where in turn there is now a progressive legalization of conflict.

Those who manage legal institutions seek continuously to legitimate the legal system. Since legitimacy is always insecure, informalism is attractive to them because, as a novel solution, its flaws are not immediately apparent, and attention given to informal, marginal institutions deflects criticism from core institutions. Moreover, the case for informalism can be persuasively expressed as a neutral concern with reducing contentiousness, technicality, cost and delay, and for compromise, through institutions which appear not to be coercive.

However, informal institutions can legalize disputes which could not be handled by formal courts. Thus the scope of state control is enlarged and existing inequalities are perpetuated. Formality has often been used to resist oppression, while informalism provides a greater opportunity for the more privileged to exert their power. Informal institutions are in reality coercive. They foster dependence on the state because they expand the incidence of the relationship between helpful professional and needy consumer. They individualize and trivialize disputes, thereby obscuring the principal struggles in contemporary society.

Thus liberal legalism, in its constant striving to mediate the contradictions of capitalist society, has recently shifted away from the extension of formal rights and protections, towards the promotion of informal processes. Despite superficial differences, both formalism and informalism are mechanisms for legalizing conflict. It is essential to consider ways of repoliticizing it.

REFERENCE

Abel, R.L.
   1981   'Conservative conflict and the reproduction of capitalism: the role of informal
                 justice', *International Journal of the Sociology of Law*, 9, 245.

Toward the development of a Northwest Territories law reform capability
to enable the development of proposals for new legislation to meet the special needs and circumstances of northern peoples

John U. Bayly

I. WHAT LAWS? WHAT PEOPLES?

In the Northwest Territories Legislative Assembly session in March, 1980, Dennis Patterson, Member of the Legislative Assembly for Frobisher Bay, made a motion that the Government of the Northwest Territories develop a strong law reform capability. It was a good idea. It was suggested by a man who, although brought up in southern Canada as a middle class white Ango-Saxon Protestant, has adopted the North as his home and has developed a northern outlook on problems; an outlook based on his sensitivity to native peoples, their values and outlooks.

A year has passed. In that time, nothing has been done to put Mr. Patterson's very good idea into action. Why not? Mr. Patterson did, after all, recognize as many people have, that law review and law reform are especially necessary in a territory with emerging native peoples both of Inuit and Dene (Amerindian) cultures - people who recently have begun to make their legislative needs and desires known.

If law reform is necessary, why has nothing been done since the Legislative Assembly passed the Patterson motion? It does not appear to be because of opposition to law reform. Spending restraints are not so very tight as to make the motion impossible to turn into a publicly funded program. I believe the problem has several causes.

In the first place, the development of a strong law reform capability is not the first good idea to blossom forth from the Legislative Assembly only to wither on the vine of northern administration before bearing fruit. Giving evidence before the Mackenzie Valley Pipeline Inquiry presided over by Mr. Justice Thomas Berger, Professor Louis E. Hamlin stated:

> "... the debates of that council [N.W.T. Legislative Assembly] show an inexhaustible stock of northern good ideas. Nowhere in Canada could we find a better collection of northern expertise on every subject dealing with the north. Specifically I am referring to works made by Rea Wonders, David Judd, the Carrothers Commission, the 1972 Jean Chretien statement, and the Northwest Territories Report on Provincial Type Responsibilities.

> However, I will try to view this massive factual information from two major perspectives. The first is a principle which considers the new ideas of northness or nordicity in men and things; this means if we do something in the north, let us do it according to a northern spirit, a northern mentality. This very northern approach cannot be taken for granted among the powerful southerners who usually manage the major decisions affecting the north ... [The second principle of southness or sameness] is the principle of Canadianity or the quality of going along with national values.
>
> In accordance with this standard, one establishes what is good for a northern region in accordance with whether it's good for the whole country. If the nation is not interested in such and such a northern program, that program is not accepted by the south as an 'A' or 'B' priority budget item, not regularly financed, that program will probably never be carried out" (Mackenzie Valley Pipeline Inquiry Transcript Vol.XIII, March 7, 1975:1399-1403).

Professor Hamlin recognised that the northern region is very poorly represented within the agencies which decide the nature of the common good. In further commenting on the people who decide what policies, strategies and experiences will apply to the north and its inhabitants, Professor Hamlin questioned:

> "How can optimum nordicity be derived from a population almost totally southern and non-Amerindian in its outlook?" (Mackenzie Valley Pipeline Inquiry transcript Vol.XIII March 7, 1975:1399-1403).

That inexhaustible stock of northern good ideas, therefore, seldom tends to find its way into northern policy and programs. It is the antithesis of Canadianity to support unique northern ideas.

As a result, the laws which have developed to govern northern native peoples derive not from their cultural values, social customs and behavioural rules, but are borrowed and often copied verbatim from laws in force in southern Canada, laws which have grown out of British traditions, history and experience. It should come as no surprise that the territorial justice administration which has taken no steps to implement the Patterson motion has, nonetheless, a history of active participation in the Canadian Uniformity of Laws Organisation and has even hosted a national conference of the Uniformity of Laws Organisation at Yellowknife since Professor Hamlin gave his evidence to Mr. Justice Berger.

In the second place, the Northwest Territories has within its borders a huge land mass - approximately 1.3 million square miles, a small population made up of Inuit, who speak several dialects of the same language, Dene, having several distinct languages, Slavey, Chippewyan, Dogrib and Loucheaux and a white English-speaking, largely transient, population with roots in the provinces and the British system of law and Parliamentary democracy. Given that there are so many distinct peoples, such a vast area and so small a population, the task of making laws to reflect folk-law tradition is formidable.

In the third place, many of the activities to be regulated such as oil and gas exploration and production, mining, commercial fishing, the administration of justice, the management of the environment, the licensing of the use of inland waters, the prevention of pollution of Arctic waters, the regulation of Air Transport, are matters within the federal domain and therefore beyond the jurisdiction of Mr. Patterson and the Territorial Legislative Assembly. The legislative powers of the Assembly are enumerated in Section 13 of the Northwest Territories Act R.S.C. 1970 c N-22 and amendment thereto. It is noteworthy that section 16(2) of the Act gives to the Government of Canada the power to disallow any ordinance passed by the Legislative Assembly within a year of the passage of that ordinance notwithstanding that such ordinance is within the legislative competence of the Assembly.

II. SOME ILLUSTRATIVE EXAMPLES

Accepting that the task is a formidable one, let us examine the problem by way of examples to discover whether the need for law reform to accommodate the special needs of northern aboriginal peoples is sufficiently important to be worthy of attention and work.

1. In the first legal case in my experience in the Northwest Territories, *The Queen* v. *Noah and Martha Komadjuak re: Nancy Okotok Komadjuak* (unreported decision of J.P. Ron Milligan, July 1967) a case involving an Inuit couple charged with child abuse and neglect under the Northwest Territories Child Welfare Ordinance, I had my first exposure to the utter bewilderment of people trying to cope with a problem in a forum totally foreign to them according to rules of which they had no idea. The child had been ill and, shortly after she was born, was taken by airplane to hospitals in Manitoba where she spent almost three years recovering under the care of English speaking white nurses and doctors. She returned speaking only English, a language not spoken by her parents. She had acquired habits, likes, dislikes and values they did not share or understand. As a result, they resented her, feared and abused her. The authorities stepped in and apprehended the child for her own safety. The parents were then tried for assault upon their daughter. The court took no steps to find out whether what they had done was in any way "criminal" in the eyes of the accused. They appeared neither to want the child who was such a stranger to them nor to have any idea that their behaviour was wrong or unacceptable.

As an interesting follow up to this case, the baby was later adopted by a white anthropologist and his family notwithstanding the fact that she was enjoying better than adequate foster care in the home of another Inuit family in Rankin Inlet where her natural parents resided. I shall refer again to aboriginal child welfare laws in another section of the paper.

2. In the tiny settlements of the Northwest Territories populated by Inuit and Dene, people know one another very well. "Everybody is related to everybody else", I was told by a young girl from Sugluk in Arctic Quebec. There are no locks on the doors of the houses. Nobody knocks before entering, and, unless somebody has been away from the community, greetings are perfunctory or non-existent. Under these circumstances, if somebody enters a dwelling and steals a pound of tea which does not belong to him, a charge of "break enter and theft from a dwelling house", which carries a maximum penalty of life imprisonment hardly seems an appropriate charge to lay. And yet, the Criminal Code of Canada, which applies throughout the entire country, defines the crime in Section 308 as:

> "308. (b) A person shall be deemed to have broken and entered if:
> i. he obtained entrance by a threat or artifice or by collusion with a person within, or
> ii. he entered without lawful justification or excuse, the proof of which lies upon him, by a permanent or temporary opening."

The police would be perfectly correct to lay a charge of break enter and theft in the example I put forward. If it were not for a policy of the regional office of the Department of Justice in the Northwest Territories which instructs the police to lay only theft charges in such circumstances, the police would have continued to lay the more serious charge of break enter and theft as a matter of course.

The example has another aspect of interest. Break enter and theft from a dwelling house is a potentially serious crime. Because of its maximum penalty being life imprisonment, it confers upon an accused person the right to a trial by a Supreme Court judge with a jury or a trial by a Territorial Court judge (magistrate). It precludes, because of its potential seriousness, trial and plea before a Justice of the Peace who can be, and often is, a local native person. In terms of the administration of justice, the results of a man walking into the house of a neighbour and stealing a pound of tea can be that a charge of break enter and theft is laid, a legal aid application taken, a lawyer assigned, crown attorney briefed by the police, a court circuit arranged, an airplane chartered, five people (a territorial court judge, clerk, a court reporter, a prosecutor and a defence lawyer) attending, an election of mode of trial taken, a plea, a trial or preliminary hearing held, a transcript ordered and a re-attendance if a trial before a Supreme Court judge is elected, and a final verdict rendered. If a charge of theft is laid in the same circumstances, the local Justice of the Peace would have jurisdiction to hear the case under almost all circumstances. The accused person could represent himself or be assisted by a native court worker with minimal legal training. More importantly, the small community could deal with the problem internally without the help of, or interference by, outside authorities. The rights of the accused person are further protected by his right to appeal to the Supreme Court of the Northwest Territories in the event that the Justice of the Peace appears to have committed an error in law. The appeal mechanisms are straightforward and the rules are relaxed in their application. As an aside, these appeal rules are "judge-made laws". Their practicality has reflected the experience of the judges in the administration of justice in the Northwest Territories.

3. In urban Canada, gun control is an important issue. Amendments were made to the Criminal Code which came into force in 1978 providing for prohibition orders preventing persons who have been convicted of crimes of violence from owning or having in their possession firearms, ammunition or explosives. Before the law was passed, representations were made to the Government of Canada by officials involved in the administration of justice in the Northwest Territories recommending that, at least in the North where so many people rely on firearms to make their living, the orders be discretionary to be applied by the judge hearing the case only where and as appropriate. The recommendations were not followed. Section 98 of the Criminal Code which applies throughout Canada reads in part:

> "98(1). Where a person is convicted of an indictable offence in the commission of which violence against a person is used, threatened or attempted and for which the offender may be sentenced to imprisonment for ten years or more or of an offence under section 83, the court *shall*, in addition to any other punishment that may be imposed for that offence, make an order prohibiting him from having in his possession any firearm, or any ammunition or explosive substance for any period of time specified in the order that commences on the day the order is made and expires not earlier than:
> (a) in the case of a first conviction for such an offence, five years, and
> (b) in any other case, ten years
> after the time of his release from imprisonment after conviction for the offence."
> (Emphasis added)

Thus for offences which include prison breach, rape, attempted rape, incest, buggery, bestiality, indecent assault upon a male person, causing death or bodily harm by criminal negligence, murder, attempted murder, manslaughter, aiding a person to commit suicide, causing bodily harm with intent, impeding an attempt to save a life, kidnapping, abduction of female person or a child, a judge *shall* upon conviction prohibit the convicted person from possessing firearms, ammunition or explosives for at least five years.

The potential effects of this prohibition on the rehabilitation of an offender who makes his living from hunting and trapping are profound. Whereas the problem perceived by the legislators and enforcement personnel was an urban one - guns with no other purpose but to threaten and harm persons - the solution was universal and applies more harshly where the problem is less serious or not serious at all. The results can be absurd. A father who abducts a child from his estranged wife's lawful custody, threatening to punch her in the nose if she resists, if found guilty cannot possess firearms for five years following his release from any prison sentence for the offence. A hunter makes immoral advances on his would-be lover and is convicted of attempted rape, loses his right to possess rifles or shotguns for at least five years notwithstanding that no firearm or weapon of any kind was used in the commission of the offence. This kind of law makes no sense to the native hunter or to his community which the law purports to protect. The concerns of the native hunters are most eloquently expressed in the words of Peter Simonie, a witness in the trial of Thomasie Panniluk, charged with non-capital murder of Johannasee Kalluk in Clyde River on the north coast of Baffin Island in 1974. It was Peter Simonie's rifle which had been used to kill Johannasee Kalluk and he was concerned that the people of the community would lose their right to possess firearms which had become so very important to their subsistence way of life.

> "Peter Simonie:
> I would like to if I may say a few things. These are some of the problems of those of us who live off the land. For those of us who live off the land or do a lot of hunting, we would like to get some rifles from the Hudson's Bay Company. Yes, in the past, as we all know, the majority of us anyway, people that were existing ahead of us never used rifles, but people today in this generation are not capable of doing things that they used to do a long time ago ... As we all know, as I indicated before, we would like to get rifles from the Hudson's Bay Company for purpose, for the purpose of using them on dangerous animals, such as wolves, polar bears and other animals that are bigger than us. I am sorry, there was one small item where I missed out. At the end of that he indicated not for the use of human beings, okay." (*R. v. Thomasie Panniluk*. Preliminary Hearing transcript, Vol. 3, pp 251-252, Nov. 6, 1974)

4. When she was close to her delivery date, a young woman from Lac La Martre was sent to Yellowknife to have her baby. She and her common law husband had two children already and, since they shared a small house with her parents, living conditions were already very crowded. The social worker from Yellowknife had visited not long before she went out to hospital and he had not liked the look of the housing conditions to which the baby would be returning.

The young woman delivered a healthy baby girl without medical complications. She had tried to contact her husband, but the radio reception was very bad. She had no friends or relatives in Yellowknife. The only visitor she had was from the Social Services Department of the Northwest Territories Government who expressed the departmental concern over the crowded little house she would be returning to with her baby. Wouldn't it be better, the social worker reasoned, to give this child up for adoption. After all, she had enough to cope with rearing the two others. Depressed anyway, without family or friends to consult, the young woman signed her consent to the adoption and gave up her baby before it was five days old.

When she returned to her village, her family was there to meet the airplane. They were surprised and shocked to hear that she had given the baby up. If she had not wanted the baby, they told her, there were plenty of people in the settlement, her own people, who would gladly have adopted her. She explained what had occurred. When she and her husband contacted the social worker, they were informed that it was too late. There was nothing that could be done.

Meanwhile, back in Yellowknife at the Social Services Department, the social worker received legal advice that the consent had been obtained from the mother before the child was five days old contrary to a provision of the Child Welfare Ordinance. In an attempt to correct the error, the social worker went to Lac la Matre and served the young woman and her husband with notice of the application for permanent crown wardship. The hearing was to be held in Yellowknife several days later. No explanation was given to the couple of the process or their rights or of the earlier error.

By borrowing money from relatives, they were able to gather sufficient funds to charter an airplane to Fort Rae and a taxi from Fort Rae to Yellowknife. They arrived at the court house in mid-afternoon. The hearing had been held in the morning. They went to see the judge who took an interest in their case and sent them over to the Native Courtworkers. By that route, they received legal assistance and an appeal was launched. Rather than oppose the appeal, the Commissioner of the Northwest Territories ordered that the child be returned to her parents as he is empowered to do under the legislation.

Although the story has a happy ending as far as the parents of the young child are concerned, it very nearly did not. One should remember that this took place in a jurisdiction which recognises aboriginal custom adoption as valid and sanctions it with legal orders. This took place notwithstanding a liberal legal aid scheme available to all residents and a court with a tradition of travelling to the various settlements to take "the law to the people". And it happened in 1977.

These examples are indicators of a variety of problems faced by aboriginal peoples who come into daily contact with laws imposed upon them by Euro-Canadian Society. Some of the problems are those faced by people of all cultures who are ignorant of the laws they are "deemed to know" and powerless to influence or cause changes to be made in these laws. But some of the problems are unique to northern aboriginal peoples and any law reform capability should be directed to the types of reform which will consider and preserve the aboriginal customs, laws and imperatives wherever that is possible.

III. QUESTIONS ARISING

A number of questions arise from these examples:
1. Do we write separate laws for Euro-Canadians and aboriginal Canadians?
2. Do we need more laws for aboriginal peoples, or should we have fewer in recognition that they have their own values and systems for working things out?
3. Do we recognise the aboriginal peoples' right to make and enforce their own laws?
4. How do we conduct our search for the answers to the above questions? Where do we look and whom do we ask?

Let us examine these questions, keeping in view that we want to know whether a strong law reform capability can be achieved in the Northwest Territories and how such a capability could be made to serve not only Euro-Canadians but also aboriginal peoples.

1. Do we write separate laws for Euro-Canadians and aboriginal Canadians?

The country most widely known for its experiments in writing separate laws for separate races is South Africa. But apartheid is not the only model. In Canada, there are a number of such laws, the most obvious being the Indian Act.

Under the terms of the Indian Act, the Government of Canada has sought to fulfil its role of protector of Indians and Indian lands which is one of its enumerated responsibilities under the Canadian Constitution. It is a much criticised statute, largely for the powers exercised over Indians and the manner of exercising these powers. Pleas for its revision and repeal have been made by native and non-native people alike (Bartlett 1978, Lysyk 1967).

Putting the criticism to one side, what is significant under Sections 81 and 83 of the Indian Act is that Indian bands on reserve lands have law making powers. Limited in scope, under-utilised, and confined in their application to the geographical limitations of reserve lands, these powers nonetheless exist and establish in principle a possible avenue to pursue. (Morse 1980).

The Spelumcheen Indian Band in British Columbia has used the powers granted to it under the Indian Act to enact a Child Welfare by-law which takes into account the traditions and laws of the band members. At the same time, the by-law is not inconsistent with the provincial Child Welfare Act so that constitutional controversies are not likely to arise as the result of its application. By enacting this by-law, the Spelumcheen Band has entered a field of law which is of vital concern to aboriginal people, namely the care and adoption of children. With lawmaking "powers" of this kind, aboriginal people can not just influence but control the placement of children and limit the fostering and adoption of their young people by non-native and sometimes non-Canadian families.

There are problems in the enactment and enforcement of separate laws for aboriginal people (Morse 1980). This separate approach does not solve many of the problems. Most of the laws which govern Canadians including aboriginal people are laws of general application. Virtually all law enforcement is in the hands of others.

But the ability to pass the separate laws is a place to begin. Furthermore, with the development of aboriginal rights positions by the Inuit, the Inuvialuit, the Dene and Metis of the Northwest Territories, there is increasing talk of aboriginal peoples taking control of their own lives and developing legislative capabilities as distinct peoples or nations.

2. Do we need more laws for aboriginal peoples?

This is a question aboriginal people should answer for themselves. In my discussion, I will not presume to substitute my answers for theirs. Instead, I should like to observe that Europeans and Euro-Canadians are compulsive law makers. Twentieth-century western civilisation may well be remembered for its inability to resist the temptation to make laws for everything. Our "thou shalt nots" are written everywhere. Governments, realising that law writing is getting out of control, have looked for ways to get rid of unwanted, redundant, obsolete and unnecessary laws. Sunset laws are written to deal with the unwanted statutes. It was not always so, for we have our roots in simpler times. Ten commandments were all God gave to Moses. Writing of a time within living memory, British essayist Laurie Lee recalls his boyhood upbringing in the Cotswolds between the wars:

> "This advantage was shared by young and old, was something no town can know. We knew ourselves to be as corrupt as any other community of our size - as any London street, for instance. But there was no tale-bearing then or ringing up 999; transgressors were dealt with by local opinion, by silence, lampoons or nicknames. What we were spared from seeing - because the village protected itself - were the crimes of our flesh written cold in a charge sheet, the shady arrest, the police-court autopsy, the headline of magistrate's homilies.
>
> As for us boys, it is certain that most of us, at some stage or other of our growth, would have been rounded up under present law, and quite a few shoved into reform school. Instead we emerged - culpable it's true - but unclassified in criminal record. No wilder or milder than Battersea boys, we were less ensnared by by-laws. If caught in the act, we got a quick bashing; and the fist of the farmer we'd robbed of apples or eggs seemed more natural and just than any cold mouthed copper adding one more statistic for the book. It is not crime that has increased, but its definition. The modern city, for youth, is a police trap.
>
> Our village was clearly no pagan paradise, neither were we conscious of showing tolerance. It was just the way of it. We certainly committed our share of

statutory crime. Manslaughter, arson, robbery, rape cropped up regularly throughout the years. Quiet incest flourished where the roads were bad; some found their comfort in beasts; and there were the usual friendships between men and boys who walked through the fields like lovers. Drink, animality and rustic boredom were responsible for most. The village neither approved nor disapproved, but neither did it complain to authority. Sometimes our sinners were given hell, taunted, and pilloried, but their crimes were absorbed in the local scene and their punishment confined to the parish." (Lee 1979:205-6).

It is observations of this kind of our own folk roots which should temper any discussion of how many codified laws are appropriate for other peoples. Law reform capability should include the option to refrain from making laws as well as the options which will fill new statute books. It should also include the option to avoid the proclamation in force of laws of more universal application. This principle is not without precedent in Canada. The Juvenile Delinquents Act, a federal statute dealing with young criminals, is only proclaimed in force in those communities which specifically request it. (Juvenile Delinquents Act R.S.C. 1970, Chap. J-3 ss. 41-43).

In small northern communities, plebiscites can be held regarding liquor prohibition or rationing. If sufficient eligible voters agree, the community can petition the Commissioner of the Northwest Territories to enact regulations prohibiting possession of liquor within the municipal boundaries of the village (and sometimes beyond) or the rationing of the quantity of liquor a person may purchase or the means of access to purchase.

Such laws, while they are often a great benefit to the small communities, do not always enhance the traditional methods of decision making. In some instances, the young people have voted against the elders whose opinions were formerly the expression of community consensus. Thus, while the result may benefit the community and its people, the process may erode the aboriginal ways of arriving at decisions. Care must be taken not just to devise laws which communities at a very local level can adapt to their own needs but also to consult those communities prior to setting up the means to choose whether or not to have the laws.

3. Do we recognise the right of the aboriginal peoples to make and enforce their own laws?

In review of an earlier question, I discussed the powers under the Indian Act to make laws which apply on reserve lands. As a country, Canada has accepted in principle that aboriginal people have the right to make their own laws. The right is limited. The approach of government has been to treat aboriginal peoples' law-making as analogous to the passing of municipal by-laws. In fact, the Northwest Territories government has recently permitted the Dene Band Council of Fort Good Hope to take over the functions of the settlement Council, one of the municipal government structures set up under Territorial jurisdiction. This was a major breakthrough for aboriginal people who have long and unsuccessfully tried to convince the Territorial Department of Local Government that they should be allowed to govern and make rules for their predominantly native communities through their preferred institutions. It remains to be seen whether this precedent will be extended to other communities.

It is not the only experiment. In Rankin Inlet where there were not band or tribal councils, the Inuit have taken over the hamlet administration and have adopted it as their own. Meetings are conducted in Inuktitut and the hamlet is well looked after. In a high profile arson case a few years ago, the Hamlet Council played a crucial role in the process of sentencing Henry Inukshuk, a local man with limited intelligence who had burned down the school and several other buildings. The Council offered to look after Inukshuk, to give him work to keep him out of trouble, to supervise his probation if the court would see fit to leave him in the community. The judge agreed, and the Hamlet Council and administrators were better than their word and have done a fine job of looking after this young man during his probation.

The band and community councils are not reluctant to make laws. Where they have status under territorial legislation, the by-laws are enforced and obeyed. Unfortunately, where the band councils have no jurisdiction under territorial legislation, the band council regulations have been ignored particularly by government and industry. For both band and community councils, what is especially frustrating is that they have no recognized jurisdiction beyond their community boundaries. The land they want so very much to protect is the very area where they are completely without recognized authority.

4. How do we conduct our search for the answers to these questions? Where do we look and whom do we ask?

The search can begin where this paper began in that record of good ideas, the debates of the Territorial Legislative Assembly. We can easily catalogue those laws which are recommended as needed and those which are complained of as being unsuitable. Since Professor Hamlin made his views known to Mr. Justice Berger, we have northern good ideas recorded in the transcript of the proceedings of that very valuable inquiry at which not only world renowned experts spoke but also more than one thousand witnesses in the northern communities. It was these witnesses in particular who told us through their evidence what it was they wanted to control in their lives, what it was about their powerlessness that frustrated them and impeded their development as people.

In addition, we have the report of the Berger Inquiry in two very readable volumes. Subsequently, other sources have been developed which include the proceedings of an environmental assessment review panel into the effects of the proposed expansion of the Norman Wells oilfield, transcripts of evidence taken before the National Energy Board at two hearings into northern pipelines and the Drury Commission report into the constitutional development of the Northwest Territories.

Perhaps the best source of information we have, however, is the aboriginal rights negotiations which are presently underway throughout the Territories. Through these negotiations, aboriginal people are seeking to entrench their rights, protect their land, their customs and their values. Their proposals are clear signposts indicating the direction law reform must take and the priorities it must adopt if law reform is to be for northern peoples.

The negotiations are between the aboriginal peoples and the government of Canada. The Territorial governments are seated at the table with their federal counterparts. They hear first hand what are the goals and aspirations of aboriginal peoples. The opportunities to use this first hand information are there for the taking. Whether the government of Canada and the government of the Northwest Territories will take advantage of this unique situation to develop a strong and innovative capability for law reform remains to be seen.

The two principles of nordicity and Canadianity continue to be juxtaposed. There is a new urgency and a new antagonism between these principles. National attention has focussed on the Canadian constitutional debate in which those who champion nordicity are seen as being opposed to the preservation of a strong Canadian federal state. Hopefully, we will live through this fierce and angry period so that to espouse northern good ideas for the good government of northern people will not be seen as somehow un-Canadian. We should keep before us the final observations of Mr. Justice Berger at the Mackenzie Valley Pipeline Inquiry.

"What we do here in the northern homeland, here on the northern frontier will tell us what kind of a country this is, what kind of people we are."

This observation applies as much to the development of a strong law reform capability for northern peoples as it does for northern non-renewable resource development.

REFERENCES

Bartlett, R.H.
1978   'The Indian Act of Canada', *Buffalow Law Review* 27: 581-615.
Lee, L.
1979   *Cider with Rosie*, Harmondsworth: Penguin Books.

Lysyk, K.
   1967   'The unique constitutional position of the Canadian Indian', *Canadian Bar Review* 45: 513.
Morse, B.W.
   1980   'By-law enforcement options', *Canadian Native Law Review* 2: 63.

Alaskan bush justice: legal centralism confronts social science research and village Alaska

Stephen Conn

THE ENVIRONMENT FOR RESEARCH

In 1970 the Chief Justice of the Alaska State Supreme Court sought to adjust the state justice process to the needs of village Alaska[1] through a process of team research by a lawyer and an anthropologist which he hoped would lead to an agenda for reform. Justice Boney spoke of reforms which acknowledged the local village role in the legal process. He influenced the conclusions of Alaska's first Bush Justice Conference that "the locus of decision-making in the administration of justice in village Alaska must move closer to the village", and its calls for "greater Native participation at all levels of the administration of justice". The conference stated that "strengthening of village councils is central to the administration of justice in remote Alaska" (State of Alaska Judicial Council 1970:2).

Professional justice was also to be improved. Trials were to be held in more rural locations, police and judicial travel budgets were to be increased, and education and recruitment of Natives in each justice bureaucracy was to be accomplished. The Conference suggested that "(T)he cultural context and impact of judicial administration must be thoroughly understood by all involved in the system of bush justice" (State of Alaska Judicial Council 1970:4). Court arraignments were to be conducted in Native languages and bilingual attorneys or para-professionals were to be recruited. That an act was committed pursuant to Native custom was to be considered as a mitigating factor in sentencing (State of Alaska Judicial Council 1970:6).

The University of Alaska was requested to establish an institute to train legal personnel in both rural and urban areas in Native culture and languages. The University, state administration and judicial council were to initiate programs of research concerning such areas as the character and processes of village law-making, judicial administration and law enforcement (State of Alaska Judicial Council 1970: 3,5). This last recommendation is particularly important because it led to my invitation to join the University of Alaska.

These reforms of bush justice were in turn to be implanted in an environment hostile to local innovation or dispersal of power to villages. The constitution established a centralized court system (with no pockets of local autonomy such as county courts); a Department of Public Safety; a Division of Corrections within the Department of Health and Social Services; a Department of Law; and a state Public Defender Agency. Each of the last agencies was headed by an appointee of the governor. These state agencies had some limited competition from incorporated cities and organized boroughs. But in bush Alaska, it is fair to say, they had free rein over the local level and quality of service.

State agency heads sat on the Governor's Commission for the Administration of Justice headed by Chief Justice Boney. State law and order money was directed to state agencies not local communities. Village Alaska had Native representation but no strong advocate for federal dollars.[2]

The era was marked by the conclusion of the Native land claims debate. The settlement resulted in a prolonged process of land selection and distribution of funds among regional corporations in Alaska. Native legislators did not focus upon bush justice in village Alaska. Regionalization was the byword of Native political organization (Conn and Garber 1981).

With Boney's untimely death in 1972, the impetus for direction of the justice system and its content passed back to the discrete departments charged with policing, prosecution, defense and corrections and their professional administration. Continuance of meetings of the Governor's Commission was for little more than a mutual division of the federal spoils. Villages were to remain legal colonies, subject arbitrarily to either inadequate police assistance or, in other cases, gross overpolicing. Neither village autonomy nor professional service improved. The relationship between village and state law suffered.

For the researcher, then, an evaluation of his role in this process must include very serious professional soul searching. Did his emphasis upon cultural adaptation understate and conceal the political imperatives which dictated the allocation of resources throughout the period? Did "cultural difference" provide the excuse for justice decision-makers to avoid hard decisions within their own realm? Did some spurious allegiance to village autonomy and its local law provide a continuing justification for inadequate state intervention to deal with violent crime?

WHAT IS THE BUSH JUSTICE SYSTEM IN ALASKA?

It is a constitutional scheme of rule making, law enforcement, adjudication, defense and correctional activity which feeds through separate and highly centralized bureaucratic channels from urban Alaska to small towns. From small towns fledgling governmental services flow to networks of rural villages. These 150 villages of 300 persons on the average are predominantly Eskimo or Indian. Village legal connections with the towns are formed in some instances by paraprofessional judges, police or ex-official bodies such as village councils who report some serious cases to state field operatives in towns.[3] More often connections are triggered by reports of serious crime and removal of offenders and victims to towns by the appropriate agencies.

In Eskimo village society all law jobs and institutions have been designated by whites. Villagers, however, implemented and developed them. Thus although the "state legal system" and the "village legal system" are both white creations from their inception, each has a differing ongoing creative core. No Eskimo person in Alaska would suggest that village justice systems were constructed to handle all matters, serious and unserious; they are components of the state system whether the state system chooses to acknowledge it or not.

Those with deepest involvement in matters of bush justice must be divided into three camps. The first camp is that of the legal professionals. They may be divided into policymakers at the top and field operatives at the bottom. At the top of the supreme court is the chief justice, a man deeply concerned with the ideology of due process.[4] He is particularly concerned with the image of his court. His lieutenant, the administrator of the state court system, is concerned with the health and welfare of his own growing bureaucracy and its competence as measured by the legislature, by practising attorneys and by high court judges. Their counterparts in the Department of Law are the attorney general and the chief prosecuting attorney. The chief public defender combines the ideological and administrative perspectives.

Field operatives represent the agency in town locations which serve as service centers. A single corrections officer in the town of Bethel, for example, provides juvenile intake and disposition, probation, parole, and pre-sentence reports for convicted felons for a region about the size of the state of Oregon, with 57 villages and 29,000 persons. The town's public defender and assistant district attorney each have the same position within their own bureaucracy and the same village clientele.

The field operatives have direct contact with villages and their justice systems, both official and extraofficial. Their mandate is to keep their agency's service record clean, "to keep the lid on". Although they have usually very clear perspectives of bush justice, their propensity to blow the whistle on inadequate service and lack of sufficient funds from their agency or from others must be weighed against career considerations.[5] They are not in a position to change the allocation of resources of their own agencies or of others. Discrete agencies are also not prepared to collaborate at the top though necessity may compel collaboration in the field. Thus, in 1975 in Nome, it could be said that the justice system played basketball on Thursday nights. Each system agency views his service and village connections as separate from the other. Only the village views all contact from justice agencies as *coming from a single source.*

The second camp is comprised of consumers. In 1974 and in 1976 they were given a chance to express their concerns to justice professionals through Bush Justice Conferences. More often, usually around election time, they have aired their complaints to visiting agency heads in what have been termed "dog and pony shows" (Easely 1973).

Those members of this village constituency nominated as magistrates, village police, or correctional aides are set apart from field professionals because they do enjoy limited professional lines of communication which stretch from town to urban bureaucracies. Village magistrates and village police exist in a nether world, making loose connections between the power structures of state justice and village justice.

The researchers are in a third camp. They were called upon to study the relationships between the state and village justice processes. They also zeroed in on the relationships of Natives to one or both systems each from legal perspectives, historical perspectives, anthropological perspectives, but rarely from political perspectives. Over ten years they researched, tested and recommended solutions to policymaking professionals. In short, the work of researchers tended to concentrate around the delivery of services to villages and the interplay of village and state legal process.

As with the paraprofessionals, researchers reported to both systems but had a power base in neither.[6] Outside of the justice bureaucracies they operated somewhat out of control of all key participants but had access to any and all.

THE EARLY YEARS OF THE RELATIONSHIP

In Alaska, village councils, locally elected bodies, have now had 60 years of experience in the business of dispute adjustment (Conn and Hippler 1973a) or 35 more than the state legal system. Teacher-missionaries introduced these institutions. Their intent appears to have been to use the councils to advance their own agenda: to suppress the manufacture of hootch, to seek out and punish sinners and to urge upon parents the discipline necessary to operate village schools in communities still geared to the rhythms of hunting and fishing. Councils over time cut loose from teachers and found a place within the larger web of white and Eskimo social control.

In the Eskimo communities, representatives of leading families formed a consensus within councils. Village councils fitted within the process of community and state law. Councils back-stopped and extended dispute adjustment. Their early style reflected the classic approaches of conflict avoidance - conciliation, gossip, ostracism and counseling among Eskimos. But, as important, they were supported from the outset by white village residents, teacher-missionaries deputized under federal law, the board of elders in Presbyterian and Moravian communities, occasional resident U.S. Commissioners and nonresident marshalls, Coast Guard cutters and even a distant court system (Milan 1964; Case 1978).

Councils were the last stop in a process of evolving interpersonal customary law ways and the first step in a process of Western intervention that could result in referral to a police and court process outside of the village. Western legal intervention had made impossible (or at least more dangerous) killing or banishment as final steps in a customary legal process. However, to a certain extent it had replaced these ultimate steps with removal into its own legal process in a distant place at the request of village councils.

Councils were most often an Eskimo institution of last resort; even within its processes of case adjustment were opportunities to admit one's guilt, ask forgiveness and be reintegrated into the community. Orientation and not punishment was the usual result of the process. Two or three appearances before a council could be anticipated before it sought to draw in outside police authority. Intervention by marshall, Indian police, liquor suppression agents and later territorial police, while limited by geography and state resources, was sufficient in territorial days to reinforce the council when it responded punitively. By reacting to incipient conflict or to the seeds of later conflict, councils avoided confrontation with either villagers or with agents of the official legal system (Conn and Hippler 1975).

THE LATER YEARS

A variety of factors destabilized the council as a mechanism for dispute adjustment in the years immediately following statehood (1959). In meetings with state officials, council presidents learned that state officials would not support bans on liquor possession or manufacture (Conn 1981a). "Village rules" were distributed by district attorneys, rules easily transferable into state violations.

Two factors made this arrangement unworkable. First, promised supportive intervention by the troopers when councils requested it was not forthcoming. In the Bethel region alone, for example, in 1963 a single trooper provided service to 57 villages. Villages were informed that they were to handle matters on their own and notify the police only when violent felonies had occurred. Letters to police during the period demonstrate that detailed descriptions of repeated violence were often left unanswered. A survey conducted by researchers and troopers in 55 villages in 1977 revealed that on the average it took three days for the troopers to respond to a request for assistance (Angell 1981a). The head of the Department of Public Safety, when confronted with this data, suggested that trooper involvement in the survey had caused village officials to minimize the actual length of time necessary to respond. He suggested that seven days was a more likely figure (Nix 1977). Inadequate trooper response even after villagers had attempted (on the field operative's instructions) to deal with less serious problems, destroyed the credibility of village law within its own realm. That credibility was, in part, state determined.

Second, in the early 1970s drunken behavior in public or in private was decriminalized. Service centers such as Bethel became ready sources of wage opportunities and bootleg liquor. Youthful populations rose dramatically, partially as a result of improved health care, and populations shifted from villages more distant from towns to those within relatively close proximity to towns.

IMPACT ON COUNCIL JUSTICE IN THE 1970s

Councils as institutions have continued to play a central role in dispute processing in more than a hundred villages without magistrates. Yet to continue that activity councils were forced to become less "council-like", by earlier definitions, and more court-like by magistrate terms.

Councils confronted a more persistent stream of conflicts of a magnitude and severity unlike the immediate past. With external punitive intervention less reliable, many councils shifted from bodies of reconciliation to bodies which directed fines and other sanctions at offenders. This shift from council-like to court-like approach was never completely successful. Fines were not collectible. Official support for fining was verbal but never explicit. Young persons challenged council authority (Conn 1976).

In the late 1960s, the court system introduced appointed Native justices of the peace (called magistrates) into about thirty Native villages. Where this occurred, village councils deferred to this official authority and refused further complaints (Conn and Hippler 1973b). Yet because matters heard by councils were often pre- or sublegal in Western terms, because complainants did not wish to confront fellow villagers, and because village policing was unstable, transfer of authority did not induce a transfer of the legal activity. Most villages did not receive magistrates, and could not appoint them without court approval.

Reports from police indicated that by the mid-1970s 80% of their arrests still resulted in council and not court disposition.[7] In a 1977 survey of 55 villages a quarter of all matters processed as criminal law violations resulted in council or problem board disposition (Angell 1979a). In other words, village police appended themselves to councils, as adjudicative bodies for minor offenses despite the fact that for the judicial system, councils were illegal institutions.

The irony of the position of the village council by the early 1970s should not be overlooked. As an official matter, the state legal system viewed village council process as an anachronism, a fixture of law ways of a distant past. As an unofficial matter, field professionals armed with mandates from their superiors to carry out impossible tasks of representation, prosecution and law enforcement over distant villages were vocal in their support of what they perceived to be continuing examples of Eskimo justice. Yet this very encouragement of village justice demanded that the village system shift from a preventative process, capable of anticipating problems, to one that reacted very much like Western systems. The balance of outside intervention with inside deliberation was lost and village councils found their council process mutated out of its original form as it was forced to handle both parts of the process.

When magistrates and village police were offered to villages through appointment and training, the issue was not best articulated as a conflict between law systems, Western and non-Western. Rather, the issue was whether villagers could adequately address their present problems with new Western resources inferior to the working arrangement between formal law and village law of earlier days. The earlier arrangement worked in part because there were fewer problems. But it also worked because it contained supportive elements. It allowed legal levels, one consensual, another punitive, to interact. But more than this, by circumstance if not by political intent, it placed in Eskimo hands the authority to draw in external force. Put baldly, Western police did not intercede unless called. Yet under this new arrangement what appeared to be more de facto control of village affairs was less.

VILLAGE EFFORTS

The record shows persistent attempts by villagers to construct their own system as a component of the state process. Villagers were told to turn back to "the old ways" and draw upon a village consensus for enforcement of village law. But the "old ways" were formed out of a coalition of white and Native authority. The "old ways" did not contend with prepaid liquor orders by telephone, improved air and land transport and wage opportunities of a younger generation as demanding of their official legal rights as other Alaskans. Villages requested assistance in the drafting of their own town statutes. They realized that some skilled professional advice was necessary in order to make the laws enforceable within the state system.

When ordinances were sent to Juneau to an agency constitutionally obligated to help towns and villages, they were filed away without comment.[8] Villages were left in a legal never-never land as troopers and state officials refused to apply village ordinances. Even village magistrates scorned village ordinances. What village justice systems have had to undertake has outstripped their capacity to deal with it pre-emptively. Problems have also overrun their capacity to deal with them in Western terms through policing, judging and jailing (Angell 1981a).

PROFESSIONAL PERSPECTIVES

The reality of a relationship between white legal agents representative of first military, then territorial, then state authority to small villages has changed little, if at all, in more than a hundred years of contact (Conn 1981b; Jenness 1962; Murton 1965). What has changed are professional attitudes toward the relationship.

Professional policymakers fail to understand village justice as a component of their own justice system. They view village process as a separate reality from which they, with lesser or greater capacity, remove cases to be dealt with in the thorough-going process that they know to be the "real" justice system, real justice being a process of adversary justice leading to state corrections. Professional operatives in towns understand the relevance of matters left to village justice. But, for them, these matters are simply problems happily left outside of the realm of their own professional caseload. "Progressive villages" or "villages which handle their own problems" are admired by town-based professionals out of relief more than out of respect (Nix 1973; Timbers 1973). Yet few would not concur that real justice as delivered would not be preferable if it could flood the villages.

What professionals fail to perceive is that the interplay of state and village justice must be nurtured and adapted to survive. For villagers engagement of the systems is an historical fact. They have sought collaboration on terms reflective of the stronger aspects of the village justice process and those of the state. This implies shared control of the process. A working justice process has been the objective of the researchers and, they believe, the village.

Yet does this global objective translate readily into compartmental ideological and administrative considerations of separate justice agencies? Can it be achieved if the idealized goal of planners is a fully articulated western justice system, capable of providing checks and balances, capable of providing due process and law enforcement typical of urban Alaska and urban America whether or not that goal is feasible or desirable? On what terms then could reforms of bush justice be made? Perspectives and interpretations of "improvement" vary as one isolates interested constituencies. Institutional perspectives and ideological perspectives guide professional judgment. The administrator of the court system is said to have referred to bush Alaska as a "can of worms". Implantation of a centralized judicial system in farflung town and village Alaska was problematic. Costs were high. Discovery of persons to fill positions was difficult.

After the state constitution went into effect, the only official judicial activity tolerated was through court personnel. Towns and villages without judges or magistrates could not officially appoint a judge or employ a council as court (State of Alaska Constitution 1959: Art. 4 Sec. 1). From an administrator's perspective allocation of judicial resources presented several problems:

(1) dangers of autonomy borne from distance, lack of supervision and lack of indoctrination into Western legal perspective;

(2) dangers of community influence on decisions made appropriate to resolution in terms of higher law; and

(3) problems of management and supervision.

Village magistrate activity displaced judicial activity if cases were heard by magistrates at defendant's request. It was not easily controlled. Magistrates were appointed by presiding superior court judges of judicial districts who jealously guarded their authority from intrusions by central administration. The court's magistrate supervisor lacked the power to hire and fire magistrates as did villages affected.[9] Yet for all of these problems, bush magistrates (along with village police) comprised the lion's share of Native participation in the justice system. With a single exception, there are no Native judges or high administrators in any state justice bureaucracy (State of Alaska Court System 1981).

The professional bureaucratic perspective emphasized supervision and control from higher levels to lower levels. It was difficult if not impossible to establish a system of justice in smaller Native communities satisfactory to this objective. The village perspective seemed to be a desire for control sufficient to deal with matters early and efficiently and to employ the professional justice system for support when necessary. It implied an autonomy which the centralized system rejected.

MAGISTRATES AS GUARDIANS OF DUE PROCESS

The court looks to its rural magistrates and Native court personnel for interpretation of Western meaning and values underlying instructions in Native languages in criminal and civil cases in rural Alaska.

Yet the Native magistrate's actual capacity to try cases, to advise clients and to reject overtures by police who might attempt to influence the justice process has been a matter of ongoing bureaucratic concern by the state court system in the past ten years. Two advisory committees of lawyers headed by the chief justice mulled over the problems of that component (Second Magistrates Advisory Committee 1979). Of primary concern was the challenge of authorizing persons with lay education to adjudicate cases in villages ill-equipped to sustain a judicial officer. Magistrates often lacked proper "facilities" (courtrooms and jails) and support from police regularly hired.

The Supreme Court's Second Magistrates Advisory Committee considered but then rejected ideas such as (1) that village magistrates would accept guilty pleas only, (2) that representation would be afforded in each village case; or (3) that magistrates' cases would be subjected to special ongoing review (Second Magistrates Advisory Committee 1978) because each would single out Native magistrates from non-Native. Researchers pointed out that these lay judges were poorly trained in Western law and operated in isolation of Western justice systems. The court responded by upgrading its internal training program. Yet what they could not create through training was the direct experience of adjudication or court business.

From an administrative point of view, the 28-odd Native magistrates represented a needless drain on resources. The administrators argued that magistrates did not generate caseloads sufficient to be in every village or even in those villages previously selected for magistrate posts. People did not bring many complaints to magistrates. More importantly, most villages lacked facilities and all lacked attorneys, Thus they pressed for these prerequisites to placement of further magistrates. These criteria, it was suggested, would automatically bar placement of magistrates in most Native villages. The criteria were adopted by the committee as advisory and not mandatory (Second Magistrates Advisory Committee 1979:2). Unofficially accepted by the court administration, their application since 1977 has resulted in no new magistrate posts in 112 Native villages without courts and in removal of five former posts since the committee issued its recommendations in 1979.

To remove magistrates would leave what alternative? The court system has adamantly refused to recognize village council justice as an acceptable component of the process. It ignored a suggestion by researchers that councils act as lay assessors at the sentencing phase (Second Magistrates Advisory Committee 1978).

What else could be suggested? The presiding judge of the Fairbanks court suggested that superior court judges, freed from urban court calendars, be assigned to regular village circuits. The circuit proposal was drawn from some limited understanding of the Canadian scheme of judicial service (Morrow 1974). Yet what committee members failed to understand was that the "flying courts" of Canada dealt with a tiny percentage of cases left unhandled by justices of the peace in most settlements. Maps were drawn for the circuits and the idea found its way into the committee's final recommendations. There the plan disappeared with other recommendations, never to reappear on budgetary requests and never to be adopted by the state court system. The Canadian scheme did not speak to the issue which the court administrators so desired to define out of existence. On what terms would the state provide officially for the *daily* business of law in small villages?[10]

What the court has left in place by near-inaction is a limited allocation of magistrates in 28 of 140 villages, officially prepared to adjudicate cases, but in fact capable of and positioned only to turn arrests into guilty pleas.

We researchers pointed out that magistrates displaced but did not actually replace village justice systems in Eskimo villages. We and Native organizations advocated and tested variant forms of dispute adjustment more reflective of small villages' needs and capacities ranging from mediation panels which might operate alongside a fining or adjudicative authority to councils or boards vested with the limited judicial authority which the magistrate possessed (Case 1977). As will be seen, the court system toyed with the concept of alternative forms of dispute adjustment, following the first bush justice conference, but then rejected it explicitly as a court function (Second Magistrates Advisory Committee 1979:19).

THE RESEARCHERS' PERSPECTIVE

As researchers, we viewed ourselves as legal culture brokers, prepared to make comprehensible, practical adjustments to both the village and state sides of the justice system.

Our primary target was not a law process as measured by either ideological Western considerations or perceived Native law ways, but what we viewed to be an amalgam of both with adjustments necessary on both sides. Our focus was on the bottom of the system. Our goal was to improve the daily operation of law as reflected in perceived village needs by developing methods for enhanced interaction between state and village processes as we had come to understand them. These methods were to be sustainable and acceptable to village consumers and justice policymakers and field operatives. We satisfied consumers and field operatives but not policymakers.

THE PROBLEM BOARD EXPERIMENT

The problem board experiment was grounded in careful study of the village council process, both historical and contemporary, throughout the 75 villages which comprise Eskimo Alaska. Assessment of village councils through study of their records and on the scene investigations led to our proposal to the court to test the proposition that a non-adversarial mediation panel could be established in villages. It would deal with matters then deemed inappropriate for either modern councils engaged in fining and jailing extralegally or magistrates (Conn and Hippler 1974a).

In association with the Eskimo village of Emmonak we worked on the process. It was in fact a process of rediscovery since Emmonak had only recently delegated its dispute adjustment to village police and a magistrate. The state had provided these Western law figures with a portable "holding facility" (jail). The council had been able to drop its role as fining and jailing council. It had done this with some relief. Nevertheless villagers recognized that an element of the earlier process was missing. The magistrate spoke of the family counseling she was called upon undertake. She desired something like the old council to take up this activity. Problems with juveniles and other problems not clearly legal were mentioned. These were reflective of disputes heard by the village council.

With the village we devised what we called conciliation boards (drawing upon literature on village complaint boards in Ceylon). Villagers changed the name to problem boards. Villagers selected persons capable of problem solving, young and old, all Yupik speaking. They rejected the village priest when he volunteered. The researchers determined that voluntary conciliation under Alaska law could be used as an alternative to prosecution for misdemeanors in most cases. They emphasized that the board would not and could not fine or jail persons. This would be left up to the magistrate (Conn and Hippler 1974b). The village developed the concept on its own. We had anticipated that matters would flow naturally from police to the magistrate and then be diverted by her to the problem board. In fact, what occurred was that matters moved directly and independently to the board (Conn and Hippler 1975).

The problem board during its test phase dealt with matters which did not have clear legal remedies. These often involved situations involving alcohol which, if left uncounseled, were expected to result in violence. For example, the board counseled A who gave liquor to B, causing family chaos. It counselled C who teased D for using welfare money to play bingo. When E, a teacher aide, kicked F, a student, it drew E and G (F's parent) together to work out a compromise. It dealt with difficult family problems involving drinking, wife beating and child abuse. Juvenile matters were often considered. In the main, it anticipated violence. It had no power to fine or jail but could refer (and be referred) cases to and from the magistrate and the police.

THE COURT EXPERIMENT WITH PROBLEM BOARDS

When the model became an experimental "program" within the court system, the court personnel in charge selected test villages with little concern for institutional relationships with councils or magistrates. While the problem board provided a mechanism for Native language speakers of all educational backgrounds to participate, only some villages were given to understand that one's skills at negotiation and conciliation and not youth and education were primary criteria. Others selected callow untrained youth for their boards.

Court personnel did not feel comfortable with village experience at dispute adjustment. They held a workshop for problem board members at an urban resort and had members of the American Arbitration Association employ models of conciliation drawn from labor, prison and other urban settings to teach the Eskimos how to resolve disputes.

Some test villages on their own grafted the board into their process with varying degrees of success. In village X near Bethel the board found a niche between the police and now-fining and jailing council (Conn 1975b). Others saw the problem board as a weak substitute for either a magistrate or council.

The court hired an attorney and anthropologist to evaluate the boards. Although the report was favorable to those boards which had been active, it stressed the limited number of matters heard (Marquez and Serdahely 1977) and not problems avoided by board activity. The court's response was to end its association with the experiment. From its perspective, the boards had failed because they had not replaced either magistrates or extra-legal councils which fined or jailed when magistrates or outside assistance was not available.

Although the court disassociated itself from the project, a 55-village survey two years later discovered that three of the six probem boards established were still in operation (Angell 1979b).

PARALEGALS

Unlike the new, urban private law legal assistants who have evolved into a discrete professional category by taking upon themselves a variety of lawyer's tasks, we viewed rural paralegals located in towns and villages as capable of performing activities not then undertaken by either professionals or members of the village justice systems (Conn and Hippler 1973b; Conn 1974).

The town paralegal's work was to combine town and village justice. By moving out from the town to villages where crimes had occurred, the rural paralegal would investigate and report back to the professional those social facts (as well as legal facts) overlooked by policy. The police report had almost exclusive bearing on legal decisions, such as bail, screening, charges, case organization and disposition. No longer would the professional have to depend on a policy report or on conventional wisdom among field professionals to evaluate his case with an eye toward its impact on the real community affected.

Our belief in village paralegals stemmed from several considerations. First, we had recognized and reported on the dependence of the rural justice process upon paralegals in a variety of village roles (Conn and Hippler 1973b). Second, we were convinced that the state legal process would not be introduced in village Alaska with any balanced concern for the integrity of either the Western process or understanding of the village law process, its strengths and its weaknesses. We perceived that, at best, state justice agencies would make village connections with a magistrate and a policeman. The screening function so essential to the integrity of both systems, carried on previously by the council, or left to a village policeman would be ignored or left to chance (Conn 1975a). Professionalization would increase the tendency to intervene in village matters without concern for the propriety of that intervention on the single dispute or in the village law process.

PROJECTS ACCOMPLISHED AND THEIR BUREAUCRATIC RESPONSE

In the years that followed we were able to test the proposition of the town-based paralegal who worked for either a district attorney or public defender. A training-tutorial mechanism was established in both Nome and Bethel. Bush professionals, especially prosecutors, remarked that their professional collaboration with villages were enhanced. Trainees became serious members of the rural process.

Yet in this instance, as in many others where plans proposed or actually implemented at the town and village level received strong support from field professionals and village residents alike, reaction from urban bureaucracies was indifferent or hostile. LEAA representatives from Seattle questioned the use of $ 100.000 to underwrite the establishment of regional training programs whose end result was apparently four new paraprofessionals. Their concern was sufficient to induce the state Criminal Justice Planning Agency in Juneau to ignore the project.

The state attorney general had promised in writing to budget permanent positions for successful trainees. He attempted to renege on his promise. Only the threat of newspaper exposure by the Bethel trainee saved his job. He was the only Native member of the rural Department of Law. A paralegal trainee with the Public Defender Agency also received high marks. Yet when the agency was in need of a second town attorney, she was encouraged to resign. She became a magistrate. The Alaska Division of Personnel unilaterally defined paralegal positions and established testing procedures. No provision was made for rural job requirements (including language competence). The district attorney's paralegal failed the test.

The Alaska Legal Services Corporation established paralegal positions in Native villages on Alaska's North Slope. These trainees were educated to discover and investigate Western law problems and to channel cases into the state process and back into the village realm. Yet, when Alaska Federation of Natives funding from its federal CETA program disappeared, the village paralegals lost their positions, becoming more in a long line of Native men and women "trained into oblivion".

What do these experiments suggest about rural justice? It would appear that no experiment, however well attuned to village needs or cultural values, however well-received by villagers and however useful to field operatives and their limited resources will succeed without overcoming priorities both ideological and institutional which are more important than a rural justice system that works.

THE PRESENT

A 1977 study of 55 villages indicates that the carnage of village Alaska is now truly impressive with murder, rape and violent crime rates two and three times the state average and many times those of the nation (Angell 1981a).[11]

Village councils persevere in 25 percent of the sample surveyed, skewed in fact to favor villages with magistrate service (Angell 1981a). Villages depend upon outside police service or service of constables who act as liaisons to state troopers. Village control has been weakened and not strengthened. The court system has disavowed rural trials where facilities are inadequate to house personnel (State of Alaska 1973:rule 18-1). It has disavowed experiments with alternative forms of dispute resolution. It has not acted upon plans proposed to it to attempt circuit riding. It trained and then forgot court interpreters (State of Alaska Court System 1981).

When its developed in-house research organ discovered that Natives in urban courts received longer prison terms for non-violent offenses (State of Alaska Judicial Council 1980), its judges attacked the problem by bringing up to the level of Natives, non- Natives' sentences and not by encouraging correctional alternatives (State of Alaska Judicial Council 1980).[12]

Magistrates placed in earlier days exist as curious anachronisms in rural villages, hearing fewer cases than councils did in their extra-legal state or even than the problem boards rejected by the court (State of Alaska Court System 1981). Paralegals trained to work with bush district attorneys and public defenders have been forced to resign by their bureaucracies even in the face of support by field personnel. The state personnel department has developed a test for such state positions which ignores language and job competence and emphasizes skills in math competence.

The Department of Public Safety has received funds to place village police in villages along with detention systems, creating a partial Western system. The Division of Corrections has provided no new correctional personnel to rural Alaska in ten years. Its dubious contribution has been to make old town jails (in Bethel and Nome) over into modern town jails. Since police are more mobile than other components of the system, and more receptive to bush service, this means construction of law systems that could make of villages "closed institutions" with guards and cells (Goffman 1961).

We as researchers, fascinated both with cultural pluralism and committed to research leading to reform, must search our souls and consider whether or not the fruit of our labor has resulted in a legal process acceptable to any standard of justice or to none at all. Those of us who are lawyers first and anthropologists second must consider whether we should steer away from research and lend our skills to law reform and political pressure and not to adaptation of the legal process and roles to fit small village situations.

Were researchers deceived or did they allow themselves to be deceived? Were they blind to overriding political considerations that made of "cultural relevance" a convenient excuse for bureaucracies to employ unless or until they were prepared to establish a partial copy of their system in village Alaska, a system unacceptable by either state or village standards? We who are infatuated with the opportunities for redefining a state law process to benefit an environment marked by cultural pluralism may find our work manipulated by those who underwrite it and apparently embrace it. From our global perspective should we not be impressed by the political imperatives that govern the entire process of bush justice? Chief among these is a battle for control of resources and populations which relinquishes none of that control to indigenous minorities on any terms without a fight.

In Alaska, for example, *it must be asked whether state authorities want village Alaska to survive.* Is it not likely that state authorities would prefer an in-migration of Natives into its cities, that in 1991 Natives sell their shares of land claims awards and rest easily on their dividends in Anchorage condominiums? Destabilization of village life may in the end be desired over improved service. Despite the historical adaption of Western law process to changing social and economic needs, present policymakers and field operatives believe that the systems in which they function are a kind of evolutional by-product, natural and appropriate to all places and persons within the American political domain.

Though we may have scholars and historians who decry the phenomenon, is it not the underlying message of Alaska legal development that the consumers and their problems must fit the process and not the converse (Friedman 1973)? The force of legal assimilation is the dominant force and adaptations in the name of cultural imperatives are mere pauses (or worse than this, excuses) which conceal a longer term trend.

As researchers, we in Alaska have tinkered with the system. We have listened and attempted to innovate within the system. What we did not accomplish was to draw Natives into the process as players, capable of negotiating change, possessing power and ultimately manipulating the system as co- or near- equals to other players. Manipulation and partial control of the system does not mean participation in bush conferences, seats on advisory committees or even membership in lower ranks of justice or police bureaucracies. It means negotiating on legal process from positions of power.[13]

NOTES

1.   In the 566,000 square mile state of Alaska, half of the population live in towns and villages usually accessible only by river, sea or air. Within the latter rural population are 55,000 Indians, Eskimos and Aleuts who reside in about 140 villages with populations from 25 to 700 persons and 300 persons on average. Another half dozen Native towns have populations from 1,500 to 3,000 persons. "Bush justice" is the Alaskan term for legal process which affects these predominantly Native villages and towns.

2.   Criminal Justice Planner Butch Schwartz reported that only 10.8% of Alaska's LEAA block grants and 11.1% of all LEA funds directly benefited bush areas. 80% of this amount went to construct five jails and to police programs (Schwartz 1973:4). Angell reports that while small white communities are isolated for purposes of data collection in police statistics, village Alaska is included in a catchall category. Nearly all white communities have a judicial officer (Angell 1981a).

3.   There are at least 112 small predominantly Native Alaskan cities (termed "Native villages") without resident state judicial officers. John Angell reports that only half of about 55 villages surveyed had even a part time policeman (Angell 1981b).

4.   Said the State Supreme Court in *Gregory* v *State* (1976), "We ... recognize that the trial court is obligated to be certain that each citizen, when involved in a criminal matter, is aware of the various rights guaranteed him by the Alaska and United States Constitution". To this was footnoted the following:

> "The Anglo-American system of justice differs substantially from the traditional Indian, Eskimo and Aleut systems, which pre-dated Western cultures by hundreds of years. The cultural difficulties experienced by many of the Alaska Natives as the contemporary Anglo-American institutions reach out to the bush communities require that the State legal system use extreme care in cases of this nature. Therefore, in those areas where a substantial portion of the populations consist of Native Alaskans, we urge the administrative office of the court system to develop bilingual explanations of basic rights for those who appear in criminal proceedings so that all citizens are clearly aware of their constitutional rights". (*Gregory*: 380).

5.   Of course differing discoveries by researchers or journalists or complaints lodged in higher courts had differing impacts on state bureaucracies.

For example, the Department of Public Safety actively supported research which discovered that violent crimes had overrun limited village and state resources. Its desire was to shift resources from urban areas (where they competed with urban police) to rural sectors. Village police were taken under the wing of the Department of Public Safety (and even funded in 1981 by them) as useful aides capable of dealing with minor drunken behavior without usurping primary police activities when major crime occurred.

6.   Annotated descriptions of twenty articles, books, and papers written by Conn on rural justice appear in Kydd 1979.

7.   "During ... [1972] the Village Policemen handled ten felony cases, 418 misdemeanors, and numerous noncriminal complaints. Seven of the felonies resulted in court action and 128 of the misdemeanors resulted in court action. One hundred and fifty-one of the misdemeanors were handled by the Village Policemen without court or Council action". (Village Police Training Annual Report 1972: 1.)

As the project director described it in presenting other statistics for the year which showed court action on 63 cases and council action on 171, "[They] also illustrate a unique relationship of two branches of government within the Criminal Justice system". (Nix 1972:2) He noted:

"The *council* had levied $1,835.00 in fines, and 38 days of jail time. In almost every case, days of work for the village satisfied council sentences".

8.   In 1973, the Department of Law passed over protest passages of a book on formation of a second class city to be used by many villages. The book stated that councils could fine or jail persons for violation of local ordinances if the offender agreed to the punishment. Cooperative Extension Service 1972:2-3.

9.   When, for example, it was discovered by the Alaska Federation of Natives that the Dillingham magistrate was a racist missionary who demanded that Natives swear off drink, who persuaded them not to request an attorney and who refused to visit surrounding villages, the court could do nothing. His refusal to send in documentation of his cases also promoted no disciplinary action.

Ironically when magistrate A retired and was replaced by B, a legal services attorney, B was fired by the presiding judge for living with a mate in an unmarried state. The supreme court upheld the presiding judge.

10.   Angell estimates that in villages he surveyed, legal professionals, other than troopers, appeared once a year or less (Angell 1981a). His conclusions seem to be reflected in an evaluation by village officials of state government agents. See Angell's chart reproduced as Appendix 1.

11.   See Appendix 2, Appendix 3.

12.   Alaska Native adult males comprised 32.2 percent of the state jail population in 1980. Native population (average age 16) comprised 16 percent of the population.

13.   Research discussed in this paper was funded by the Law and Social Science Program, National Science Foundation; the Ford Foundation; the National Institute on Alcohol Abuse and Alcoholism; the Alaska State Court System; the Law Enforcement Assistance Administration; and the University of Alaska. The author remains entirely responsible for conclusions expressed in this paper.

REFERENCES

Alaska, State of
    1959   *Constitution of the State of Alaska,* Juneau, Alaska: Lieutenant Governor.
    1973   *Supreme Court, Rules of Court,* Seattle, WA: Book Publishing Company.
Alaska, State of, Court System
    1981   *1980 Annual Report of the Alaska Court System,* Anchorage: Alaska Court System.
Alaska, State of, Judicial Council
    1970   'Conference Resolutions', of the First Bush Justice Conference, Girdwood, Alaska (unpublished paper).
    1980   'Report of the Advisory Committee on Minority Judicial Sentencing Practices, Ch. 42, SLA 1979' (unpublished paper).
Angell, J.E.
    1979a   *Alaskan Village Justice: An Exploratory Study,* Anchorage: Justice Center, University of Alaska.
    1979b   *Public Safety and the Justice System in Alaskan Native Villages,* Anchorage: Justice Center, University of Alaska.
    1981a   *Public Safety and the Justice System in Alaskan Native Villages,* Jonesboro, TN: Pilgrimage.
    1981b   Interview with Stephen Conn.

Bayley, B. et al.
1980   *A Statistical Analysis of Discrimination in the Alaska Criminal Justice System*, Vancouver, WA: Cascade Research Center.

Case, D.S.
1977   *Twenty Four Ordinances to Enforce Local Laws Through the Alaska 'Village' Council*, Anchorage: Alaska Federation of Natives, Bush Justice Committee.
1978   *The Special Relationship of Alaska Natives to the Federal Government; an Historical and Legal Analysis*, Anchorage: Alaska Native Foundation.

Conn, S.
1974   'Report to the Chief Justice', recommendations for reform of the court system in rural Alaska (unpublished paper).
1975a   'Perspective on Small Village Justice Systems', prepared for the Alaska Judicial Council (unpublished paper).
1975b   'Napakiak, Selawik, Gambell and Savoonga, Wainwright and Manokotak: Five Research Monographs on the Operation of State Criminal Justice System', prepared for Alaska Judicial Council (unpublished paper).
1976   'Village Life on Trial: Corrections and the Bush', narrative report for the Alaska Bar Association for Improvement of Corrections (unpublished paper).
1981a   'Satellite Villages, Bethel and State Liquor Policy in the Modern Era', report pursuant to NIAAA grant (unpublished paper).
1981b   'Alcohol Control and Native Alaskans - From the Russians to Statehood: the Early Years', report pursuant to NIAAA grant (unpublished paper).

Conn. S. and B.K. Garber
1981   *Moment of Truth: The Special Relationship of the Federal Government to Alaska Natives and Their Tribes*, Anchorage: Justice Center, University of Alaska.

Conn, S. and A. Hippler
1973a   'Traditional Northern Eskimo Law Ways and Their Relationship to Contemporary Problems of Bush Justice', *Occasional Papaers, Institute of Social, Economic and Government Research* 10, Fairbanks: University of Alaska.
1973b   'Paralegals in the Bush', *UCLA-Alaska Law Review* 3-1: 85-102.
1974a   'Conciliation and Arbitration in the Native Village and the Urban Ghetto', *Judicature* 58-5: 229-235.
1974b   'Final Report, Emmonak Conciliation Board, A Model for a New Legal Process for Small Villages in Alaska', Report of National Science Foundation project prepared for presentation to the Alaska State Supreme Court (unpublished paper).
1975   'The Village Council and its Offspring: A Reform for Bush Justice', *UCLA-Alaska Law Review* 5-1: 22-57.

Cooperative Extension Service
1972   *What's a Second Class City?*, University of Alaska in cooperation with the Department of Community and Regional Affairs, State of Alaska.

Easley, P.P. (ed.)
1973   *The Administration of Justice in Village Alaska (Barrow, Bethel, Dillingham, Fort Yukon, Nome and Kotzebue)*, Juneau: Alaska Criminal Justice Planning Agency.

Friedman, L.M.
1973   *A History of American Law*, New York: Simon and Schuster.

Goffman, E.
1961   *Asylums*, Garden City, NY: Anchor Books and Doubleday and Company.

Jenness, D.
1962   *Eskimo Administration: I. Alaska*, Arctic Institute of North America Technical Papers, 10, Ottawa.

Kydd, D.L. (ed.)
  1979   *Towards a Legal Education and Information Program for Natives*, Saskatoon:
              Native Law Center.
Marquez, J.E. and D.J. Serdahely
  1977   *Alaska Court System Village Conciliation Board Project Evaluation*, Anchorage:
              Alaska Court System.
Milan, F.
  1964   'The Acculturation of the Contemporary Eskimo of Wainwright, Alaska', *An-
              thropological Papers of the University of Alaska* 11: 1-95, Fairbanks: University of
              Alaska.
Morrow. W.G.
  1974   'Riding Circuit in the Arctic', *Judicature* 58-5: 236-241.
Murton, T.O.
  1965   *The Administration of Criminal Justice in Alaska, 1867 to 1902*, Berkeley: School
              of Criminology, University of California (unpublished Master's thesis).
Nix, W.
  1972   'Subgrantee Professional Report', Juneau: Alaska Department of Public Safety
              (unpublished paper).
  1973   Interview with Stephen Conn.
  1977   Interview with John E. Angell.
Schwartz, B.
  1973   'CJPA to Hire Native Criminal Justice Planner', *Alaska Criminal Justice Report-
              er* 3-4, Juneau: Alaska Criminal Justice Planning Agency.
Second Magistrates Advisory Committee
  1978   'Tentative Draft Recommendations of the Second Magistrates Advisory Com-
              mittee', prepared for the Alaska Supreme Court (unpublished paper).
  1979   'Recommendations of the Second Magistrates Advisory Committee', prepared
              for the Alaska State Supreme Court (unpublished report).
Timbers, B.
  1973   Interview with Stephen Conn.

CASE CITED

Gregory v. *Alaska*, 550 P.2d 374, 1976.

APPENDIX 1

Public officials' assessments of quality of justice and selected public services

	Good		OK		Needs improv.		Inadequate		No service		N.R./ Don't know	
	#	%	#	%	#	%	#	%	#	%	#	%
Village police	7	13.7	6	11.8	20	39.2	5	9.8	13	25.5		
AST	13	25.5	12	23.5	14	27.5	10	19.6	1	2.0	1	2.0
AF & W	7	13.7	6	11.8	17	33.3	13	25.5	4	7.8	4	7.8
Magistrates	14	27.5	7	13.7	8	15.7	3	5.9	14	27.5	5	9.8
Legal services	8	15.7	10	19.6	7	13.7	7	13.7	14	27.5	5	9.8
Prosecutor	3	5.9	11	21.6	9	17.6	5	9.8	11	21.6	12	23.5
Defense services	4	7.8	9	17.6	3	5.9	4	7.8	20	39.2	11	21.6
Probation/Parole	8	15.7	8	15.7	7	13.7	8	15.7	12	23.5	8	15.8
Local jail	2	3.9	3	5.9	11	21.6	9	17.9	22	43.1	4	7.8
Mental health	4	7.8	3	5.9	6	11.8	4	7.8	29	56.9	5	9.8
Medical services	15	29.4	11	21.6	17	33.3	4	7.8	2	3.9	2	3.9
State jail	6	11.8	13	25.5	2	3.9	2	3.9	16	31.4	12	23.5
Educational services	22	43.1	9	17.6	18	35.3	2	3.9	0	0	0	0
Fire	0	0	3	5.9	19	37.3	9	17.6	19	37.3	1	2.0
Welfare, unempl.	10	19.6	16	31.4	13	25.5	6	11.8	2	3.9	4	7.8
Youth services	0	0	1	2.0	7	13.7	13	25.5	28	54.9	2	4.0

Source: Angell, 1981a: 39.

APPENDIX 2

Comparison of Alaska village, Alaska statewide and United States crime rates

Category of crime	Rates*		
	Alaska villages	Alaska statewide	United states
Homicide	28.4	10.9	8.8
Rape	99.2	50.3	26.4
Robbery	127.6	96.5	195.8
Aggravated Assault	326.0	286.5	228.6
Burglary	936.8	1310.2	1439.4
Vehicle Theft	446.5	3272.6	2921.3
Simple Assault	354.3	783.7	446.1

* Per 100,000 population in 1977.
Source: Angell 1981a: 27.

APPENDIX 3

Statewide juvenile arrest rate per 100,000 individuals

1978 Statewide count

	White	Black	American Indian	Other	Total
Burglary	368	12	98	67	545
Larceny	1,361	85	304	43	1,793
Drug abuse	419	15	57	19	510
Liquor laws	403	3	308	183	897
All other offences	230	7	67	15	319
Curfew & loitering	173	2	32	19	226
All crimes	3,998	149	1,300	500	5,947

1978 Statewide arrest rate per 100,000 individuals

	White	Black	American Indian	Other	Total
Burglary	245.7	212.6	951.8	275.7	286.9
Larceny	908.9	1,506.5	2,952.6	176.9	943.8
Drug abuse	279.8	265.8	553.6	78.2	268.4
Liquor laws	269.1	53.1	2,991.4	753.2	472.2
All other offences	153.6	12.4	650.7	61.7	167.9
Curfew & loitering	115.5	35.4	310.8	78.2	118.9
All crimes	2,670.1	2,640.9	12,626.3	2,057.8	3,130.5
Base population	149,735	5,642	10,297	24,297	189,970

Source: Bayley et al. 1980.

The role of traditional Inuit measures for social control in correctional policy and administration

Harold W. Finkler

I. INTRODUCTION

Within the context of the development of a Northwest Territories (Canada) law reform capability, this paper explores the potential application of the revitalization of traditional Inuit measures for social control in correctional programming and planning in the Eastern Arctic. Beginning with a brief summary of the traditional system of social control, we examine the current level of tolerance toward offenders as the point of departure for our assessment of the continuing role of traditional measures in the resocialization of offenders within a prison environment.

Recent field research related to a review of the Baffin Correctional Centre, predominated by three months of community consultation in the Baffin region, provided the opportunity for the expression of community views regarding offenders, social control, the Centre's program, and expectations and potential for involvement. It was within the context of the need to re-establish that vital level of community involvement that we endeavoured to ascertain the possible application of traditional measures as an alternative approach in existing correctional policy and administration.

Before considering the current level of tolerance toward offenders in the Baffin region, it may be noted that traditionally the normative structure of Inuit society, while not codified, was characterized by generally recognized customary laws that focussed on a person's obligations in regard to hunting and the sharing of food, natural resources and material goods (Balieki 1970; Birket-Smith 1929). Furthermore, in reference to an earlier summary of Hoebel's (1954) evaluation of beliefs and practices inherent within the Inuit system of social behaviour, the existence of several underlying jural postulates and corollaries has been established.

"Specifically, these postulates expressed a multitude of taboos as well as beliefs, such as that no one should be a burden on the community; obligations concerning the sharing of natural resources as well as material goods; the affirmation of a person's individualism; male-female roles in addition to that of the family; and the need to be able to predict a person's behaviour. In Hoebel's opinion, these postulates constitute the bases of legal or quasi-legal principles and norms, whose violation may evoke a varying pattern of reactions and sanctions" (Finkler 1976:10).

The reaction to interpersonal conflict, devoid of any authority for the administration of customary laws, yet maintaining an emphasis on restoring the peace within the community, ranged from avoidance (Balieki 1970; Graburn 1969; Hall 1864; J.J. and I. Honigmann 1965; Steenhoven 1956) to murder (Graburn 1969; Weyer 1932). Other responses to private conflict included gossip and derision (Balieki 1970), as well as song duels (Hoebel 1954; Steenhoven 1962). Group action, a collective response when an offender's actions threatened or undermined the social equilibrium of the entire community, included ostracism (Birket-Smith 1929; Steenhoven 1962; Vallee 1962), or in serious situations, his exclusion from the camp (Birket-Smith 1959; Goldschmidt 1956; Hoebel 1954; Vallee 1962), and in instances of intolerable stress, homicide (Hoebel 1941, 1954).

Interestingly, despite the absence of forensic institutions, both Balieki (1970) and Hoebel (1941, 1954) refer to examples where an informal gathering of members from the community emerged to deliberate as to the appropriate course of action in response to unacceptable behaviour. However, in reference to the previous literature, and especially Goldschmidt (1974), it must be asserted that the traditional system of social control with its emphasis on the restoration of peace rather than justice, was characterized by a flexibility in reaction to conflict, dependent on the community's assessment of the offender's value to the group rather than on the determination of guilt and punishment.

II. LIMITS OF TOLERANCE TOWARD OFFENDERS

In our opinion, the success of any intervention for the resocialization of offenders is dependent on public acceptance and support. Consequently, prior to any consideration for action in institutional programming and planning it is essential to determine the prevailing level of tolerance toward offenders. During the course of our community consultation in the Baffin region, this level of tolerance was reflected in people's expectations and reactions in regard to the value of incarceration at the Baffin Correctional Centre, an institution for predominantly Inuit adult male offenders, situated in Frobisher Bay. The following comprise community reactions as to the effectiveness of the Baffin Correctional Centre.

> "First, they felt that the Centre's existing liberal or lenient approach to inmate administration and treatment undermined their expectation of the deterrent value of the incarceration. They identified the issues of unsupervised movement within the community, the material comforts of the environment, inmate allowances, the hunting program, employment with pay, recreation, and other activities as potential incentives to recidivism.

Regarding the Centre's ability to effect change in an offender's behaviour, many began with expressing their appreciation for the availability of such a service and the rehabilitation orientation of its program. Nevertheless, other than the provision of safe custody, many were not encouraged with the results of the incarceration in terms of having any significant rehabilitative, deterrent or preventive value...

Consequently, several advocated a more punitive approach in the Centre's administration and operation, including some reduction in its environmental standards. This evolved from the expectation of sentencing to imprisonment for punishment, as opposed to the view that the deprivation of liberty, in itself, was sufficient to achieve this end. Furthermore, these feelings stemmed from the community's unrealistic expectations about the effectiveness of prisons" (Finkler 1981: 86, 91-92).

However, it is interesting to note that

"the majority of offenders did not feel that their communities were concerned about their welfare, or sensitive to their problems and needs, or prepared to assist in their adjustment or re-entry into community life" (Finkler 1981:89).

III. THE CONTINUING ROLE OF TRADITIONAL MEASURES FOR SOCIAL CONTROL IN CORRECTIONS

While the current legislation, i.e. the Northwest Territories Corrections Ordinance, neither encourages nor discourages community participation, it does not impede the establishment of a community advisory group in corrections programming and planning. The difficulty lies in determining the parameters of its involvement and decision-making authority in the administration of the institution. Furthermore, existing legislation, through its entrenchment of basic rights as well as standards for the care and custody of offenders, prevents the implementation of the full range of traditional measures. Nevertheless, the mechanism of a citizens' advisory group enabling community involvement in direct service in the Centre's programs, or in the formulation of general correctional policy, provides the opportunity for the application of traditional measures of resocialization.

Specifically, with regard to community participation in the Centre's programming, there exists the potential for the continuing role of traditional measures for social control through direct service in the following areas:

"The teaching of traditional skills as part of the land or evening program; providing apprenticeship opportunities for inmates within the context of vocational training, work release, or community service; participation in the evening program through a contribution of their knowledge; resource persons for an alcohol and drug information/counselling program; providing counselling or spiritual guidance; assistance in pre-release planning; and after-care" (Finkler 1981:101).

Community involvement in these service functions provides the opportunity for the acquisition of traditional skills and consolidation of community values, as well as impressing upon inmates the boundaries of acceptable behaviour and responsibility for their actions.

> "Presently, the offender's removal from the community precludes this opportunity for his accountability to the community or his confrontation with self. Consequently, the involvement of leaders, elders, and church people in counselling, through the traditional means of group confrontation, enables the community to emphasize to the offender that his actions are disrespectful of Inuit life style and culture, and that he must learn to be accountable for his behaviour" (Finkler 1981:101).

Through the community's involvement in the formulation of regional correctional policy encompassing the content, direction, and delivery of the Centre's programming, the potential exists for the application of traditional measures in creating an environment conducive to inmate development and responsibility.

IV. CONCLUSION

At first glance, with the emergence of a more punitive and less tolerant attitude towards offenders, the potential for the continuing role of traditional measures for social control in correctional policy and administration does not look encouraging. Furthermore, the general demise of primary relationships, the development of a less homogeneous population, a decline in people's dependency on one another, the breakdown of traditional family control and respect, along with increased contact with Euro-Canadian culture, all characteristic of current town life, have significantly eroded the basis for such community involvement in resocialization. In addition to a change in the traditional normative structure, there has been an increasing tendency to refer disputes or instances of unacceptable behaviour to the formalized agencies of socio-legal control for conflict resolution or action. However, as we have seen, the potential application of traditional values and measures in correctional policy is dependent on the community's sharing its responsibility for social control. It is within this context, in conjunction with the development of the appropriate mechanisms facilitating community participation in corrections programming and planning, that the revitalization of traditional measures for social control may be considered as a viable approach in corrections as well as in the development of community-based alternatives to sentencing and non-institutional sentencing options.

REFERENCES

Balicki, A.
1970   *The Netsilik Eskimo*, Garden City: Natural History Press.
Birket-Smith, K.
1929   'The Caribou Eskimos', *Fifth Thule Expedition*, 5.
1959   *The Eskimos*, London: Methuen.
Finkler, H.W.
1976   *Inuit and the Administration of Criminal Justice in the Northwest Territories: the Case of Frobisher Bay*, Ottawa: Indian and Northern Affairs, Government of Canada.
1981   *The Baffin Correctional Centre: A Review of Current Programs and Alternatives*, Ottawa: Indian and Northern Affairs, Government of Canada.
Goldschmidt, V.
1956   'The Greenland Criminal Code and its Sociological Background', *Acta Sociologica*, 1, 217-254.
1974   'The Decriminalisation as a Resource Problem', Paper presented at the VIIIth World Congress of Sociology, Toronto.
Graburn, N.
1969   'Eskimo Law in Light of Self and Group-Interest', *Law & Society Rev.*, 4, 45-60.
Hall, C.F.
1864   *Life with the Esquimaux*, Edmonton: Hurtig.
Hoebel, E.A.
1941   'Law-Ways of the Primitive Eskimos', *J. of Criminology and Criminal Law*, 31, 663-683.
1954   *The Law of Primitive Man*, Cambridge: Harvard University Press.
Honigmann, J.J., and Honigmann, I.
1965   *Eskimo Townsmen*, Ottawa: Canadian Research Centre for Anthropology.
Steenhoven, G. van den
1956   *Research Report on Caribou Eskimo Law*, Ottawa: Northern Affairs and National Resources, Government of Canada.
1962   *Leadership and Law Among the Eskimos of the Keewatin District, Northwest Territories*, unpublished doctoral dissertation, University of Leiden.
Vallee, F.G.
1962   *Kabloona and Eskimo in the Central Keewatin*, Ottawa: Northern Co-ordination and Research Centre, Indian and Northern Affairs, Government of Canada.
Weyer, E.M.
1932   *The Eskimos*, New Haven: Yale University Press.

Australian aboriginal customary law: progress report

Justice M.D. Kirby

[*Editorial Note*: The progress report presented to the Bellagio symposium has been superseded by a number of papers published by the Australian Law Reform Commission at later stages in its work on the subject. The following summary has been prepared by Gordon Woodman.]

From the commencement of British settlement in 1788 until recently, little respect was shown by the laws of the Commonwealth and States of Australia for the laws and customary rules of Aborigines, who have inhabited Australia for more than forty thousand years. Legal developments in the past twenty years display changing attitudes, and have been accompanied by the growth of political awareness, cultural pride, and political organisation on the part of Aborigines. Against this background the Federal Attorney-General in 1977 asked the Australian Law Reform Commission (ALRC) to report on the recognition of Aboriginal customary laws. It was considered that this raised two essential issues: the extent to which Australian law should accommodate Aboriginal customary law; and the extent to which Aboriginal communities should be able themselves to apply traditional laws and punishments.

The ALRC's first discussion paper listed a number of options for reform, including:

recognition of some aspects of Aboriginal customary law in Australian courts;

special provisions for the composition and procedures of courts sitting in predominantly Aboriginal districts;

the provision of Aboriginal courts with Aborigines sitting as Justices of the Peace and exercising jurisdiction in minor breaches of the peace and small civil disputes;

the use of traditional authorities to resolve disputes by means of community-established law councils, at least in some remote Aboriginal communities;

improvement in the relations between Aborigines and the police.

A Commissioner and Commission staff toured all parts of Australia to consult both white and Aboriginal Australians on these issues through public meetings, informal gatherings and use of the media.

The ALRC have found certain features of Aboriginal lifestyle, which evidence the existence of customary law, to be most apparent in the more remote communities. However, it was pressed upon the Commission that customary law existed also in the urban environment, and that most Aboriginal communities had developed practices and laws to accommodate white society.

A number of manifestations of Aboriginal customary law have been specially considered. Traditional punishments appear to survive in many communities, and it has been argued that, while payback killing must be rejected, there is a case for retaining spearing and certain other punishments. The hearings seem to confirm that Australian law should not interfere with tribal marriage law except to recognise tribal marriages for certain purposes. It was argued that there should be reconsideration of legal restrictions which prevented Aborigines from catching their traditional food if they no longer lived on reserves, that registration or licensing of tribal doctors would be useful, and that interference with Aboriginal funerary customs should be avoided.

The Commission has considered aspects of the criminal justice system as they affect Aborigines. Alcohol is a major reason for Aboriginal involvement in the system. Evidence has been given of the effects of prohibition and of control of alcohol availability, and of various methods of dealing with drunkenness. Juvenile offenders, it was frequently suggested, should be kept within the Aboriginal community, and might be placed in the care of their extended families.

Great interest was expressed in the possibility of special Aboriginal courts. Existing justice mechanisms in Aboriginal communities were described. It appears that any proposed model would have to be very flexible, since communities have different ideas on the relevant laws, the range of crimes, and the punishments which would be appropriate for such courts. It was agreed that they could operate only in areas of Aboriginal reserves or of more remote Aboriginal communities. The Commission also heard proposals for involving Aborigines more fully in the administration of the Australian legal system in urban areas where they reside.

If the Australian legal system is to recognise Aboriginal customary law, it will be necessary to define who is an Aborigine. The Commission has suggested that a sufficient criterion would be descent as an Aborigine, but a number of other proposals were presented. There was widespread support for the ideas that judges should take account of customary law when sentencing convicted Aborigines, and that customary law advisers or assessors should be appointed to assist judges.

Finally, there was considerable discussion of Aboriginal-police relations. There was support for Aboriginal-police liaison committees, provided that they were localised and taken seriously by the police. The Commission heard various views on the possibilities of increasing Aboriginal membership of State and Territory police forces and of establishing Aboriginal police forces. Procedures for the protection of Aborigines during police interrogation were considered. There were proposals for changes in the training of police generally and of Aboriginal police and police aides.

Unfortunately non-Aborigines hostile to the approach of the discussion paper were apparently reluctant to express their criticisms, although a variety of objections were set forth in the discussion paper. They include the views that Aboriginal laws are unnecessarily harsh, that legal pluralism entails excessive complexity and inequality, and that genuinely traditional laws no longer exist. On the other hand many Aborigines question the right and competence of non-Aboriginal Australians to determine or even investigate the issues before the Commission.

This has been a particularly complex, sensitive and controversial enquiry. The task was assigned to the Commission as part of the mosaic of efforts by Australian governments to establish a new accord with the Aboriginal people. The public debates and hearings on the discussion paper have focused attention on a number of difficult moral, philosophical and legal questions. The Commission is not permitted to conclude that the problems are too hard. It must complete its enquiry, deliver its report, and draft any legislation it proposes. It is expected that a report will be completed in late 1984.

Recognition of folk institutions for dispute-settlement in Lombok, Indonesia

F. Strijbosch

I. INTRODUCTION

This paper consists of two main parts. The first is concerned with a sketch of institutions for dispute-settlement in Lombok, one of the islands of Indonesia.[1] The sketch comprises the official courts as well as the native forms of dispute-settlement, which are not recognized legally and operate beside the former. In this description attention will be paid to the composition, the procedure and the relation to one another of the various institutions of official and unofficial justice.

In the second part of the paper a short account will be given of the issue of legal recognition of unofficial, non-state law courts. This account will refer to the above-mentioned description of the institutions for dispute-settlement. In 1970, when Act No. 14 came into force, a unified administration of justice was introduced in Indonesia. Lately administrators as well as scientists have nevertheless been considering the possibility of utilizing unofficial procedures in dispute-settlement. I intend to contribute to this discussion and to investigate if it would be advisable to recognize non-state institutions for dispute-settlement in Lombok, and, if this question can be answered positively, to find out how this might take place.

The various aspects of the issue of recognition will be regarded from the point of view of the Indonesian government. In the 1970 Act criteria are given for the Indonesian administration of justice. I will use these criteria in forming a judgment of the quality of justice in the official and unofficial spheres. With regard to the notion of recognition I shall refer to arrangements which are laid down in the older legislation, which has now been replaced by Act No. 14 of 1970, but which nevertheless, as we shall see later, has not yet lost its meaning for the present-day administration of justice. In the next section the various Indonesian legal regulations in this field will be mentioned and annotated.

This paper may also be of importance for the political and scientific discussion of matters of recognition which are much more widely discussed at present. In many parts of the world interest in alternative procedures, in indigenous or informal forms of dispute-settlement, is growing. In the '60s and '70s this informal justice was one of the most important topics in sociological literature. The inadequacy and inhumanity of the state's "assembly-line justice" were severely criticized, while much attention was paid to the "superior qualities of non-state, informal people's law" (Baxi 1979: 102). A similar tendency is present in the literature about issues concerning "law and development". Before the '70s it was characterized by a spirit of "liberal legalism": belief in modernization, westernization and introduction of unified law and unified administration of justice (Snyder 1980: 730-32). These views have changed in the past decade. Experts on legal development came to prefer a more historically directed approach to the issue. According to them models of development were to be founded on the specific, existing indigenous values and institutions of a certain community in the field of law. In western countries state justice is also criticized. Nader comes to the conclusion that the legal apparatus in the USA is overburdened, and that, as a result, there is a tendency to settle disputes outside the official system (1978:3). The inefficient operation of official law courts induced the government of the USA to establish informal institutions for dispute-settlement: dispute mediation centres.[2] In other western countries (Canada, Australia) the same problem occurs in a different form. There the question arises of whether and to what extent the law and justice of ethnic minorities should be recognised.[3]

In the literature one is nevertheless warned against too much optimism, even by those who in principle favour the recognition of folk institutions. "Indigenous law often reflects narrow and parochial concerns; it is often based on relations of domination" (Galanter 1981:25). Van den Bergh expresses a similar view (1975:25). Baxi states that the folk law may frustrate the solution of certain development problems (1979:112).

Although views on the issue of "recognition" and the solutions suggested with reference to it differ from country to country, one can assume that they all stem from a more or less identical thought: that state justice is expensive, inefficient, alien or incomprehensible, and that disputes should be settled as much as possible within the social and ethnic setting in which they have arisen, and by institutions which exist within this setting or should be introduced there.

I hope that my paper can be a contribution to the above-mentioned general discussion of the pros and cons of the issue of recognition.

The paper consists of six parts. After the introduction, in Part II an amplification of Indonesian legislation in the field of administration of justice will be given. In Part III I will give some ethnographic information about the island of Lombok. In Part IV there will be a sketch of a case-history. Part V concerns an inventory and description of the official and unofficial institutions for dispute-settlement. The information on dispute-settlement by informal institutions has principally been gathered in the village of Rembiga on West Lombok. There are strong indications that the description is relevant for a much larger area of Lombok. Data provided by Hartong on matters of dispute-settlement in other parts of Lombok (Hartong 1974) are in agreement with mine in many respects. In Part VI the operation of the official and unofficial institutions for dispute-settlement will be investigated and problems concerning recognition of folk institutions will be discussed.

II. LEGISLATION AND POLICY CONCERNING ADMINISTRATION OF JUSTICE

In 1970 Act No. 14 became operative, containing basic provisions for the regulation of the judicature in Indonesia.[4] In this law general starting-points and fundamental values are laid down with reference to the administration of justice, particularly in the second section (articles 3 to 9), headed *Ketentuan Umum* (General Provisions). These values will be mentioned and partly commented on hereafter. In the last Part they will be used as a guide in the discussion of issues of recognition.

In article 3(2) of the Act unity of justice is proclaimed: "All administration of justice in the entire area of the Republic of Indonesia is state administration of justice and is settled in the law". In the amplification of this clause it is repeated copiously that the law does not leave any room for administration of justice outside state courts (Intibuku Utama 1971:26). In this amplification the existence of non-state forms of dispute-settlement is expressly tolerated, but they are not referred to as "administration of justice", but as "arbitration" (*perdamaian*). It is determined explicitly that the state will not confer legal authority on decisions given by non-state institutions. We will come back to the importance of this clause later.

Article 4(2) says: "Justice is administered in a simple and quick manner and at low charges".

Article 5(l) says "Justice is administered according to the law, irrespective of persons". The contents of these two articles need not be commented upon yet. We will return to them at the end of this paper. Articles 6 to 9 will not be discussed. They provide regulations for the protection of the position of the accused in a suit. They are not important for the purpose of this paper.

The introduction of Act No. 14 in 1970 implied, at least formally, the end of a period in which folk institutions in Indonesia were legally recognized. This period started in colonial times in 1935, when, at least in certain parts of the archipelago, indigenous village-justice was recognized[5] by the insertion of an article (3a) in the Regulations for the Judicial Organisation (*Reglement voor de Rechterlijke Organisatie*) which has been summarised thus (Ter Haar 1950: 563):

"Without detracting from the legal power of the state judges, the trial of lawsuits by headmen who are responsible for the legal order of the small indigenous communities, was thus legalized, as far as those lawsuits fell under their competence in the organisation of their own community [in accordance with *adat* law], and a procedure was drawn up [in the regulations] for the delegation of suits by state councils to the village judge, in order to have the latter's decision precede the former's".

Van den Steenhoven (1974:256) remarks that in the colonial period, at least de facto, a complete separation between state and folk law had been realised with reference to a certain category of cases, mainly concerning specific delicts of the native legal order. With reference to general issues in the field of civil law there existed a procedure, laid down legally for co-operation between both legal spheres (see article 135a of the Revised Indonesian Regulations - *Het Herzien Indonesisch Reglement*). The first subsections of this article state:

"(1) If the claim concerns a suit in which judgment has been given by a village judge, the judge of the state court informs himself of the verdict and as much as possible of the motives for it.

(2) In case the claim concerns a suit in which judgment has not been passed by a village judge, but in which the state judge thinks such a judgment useful, he notifies this to the plaintiff by reason of a written document in support, and the trial of the suit will be adjourned until a later date.

(3) If the plaintiff wants the suit to be continued after the village judge has given judgment, he should notify this to the state judge, if possible by means of a document, after which the hearing of the case will be pursued."

After Indonesia's independence the legal recognition of village justice was once more affirmed in 1951 in article 1(3) of the so-called "Emergency Act". This Emergency Act was finally replaced by the above-mentioned Act No. 14 of 1970.

Even after 1970, however, folk institutions de facto enjoy a certain form of recognition by state courts in some parts of Indonesia. Hazairin (1972:3) remarks that these institutions have indeed not been abolished explicitly and also that by virtue of the still valid Revised Indonesian Regulations, clauses 120a and 135a, they came to operate throughout the entire Indonesian territory. Van den Steenhoven (1974:247) comes to the conclusion that the legal provision that all justice should be administered by state courts does not prevent a considerable number of regular disputes in fact being settled outside the state courts. He also observes that certain state courts (e.g. in East Borneo) have formed a sort of co-operation with village justice which is largely in agreement with the above-quoted directives of the Revised Indonesian Regulations. With reference to a case-history recorded by him, he reports how official and unofficial courts co-operate in the area of Karo-Batak. He concludes that *"Adat* law is alive at the village level ... the *adat*-procedure for dispute-settlement exists in all of these places, is preferred by the population and is at least tolerated by the state judge and at best promoted or used by him" (1974:255).

Despite the above-mentioned examples, co-operation at present between state and folk institutions is definitely not an established practice in Indonesia. As far as I know, this form of recognition is not present in most parts of the country. As we will see later, this also applies to the island of Lombok. Nevertheless it is equally wrong to discard these forms of co-operation as mere incidental initiatives developed by judges or courts which happen to be interested in folk law. These initiatives indicate an increasing interest in issues of recognition in Indonesia, from the side of the state as well. During two symposia, organised by the Government, it was concluded that it would be advisable for the state courts to involve the still functioning village justice in the settlement of disputes (Lim 1979:1). As yet, however, these conclusions have not led to actual changes in the policy of the courts.

III. ETHNOGRAPHIC BACKGROUND DATA

Narrow straits separate the island of Lombok (area: about 5,000 km²; compare The Netherlands: about 35,000 km²) to the west from Bali and to the east from Sumbawa. Together with other islands they form the so-called Lesser Sunda islands. Geologically Lombok consists of three parts. About half of the area is taken up by young volcanic highlands in the north (highest peak Rinjani, 3,736 m). Apart from some coastal villages, this part is hardly inhabited. At the south of the island there is a similarly relatively sparsely populated area: barren, hilly country, of limestone composition. Between these two areas the very fertile middle zone of Lombok extends, being about 60 km long and 35 km wide. Up to 90% of the total population of about 1½ million souls is packed together here. The density of population in this area is 667 per km² (Hartog 1974:2).

The population of the island mainly consists of an ethnic group called *Orang Sasak* (Sasak people), with a language and a culture of their own. Their religion is predominantly Islamic. Agriculture, viz. rice-growing, is by far the most important means of subsistence and is especially practised on wet fields (*sawah*) in the middle zone. Two-thirds of the population owns land. The landless usually farm the fields of other people as sharecroppers or as wage-earners. Animal-breeding (horses, cows, goats) is second as a means of subsistence. Industry is almost entirely lacking.

Together with Sumbawa Lombok forms the *propinsi* (province) Nusatenggara Barat (capital Mataram). The island is divided into three administrative units, *kabupaten*. In their turn they are divided into districts, *kecamatan*, each headed by a *camat*. On the lowest administrative level there are the villages, *desa*, which are each governed by a *kepala desa*; these *desa* are divided into quarters, *kampung*, the heads of which are the *kepala kampung*. All leaders of the above mentioned units are to be considered as officials appointed and paid by the state.

Unless stated otherwise, the data in this article relate to the situation in Lombok in or about the year 1973. It is important to know that then a rupiah was approximately 0.2 cents (US), that a *sawah* (first class) cost about 250,000 rp., and that a judge earned 7,000 rp. a month.

IV. A CASE-HISTORY

In the year 1946 Saleh received written permission from the then government of Lombok to cultivate a piece of land lying some kilometres from his dwelling-place, the *desa* S., at the border of the northern highlands. In 1947 Saleh refused to pay land-tax for the land, saying that he did not want it any longer, because it was too far away and needed too much looking after. In the same year five fellow-villagers declared themselves to be prepared to divide the land among themselves and cultivate it. These five will be called Anji et al. They improved the land considerably, and changed it into a *sawah* and each year they paid land-tax for their shares, for which they received a tax receipt.

In 1961 Anji et al. were summoned to depart from the plot by Saleh's son, Agus, who argued that on account of the cultivation certificate it still belonged to his father. Anji et al. refused to leave and a dispute arose, which was put before the *kepala desa*. His arbitration failed, and he sent the parties to the *camat*, whose effort was also in vain. The land remained where it was. The dispute remained unsolved and simmering.

In the same year 1961 Agus was visited by a *pokrol*. (In Lombok, as elsewhere in Indonesia, the term *pokrol* refers to a sort of informal solicitor, mostly unqualified, who renders legal aid in the widest sense of the word to litigants.) The *pokrol* moved Agus once more to take up the dispute, now under the former's guidance. Agus agreed. On the *pokrol's* advice they again brought the dispute to the *camat's* notice. The opposing parties were called up, but arbitration attempts failed up to five times. Each time Agus had to pay 2,000 rp. to the legal adviser. The latter proposed a new action; he advised Agus to take matters into his own hands and to take possession of the land. Literally on the ground itself there was a major argument. The police had to step in. The parties again appeared before the *camat*, who sent them on to the police in Selong. Meanwhile the disputed plot was confiscated (*sita*) by the *camat*. From that moment on the land was cultivated by a sharecropper, who took a part of the produce himself and deposited the rest with the *camat*. At the police-station the parties were detained for two days. They were heard and the police attempted arbitration. The *pokrol* was at Agus' side all the time. The attempt failed and all went home. The *pokrol* had to be paid 10,000 rp. He advised his client once more to seek justice with the police. Again they all went to Selong, again in vain. At the office the litigants agreed to follow the *pokrol's* proposal and put the matter before the state court, the *pengadilan negeri*.

The *pokrol* had to be paid 15,000 rp. Then he asked Agus for a *surat kuasa*, a warrant to be allowed to represent him before the state court, at a cost of 5,000 rp. Next he asked for 20,000 rp. to take the matter up with the court. The *pokrol* wrote a summons. At the end of 1963 the lawsuit started. It took up nine sessions spread over many months, because now one and then the other party - and sometimes the judge - did not appear. Each time Agus had to pay the *pokrol* 5,000 rp. The latter gave him advice, but did not appear in court. Anji et al. had not called in any legal aid. Both parties, each time starting afresh, had incurred great expenses on behalf of their witnesses, about 2,000 rp. per session for travel and lodging.

Judgment was in favour of Agus. The *pokrol* asked for 30,000 rp. and later 40,000 more to influence the court to publish the judgment quickly. Eventually the verdict was released after $1\frac{1}{2}$ years. Anji et al. appealed against judgment (*ngapel*). They did not feel *puas* (satisfied) with it. They also called in the help of a legal adviser. A judge of the same court at which judgment had been passed functioned as such. This judge wrote a memorandum of appeal (costing 18,000 rp.). Agus engaged a new adviser: an academic, a jurist from the capital of the island. He thought the old *pokrol* too expensive. The new adviser asked for 50,000 rp. in advance for his help. The appeal took place before the *pengadilan tinggi* (the court of appeal) in Denpasar on the island of Bali. Agus and his lawyer went there. The latter did hardly anything at the court. Agus had to pay 5,000 rp. to the clerks to accelerate the legal proceedings. Later Anji also went to Bali without a *pokrol*, but with one of his fellow-plaintiffs. They were allowed into the clerk's room but did not get the opportunity to plead their case any further. They also paid the clerk 5,000 rp. to hasten the process. Anji and his friend did not return home by (cheap) boat, but by aeroplane, which was much more expensive. They were very eager to experience this for once.

In 1972, after about nine years, judgment was given. Agus again won. Costs of the lawsuit, to be paid via the *pokrol*, were 200,000 rp. In the same year, however, Anji et al. decided to submit their case to the higher court of Indonesia, the *Mahkamah Agung* in Jakarta.

At that moment, in 1973, I lost sight of the case. The story was told to me by the two opponents Anji and Agus, who were sitting next to each other during the narration, amplifying and correcting each other back and forth. They were no longer at odds with each other. The case was in Jakarta and they just had to wait. The disputed land was still confiscated. I also got some information from one of the clerks of the court.

V. INVENTORY AND DESCRIPTION OF THE INSTITUTIONS OF DISPUTE-SETTLE-MENT

1. Institutions at Village Level

The case-history shows that both parties, Anji et al. and Agus, first tried to settle their dispute within the village before the headman. In Lombok it is customary to deal first with a dispute at this level, although it is not an absolute requisite. I know of cases which have been put before the state court immediately after arising, passing over many other official bodies. Mostly, however, the institutions within the village will be approached first. These institutions can be divided into three categories:
a. civil authorities: the *kepala kampung* and the *kepala desa*;
b. religious authorities: the *kijaj*, the *penghulu* and the *P. 3 NTR*;
c. various officials and other people: police and military functionaries, titled and socio-economically powerful people. Each of the institutions mentioned will be commented on below.

a. The *kepala kampung* deals with all sorts of disputes of daily life. As far as persons are concerned, his jurisdiction is basically unlimited, but mostly he does not deal with disputes in which big financial interests are at stake. He is especially approached if the parties are from the same *kampung*. If he hears about a dispute, he does not usually summon the opposing party, but goes to them. He tries to settle the dispute by functioning as an intermediary. It is his aim to effect a compromise. In his search for a solution he is guided by rules and ideas of the folk law applying in the *kampung*. The *kepala kampung* cannot impose or enforce a solution, he is just an arbitrator, a mediator. If his intervention is fruitless, the *kepala kampung* refers the parties to one of the other above-mentioned bodies, mostly to the *kepala desa*.

Generally the arbitration attempt of the *kepala kampung* does not cost much. As an arbitrator he enjoys a good reputation. True, he is a state official, but almost invariably he is born in the same area. He is considered a confidential agent who is well-informed about the existing relations and rules.

Like the *kepala kampung* the *kepala desa* has jurisdiction to hear all disputes. In practice he deals with the more important matters in which much money is at stake. These matters are practically always about land. The *kepala desa* is much less frequently called upon in matters of kinship, marriage and divorce. Disputes about these are usually brought to the notice of religious authorities. The working method of the *kepala desa* can vary considerably, depending on the nature of the affair, his own ideas and tastes and on the customs in this respect of the village. In the majority of cases his method appears to be similar to the approach of the *kepala kampung*, described above. The *kepala desa* does not summon parties, and he does not organise a meeting or a session, but he visits the parties, and possibly their relatives, neighbours and others notably the *kepala kampung*, who according to him would supply information about the case. In this way he tries to carry the conflict to a happy conclusion as an intermediary. The *kepala desa* also tries to reach a compromise between the parties, in the process of which he is mainly guided by the ideas of folk law. His intervention likewise implies only arbitration. He is not able to enforce a decision. The authority of the chief of the village is not absolute or unchallengeable. One of the reasons for this may be the fact that his arbitration work is not free of charge.

For the *kepala desa* dispute-settlement is one of the most important sources of (subsidiary) income (also compare Hartong 1974:80). For a successful arbitration attempt he asks a considerable sum of money. The kind of solution he proposes may be affected by corruption. Sometimes he lets himself be paid by one of the parties for a favourable decision. In such a case the *kepala desa* tries to persuade the opposing party to accept the decision. If the latter belongs to the less competent or socio-economically weaker class this is likely to be successful.

It may also happen that the *kepala desa* devotes a sort of public meeting, a session, to a certain problem. Then the problem is discussed, and, if possible, solved during the meeting, in the presence of the parties involved, and sometimes also of other village officials. In this case too, however, the parties are free to refuse the decision offered.

b. In principle the religious functionaries have a restricted jurisdiction relating to matters of kinship, marriage and divorce. They may also give their opinion upon matters concerning inheritance of land. Especially in this field the jurisdiction of the civil and religious authorities may overlap. The principles of Islamic law are used in the settlement of a dispute. This form of dispute-settlement is not so much directed to finding a compromise as to the application of the rules in question.

c. In addition to the above-mentioned institutions, at present all sorts of people, whether or not having official functions, also act in the solution or settlement of disputes in many villages in Lombok. Basically their jurisdiction is unrestricted, but they are primarily concerned with disputes about land. Disputes are especially put to military and police functionaries. Furthermore, socially and economically powerful people, landed gentry, important traders and titled people, are generally available for the solution of problems.

Dispute-settlement of this type is, however, not always regarded favourably. In the majority of cases military and police officials and successful traders come from outside the village, and often from outside the island. They mostly stay in a certain village for a limited period of time and they are not well informed of the operative relations. As a rule they are very sensitive to payment by the parties. They use their power, based on their official positions, to induce the parties who "lose" as a result of their efforts, to accept their decisions. In certain cases they are successful, but in the long run their decisions do not have a lasting effect. When the functionary concerned is transferred, which happens regularly, his decision loses power and the losing party once more feels capable of disputing the solution offered.

In the villages various institutions for dispute-settlement are operating, but there is no common understanding about the limits of their respective jurisdictions. This makes it possible for people seeking justice to make a choice. The same matter can be put before various institutions. In the choice of which institutions to go to, two factors can play a role:

a. Religious considerations can induce parties to put their disputes before Islamic functionaries. Orthodox Muslims will, if the nature of the affair lends itself to it (e.g. if it lies in the field of kinship, marriage, divorce or inheritance) as a rule bring their disputes before them, ignoring all other alternatives.

b. Then litigants have the possibility of "shopping"; the issues are put before the institution from which most advantage is expected. The occasion for "shopping" arises e.g. in the field of inheritance. The rules concerning this issue in the traditional folk law of Lombok differ considerably from those in Islamic law. According to folk law a woman cannot claim land from an undivided estate. She can only, if she is destitute (e.g. because she is single, divorced or a widow), ask her relatives for support (*sanggu*). According to Islamic law, however, women are entitled to a certain part of the legacy. Therefore women often choose the Islamic institutions in the village, as these base their decisions on Islamic law.

2. Informal Justice Between Village and State Insitutions

Cases which are taken beyond the borders of the village are seldom directly submitted to one of the state institutions. Before they enter the official legal sphere litigants resort to all kinds of informal institutions (military and police functionaries, district officials, etc.) functioning at the level of the district, between the village and the state. Their justice has no legal recognition, and is directed at reconciliation.

Outside the village, most litigants need legal advice, which is delivered by unofficial legal aids, the *pokrols*. These *pokrols* function as guides in the opaque world of legal institutions on Lombok. They influence nearly all the litigant's decisions later during the course of the process of litigation, at the district level as well as at the state level.

3. The State Courts

The state courts operating in Lombok can be divided into two types, namely religious state courts (*pengadilan agama*) and common courts for civil and criminal justice at first instance (*pengadilan negeri*). Both types will be commented on below.

a. The religious administration of justice is regulated in Indonesian Act No. 14 of 1970 concerning *Kekuasaan Kehakiman* (the judicature).

In Lombok one court of this type is operative in Mataram. This court follows the rules of Islamic law. I have never attended sessions of this court, nor have I read any of its judgments. Yet one can expect that the *pengadilan agama* concentrates especially on the strict application of the Islamic law and is less inclined to effect a compromise.

Hartong has collected all 165 judgments pronounced by this court in the year 1972, as well as the first 50 of 1973. Of these 167 dealt with marriage and divorce and 45 with inheritance. In the inheritance cases the plaintiffs generally belonged to the category of wives, daughters and children of predeceased daughters of the testator (Hartong 1974: Appendix U).

Although the *pengadilan agama* is legally recognized and regulated, it lacks the power to enforce the execution of a given decision. For this purpose the winning party should apply to the *pengadilan negeri* for a new decision and obtain one. Because of this lack of power the *pengadilan agama* should be considered as a body for arbitration, not for adjudication.

b. The administration of justice by the *pengadilan negeri* is based on the same Act (No. 14, 1970) as the religious one.

In 1973 two of these courts were operative in Lombok, one in the *kabupaten* and one in East Lombok. A third court for the *kabupaten* of central Lombok was in the process of being established.

In the state courts in Lombok there are in total about six or seven judges working. A small majority of them comes from Lombok, the rest come from all parts of the archipelago. At present only graduates of law are appointed. The judges are assisted by clerks. Altogether twelve of them are working at each court. They are all natives of the island. The courts have their seats in stone buildings. The sessions take place in small halls, in which there are a few benches as a public gallery. During the sessions the parties are seated on separate chairs, placed in front: their witnesses and the rest of the public sit on the benches of the gallery. The windows and doors of the building are wide open, and are used frequently by all sorts of interested people to follow the course of the session.

If the judge has command of the language of the island, Sasak, then Sasak is spoken; otherwise they speak Indonesian (*bahasa Indonesia*). Most of the parties to a dispute and witnesses have a reasonable command of the two languages. If, nevertheless, language problems arise, the judge and parties are assisted by bilingual clerks. In addition, by the Act of 1970 the course of the session is determined by the afore-mentioned rules, dating back to colonial times, notably the provisions of the so-called Revised Indonesian Regulations and the Legal Regulations of the Outer Districts (Engelbrecht 1960:1723 ff).

In 1969 the number of civil cases was 142; in 1970, 172; and in 1971, 149. These cases can be divided into two groups, namely bank cases and others. Bank cases include claims brought by banking institutions directed at the execution of pledges, mostly of pieces of land, because of non-repayment of loans given by the bank. In 1963 the number of such cases amounted to 31, in 1970 to 40, and in 1971 to 42. These cases are determined according to the provisions of the Civil Code of Indonesia dating from the colonial period. In the records kept by the clerk the second group of civil cases heard by the court is almost invariably referred to as *minta kembali tanah* (request restitution of my land). This description comprises all sorts of issues concerning land transactions (hereditary transmission, sale, donation and mortgage). With reference to this category of cases Lombok folk law is applied.

The session starts with the judge's question whether the parties are prepared to compromise. This is a formality which is hardly ever responded to. Then the judge will proceed with an investigation in which he tries to determine the true facts and events leading to the dispute. (Most disputes are not based on disagreement about rights but about facts: see Van Vollenhoven 1931.) Parties and their witnesses are heard; if necessary it is decided to call new witnesses. Mostly the witnesses are village authorities, *kepala desas, kepala kampungs*, etc., relatives and neighbours. In determining the facts much importance is attached to written evidence. In general the investigation is only concerned with the dispute as it is expressed in short juridical terms in the summons. Less attention is paid to the social conflicts in the background. A more thorough investigation would have to be accompanied by a judicial inspection of the place where the dispute had arisen and a new investigation on the spot. Such a time-consuming approach is hardly ever pursued. At the end of the investigations, which can extend over some tens of sessions (although it mostly ends more quickly), judgment is given and eventually put into writing.

Above the *pengadilan negeri* are the *pengadilan tinggi* and the *mahkamah agung* (Supreme Court) as courts of appeal. The *pengadilan tinggi* for Lombok suits resides in Denpasar on the island of Bali, the *mahkamah agung* being in Jakarta. As soon as a matter has been appealed to a higher court, the parties lose sight of it. The hearing will go on the basis of the documents. No new investigation will be started, except very rarely, if the *pengadilan tinggi* orders the *pengadilan negeri* to make an additional investigation.

The high percentage of appeals is remarkable. I do not have any exact figures on this point - they were not recorded - but one of the clerks told me that it amounted to over 50%, a judge even made an estimate of 90%. Often parties go to a higher court because they are persuaded to do so (details of this problem will be discussed below). It does not seem very advantageous. One of the judges said he believed that the higher courts adopt the decision of the lower court in the vast majority of cases. A small group of cases is eventually taken to the *mahkamah agung*.

The delays one must expect for appeals are long. For appeals submitted to the *pengadilan tinggi* in Bali it is two to five years. If a case is submitted to the *mahkamah agung* it will take even longer. In 1973 no suit since 1959 had been received back from the highest court. These delays are partly due to problems of organisation, partly also to the delaying tactics applied by the courts. Judgments are only handed to the parties after they have paid considerable amounts of money for them.

4. Costs of a Dispute

The costs incurred by the parties in the case-history described were considerable. Notably the complainant at first instance, whom both state courts decided was entitled to the land, had to pay a great deal. According to the calculations given, this was in total 423,000 rp. (cf. the price of a plot of *sawah*-land of 1 ha.: 250,000 rp.). Yet not all costs incurred by the parties have been mentioned, due to lack of certain details. The costs can be categorized as follows:

a. people or functionaries connected with institutions for dispute-settlement ask for money or goods as compensation for the various services they render. The winner is, for instance, asked to pay a certain percentage of the land "won" by him. One or both parties may also pay to get a favourable decision. Finally, a sort of entrance-fee has to be paid in many instances, especially outside the village-domain. Then the winner of a dispute which has been put before a state court is sometimes confronted with high costs to get the judgment in his hands. Before this, he often has to make several payments to speed up the proceedings, with reference to the judgment concerned.

Frequently the payments mentioned are not directly given to the functionaries by the parties, but the *pokrol* acts as an intermediary. In the name of his client the *pokrol* negotiates the level of fees. From the negotiated fees he again takes a certain percentage as payment for his negotiation.

b. Besides the above-mentioned fees for negotiation (which mostly are not specified any further) the *pokrol* receives "wages". Often the *pokrol* also asks a part, about 20%, of the "gain" after a dispute has been determined favourably.

c. Especially at the state courts it is necessary for the parties to take witnesses with them. Customarily the parties pay their witnesses' expenses. They pay their travel and lodging expenses, and, moreover, they give them something extra, the so-called *uang rokok* ("money for cigarettes"). Needless to say these costs can become considerable. Often one has to appear in court several times (nine times in this case) with a group of witnesses (and supporters), which implies having to travel far and possibly even to stay overnight.

d. The parties have to count on considerable travel and hotel expenses for themselves.

e. Finally the authorities (the *kepala desa*, the *camat*, the police judge) may proceed to confiscation of the land in dispute. The land will then be cultivated by someone else pending the decision (which may not be forthcoming for years). Meanwhile the proceeds will be divided between the farmer and the confiscating body. The latter are in theory obliged to hold the proceeds in trust, but in practice restitution hardly ever takes place.

Usually the parties obtain money for the above-mentioned payments by selling or pledging plots of land. Because of the often urgent nature of these transactions the parties may well sustain loss as a result of the forced reductions in price they have to give.

Shrugging his shoulders, an informant to whom I expressed my concern about the proceedings, feeling sorry for the fate of the parties in a lawsuit in Lombok, answered: *"Si menang menjadi abu, si kalah menjadi arang"* ("who wins becomes soot, who loses becomes ashes").

VI. PROS AND CONS OF RECOGNITION

From the survey made above it appears that the institutions for dispute-settlement in Lombok form an extensive and complex body. The legally recognized state justice is only the tip of the iceberg. Under or next to it numerous other institutions, referred to as "arbitration" in the 1970 Act, operate in the informal sphere. The name "arbitration" seems to be quite correct in this connection, if one takes into consideration that the informal institutions do not usually have the means actually to put a given judgment into effect.

We will now carry out the intention mentioned in the first section and investigate how the official judicature functions, whether it is advisable to recognize informal institutions, and what problems such a recognition will entail.

1. Problems with respect to the Official Administration of Justice

The state administration of justice in Lombok is not always in complete agreement with the legally formulated ideals. It is possible that parties involved in a lawsuit are not always faced with as much adversity as those in the case described. Nevertheless, a suit seldom proceeds successfully and without blemish. The defects of the administration of justice on Lombok will be summarized.

a. Official justice proceeds slowly. We have seen that it takes three to ten sessions before the *pengadilan negeri* gives a decision. After that it still takes a considerable time (about three months to two years) before the parties can actually lay hands on the judgment. It is even more time-consuming to appeal. We have seen that, because of various circumstances, it may take a long time, sometimes even ten years, before a particular matter is settled.

b. The administration of justice is perceived by ordinary people to be complicated. The proceedings are governed by written law of Dutch origin. People from Lombok seeking justice feel helpless. Moreover, because many of them (probably 50%) cannot read or write, they are not able to go more deeply into the proceedings. They can neither read the law nor the documents of the suit (summons, judgment, letters in evidence, deeds and documents). Without the help of a *pokrol* they cannot take legal action.

c. Undertaking legal action is expensive ("who wins becomes soot, who loses becomes ashes"). The expenses of the parties in the case described have been discussed. Two factors in particular are responsible for the considerable cost of legal action: (i) legal assistance (*pokrols*) is expensive; (ii) judges and court personnel are susceptible to bribery. Additionally the parties involved in a lawsuit have to make many payments to keep the proceedings going.

d. Susceptibility to bribery implies that judicial decisions are not always given "irrespective of persons".

A final problem is not based on any legal provision. It is the relative ignorance of many judges of local justice and the local language and culture, resulting from the fact that many judges are strangers in the community of Lombok as a result of the system of circulation.

The administration of justice in Lombok has to face considerable problems. It seems improbable that these can be solved in the near future. The problems are structural and are typical of the official jurisdiction in most countries of the Third World (Könz 1969:97) (and maybe even of the whole world). It is therefore natural, considering the specific state of affairs within the state administration of justice of Lombok, to investigate how folk institutions might be involved in the process of dispute-settlement.

2. Problems with Respect to Folk Institutions

A policy directed at the solution of disputes outside the state court system, in the social sphere in which the issues have arisen, can in general lead only to an improvement. Two advantages of dispute-settlement by folk institutions are foremost.

Firstly, time is gained. The unofficial institutions work fast; they do not know the extremely long delays typical of state courts, especially for appeals.

In the second place folk institutions are relatively cheap, notably because of the absence of delay.

The partial delegation of the administration of justice to, or its retention by, folk institutions, however, leads only to a relative improvement of quality. Folk jurisdiction also is not in all respects conformable to the ideals set out in the Indonesian legislation. Generally speaking one can say that almost all above-mentioned problems of official jurisdiction return on a smaller scale in folk institutions.

a. Within the folk sphere also considerable amounts of money may be asked for dispute-settlement (notably by village headmen, *camats* and diverse functionaries): it has become a means of income for judges and arbitrators.

b. The proceedings are not always fair. Especially members of the aforementioned group of "diverse" functionaries are inclined to find for the party who pays most.

c. Neither can one be sure, at the lower level, of being tried by an expert judge. In particular the group of diverse functionaries consists of officials who mostly come from other parts of Indonesia and who have hardly any knowledge of local justice. The same applies, in a somewhat lesser degree, to the *kepala desas* and *camats*.

If, despite these problems, the state would consider the recognition of folk institutions in Lombok, with the aim of realising co-operation according to the procedures laid down in the provisions of article 135a of the Revised Indonesian Regulations quoted in Part II, there will still remain technical problems requiring prior solution.

In this article the state judge is required to take into account the decisions of the "village judge". In case this judge has not yet given a decision, a suit should be sent back to him. The question arises, who can function as a village judge in Lombok, as a counterpart of the state judge. We have seen that within the village several institutions for dispute-settlement operate next to each other. These institutions have not set complementary limits to their respective jurisdictions. They apply different sorts of law (in general, folk law and Islamic law). Moreover, they enjoy little respect from people seeking justice. The problem becomes even more complicated if one takes into account that outside the village as well a great variety of unofficial institutions and people are involved in dispute-settlement.

Taking into consideration what I have said, one can only come to the conclusion that, as far as Lombok is concerned, the issue of recognition is extremely complicated. The Indonesian government can successfully incorporate folk institutions into the judicial organisation only when it has thoroughly studied the above-mentioned problems and has solved them.

NOTES

1.   Information for this article was assembled during a period of fieldwork in Lombok between December 1971 and September 1973. This investigation took place within the framework of a concerted action of the Catholic University of Nijmegen and the Airlangga University in Surabaya. The project was financed by the Netherlands University Foundation for International Cooperation (NUFFIC).

2.   See: McGillis and Mullen 1977; Galanter 1981; Abel 1981.

3.   See the papers by Bayly, Conn and Finkler in this volume.

4.   In full the law is called *Undang-undang Tentang Ketentuan-Ketentuan Pokok Kekuasaan Kehakiman* (Act concerning Basic Provisions for the Judicature). In this paper the Act is quoted from an edition of Intibuku Utama 1971.

5.   This term refers to the indigenous justice administered under supervision of traditional authorities and bodies - headmen, village councils, priests, etc. - which were present on each level of a village in most parts of Indonesia.

REFERENCES

Abel, R.L.
1981   'Conservative Conflict and the Reproduction of Capitalism: the Role of Informal Justice', *International Journal of the Sociology of Law*, 9, 245; and see Abel in this volume.
Bergh, G.C.J.J. van den
1975   'Eenheid en Veelheid van Recht in de Moderne Wereld', 't Exempel dwinght, Bundel Kisch, 17-26.
Baxi, U.
1979   'People's law, Development, Justice', *Verfassung und Recht in Ubersee*, 12, 2, 97-114.
Engelbrecht, E.M.L.
1960   'Het Herziene Indonesische Reglement', *De Wetboeken, Wetten en Verordeningen benevens de Grondwet van 1945 van de Republiek Indonesie*, Djakarta, pp. 1724-95.
Galanter, M.
1981   'Justice in Many Rooms', *Journal of Legal Pluralism*, 19, 1-48; and see Galanter in this volume.
Haar, B. ter
1950   Verzamelde Geschriften, II, Jakarta: Noordhoff-Kolff.
Hartong, A.
1974   'Eindrapport', unpublished MS in Library, Institute of Folk Law, Nijmegen.
Hazairin
1972   'Introduction' in: Soepomo, *Pertautan Peradilan Desa Kepada Pengadilan Gubernemen*, Djakarta.
Intibuku Utama
1971   'Undang-undang tentang Ketentuan-Ketentuan Pokok Kekuasaan Kehakiman', Djakarta.
Könz, P.
1969   'Legal Development in Developing Countries', *Proceedings of the American Society of International Law*, 91-100.

Lim, T.H.
    1979   'Kedudukan Hakim Perdamaian Desa dalam Kesimpulan Seminar Hukum
                Nasional ke-IV', *Kompas*, 28-6-79
McGillis, D., and J. Mullen
    1977   *Neighbourhood Justice Centers: an Analysis of Potential Models*, prepared for the
                National Insitute of Law Enforcement and Criminal Justice, Law Enforcement
                Assistance Administration, US Department of Justice, Washington D.C.
Nader, L., and H.F. Todd Jr.
    1978   'Introduction: the Disputing Process', in: L. Nader and H.R. Todd Jr. (eds.), *The
                Disputing Process in Ten Societies*, pp. 1-40, New York: Columbia University
                Press.
Snyder, F.G.
    1980   'Law and Development in the Light of Dependency Theory', *Law and Society
                Review*, 14, 723-804.
Steenhoven, G. van den
    1974   'Formele en Informele Rechtspleging: de Dorpsjustitie in Indonesie', *Rechtsple-
                ging, Jubileumbundel Katholieke Universiteit Nijmegen, 1923-73*, Deventer.
Vollenhoven, C. van
    1931   *Het Adatrecht van Nederlandsch-Indie*, II, Leiden: Brill.

The authors

Richard L. *Abel* is Professor of Law in the Law School of the University of California, Los Angeles. He is a graduate of Yale Law School, and gained a Ph.D. from the University of London in 1974 for a thesis on customary law and dispute processes in Kenya. He has been the editor of the *Law and Society Review* and editor-in-chief of *African Law Studies* (now the *Journal of Legal Pluralism*), of which he remains an associate editor. His publications include: *Western Courts in Non-Western Settings: Patterns of Court Use in Colonial and Neo-Colonial Africa*, Academic Press: New York (1979); and (as editor) *The Politics of Informal Justice* (2 vols.), Academic Press: New York (1982).

Antony *Allott* is Professor of African Law at the School of Oriental and African Studies, University of London, and a Magistrate in London. He gained his Ph.D. for a thesis on "Akan Law of Property" from the University of London in 1954 after fieldwork in Ghana. He was the founding editor of the *Journal of African Law*, of which he remains an editor. His books include: *Essays in African Law with special reference to the Law of Ghana*, Butterworths: London (1960); *New Essays in African Law*, Butterworths: London (1970); and *The Limits of Law*, Butterworths: London (1980).

Rolando A. *Alum* Jr. is Professor at the John Jay College of Criminal Justice, City University of New York. He studied law and political anthropology at the Universities of Pennsylvania and Pittsburgh, and has taught at various universities in the Dominican Republic, Puerto Rico and the continental U.S.A. He has written about anthropological research and theory, and about the Dominican Republic.

Upendra *Baxi* is Professor in the Faculty of Law, University of Delhi, and a University Grants Commission National Fellow in Law. He is a former President of the Australian Society of Legal and Social Philosophy, and is a fellow of the International Academy of Comparative Law. His publications include *The Indian Supreme Court and Politics* (1980), and *The Crisis of the Indian Legal System*, Delhi: Vikas Publishing House (1982).

John U. *Bayly* is a barrister and solicitor based in Yellowknife, Northwest Territories, Canada. He is engaged in general law practice throughout the Northwest Territories, and is counsel to the Dene Nation.

Franz von *Benda-Beckmann* is Professor of Agrarian Law of non-Western Societies in the Agricultural University of Wageningen, The Netherlands. He holds a Dr. Jur. from the University of Kiel, West Germany. He has carried out research in Zambia and Malawi (1967-68) and West Sumatra (1974-75). He has taught ethnology and legal anthropology at the University of Zürich and been Director of the Netherlands Research Centre for the Law of South-East Asia and the Caribbean, Leiden. He is an associate editor of the *Journal of Legal Pluralism*. His publications include *Rechtspluralismus in Malawi* [Legal Pluralism in Malawi], Munich: Weltforum Verlag (1970), and *Property in Social Continuity; Continuity and Change in the Maintenance of Property Relationships Through Time in Minangkabau, West Sumatra*, The Hague: Martinus Nijhoff (1979).

Keebet von *Benda-Beckmann* is Lecturer in the Sociology of Law and Social Law in the Law Department, Erasmus University, Rotterdam, The Netherlands. She has carried out research in West Sumatra (1974-75), and published a number of papers on law in Indonesia and on Minangkabau state courts and village dispute processing institutions. She received her doctoral degree at the University of Nijmegen for a thesis on 'The Broken Stairways to Consensus: Village Justice and State Courts in Minangkabau', Dordrecht: Foris Publications (1984).

Ralph *Bolton* is Professor in the Department of Anthropology, Pomona College, Claremont, California. He gained his Ph.D. in anthropology from Cornell University, U.S.A., in 1972 for a thesis on "Aggression in Qolla Society", and has subsequently continued to conduct research among and to write on the Qolla, Peru.

Masaji *Chiba* is Professor of Jurisprudence at the Tokai University Research Institute of Law, Tokyo. He was formerly Professor at the Faculty of Law, Tokyo Metropolitan University. He has published a major work on the history of legal ideas, and also *Gakku-Seido no Kenkyu: Kokka-Kenryoku to Sonaaku-Kyodotai* [A Study of the School District System: State Power versus Village Community], Tokyo: Keiso Shobo (1962), summarised, "Relations between the school district system and the feudalistic village community in nineteenth-century Japan", *Law and Society Review*, 2, 229-40 (1967-68).

Stephen *Conn* is Professor of Alaska Bush Related Studies and Rural Justice at the Justice Centre, University of Alaska, Anchorage. He holds degrees in law and international affairs from Columbia University, New York, and in anthropology from the University of California, Los Angeles. He has been Visiting Professor at the Department of Law, University of Brasilia. He has conducted research on rural and urban Brazilian Indian law matters, and on "bush justice" in Alaska.

Harold W. *Finkler* is Co-ordinator, Social Research and University Affairs in the Office of the Northern Research and Science Advisor, Ottawa. He is conducting socio-legal research on issues concerning northern natives and the criminal justice system in the Canadian arctic, with an emphasis on the impact of major resource development projects in the area.

Peter *Fitzpatrick* is Senior Lecturer in Law and Interdisciplinary Studies at the University of Kent, Canterbury, Britain. He holds degrees in law from the Universities of Queensland and London. He has taught law at the University of Papua New Guinea and worked in the office of the Prime Minister of Papua New Guinea on development matters and legal projects. His publications include *Law and State in Papua New Guinea*, London and New York: Academic Press (1980).

Marc *Galanter* is Professor of Law and of South Asian Studies at the University of Wisconsin, and President of the Commission on Folk Law and Legal Pluralism. His university education was at the University of Chicago. He has written on the development of the legal system and on the relation between law, caste and religion in India, and on lawyers, litigation and courts in the U.S.A. He has been editor of the *Law and Society Review*. His publications include *Competing Equalities; the Indian Experience with Compensatory Discrimination*, Laguna Beach, California: University of California Press (1983).

John *Griffiths* is Professor of Sociology of Law at the University of Groningen, The Netherlands. He is editor-in-chief of the *Journal of Legal Pluralism*. He holds a law degree from Yale University, U.S.A., and has taught law there and at New York University and the University of Ghana. He has written on a variety of legal subjects, many of his more recent papers being concerned with descriptive theory in the anthropology and sociology of law.

Mr. Justice M.D. *Kirby* is a Judge of the Federal Court of Australia, and Chairman of the Australian Law Reform Commission, established in 1975. In this office he has been responsible for inter alia research following on the Federal Attorney-General's reference to the Commission on the extent to which Aboriginal customary laws should be recognised in the Australian legal system.

A.K.P. *Kludze* is Professor of Law at the School of Law, Rutgers University, Camden, New Jersey. He holds law degrees from the University of Ghana, and gained a Ph.D. from the University of London for a thesis on the law of property of the northern Ewe of Ghana. He has taught law at the Faculty of Law, University of Ghana and Temple University School of Law, Philadelphia, Pennsylvania. His publications include *Ewe Law of Property*, London: Sweet and Maxwell (1973).

Mohammed *Koesnoe* is Research Professor of Adat Law in the University of Surabaya, Indonesia. He has been a Visiting Professor at the Institute of Folk Law, Catholic University of Nijmegen, The Netherlands, and was a leader in the Bali-Lombok Project of the Institute (1969-74). He has written extensively on Adat law.

Etienne *Le Roy* is a Research Officer of the Centre National de la Recherche Scientifique, Paris. He holds doctorates in law and in ethnology from the University of Paris. He is a founding member of the Laboratoire d'Anthropologie Juridique, Paris. He has conducted research in Senegal and the Popular Republic of the Congo. He is a co-editor of *Enjeux Fonciers*, Karthala (1982).

Adam *Podgorecki* is Professor of Sociology of Law in the Department of Sociology, Carleton University, Ottawa. He holds a Ph.D. in law, and was formerly Professor at the University of Warsaw. He is the author of several books in Polish and in English, including *Law and Society*, London: Routledge & Kegan Paul (1974), and *Practical Social Sciences*, London: Routledge & Kegan Paul (1975).

E.A.B. *van Rouveroy van Nieuwaal* is Professor of African Constitutional Law at Leiden University, The Netherlands. He holds a law degree from the University of Groningen, The Netherlands. Since 1969 he has spent periods conducting research in northern Togo, producing a number of papers and films on socio-legal processes. His publications include *A la Recherche de la Justice - Quelques Aspects du Droit Matrimonial et de la Justice du Juge de Paix et du Chef Supérieur des Anufòm à Mango dans le Nord du Togo* [In Search of Justice; some Aspects of Matrimonial Law and the Justice of the Justice of the Peace and of the Paramount Chief of the Anufòm in Mango, Northern Togo], Leiden: African Studies Centre (1977).

Rüdiger *Schott* is Professor of Ethnology at the Seminar for Folk Knowledge, University of Münster, West Germany. He has studied ethnology, geography, prehistory, comparative religion and psychology at the Universities of Bonn and Göttingen, West Germany, and of London. He gained a

Ph.D. for a dissertation published in 1955 entitled *Anfänge der Privat- und Planwirtschaft; Wirtschaftsordnung und Nahrungsverteilung bei Wildbeutervölkern* [Origins of Private and Planned Economy; Economic Order and Food Distribution Among Hunters-and-Gatherers]. He has conducted fieldwork among the Bulsa of northern Ghana in 1966-67 and 1974-75, and has written extensively on questions of legal ethnology.

Norman J. *Singer* is Professor of Law and Anthropology in the Department of Anthropology, University of Alabama. He has worked for the Ford Foundation in the Sudan, and has also carried out fieldwork in Zambia.

Francis G. *Snyder* is Reader in Law at the School of Law, University of Warwick, Britain, and a member of the Laboratoire d'Anthropologie Juridique, Paris. He holds a law degree from Harvard University, and a doctorate from the University of Paris I. He has taught and conducted research at: Yale University Law School; Osgoode Hall Law School, Toronto; the Division of Social Science, York University, Toronto; the African Studies Centre, Leiden University, The Netherlands; and the Institute of Development Studies, University of Sussex, Britain. He has conducted fieldwork in Mali and Senegal. His publications include *Capitalism and Legal Change; an African Transformation*, London and New York: Academic Press (1981).

June *Starr* is Professor of Anthropology at the State University of New York, Stony Brook. She has studied at Smith College and Columbia University, U.S.A., and gained a Ph.D. in anthropology from the University of California, Berkeley, in 1970. She has been a post-doctoral fellow at Harvard University and Yale Law School, and Professor of Sociology of Law at the Faculty of Law, Erasmus University, Rotterdam, The Netherlands. She has carried out fieldwork in Bodrum, Turkey. Among her publications is *Dispute and Settlement in Rural Turkey; an Ethnography of Law*, Leiden: E.J. Brill (1978).

Fons *Strijbosch* is Research Officer at the Institute of Folk Law, Catholic University of Nijmegen, The Netherlands. He gained a doctorate in law in 1980 for a dissertation entitled *Juristen en de Studie van Volksrecht in Nederlands-Indie en Anglofoon Afrika* [Lawyers and the Study of Folk Law in the Dutch East Indies and Anglophone Africa]. He conducted research in Lombok, Indonesia, from 1971 to 1973.

Gordon R. *Woodman* is Lecturer in the Faculty of Law, University of Birmingham, Britain. He holds law degrees from the University of Cambridge, Britain, and gained a Ph.D. from the same University in 1966 for a thesis entitled "The Development of Customary Land Law in Ghana". He has taught and conducted research at: the University of Cambridge; the University of Ghana; Ahmadu Bello University, Nigeria; and the University of London. He is an associate editor of the *Journal of Legal Pluralism*. He has written on Ghanaian and Nigerian law with special reference to the judicial enforcement of customary law.

The IUAES Commission on folk law and legal pluralism

The Commission on Folk Law and Legal Pluralism was created in December 1978 by the International Union of Anthropological and Ethnological Sciences (IUAES), and affiliated with the International Association of Legal Science (IALS) at Unesco's head office in Paris, upon an initiative of Professor G. van den Steenhoven (Institute of Folk Law, Nijmegen, The Netherlands).

By June 1983, approximately 175 lawyers/jurists and anthropologists/ sociologists from all over the world were participating in the activities of the Commission. They are all, from their desks or in the field, concerned with or involved in theoretical and practical questions of folk law. This study gains a new perspective owing to the awareness of the contemporary existence of legal plurality, not only in countries with ethnic minorities and autochthonous populations, but also in the industrialized societies.

The goal of the Commission is to further knowledge of folk law and legal pluralism in general, and of theoretical and practical problems resulting from the interaction of folk law and state law in particular, and to make a sympathetic and constructive contribution to the solution of these problems, and, hence to the future of ethnic and social groups, governed by folk law, in the modern world.

The Commission's programme consists of three major clusters of activities: issuing Newletters (3 times during a period of two years), organising symposia, and stimulating Regional Working Groups in different parts of the world (S.E. Asia, Indonesia, Canada, Australia, The Netherlands, and South America).

Those who feel motivated to join this multi-disciplinary working group may write to the Commission's secretariat, c/o Institute of Folk Law, Catholic University, Thomas van Aquinostraat 6, Postbus 9049, 6500 KK Nijmegen, The Netherlands.